John Eliot's Mission to the Indians
before King Philip's War

· · ·

John Eliot's Mission to the Indians before King Philip's War

· · ·

RICHARD W. COGLEY

HARVARD UNIVERSITY PRESS
Cambridge, Massachusetts, and London, England   1999

Copyright © 1999 by the President and Fellows of Harvard College
All rights reserved
Printed in the United States of America

Library of Congress Cataloging-in-Publication Data
Cogley, Richard W., 1950–
  John Eliot's mission to the Indians before King Philip's War /
Richard W. Cogley.
     p. cm.
  Includes bibliographical references and index.
  ISBN 0-674-47537-2 (hardcover : alk. paper)
     1. Eliot, John, 1604–1690. 2. Indians of North America—Missions—Massachusetts.
3. Missions—Massachusetts—History—17th century. 4. Missionaries—Massachusetts—
Biography. 5. Puritans—Massachusetts—Biography. I. Title.
E78.M4C64   1999
266′.58′092—dc21
[B]   98-45386

*For my mother and
to the memory of
my father*

Preface
. . .

I first met John Eliot, the "Apostle to the Indians," as a student of Puritan eschatology. My dissertation, as well as the articles that emerged from it, investigated Eliot's interpretation of biblical prophecy with little or no regard for the historical development of his missionary work. In this respect my earlier publications resembled those of other scholars who have been intrigued by Eliot's eschatological writings. I bid farewell to Eliot as an historian of his mission.

There is an extensive secondary literature on the history of Eliot's mission, and I have benefited greatly from it. Nevertheless, the existing discussions are inadequate for one or more reasons: they do not incorporate eschatology into the history of the mission, they do not pay attention to the biographies of the proselytes (the "praying Indians") or to the individual histories of the Christian Indian settlements (the "praying towns"), and they misperceive the mission's role in English expansion.

Although it includes many discussions of Eliot's eschatology, this book is not an intellectual-historical study of Puritan eschatology. It offers a narrative history of the mission until the start of King Philip's War in June 1675. An equally thorough evaluation of the wartime and postwar periods in the missionary history of colonial Massachusetts would require a book of similar length.

Various conventions are observed throughout the narrative. Native Americans are sometimes called "natives" or "Indians" for stylistic variation. Quotations from seventeenth-century sources have been modernized except for titles of books and for English-language statements written by Native Americans. Dates between January 1 and March 25 in the Old Style calendar have been converted to the New Style year without further adjustment; hence, March 1, 1662, becomes March 1, 1663. Years of publication for seventeenth-century titles remain in the Old Style unless otherwise noted. Biblical quotations are from the King James Version, the translation Eliot used. The praying towns are designated by their Indian place names and not by their English counterparts. The designation "no longer extant" is based on my knowledge of the printed and unprinted sources. In bibliographical citations, "Cambridge" is Cambridge, Massachusetts. The words "Commissioners" and "confederation" refer to the Commissioners of the United Colonies, and "Company" and "corporation" to the New England Company. Sums are given in New English money except when otherwise indicated; in the seventeenth century, the pound was more valuable in Old England than in New (typically, £4 in England were worth £5 in New England).

I wish to thank Alden Vaughan for reading all of the manuscript, and Dwight Bozeman, Eric Cheyfitz, Edward Countryman, and Peter Onuf for reading portions of it; my friends Susannah Heschel, James Hopkins, Thomas Knock, Ann Rives, Martha Ann Selby, Mark Valeri, and Kathleen Wellman, as well as my sisters Elizabeth and Emily, for their many words of encouragement; and James F. Jones (former Dean of Dedman College at Southern Methodist University), Joseph Tyson and Lonnie Kliever (past and present chairs of SMU's Department of Religious Studies), and faculty colleagues William Babcock, Charles Curran, William F. May, and the late Frederick Streng for guiding and supporting my career. I acknowledge older debts to John Biddle and the late Sydney Ahlstrom of Yale University, and to Horton Davies, Emory Elliott, John Murrin, and John F. Wilson of Princeton University. Thanks also to Aïda Donald, Elizabeth Suttell, and Donna Bouvier of Harvard University Press; four present or former administrators of SMU's Department of Religious Studies (Tina DeLeon, Gwen Harris, Marlene Palmer, and Ann Wilson); and the many student workers in the department (especially Melanie Harber, Karen Kennedy, Allison Knox, Kim Parrish, Todd Philips, and Marc Shook).

Finally, I owe a personal debt to the courageous example of the late Mary Ann Denisar Tysver.

I have utilized the collections of the following libraries: Fondren, Bridwell, Underwood, DeGoyler, and ISEM (Southern Methodist University); Widener and Houghton (Harvard University); Mugar (Boston University); Sterling and Beinecke (Yale University); Firestone (Princeton University); Speer (Princeton Theological Seminary); Baker (Dartmouth); John Carter Brown (Brown University); van Pelt (University of Pennsylvania); Butler (Columbia University); Perry-Casteñada and Tarlton Law (University of Texas); Natick Historical Society; Boston Public; New York Public; New-York Historical Society; the Historical Society of Pennsylvania; the American Philosophical Society; and the Library of Congress. The staffs at the Massachusetts Historical Society, the Massachusetts State Archives, the New England Historic Genealogical Society, the American Antiquarian Society, the University of Massachusetts Archaeological Services, and the Boston Athenaeum have provided helpful assistance. A special word of gratitude is reserved for Billie Stovall of the interlibrary loan office at SMU's Fondren Library.

The dedication is an expression of my love for the two people who have most enriched my life.

Contents

1 The Context of the Mission   *1*

2 The Submission of the Sachems and the Birth of the Mission   *23*

3 The Early Development of the Mission   *52*

4 The Mission and the Millennium   *76*

5 The Natick Mission   *105*

6 The Remaining Praying Towns   *140*

7 Missionary Work outside Massachusetts Bay   *172*

8 The Supervision of the Mission   *207*

   Conclusion: The Apostle and the Indians   *240*

Appendixes

1 John Cotton's Lectures on Revelation and Canticles   *251*

2 Variant Indian Personal and Place Names in the Missionary History of Massachusetts Bay   *253*

3 Population Figures and Permanent and Temporary Personnel in the Prewar Settlements   *256*

4 Principal Nonantum and Neponset Indians   *259*

5 Eliot's Massachusett Publications   *260*

Abbreviations   *261*

Principal Printed Sources   *263*

Notes   *267*

Index   *323*

Maps

1   Pertinent Indian settlements in the missionary history of Massachusetts Bay   *xiv*

2   Natick and Dedham   *108*

Tables

1   Formal steps in the creation of the Natick church   *137*

2   Publication costs and press runs of Eliot's Cambridge imprints, exclusive of the Indian Bible   *218*

John Eliot's Mission to the Indians
before King Philip's War

· · ·

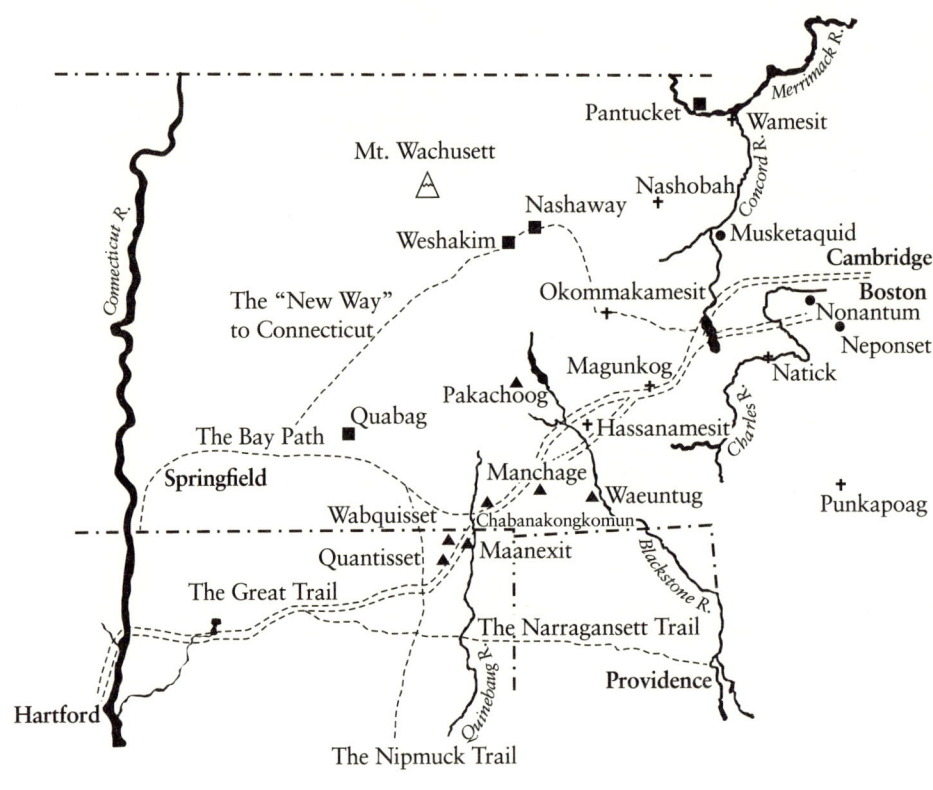

Map 1 Pertinent Indian settlements in the missionary history of Massachusetts Bay. Circles, the original Christian Indian settlements; crosses, the old praying towns; triangles, the new praying towns; squares, other settlements. Adapted by Matthew Offield from maps in Harral Ayres, *The Great Trail of New England* (Boston: Meador Publishing Co., 1940).

CHAPTER ONE

. . .

The Context of the Mission

Governor John Winthrop's first night in the New World was spent on board the *Arbella* as the ship lay anchored off Plum Cove in the summer of 1630. To his north were the ruins of the settlement on Cape Ann that the Dorchester Adventurers had operated from 1623 to 1627, and to his west stood the town of Salem, now under the control of the Massachusetts Bay Company. Among the other persons sleeping on the *Arbella* that night was an Indian who had come on deck earlier in the evening to greet the latest English arrivals to the Massachusetts coast. The next morning two more natives boarded the vessel and stayed for the remainder of the day. Winthrop probably had not expected to encounter living reminders of the colony's missionary obligation before he had even established residence on the mainland; nevertheless, he could scarcely have forgotten the obligation itself. Prior to his departure from England, he had pledged in the governor's oath of office "to draw . . . the natives of this country . . . to the knowledge of the true God." He had set sail for a destination where there were already two ministers, Samuel Skelton and Francis Higginson, who had promised the Massachusetts Bay Company to do "their uttermost to further the main end of this plantation, . . . the conversion of the savages," and where there was also a presiding magistrate, John Endecott, who had been told by Matthew Cradock, Winthrop's predecessor as the Company's governor, that "the main end of our plantation" was "to bring the Indians to the knowledge of the Gospel." Winthrop had carried across the Atlantic the autograph copy of the colony's royal charter, which stated that "the principal end of this plantation" was to "win and incite the natives of [the] country to . . . the Christian faith," as well as a duplicate copy of the colony's seal, which depicted an Indian imploring the English to "come over and help us" (Acts 16:9).[1]

These official professions of missionary purpose raise two historical-critical problems. The first is determining whether or not this missionary idealism was the primary motive that led Winthrop and others to settle New England in the late 1620s and the 1630s. There is some evidence that it was. Winthrop, for instance, placed Indian evangelism at the top of several of the lists of reasons for emigration that he prepared in 1629. Moreover, Hugh Peter, Increase Nowell, William Pynchon and several other future colonists were members of the Massachusetts Bay Company when the charter was drafted, the seal designed, the governor's oath composed, and the articles of agreement with Skelton and Higginson signed. Finally, John Cotton explained in his farewell sermon to the Winthrop fleet, *Gods Promise to His Plantations*, that the colonists should "win . . . [the Indians] to the love of Christ" and remember that God may have "reared up this whole plantation for such an end."[2]

This body of evidence notwithstanding, it is unlikely that Winthrop, Cotton, John Eliot, and other lay and clerical leaders moved to Massachusetts Bay because they considered missionary work to be the principal, or even a principal, reason for emigration. The evangelization of the natives was, in the words of Andrew Delbanco, "a public motive with a long history" that stretched back into the late Elizabethan period and appeared in many royal and proprietary charters and gubernatorial commissions throughout the colonial period. The missionary idealism enshrined in the Massachusetts charter and other official expressions of purpose clearly reflected a regnant convention in the literature of colonization rather than the central priority for the leading planters. Dwight Bozeman, in a 1988 survey of the motives for emigration that appeared in first-generation sources, found that professions of missionary purpose surfaced "occasionally but not frequently." The commonly expressed objectives were to escape the anticipated visitation of divine wrath on a wayward England and to establish the biblical ordinances without Anglican interference. There are no references to a mission, or to the Indians for that matter, in such celebrated statements of purpose as Winthrop's "A Modell of Christian Charity" (1630) and the systematic presentations of the reasons for emigration prepared by John Cotton and Richard Mather in the mid-1630s.[3] On several occasions after the birth of the mission in 1646, Eliot asserted that the evangelization of the Indians was "one end" or "one great end" of emigration. Other colonists made similar statements after the fact, sometimes for transparently political reasons. But no seventeenth-century Bay Puritan, as far as I have been able to determine, ever stated that the conversion of the Indians to Christianity was *the* "main" or "principal" purpose of settlement.[4]

The second problem created by the Bay Colony's official statements of objective is the nature of missionary idealism itself. This issue has been forcefully raised by Francis Jennings, who argues that the colony did not conduct the kind of mission advertised in the charter and in other expressions of purpose. Jennings's underlying assumptions are that the purpose of a mission is to redeem nonbelievers and that any missionary idealism worthy of the name cannot be mixed with self-interest. The "professed goal of European colonization," he writes, was to "convert the heathen to doctrines of truth rather than to learn from them the errors of evil." While some missionary programs in the New World properly endeavored "to save the heathen for the heathen's sake," the mission in Massachusetts Bay was "a means to an end rather than . . . an end in itself." He maintains that the actual purpose of the mission was to enhance the colony's political and economic power at the natives' expense, and that the Bay Puritans tried to conceal the fact that they were not running a proper mission by misrepresenting the Indian work as "an altruistic outpouring of religious benevolence." Jennings's account of Eliot's work reads like the record of one breach of missionary propriety after another.[5]

Jennings has a higher standard of missionary idealism than the Massachusetts Puritans did. The colonists never imagined that the purpose of a mission was simply to "save the heathen for the heathen's sake." The Massachusetts sources contain many acknowledgments of the advantages of a mission. The redemption of the Indians, for example, would advance the glory of Protestant England at the expense of Catholic France and Spain. Thus Winthrop wrote in 1629 that a mission would remove the "scandal to our religion that we show not as much zeal in seeking the conversion of the heathen as the papists do" and also "raise a bulwark against the kingdom of Antichrist which the

Jesuits labor to rear up in all parts of the world"; and Richard Saltonstall, Jr., observed in 1632 that "propagating the Gospel to these poor barbarous people" would work to "the honor . . . of Old England (to which we owe the fruit of our best endeavors)" as well as to the colonists' "own eternal glory." The benefits could also be diplomatic. Winthrop anticipated that a mission would help to exonerate the planters from the charge of abandoning the Puritan cause at home. "He that does good in any place does serve the church in all places . . . It is the revealed will of God that the Gospel should be preached in all places and nations," he explained in 1629. Another advantage was that a mission would justify the dispossession of the Indians. Cotton said in *Gods Promise to His Plantations* that "as you partake in their land, so make them partakers of your precious faith; as you reap their temporals, so feed them with your spirituals." The same "spirituals" for "temporals" argument appears in one of Winthrop's pre-emigration sources. The gains could also be economic. The authors of *New Englands First Fruits* (1643), who were almost certainly Thomas Weld, Hugh Peter, and Henry Dunster, explicitly used the prospect of a mission to secure contributions for Harvard College. These are the instrumental benefits of a mission listed in the standard Massachusetts sources. The larger body of English Protestant promotional literature identifies additional advantages that surely appealed to Bay Puritans, such as the role of a mission in making natives peaceful and loyal, and in eliciting providential favors from God.[6]

Once the mission began in 1646, there was an ever present possibility that its function as an instrument for Puritan self-aggrandizement would overshadow its role as a vehicle for Indian redemption. This possibility never came to pass, in large part because Eliot refused to allow it to happen. Jennings and other historians have exaggerated the political and economic advantages that the colony derived from the mission.

Eliot viewed the mission primarily as a program for instructing Indians in "civility" and "religion" so that some natives could experience "conversion" and enter into "full" church membership. He did not understand the Indian work exclusively in these terms (which are defined in the next section). For a period of time in the 1650s, he thought that the mission could also establish the millennium among the natives; and once he became better acquainted with the Indians and more sympathetic to their problems, he regarded the mission as a way of protecting Native Americans, whether Christian or not, from land-grabbing settlers and from Indian marauders.

Puritan Missionary Theology

Puritan missionary activity was not an early form of the aggressive evangelism so familiar to twentieth-century Americans. As several scholars have observed, the Massachusetts charter enjoined the planters to "win and incite the natives to . . . the Christian faith" through "your good life and orderly conversation." This phrasing reflected a point of view found in many seventeenth-century missionary sources, whether Puritan or Anglican. The perspective in question—which I term the "affective model" for a mission—taught that Indians would yearn to participate in the English way of life once they had witnessed the virtues of the colonists.[7]

The importance of the affective model is apparent in the Massachusetts Bay sources. In 1629 Cradock encouraged Endecott and other leaders of the advance settlement at Salem to "draw the heathen by [y]our good example to the . . . Gospel" and also explained that "their doctrine will hardly be well esteemed whose persons are not reverenced." In 1630 John White, the English clergyman who was a principal promoter of the colonization of Massachusetts Bay, wrote in *The Planters Plea* that "the example of our course of living" would "by God's blessing . . . make way for religion" among the Indians. White then discoursed about the kind of planter who would provoke the natives to cultural envy. "Men nourished up in idleness, unconstant, and affecting novelties, unwilling, stubborn, inclined to faction, covetous, luxurious, prodigal, and generally . . . habituated to any gross evil, are not fit members of a colony," he wrote. Only persons who embodied the virtues of piety, frugality, industry, constancy, sobriety, honesty, and austerity would be appropriate "patterns to the heathen." Both Cradock and White warned that the effectiveness of the English example would be severely compromised if settlers treated the natives unfairly in commercial and diplomatic exchanges. "Have a diligent and watchful eye over our own people," Cradock told Endecott in a representative passage, "that they . . . demean themselves justly and courteously toward the Indians, thereby to draw them to affect our persons, and consequently our religion."[8] The affective model continued to shape Puritan thinking after the Great Migration commenced. As we shall see, the model was used to interpret the actions of the isolated Indians who embraced Christianity before the start of Eliot's work, and also to explain the submission of six sachems to the Massachusetts General Court in 1644.

Puritans identified four stages in the missionary process that would unfold after the natives had "affect[ed] the persons" of the saints. The first was to train the Indians in what was almost always termed "civility." In James Axtell's handy summary of Puritan judgments about the matter, natives lacked three defining characteristics of the "civilized" way of life: order, industry, and manners. Colonists saw evidence of disorder in the Indians' failure to enclose their fields and establish year-round places of residence, a disregard for the virtue of industry in native subsistence practices, and improper breeding in the Indians' grooming habits. Eliot devoted much of his attention to eliminating these alleged deficiencies in aboriginal culture. The second stage was to teach the Indians about Protestant Christianity. The indoctrination of the natives required the eradication of their traditional form of animism, which colonists variously described as superstition, idolatry, and devil worship. This educational process, which was often called "instruction" in "religion," conforms to the modern usage of the word "conversion," a term that the colonists normally employed in a different sense (shortly explained). Bay Puritans were awed by the magnitude of the task of civilizing the Indians and instructing them in Protestant faith and practice. Thomas Shepard, the Cambridge minister who was Eliot's primary associate in the early years of the mission, stated that the natives stood at "a vast distance . . . from common civility, almost humanity itself," and the authors of *New Englands First Fruits* observed that the Indians' traditional religion placed them at an "infinite distance from Christianity."[9]

Puritan sources on Indian instruction invariably listed the word "civility" before the word "religion." In some cases, this arrangement clearly indicated a chronological order. White observed that "we hardly have found a brutish people won before they had been taught civility, . . . [and] we must endeavor and expect to work that in them first, and religion afterward"; and James Hopkins, a clergyman in Suffolk, advised Winthrop that the colony should "first civil the natives, and then bring some of them to know God." Eliot's practice, however, was to "carry on civility with religion." From the outset of his missionary work, he taught the Indians to "labor and work in building, planting, clothing [them]selves, etc." and also instructed them in "all the principal matters of religion."[10]

There were various reasons why Eliot and other Puritans insisted that civility had to accompany religion. One was the assumption that the latter could not endure without the former. Thus Eliot explained that the Indians were "incapable" of making proper progress in the Christian life "whilst they live[d] so unfixed, confused, and ungoverned a life, uncivilized and unsubdued to labor and order"; and Shepard observed that "in religion such as are so extremely degenerate, must be brought to some civility before religion can prosper." Another was that God had revealed the Law and not simply the Gospel. The purpose of the Law, Eliot explained in an early discussion of his missionary objectives, was "to convince, bridle, restrain, and civilize" the "rude company" of Israelites. A third reason was that the English people had been enriched by civility no less than by Christianity. Puritans often likened the natives to the uncouth inhabitants of ancient Britain. The Indians "are pagans and brutes rather than men," White remarked in drawing this analogy, "and such were ... our progenitors before us." A fourth was to protect the purity of the Lord's Supper. The saints routinely (but unjustly) accused Roman Catholic missionaries of administering the sacrament to multitudes of unwashed heathen. Indians "must have visible civility," Eliot explained, "before they can rightly enjoy visible sanctity in ecclesiastical communion."[11]

The Native Americans were not the only persons whom the colonists considered deficient in civility and religion. Many scholars have noted that the English sometimes compared the Indians to the "wild" Irish. But as Alden Vaughan points out, the Irish parallel should not be stressed to the exclusion of others. Puritans thought that all the "dark corners" of the British Isles contained ill-mannered and ignorant people. "We have Indians at home, Indians at Cornwall, Indians in Wales, Indians in Ireland," observed an "eminent person" in England whose judgment was recorded by Roger Williams. Moreover, Maine, Virginia, and the West Indies were filled with English settlers whom the authors of *New Englands First Fruits* considered "almost as dark and rude as the Indians themselves"; and Massachusetts Bay was home to unruly frontiersmen and laborers who, in Cradock's phrasing, needed to be "reduce[d] to a civil, yea, a godly life" no less than Indians did.[12]

At the same time, however, the Indians represented a special challenge. They were more "dark and rude" than reprobates in Maine and interior Massachusetts, and they did not speak English. The Massachusetts Puritans did not lack advice about how to solve the language problem. In 1632 Edward Howes, a family friend in England, told the younger John Winthrop that the colonists' objective should be "the speedy bringing of . . . Indians to the perfect understanding of our tongue and writing" and that the best way to achieve this goal was by teaching "the Indian children only to read English and to know no other." In 1639 Patrick Copeland, who earlier had been appointed rector of the stillborn Indian College in Virginia, suggested to Winthrop, Sr., that "many of your heathen . . . may be gained to the Christian faith" by educating English and native boys in bilingual schools. John White, for his part, thought that the planters would have no problems conversing with the Indians about trade and other "things subject to outward sense," but would find it difficult to teach the natives about Protestant theological doctrines, "things which have no affinity with sense." He anticipated that the linguistic barrier to religious instruction could be easily overcome only if God restored the apostolic gift of speaking in tongues. White considered this an unlikely prospect because he believed that the apostles had received the gift of tongues in order to instruct persons who had already been civilized by their exposure to the Romans. He lamely concluded that the planters would have to become "more perfectly acquainted" with the Indians' language, and "they with ours," before proper instruction could be given.[13]

There are few discussions of the language question in sources written by Massachusetts Puritans prior to the birth of the mission. The assumptions seem to have been that the instruction of adult Indians should be conducted in Algonquian rather than in English; that the persons who initially provided it were to be ministers who used interpreters or Harvard students who had studied the language; and that the work would eventually be turned over to Indians who had spent their childhoods in English homes and schools without losing their own dialects. The colony made little progress in achieving any of these objectives during the first fifteen years of settlement. Until Eliot did so in the 1640s, the only Bay Puritans who studied an Algonquian dialect for a missionary purpose were Roger Williams (before his banishment in the winter of 1635–36) and possibly Henry Dunster, the Harvard president. Nor did the plan to train Indian youths for future service produce the desired results. Many of the boys who received an English education prior to the birth of the mission—mostly Pequot War captives and children orphaned during the smallpox epidemic of 1633–34—died before they reached maturity. Those who survived were often disinclined to leave the English settlements.[14]

Like the first and second stages in the missionary process, the third and fourth were closely associated in Puritan minds. The third was often called "conversion." Eliot and his missionary associates knew that a program of civility and religion could not carry the Indians through to conversion, which was the exclusive responsibility of God. "It must certainly be a spirit of life from God (not in man's power) which must put flesh and sinews into these dry bones," Shepard explained in 1647, in an expression of the characteristic Puritan conviction that conversion was possible only through divine grace.[15] The fourth stage was church membership. A colonist who sought admission into a Puritan church had to pass an examination in Christian doctrine and deliver a conversion narrative to the members or officers of the congregation, who evaluated the testimony for signs of divine grace. Persons who offered acceptable narratives became "visible saints" or "full" church members eligible to receive the Lord's Supper and to present their children for baptism. These admission procedures were followed in the 1650s when Eliot organized the first Indian church in the colony.

Thus the final stages in the missionary process were conversion at the hand of God and communion in a church of visible saints. By the time Eliot began his Indian work in 1646, however, Cotton had delivered two series of public lectures on biblical prophecy. In the course of these lectures, the celebrated Boston preacher drew a conclusion that doomed the as yet nonexistent mission to virtual failure as a vehicle for Indian conversion prior to the redemption of the Jews.

Cotton's Millennialism

Cotton's two series of lectures were attended by Winthrop and other members of the Boston church, and by interested persons in the vicinity—including, in all likelihood, Eliot. The first set of lectures, which Cotton probably began in 1638 and probably completed in 1641, was devoted to the Book of Revelation. In these lectures he disclosed that the prophecies for the destruction of Antichrist, the redemption of the world's non-Christian peoples, and the millennium were nearing fulfillment in history. As several historians have observed, Cotton drew this conclusion from recent events in the British Isles, particularly the Scottish rebellion against Anglican attempts to impose the Book of Common Prayer and the rumored convening of Parliament. In this respect he resembled other Puritan divines in England and Holland, who were reaching the same or similar conclusions from contemporary events. The subject of Cotton's second series of lectures, probably presented in 1645, was the Book of Canticles (also called the Song of Songs or the Song of Solomon). He interpreted this collection of love poems as an allegory of redemptive history from the time of the Israelite monarchy through the dawning millennial era and on to the distant second coming, universal resurrection of the dead, and last judgment.[16]

In *To Live Ancient Lives: The Primitivist Dimension in Puritanism* (1988), Dwight Bozeman argues that the major influence on Cotton's eschatology was the English Presbyterian Thomas Brightman, whose commentaries on Daniel, Canticles, and Revelation were published on the Continent shortly after his death in 1607. Brightman was "probably the first Englishman otherwise in the mainstream of Reformed thought" to espouse the doctrine of an approaching millennium on earth. The received eschatological wisdom in England had either located the millennium in heaven or assigned it to a past historical epoch that predated the alleged corruption of Christendom by Roman Catholicism. Brightman's millennialism was slow to penetrate early Stuart Puritanism. One reason was that his commentaries were not published in England until the collapse of Anglican censorship in 1641. Prior to that time, Brightman's works were known only through foreign editions smuggled into the country or through manuscripts in circulation. Another was that millennialism was controversial among contemporary Puritans, many of whom remained under the sway of the older habits of thought. The pre-emigration Cotton was unusual among English Puritans in that he both knew Brightman's views and was sympathetic to them. In the early 1620s, Cotton delivered a series of lectures on Canticles in his Lincolnshire church. Clearly indebted to Brightman, these lectures contained what Bozeman calls an "inchoate" and "partially developed" millennialism. To judge from his literary remains, however, Cotton did not move beyond this "protomillennialism" until he delivered the lectures on Revelation and Canticles in Massachusetts Bay some twenty years later.[17]

Brightman's influence on Cotton's American lectures is most apparent in two respects. First, Cotton shared Brightman's doctrine of the "Middle" or "Bright Advent" of Jesus (see 2 Thessalonians 2:8). This doctrine, which was heterodox by Protestant and Catholic standards, originated with the twelfth-century Cistercian abbot Joachim of Fiore, who taught that there were three comings of Christ. The first had been at his Incarnation, and the third—the "second coming" of traditional Christian theology—would take place at his bodily return to earth on judgment day. The Middle Advent was to be a noncorporeal appearance that occurred centuries before the second coming. Bozeman explains that Brightman and Cotton construed the Middle Advent as "a terrific exertion of supernatural power that would revolutionize the course of world history" through the destruction of Roman Catholicism, the conversion of the Jews, the birth of the millennium, and the redemption of the world's pagan peoples. These spectacular events would be achieved by human agents, such as monarchs, soldiers, preachers, and missionaries, empowered to work wonders by the unseen Lord of the Middle Advent. Second, Brightman and Cotton envisioned the millennium as the restoration of institutions and practices that God had established in ancient Israel or in the apostolic church, and that had later been defiled or destroyed by human inventions. This vision of the millennium was a special form of the larger "primitivist dimension" that Bozeman sees as one of the three defining characteristics of Puritanism—the others being "moralism" and "pietism." All Puritans yearned "for reconnection with the paradigmatic events and utterances of ancient and unspoiled times." Brightman and Cotton, however, went beyond nonmillennial Puritans, who believed that the living could restore only approximations of the divine institutions that had once existed in history, by positing an earthly millennium that would restore these institutions in all their original purity. At the time of the Middle Advent, "the limits upon recovery were to be lifted, . . . events were to be driven by the irresistible force of miracle, . . . [and] the cycle of return to origins could achieve closure and finality."[18]

Bozeman also clarifies the place of Cotton's two series of lectures in the intellectual history of early Massachusetts Bay. Cotton was almost certainly "the first founder to expound an unequivocally millennial outlook." Bozeman argues that the absence of the millennial doctrine in the Massachusetts sources from the 1630s—including Cotton's discussions of ecclesiastical polity, fundamental law, and political organization—destroys the documentary foundation for the familiar claim that the Great Migration was undertaken in order to inaugurate the millennium in New England. Bozeman also extends his revisionist perspective into the 1640s. Cotton's public advocacy of millennialism at this time did not mean that he now authorized the colony to commence a millennium-making errand into the wilderness. The Boston preacher did not teach in either set of lectures that "New England had inaugurated, was called to inaugurate, or conceivably could inaugurate the millennium." In Cotton's judgment, the millennium "could not appear until the ruin of Rome and the rise of a Jewish church. Those were the inaugural events, and they would occur far from American shores." Nor did Cotton stand in defiance of contemporary opinion in the colony. Bozeman finds no compelling evidence in the canonical sources of the 1640s that other Bay Puritans believed that New England was or could ever be "*the* scene or headquarters of the New Jerusalem." Cotton's millennialism was nevertheless historically important in Massachusetts Bay. The lectures on Revelation and Canticles offered a "vision of protracted and world-wide millennial reign" theretofore absent in the colony, and also assured the saints in New England that they "stood in singular readiness for the great transition" even though they were unable to inaugurate it. Cotton's millennial views manifestly influenced some persons in the colony, including Eliot. But at the same time, Bozeman cautions that "it is well to avoid excessive claims." The lectures did not transport the colony into "the grip of a constant and determinative millennial enthusiasm." The surviving sources of many prominent first-generation lay and clerical leaders reveal little or no expectation of an approaching terrestrial millennium.[19]

Cotton held that there were two preconditions to the birth of the millennium. The first was the destruction of Roman Catholicism in the Battle of Armageddon. He expected that this battle would take place in Europe rather than on the Plains of Megiddo in Palestine. He also thought that the time for it "is now coming" and "hastens fast," and he suggested on one occasion that the preliminary fighting might begin in 1655. The leaders of the victorious armies would be the kings of ten European nations: "our native country for one, France, and Spain, and Navarre, Sweden and Denmark, and the rest" (the political geography of the Holy Roman Empire evidently created an insoluble exegetical problem for Cotton). He anticipated that these monarchies, which had allied with the papacy in the Middle Ages, would embrace Reformed Protestantism—some of them were already Lutheran and one, of course, was Anglican—in advance of the Battle of Armageddon. Thus the "ten crowns" that had once "worshipped the Beast" (Revelation 13:1–4) "shall hate the whore, and shall make her desolate and naked, and shall eat her flesh, and burn her with fire" (Revelation 17:16).[20] The second precondition was the national conversion of the Jews, an event that Cotton thought would commence "very speed[ily]" after Armageddon. The mass conversion of the Jews would come about through the destruction of Catholicism (he attributed the Jewish rejection of Christianity to the Catholic corruption of an otherwise irresistible religion) and through a special outpouring of divine grace of sufficient magnitude to redeem an entire people. Shortly before or soon after their conversion, the Jews—with the support of the Protestant monarchs—would liberate Palestine from an Ottoman Empire weakened by the collapse of the papacy. God's ancient people would then return to their ancestral homeland.[21]

For Cotton the coming millennial order had two institutional components. The first, which he discussed to the virtual exclusion of the other, was the restoration of the doctrine, liturgy, discipline, ministry, and (to his mind) congregational polity of the apostolic church. He believed that the apostles had carried this pristine form of Christianity to England and the other nations of the Roman Empire; that the Roman Catholics had later replaced apostolic belief and practice with human inventions such as the papacy, the episcopal polity, scholastic theology, and the canon law; and that the Waldensians and other late medieval groups had initiated a process of reformation, which was sustained and deepened by the continental and English reformers. In Cotton's estimation this historical process had reached its highest level of achievement in Massachusetts Bay, where there was "a greater face of reformation" than anywhere else in the Protestant world. He insisted, however, that the reformation of a corrupt church was not equivalent to the millennial restoration of the apostolic one. He told his auditors that they could not "see true doctrine and worship and government as it is held forth in the Gospel of Christ" before the Middle Advent and that, after the great day had come, "for any further reformation expect it not." Prior to that time, the colony could only strive to reach what Bozeman calls "the limits of religious reformation within history untransformed."[22]

The other component of the millennium was "godly magistracy." Here Cotton betrayed considerable uncertainty about institutional structure. The New Testament provided him with no endorsement of a form of political organization, and the Hebrew Bible furnished him with too many: the rulers of tens through rulers of thousands established by Moses, the charismatic leaders known as "judges," the tribal chieftains called "princes" (we might term them "sheiks"), and the monarchs. Cotton assumed that monarchy was an acceptable system of millennial government. In the lectures on Canticles and Revelation, he praised Jehoshaphat, Hezekiah, Josiah, and other Israelite kings who had been "nursing fathers and mothers" (Isaiah 49:23) to the ancient faith, and he celebrated the contributions made by the fourth-century emperors Constantine and Theodosius I to the expansion of orthodox Christianity; furthermore, Cotton took for granted that the European monarchs would remain in power after they had destroyed the papacy in the Battle of Armageddon. Nevertheless, he did not state that monarchical government was a necessary constituent of millennial organization, perhaps because he saw no need for the polity to be introduced in locations where it did not exist. He preferred instead to stress the function rather than the form of "godly magistracy." The duties of civil rulers during the millennium were to protect the restored apostolic church and to administer "the judicial laws of Moses that are built upon moral equity"—a provision that for Cotton included the capital laws of ancient Israel and excluded circumcision, diet, jubilee years, polygamy, and certain other matters.[23]

The millennium would begin in Jerusalem under the leadership of the repatriated and Christianized Jews. In Cotton's judgment, Jerusalem was the appropriate inaugural location because the city had been the capital of ancient Israel as well as the original home of the Christian church. Thus he did not teach that either of the two Englands was the destined birthplace of the millennium. From Jerusalem the millennial order would spread to England and the other nations of Europe, just as apostolic Christianity had gone from Judea into the other provinces of the Roman Empire. Massachusetts Bay would become eligible for the millennium along with the nations of Europe. Although they lived in a location never visited by the apostles, the Bay colonists were representatives of a country where apostolic Christianity had once existed. In time the millennium would reach the non-Christian Gentile nations of the world. The work of evangelizing the pagan peoples would fall to missionaries appointed by the Lord of the Middle Advent. Accompanied by the miraculous gifts and the massive quantities of grace required for the purpose, these missionaries would carry the millennial order to "the uttermost parts of the earth" (Psalms 2:8).[24] The kingdom would then endure until the traditional second coming, the resurrection of the dead, and the last judgment brought the course of terrestrial events to a close, evidently at some point in the twenty-seventh century.[25]

Cotton's points of focus in the lectures on Revelation and Canticles were the destruction of Catholicism, the national conversion of the Jews, and the millennial transformation of Palestine and the Gentile Christian world. He had little to say about the national conversions of the world's pagan peoples. Nevertheless, his brief remarks about the matter had enduring implications for the missionary history of Massachusetts Bay. He assumed that the Indians were Gentiles, a judgment shared by Winthrop, Eliot, Shepard, and probably every other Bay colonist of consequence in the 1630s and 1640s. Cotton's views about the natives' specific Gentile lineage do not surface in his extant sources. He may have agreed with Shepard, who remarked in 1646 that the "most probable" Gentile-origins theory was that the Indians were "Tartars passing out of Asia into America by the straits of Anian." This particular view had been popularized in early Stuart England by Edward Brerewood, the celebrated linguist and astronomer, and by Samuel Purchas, the compiler of travel narratives. The extent to which the Tartar theory was the accepted Gentile-origins theory in Massachusetts in the 1630s and 1640s is unclear: Shepard is the only Bay Puritan (known to me) who discussed the Indians' specific Gentile pedigree before July 1649, when Eliot endorsed an alternative Gentile-origins view.[26]

Cotton's eschatology placed the non-Christian Gentile nations at the end of the anticipated sequence of latter-day events. The destruction of Catholicism in the Battle of Armageddon and the conversion of the Jews were the prerequisites to the mass conversions of the Indians and other pagans. This perspective for the redemption of non-Christian peoples I call the "Jews-then-Gentiles sequence." Cotton qualified the rigor of the Jews-then-Gentiles sequence by teaching that "now and then" and "here and there" isolated natives could experience conversion in advance of the redemption of the Jews, just as isolated Jews would be eligible for saving grace prior to the destruction of

Catholicism. He variously quantified the number of exceptions as "sprinklings and gleanings," "no new multitudes," "some few," and the "first fruits." These scattered Indian conversions would come about through ordinary missionary means, in contrast to national conversion of the natives through miraculous means at the appointed time. Cotton did not indicate when he expected the mass redemption of the Native Americans to begin; Shepard tentatively proposed a date of 1690.[27]

In formal structure Cotton's missionary eschatology closely resembled that of Roger Williams, whose distaste for Indian evangelism after his removal to Rhode Island is well known to students of the period. Williams's eschatology took shape around the time that Cotton was delivering the lectures on Revelation. The Rhode Islander disclosed his views in works prepared for publication during his diplomatic embassies to London in 1643–44 and 1651–1654. Williams suspected that the Indians were Gentiles, probably Tartars; his flirtation with the lost tribes theory of the Indians' ancestry had waned by the time of his first return visit to England. He held that the national conversion of the Indians and other non-Christian Gentile peoples could not begin until the Lord of the Middle Advent, whom he expected would appear "shortly," had empowered missionaries—Williams usually called them "apostles"—for that purpose. He thought that the destruction of Antichrist (through preaching rather than through warfare) and the national conversion of the Jews had to occur before the millennium could be inaugurated in Jerusalem and new apostles commissioned. As he explained in 1645, in words that Cotton could have written, "God's great business between Christ . . . and Antichrist" must "first be over, and Zion and Jerusalem be rebuilt and reestablished, before the law and word of life be sent forth to the rest of the nations of the world who have not heard of Christ." Finally, Williams anticipated that isolated natives might experience conversion before the collective redemption of the Jews.[28]

Despite these similarities, Cotton's eschatology could accommodate a conventional mission and Williams's could not. As noted earlier, Cotton thought that conscientious Christians living before the Middle Advent could recover a semblance of the apostolic church, even though its full restoration had to await the millennium. In his judgment, Massachusetts Bay had recaptured enough of the primitive church to establish a standard of faith and order that could be used for a variety of purposes, including the creation of a state church, the formulation of creeds, and the persecution of heterodoxy. Other purposes were the instruction of Indians in Christian doctrine and the establishment of congregations of visible saints for the isolated converts who appeared before the Lord of the Middle Advent appointed miracle-working missionaries to accomplish the lion's share of the work. Williams, for his part, refused to participate in what he called a quest for "a finer and a finer and a yet more fine" approximation of apostolic belief and practice. He insisted that prior to the Middle Advent, Christians could never recover enough of apostolic Christianity to meet any of these purposes. Hence there was no legitimate basis for a traditional missionary program of instruction and church formation.[29]

Williams was not opposed to all forms of missionary activity. After his removal to Rhode Island, he conversed with Indians about the inadequacy of their traditional religion and about their sinful condition in order to ready them for the coming transformation. He explained in the mid-1640s that he had engaged in "many solemn discourses" with the natives, that "there is no small preparation in the hearts of multitudes of them," and that the Indians had offered "many solemn confessions" of "their lost, wandering conditions." He also anticipated that the Indians would become model Christians once the Lord of the Middle Advent had restored a standard of faith and practice and commissioned apostles to carry it to the natives. Williams stated that the Indians "are intelligent, many very ingenuous, plainhearted, inquisitive, and . . . prepared with many convictions" and that they fall "far short of European sinners." His quarrel was with traditional missionary theology. He denied that Christians could confidently instruct Indians in Christian doctrine and establish churches for the isolated Indians converted by the hand of God prior to the redemption of the Jews. He evidently thought that these converts would become free-floaters like himself, uncertain of the doctrinal content of the Christian religion and unaffiliated with any church. Williams also resisted the assumption, which was not under debate at the level of eschatology, that prospective converts had to become civilized in the English manner. The notion that an Indian convert could be uncivilized, lack a solid grounding in doctrine, and have no church in which to receive the sacraments was unthinkable to Cotton, Eliot, and other Bay Puritans.[30]

Eliot almost certainly accepted Cotton's missionary eschatology in the early years of the Indian work. The evidence for this judgment is necessarily circumstantial because Eliot's extant sources contain only one unrevealing reference to the "last things" prior to July 1649, when he began to steer his own course through biblical prophecy. There are three reasons for thinking that Eliot followed Cotton before that time. First, the Apostle's principal missionary colleague in the 1640s, Shepard, endorsed the sequence ("till the Jews come in, there is a seal set upon the hearts" of the Indians) and acknowledged the possibility of occasional conversions before that time ("if the least beginnings be made by the conversion of two or three, it is worth all our time and travails"). Second, Eliot's discussions of the Indians' ancestry in the early 1650s presupposed the validity of the Jews-then-Gentiles sequence. Third, he acknowledged a profound debt to Cotton even though he did not specify what that debt was.[31]

The mission in Massachusetts Bay began in 1646 under the shadow of Cotton's Jews-then-Gentiles sequence. Eliot and his associates worked to civilize the natives and instruct them in Christian doctrine even though only isolated natives were presently eligible for conversion and church membership. The fact that Cotton's eschatology could and did accommodate the Indian work in 1646, however, should not obscure the antimissionary implications of his perspective. Although a late comer relative to others, the Jews-then-Gentiles sequence was one of the factors that postponed the birth of the mission in Massachusetts Bay.

The Delay of the Mission

The ethnocentrism of the affective model is self-evident. To borrow words that Gary Nash has used to make a slightly different point, the model assumed that "Algonkian-speaking people for generations had been aware that their culture was worthless and had daily searched the horizon for sight of some redemptive expeditionary force." But shorn of its ethnocentric arrogance, the affective model meant that a mission could not begin until the Indians wanted to receive one. The colony's policy, as Cotton told an English correspondent in the mid-1630s, was "not to compel" the Indians "but to permit them either to believe willingly or not to believe at all." The published records of the Massachusetts General Court support Cotton's claim. Prior to the submission of the sachems in 1644, the court enacted no law that explicitly required Indians to receive Christian instruction or prohibited them from traditional religious activities. In practice, the only exceptions to this voluntaristic policy were Pequot War captives, who were assigned to Puritan homes or sent to English settlements in the Caribbean. These individuals had little alternative but to accept training in civility and instruction in religion.[32]

Several natives chose to cast their lot with the English in the period prior to the birth of the mission. The most celebrated example in Massachusetts Bay was a Pawtucket Indian called Sagamore John, who sought Christian instruction after John Wilson had cured him of an unspecified illness in 1631 or 1632. Sagamore John then "fell off and took up his Indian course of life again." In 1633 he contracted the smallpox virus, sought forgiveness for the sin of apostasy, and died "in a persuasion that he should go to the Englishmen's heaven." Well-known examples outside the Bay Colony were Squanto, a Patuxet Indian in Plymouth, and Wequash, a Pequot who lived near the Saybrook plantation in Connecticut. Squanto had been kidnapped by an English captain in 1614 and then lived in Spain, England, Newfoundland, and England a second time; he returned home in 1619 to discover that epidemic disease had depopulated his village. As his death approached in 1622, Squanto asked William Bradford to "pray for him that he might go to the Englishmen's God in heaven." Wequash defected from the Pequots during the war in 1637. By the time of his death in 1642—Pequot refugees had allegedly poisoned him—he had made such progress in the Christian life that Shepard pronounced him converted in the Puritan sense of the word.[33]

The authors of *New Englands First Fruits*, by far the richest source for missionary history prior to the start of Eliot's work, interpreted these and similar cases through the affective model. Sagamore John "loved to imitate us in our behavior and apparel and began to hearken after our God and his ways"; a Bay Colony Indian called "William" (probably the Duke William or Black William who lived on Nahant Neck) "labored to transform himself into English manners and practices"; and an unidentified Plymouth Indian, possibly Squanto, "increased in knowledge and so in affection, and also in his practice, reforming and conforming himself accordingly." The authors of the work claimed that what had "won these poor wretches to look after the Gospel" were "the dealings and carriages, which God has guided the English in our patent, to exercise toward them." These displays of virtue included the colonists' "free and fair" occupation of coastal land, their willingness to vindicate "to the utmost" natives with grievances against settlers, and the "good looks and kind salutes" the saints bestowed upon the Indians. The authors then concluded, in a perfect expression of the affective model, that those natives who have been "brought to hearken to our words and . . . to serve our God" had "first a good esteem of our persons."[34]

These Indians were clearly the exceptions rather than the rule. The authors of *New Englands First Fruits,* who wanted to construe the situation to the colony's greatest advantage, were able to list only six or seven adults who had allegedly affected the virtues of the planters in the early period of settlement: Sagamore John, Wequash, William, the anonymous Plymouth Indian, an unnamed one in Salem, and one or two others of uncertain identity and location (for good measure, the authors threw in the irrelevant example of a "blackmore maid" in Dorchester). At least two of these Indians lived outside Massachusetts Bay, and at least three of them were dead by the time *New Englands First Fruits* was written. The authors' contention that many "more might be added" does not square with the documentary record. In the 1640s Eliot, Shepard, Cotton, and Edward Winslow stated that the Indians had revealed no collective interest in the English example during the first decade and a half of colonization, and in the 1650s several of Eliot's proselytes testified to the same effect.[35]

There were occasional attempts prior to the birth of the mission to rouse the Indians from their lethargy. In 1647 Eliot reported that he had tried to interest the natives in Christian civilization before his first successful missionary sermon in October 1646 (evidence exists for only one earlier attempt, in September 1646); Wilson sometimes preached to other natives besides Sagamore John in the early settlement period; and Edmund Brown, the minister at Sudbury, and Roger Williams (before his banishment) may also have attempted to evangelize the local Indians. Most if not all of the colonists, however, were probably content to agree with Cotton, who said in the mid-1630s that because the natives had not responded to the English example, "we acknowledge and accordingly permit [them] to remain in their unbelief." The most explicit testimony to the settlers' state of mind, as well as to the Indians' sluggish response to the virtues of the saints, appeared in a letter that Eliot wrote in 1657 to Richard Baxter, who had asked him why the colony had made so little missionary progress in the early years of settlement. Eliot explained:

> For many years together when the Indians resorted to the houses of godly people, they saw their manner of life and worship in families and in public also; where sometimes they would see and observe what they did, but liked not of it—yea, so disliked, that if any began to speak of God and heaven and hell and religion unto them they would presently be gone. So that it was a received and known thing to all English that if they were burdensome, and you would have them gone, speak of religion and you were presently rid of them; and hence they often frequented the houses of loose and carnal persons who did never speak of religion to them.[36]

There were various reasons why the colonists were disinclined to adopt a more aggressive missionary posture. One was the existence of more pressing concerns in their lives, such as the construction of towns and the creation of economic, political, and ecclesiastical institutions. Another was the language problem. The planters clearly did not expect that God would restore the gift of speaking in tongues for routine missionary purposes; and Winslow, Cotton, and the authors of *New Englands First Fruits* admitted that the prospect of mastering the local dialects through ordinary means was a deterrent to missionary activity.[37] A third reason was the Jews-then-Gentiles sequence. In 1642 the repatriate Thomas Lechford observed that "some" colonists were using the sequence to justify the continued postponement of the mission. Several years after the start of Eliot's work, Cotton stated that Lechford was wrong and insisted that the sequence "hinders not but that some sprinklings and gleanings of them [Indian converts] may be brought home to Christ" before the calling of the Jews. Nevertheless, Lechford was almost certainly correct in his assessment of the role played by Cotton's eschatology before the birth of the mission. In a manuscript fragment from one of his lectures on Revelation, Cotton noted without further comment that the sequence explained "the backwardness of these Indians to be converted unto our religion."[38] A fourth reason for the settlers' nonaggressive missionary stance was the colony's ecclesiastical polity. In contrast to its episcopal and presbyterian counterparts, the congregational polity could not ordain persons for full-time missionary service. The pastoral obligations of Congregationalist ministers left them with little time to instruct the Indians. The polity's weakness in this respect is most clearly illustrated in the Cambridge Platform (1648), which defined ecclesiological orthodoxy in Massachusetts Bay. The platform contains no provision for missionary work. The reason for the silence was not that the delegates to the synod forgot about the natives: Eliot brought a group of Christian Indians to the opening session, and it was noted that their piety "did marvelously affect" the assembled worthies.[39] Moreover, the principal author of the platform, Richard Mather, was one of Eliot's associates in the Indian work. Rather, the reason was that at the level of formal ecclesiology, Congregationalism could not accommodate a mission.

These four reasons are the ones commonly cited by historians to account for the delay of the mission.[40] There can be little doubt that the exigencies of settlement, the language barrier, the Jews-then-Gentiles sequence, and the congregational polity contributed to the delay of the mission. Yet none of the four was insurmountable: Eliot and his co-workers overcame them all. To the extent that the surviving documentation permits a judgment about the matter, the major reason for the postponement of the mission was the Indians' failure to conform to the affective model. Until the natives had done so, the elders were reluctant to think about learning the Massachusett language, to steal time from their flocks and from other concerns, and to take advantage of the loopholes in Cotton's eschatology.

Thus by 1644 there were obstacles at both ends of the missionary process. The Indians' unresponsiveness to the English example delayed the first two stages in the process, training in civility and instruction in religion; and Cotton's Jews-then-Gentiles sequence placed severe strictures on the later two stages, conversion at the hand of God and full church membership. The historical problem that needs to be explained is not why Massachusetts Bay waited so long to begin the Indian work, but why the colony began it at all. The decisive event that led to the birth of the mission was the submission of six sachems to the General Court in 1644. This action must be viewed in conjunction with the Bay Colony's attempts to establish control over the "Narragansett Country" on the west shore of Narragansett Bay and with the diplomatic initiatives undertaken in 1643 and 1644 by Roger Williams and by his fellow Rhode Islander, Samuel Gorton.

CHAPTER TWO

• • •

The Submission of the Sachems and the Birth of the Mission

In 1643 Roger Williams sailed for London to seek a charter incorporating the Rhode Island towns of Providence, Portsmouth, and Newport into a single colony. He undertook the journey partly because these three settlements were internally unstable and partly because Massachusetts Bay, Plymouth, and Connecticut were trying to establish control over the lands in and around Narragansett Bay. The action most directly responsible for Williams's journey to London occurred in September 1642, when William Arnold and three other Englishmen living in the Pawtuxet reserve on the southern outskirts of Providence seceded from the town's "combination government" and placed their settlement under the authority of Massachusetts Bay. Shortly before this action, the four Pawtuxet men had secured a dubious title to the land from the local Narragansett sachem, Sacononoco, who in turn wanted to sever his ties with the paramount Narragansett sachems, Canonicus and his nephew and heir apparent, the ill-fated Miantonomi. The Bay Colony had encouraged the Pawtuxet secession for self-interested reasons. As John Winthrop explained at the time, Massachusetts Bay accepted Pawtuxet into its jurisdiction in order to "draw in the rest of those parts, either under ourselves or Plymouth," to have a base for military operations in the event that "we should have occasion of sending out against any Indians of Narragansett," and to have "an outlet into Narragansett Bay."[1]

In traveling to London, Williams found himself in the awkward position of protecting the interests of the man largely to blame for the political instability in the three Rhode Island towns and for the Pawtuxet secession. The individual in question was Samuel Gorton, an uncompromising advocate of English law and the founder of a radical spiritist sect that survived into the late eighteenth century. Gorton's career in New England began in 1637, when he arrived in Massachusetts Bay and left shortly thereafter. As Robert E. Wall, Jr., has noted, Gorton "must have known after even the most cursory observation that a man of his religious mentality would not be welcome in the Bay Colony." Gorton then moved to Plymouth, where he remained until the winter of 1638–39, when he was banished from the colony for political and theological heterodoxy. He next tried his luck in Portsmouth, Rhode Island, where, in alliance with the Hutchinsonians, he and his small band of disciples overthrew the government of William Coddington. In 1640 the restored Coddington government exiled the Gortonists, who then settled in Providence, where their actions and opinions exasperated Williams and other residents of the town. In January 1642 Gorton and his followers moved to Pawtuxet. Unable to control the Gortonists, Arnold and his associates appealed to Massachusetts Bay for help. The colony's calculated refusal to offer assistance without a legal justification for intervention led to the secession of September 1642. The Gortonists then left Pawtuxet for a site directly to its south, Shawomet (Warwick), where in January 1643 they purchased some land from Pomham, the local Narragansett sachem whom Miantonomi had pressured into making the sale. Pomham soon came to resent the Gortonists and, like Sacononoco, fell under the pro-Massachusetts influence of the Pawtuxet secessionists.[2]

During his Atlantic passage, Williams drafted *A Key into the Language of America*, a collection of Algonquian words and phrases interspersed with observations about the Indians. His decision to write a book about the natives was prudent: missionary work held a place of honor in English promotional literature, and he had sailed to England in order to win a charter. Upon his arrival in London, Williams discovered, or so he said in the preface to *A Key*, that "the great inquiry of all men" was "what Indians have been converted? what have the English done in those parts? what hopes of the Indians receiving the knowledge of Christ?" Williams did not attribute this interest in Indian evangelism—which he clearly exaggerated, given the fact that England was in the midst of a civil war—to criticism of the sorry missionary record in Massachusetts Bay. Rather, he traced the excitement about the matter to the recent publication of *New Englands First Fruits*. Williams was disturbed by the political implications of this work, for he feared that it would create the false impression that a mission already existed in Massachusetts Bay. He surely anticipated that the colony's current agents in London, Thomas Weld and Hugh Peter (who were responsible for publishing and for writing much of *New Englands First Fruits*), would oppose his design to secure a charter for Rhode Island. Williams was particularly upset about the account of Wequash in *New Englands First Fruits*. The work credited some unidentified "English[men] well acquainted with his language" with the Indian's spiritual progress. This phrasing concealed Williams's considerable role. Although he did not claim exclusive credit for the achievement, he stated in the preface to *A Key* that he had engaged in "many discourses" with Wequash about "the condition of all mankind," and that he had visited the dying Pequot and "closed with him concerning his soul." Williams further strengthened his missionary credentials by representing *A Key* as a primer for aspiring evangelists: "a man may, by this help, converse with thousands of natives all over the country; and by such converse it may please the father of mercies to spread civility (and in his most holy season) Christianity." He then promised to publish at a future date "a brief additional discourse" about the "great point of [the Indians'] conversion so much to be longed for." Williams concluded the preface with a pious expression of hope for "these Gentiles of America to partake of the mercies of Europe, and then shall be fulfilled what is written by the prophet Malachi [1:11], from the rising of the sun (in Europe) to the going down of the same (in America), my name shall be great among the Gentiles."[3]

A Key into the Language of America was published in September 1643. At the time Williams did not know the identity of the person or persons who had the power to grant a charter. His uncertainty ended in November, when the Long Parliament created the Warwick Commission for Foreign Plantations and gave it authority over the colonies. Williams's adversary in his negotiations with the commission was Weld; Peter was in Holland at the time. Weld proposed to the Warwick Commission that the Bay Colony's patent be extended southward to Narragansett Bay and westward to the Pequot (Thames) River. His arguments before the commissioners can be inferred from the fraudulent "Narragansett Patent" that he prepared during the negotiations: the need for new land to accommodate the growing population of Massachusetts Bay, the importance of "planting further into the heathen's country" so that the Gospel "may be the more speedier conveyed and preached to natives that now sit there in darkness," and the necessity of protecting orthodoxy from contamination by the Rhode Islanders. Williams's arguments before the Warwick Commission do not appear in the documentary record. He surely defended the colonists' heterodoxy and stressed their history of amicable relations with the leading Narragansett sachems. Whether he professed a missionary purpose for the proposed colony, or simply allowed *A Key* to speak for him, is unclear.[4]

In March 1644 the Warwick Commission awarded Williams a "free and absolute charter" for the colony of Rhode Island, with boundaries that stretched westward to the Pequot River, northward to the existing Massachusetts line, and eastward to the edge of Plymouth Colony. Pawtuxet and Shawomet were located within this territory even though the charter did not mention either settlement by name. Williams remained in London long enough to publish his famous polemic against Massachusetts Bay, *The Bloudy Tenent of Persecution*. Then in August 1644 he set sail for New England, armed with the charter as well as a letter signed by several prominent parliamentary leaders. The letter directed the Bay Colony to permit him to land at Boston (he had been forced to sail to England from New Amsterdam), praised him for his "great industry and travail in his printed Indian labors," and commended him for a record of missionary achievement "the like whereof we have not seen extant from any part of America." Williams left England without publishing the promised "brief additional discourse" about the "great point of the Indians' conversion."[5]

Williams did not pursue this "great point" after his return to Rhode Island. In the preface to *A Key*, he had walked a fine line between his diplomatic objectives and his eschatological convictions. He was not lying when he wrote in the preface that he "longed for" the day when Christian truth stretched from "the rising to the setting of the sun." What he concealed—surely in the interests of diplomacy—were the reasons why he was not prepared to work toward that goal in a conventional missionary fashion. In January 1645 Williams's "brief additional discourse" appeared in London. He had written the work, entitled *Christenings make not Christians*, prior to his departure from

London. The postponement of publication was probably deliberate on Williams's part, for the members of the Warwick Commission would certainly have seen reason in the work to question the missionary commitment of its author. Although it carried an orthodox anti-Catholic title, *Christenings make not Christians* was not orthodox in its contents. In the tract Williams disclosed why he was unwilling to pursue the evangelical work even though he had "such a key of language and such a door of opportunity." He explained that the "main particulars" were the eschatological reasons I described in Chapter 1. He also gave two other reasons. The first was that his knowledge of Algonquian was insufficient to "open matters of salvation" to the Indians, a surprising confession by a man who had recently published a language primer advertised as a "help" to prospective missionaries. The second, surely tinged with a measure of sarcasm, was that he would leave the Indian work to his "worthy countrymen in the Bay of Massachusetts," who had given "many expressions of their holy desires" about the matter.[6]

In the interim, much had transpired in New England. During Williams's absence, the Pawtuxet secessionists persuaded Pomham and Sacononoco to officially sever their ties with Canonicus and Miantonomi. In May 1643 William Arnold's son Benedict brought Pomham and Sacononoco to Boston for a session of the General Court. The two sachems presented the assembly with ten fathoms of wampum, a symbol of tribute worth about 50 shillings, and offered to submit to the Massachusetts government. The court temporarily declined the offer of submission and instead invited Gorton and Miantonomi to Boston for a hearing about the transactions at Pawtuxet and Shawomet. Gorton refused to attend. Miantonomi, who sought the neutrality or even the support of Massachusetts Bay in his ongoing struggle against Uncas and the Mohegan Indians in Connecticut, accepted the invitation. The purpose of the hearing was to create the semblance of justice; the outcome of the proceedings sustained the Bay Colony's interests. The court ruled that the sale of Pawtuxet was legal, thereby vindicating Sacononoco and the secessionists against Canonicus and Miantonomi, and that the sale of Shawomet was not, thus upholding Pomham against the paramount Narragansett sachems and Gorton. Pomham and Sacononoco then returned to Rhode Island, where they were soon visited by two unidentified Massachusetts deputies, who explained the terms of submission to them. These terms included obedience to the Ten Commandments. According to the deputies, the two sachems promised "to worship the true God... and not to blaspheme him," "to honor their parents and [English] superiors," "not to kill any man but upon just cause and just authority," to refrain from "fornication, adultery, bestiality, etc." and from lying and "swear[ing] falsely," to permit their children "to read God's Word," and to avoid "any unnecessary work on the Lord's Day within the gates of proper towns." Pomham and Sacononoco reportedly replied to this last injunction that they "have not much to do any day, and therefore will forbear on that day."[7]

In June 1643, Pomham and Sacononoco returned to Boston and formally submitted to Massachusetts Bay by placing their marks upon a document stating that they

> do voluntarily, and without any constraint or persuasion, but of our own free motion, put ourselves, our subjects, lands, and estates under the government and jurisdiction of the Massachusetts, to be governed and protected by them, according to their just laws and orders, so far as we shall be made capable of understanding them; and we do promise for ourselves, and all our subjects, and all our posterity, to be true and faithful to the said government, aiding to the maintenance thereof, to our best ability, and from time to time to give speedy notice of any conspiracy, attempt, or evil intention of any which we shall know or hear of against the same; and we do promise to be willing from time to time to be instructed in the knowledge and worship of God.

By this action the two sachems placed Pawtuxet and Shawomet under the jurisdiction of Massachusetts Bay (this action was soon undone by the Rhode Island charter of 1644). The provision about religious instruction was included in the terms of submission in order to justify the extension of the colony's authority into the Narragansett Country. As Winthrop explained a month later, "when we received Pomham and Sacononoco into our jurisdiction, the General Court considered how offensive it would be to the Narragansetts [that is, to Canonicus and Miantonomi], and so likely to engage us in a war with them; yet the thing being lawful and expedient for us, and giving hope of opening a door to the conversion of some of them, [we] would not let slip the opportunity of such advantages, for the fear of doubtful dangers."[8]

In August 1643, two months after the submission of Pomham and Sacononoco, Miantonomi marched into battle against the Mohegans under the leadership of their sachem, Uncas. The Narragansett sachem, encumbered by a coat of armor given him by a well-intentioned Gortonist, fell into the hands of his enemies. The Mohegans brought Miantonomi before the Connecticut magistrates, who jailed him and then turned his case over to the Commissioners of the United Colonies for adjudication at their inaugural meeting in September. The Commissioners recommended that Uncas follow a certain course of action, and the sachem gladly accepted their advice. Accompanied by English witnesses assigned for this specific purpose, the Mohegan Indians took Miantonomi beyond the jurisdiction of Connecticut and drove a hatchet into his head. The Commissioners promptly made plans to protect the orthodox colonies and the Mohegans from the anticipated Narragansett retaliation.[9]

The Bay then moved against the other victim of the hearing over Pawtuxet and Shawomet, Samuel Gorton. In September 1643 the General Court sent an expeditionary force to Shawomet to arrest Gorton and his disciples, who, according to the results of the hearing, resided within the jurisdiction of Massachusetts Bay. In October the Gortonists were tried and convicted for blasphemy and contempt for civil authority, and were sentenced to perform manual labor, in leg irons, in various towns around Boston. Some six months later, the court, convinced that the Gortonists were seducing others to their views, changed the sentence to banishment from the colony, including Shawomet, on pain of death. The Gortonists then returned to Shawomet to test the Bay Colony's resolve. After receiving a threatening letter from Winthrop, they moved to Aquidneck Island where, under Coddington's distrustful eye, they planned their next course of action.

That course was for them to seek vindication in London. In June 1644 Gorton and two of his disciples, Randall Holden and John Greene, traveled overland to New Amsterdam and boarded a ship for England, where they hoped to secure clear title to Shawomet. It is uncertain if Gorton and his companions sailed with knowledge of the March 1644 Rhode Island charter (Williams did not return to Providence until September; whether or not he sent advance news of his diplomatic success is difficult to ascertain because his correspondence for 1644 is lost). In May 1646 Gorton won his case before the Warwick Commission. Several months later, Holden sailed to Boston with a warrant from the commission that authorized him to proceed unmolested to Shawomet. Gorton chose to stay in London in the event that Massachusetts Bay renewed its quarrel with him. In the meantime he published an account of his struggle with the colony, *Simplicities Defence against Seven-Headed Policy* (1646), as well as a theological manifesto, directed largely against John Cotton, *An Incorruptible Key, composed of the CX Psalme* (1647). The wisdom of Gorton's decision to remain behind was confirmed in January 1647, when Edward Winslow, the Bay Colony's newly appointed agent in England, arrived in London to challenge the Gortonists' title to Shawomet.[10]

The situation in Rhode Island played an important role in the birth of Eliot's mission. The Bay Colony's expansionist designs on the Narragansett Country led to the submission of Pomham and Sacononoco, which set a precedent soon followed by six sachems within the colony's chartered bounds, and also obliged Williams and Gorton to travel to London to seek parliamentary protection. The leaders of Massachusetts Bay were dismayed to learn that the Warwick Commission had awarded Williams a charter and confirmed Gorton's title. As Francis Jennings has observed (in an argument evaluated later in this chapter), the commission's decision to side with two heterodox Rhode Islanders convinced the Bay Colony that it needed to rehabilitate its reputation in England.

The Submission of the Sachems in Massachusetts Bay

On March 8, 1644, the Massachusetts General Court received the submissions of five sachems who lived within the chartered boundaries of the colony: Cutshamekin, the "Squaw Sachem," Mascononomo, Nashowanon, and Wossamegon. The sachems presented the court with twenty-six fathoms of wampum (they had delivered thirty fathoms the month before). After "freely assenting" to the terms of submission, the five sachems placed their marks upon a document identical to the one that Pomham and Sacononoco had signed nine months earlier, and they also promised to heed a list of religious and moral injunctions similar to the one given to the two Narragansetts. For its part, the General Court gave each of the five sachems a coat, two yards of red cloth, a meal, and a "potful of wine." The five sachems then "went away very joyful." Some ten weeks later, a sixth sachem in Massachusetts Bay, Passaconaway, agreed to "such articles as Cutshamekin and others have formerly accepted." One or more of Passaconaway's sons accompanied him to Boston for the occasion.[11]

The submission of the sachems in Massachusetts Bay presents an interpretive problem. There is ample documentation about the negotiations that resulted in the submissions of Pomham and Sacononoco in 1643. In contrast, the published records of the General Court and John Winthrop's journal and correspondence contain no evidence that the 1644 submissions were preceded by a diplomatic initiative on the colony's part. Jennings suspects that the General Court strong-armed the sachems in Massachusetts Bay and "extorted" the wampum. "Considering what the Indians gave up," he writes, "we may harbor a small doubt about how voluntarily they laid out their sacrifice." He also surmises that the sachems were reluctant to resist the colony's aggression because they did not want to suffer the fate that befell Miantonomi.[12] Jennings's interpretation is difficult to accept. A fuller examination suggests that the impetus for the submissions came from the sachems, rather than from the Massachusetts Bay colonists, and that the Indians had their own reasons for subjecting themselves and their bands to the General Court.

Three of the signatories of the act of submission—Cutshamekin, the Squaw Sachem, and Mascononomo—lived in the vicinity of Boston. Cutshamekin was the sachem of the Massachusett Indians, who resided to the south and west of the city. He had been sachem since the death of his older brother, Chickataubut, in 1633. After Cutshamekin's passing in late 1651 or early 1652, his nephew Josias Wompatuck, Chickataubut's son, became the Massachusett sachem. The Squaw and Mascononomo belonged to the Pawtucket bands to the immediate north and east of Boston. The Squaw was the mother of three well-known Indians, Sagamore John (one of the "hopeful" natives in *New Englands First Fruits*), Sagamore James, and Sagamore George. She apparently died shortly after her submission to the General Court. Mascononomo, the "sagamore of Agawam," had been one of the three Indians who boarded the *Arbella* as the ship lay off Plum Cove in June 1630. He died in 1658. Nine years later, an Englishman was jailed, placed in the stocks, and fined for disinterring the sagamore's remains and then "carrying his skull on a pole." The culprit was also ordered to rebury "the skull and bones that can be found."[13]

The Boston-area Indians had suffered through two major epidemics by the time of the submission. The first lasted from 1616 to 1619; its nature remains a matter of debate among scholars. This epidemic had a horrendous impact on the Massachusetts and the Pawtuckets. In

1631 Thomas Dudley reported that Chickataubut had only "between fifty and sixty subjects," that Sagamores John and James "command not above thirty or forty men," and that Mascononomo had "two or three families subject" to him. These figures may represent a 90 percent population loss from the precontact period. The second epidemic (1633–34) was clearly a form of smallpox. Chickataubut and Sagamores John and James were among its victims. The two epidemics cleared a large expanse of territory for Puritan settlement, increased the Indians' fear of raiding parties, and left the sachems and their bands vulnerable to manipulation by their English neighbors.[14]

In the early 1630s the Massachusett and Pawtucket sachems donated land to the colonists in order to build a wall of protection against the Micmac Indians (the "Tarrantines"). These distant marauders, who lived beyond the Penobscot, had raided the bands in 1619, when they killed the Squaw's first husband, Nanepashemet, and again in 1631, when they burned Mascononomo's wigwam, wounded Sagamores John and James, and abducted the latter's wife. The English presence discouraged further Micmac incursions after 1631. In the mid-1630s the sachems began to sell land to the colonists instead of giving it to them. As Neal Salisbury explains in *Manitou and Providence,* the end of the short-lived fur trade along the coast led the Massachusetts and Pawtuckets to "turn increasingly to their own land, the commodity which the English coveted most," in order to satisfy their taste for European trade goods. In 1634 the General Court "reassert[ed] its land-granting authority in the face of eager Indian sellers and English buyers" by prohibiting further purchases without its approval. Most of the land transactions that took place between the 1634 action and the submissions of 1644 fell into two major categories. First, the sachems received retroactive payments for lands donated to the English in the early 1630s. For instance, in 1638 Mascononomo obtained £20 compensation from John Winthrop, Jr., and the other residents of Ipswich; between 1637 and 1639 the Squaw Sachem received a total of 36 shillings, 21 coats, 19 fathoms of wampum, and 3 bushels of corn for Charlestown (Cutshamekin received 10 shillings for a modest claim in the town); and in 1640 the Squaw was given slightly less than £25 plus an annual coat for Cambridge and Watertown. The circumstances of these transactions may explain the meager amount of remuneration—the planters probably reasoned that the sachems were fortunate to receive any payment for territory they had once given away. Second, the sachems were compensated for lands freshly settled by the English from the mid-1630s on. For example, in 1637 the Squaw; her current husband, Webbacowet; and several other Pawtuckets received an unspecified payment for the newly established town of Concord.[15]

In the transfer of land, the General Court expected the sachems to act as the representatives of their bands. This policy inflated the authority of the sachems and minimized or perhaps eliminated the traditional role of their counselors in important decisions. The officers of the court created this relationship because they preferred to deal with individuals rather than with groups and because they sometimes wrongly assumed that the sachems were the native counterparts to European monarchs. The colony occasionally awarded special privileges to the sachems in order to encourage their cooperation. Prior to the act of submission, Cutshamekin, Masconoomo, and the Squaw Sachem were apparently the only Indians in the colony authorized to purchase rifles and ammunition, and to take their firearms to gunsmiths for repair. Winthrop also gave small presents to the sachems and their relatives, and he occasionally invited them—provided they wore English clothing—to dine at his table. The purpose of these "tokens of place and dignity" was to subordinate the sachems and their bands to Puritan power. "It is a rule in war," Edward Howes told the younger Winthrop in 1632, "to aim to surprise and captivate great ones, and the less will soon come under; so win the hearts of the sachems and you win all."[16]

Prior to the act of submission, the sachems also assisted the General Court in the investigation of the disputes that arose between the two peoples. Most of these cases involved the property damage that resulted from the Indians' reluctance to fence their fields and the colonists' disinclination to corral their livestock, or from acts of vandalism. The court adjudicated these and other matters with little or no regard for native standards of justice. In instances when they assigned guilt to the Indians, the magistrates instructed the sachems to arrange for redress to the English victims and, in some cases, to beat the offending members of their bands. Like the allocation of land, the infliction of punishment was a traditional responsibility of the sachems. But as Salisbury observes, the magistrates perverted Indian custom even though they preserved the appearance of it. In the past the sachems and their counselors had sometimes assigned plots of land to families but had never conveyed territory into the permanent possession of others, and they had punished subordinate Indians in order to restore equilibrium within the bands and not to satisfy a European standard of justice.[17]

In the early period of settlement, the colony also used the sachems, particularly Cutshamekin, in its diplomacy with the Narragansetts. The Boston-area Indians may have been predisposed to this arrangement because they had an existing history of association with the Narragansetts: in 1632 the Massachusetts and Pawtuckets had sent men to Canonicus when he raised a show of force against the Pequots. Nevertheless, the sachems' diplomacy on the colony's behalf obliged them to represent English interests rather than their own. In August 1636 Cutshamekin accompanied Edward Gibbens and John Higginson on an embassy to the Narragansetts to determine if Canonicus and Miantonomi were responsible for the murder of John Oldham, an English trader on Block Island (they were not); later that month Cutshamekin went with John Endecott on a punitive expedition to Block Island, and on the way back to Boston killed a Pequot and sent his scalp to Canonicus; in October 1636 the Massachusett sachem helped to arrange a treaty between the Narragansetts and the Bay Colony against the Pequots; and in the fall of 1638, he and Macononomo participated in the advance negotiations that led to a treaty at Hartford between Connecticut, the Narragansetts, and the Mohegans.[18]

In September 1642 Massachusetts Bay accepted the Arnolds' Pawtuxet settlement into its jurisdiction. This action stranded Cutshamekin between the Narragansetts and the English. The General Court disarmed and incarcerated the sachem, and then interrogated him about his possible involvement in an alleged Narragansett conspiracy against Massachusetts Bay. "The arrest was a signal," Salisbury explains, "that the colony no longer needed the Massachusett sachem in his intermediary role and that it sought to detach him from the Narragansett altogether." The magistrates released Cutshamekin and restored his weaponry after he convinced them of his loyalty. Massachusetts Bay soon provided the sachem with an opportunity to demonstrate his allegiance to the colony. In May 1643 he testified against Miantonomi in the hearing about the transactions at Pawtuxet and Shawomet. Cutshamekin stated that Pomham and Sacononoco were "free sachems" whose autonomy permitted them to dispose of their lands as they pleased. This testimony, as Salisbury notes, "grounded the colony's argument in native custom as well as English law."[19] In order to secure this testimony, however, the magistrates forced Cutshamekin to repudiate the Narragansett Indians in the daunting presence of Miantonomi.

Salisbury terminates his narrative in *Manitou and Providence* with the murder of Miantonomi in September 1643. For this reason, he offers no interpretation of the submissions of Cutshamekin, Mascononomo, and the Squaw in 1644. The Puritan magistrates had committed three acts of provocation against the main body of Narragansetts: the establishment of the settlement at Pawtuxet in September 1642, the hearing over the sales at Pawtuxet and Shawomet in May 1643, and the murder of Miantonomi in September 1643. The Winthrop sources, as well as the records of the Massachusetts General Court and the Commissioners of the United Colonies, contain numerous expressions of concern for the security of the orthodox colonies and their Indian allies Pomham, Sacononoco, and Uncas. Yet these same sources reveal, through their silence about the matter, a callous disregard for the safety of the Massachusett and Pawtucket sachems, who were also vulnerable to Narragansett reprisals, and who could not reestablish relations with the Rhode Island Indians without alienating Massachusetts Bay. Jennings is probably right that the execution of Miantonomi terrified the Massachusetts and Pawtuckets, and probably wrong about the reason for their alarm: they feared the Narragansetts, not the saints.

In an important journal entry dated February 5, 1644, Winthrop reported that Cutshamekin, Josias Wompatuck, and Mascononomo had recently paid him a visit. The Indians presented Winthrop with thirty fathoms of wampum and then offered to submit to the Bay Colony at the next session of the General Court, which proved to be the one in March, when they made formal submission and contributed another twenty-six fathoms of wampum. Winthrop did not attribute the Indians' visit—which constitutes the only hint in the standard sources of the coming submissions—to any direct negotiations on the Bay Colony's part. The submission was probably the idea of Cutshamekin, who was surely familiar with the precedent set by Pomham and Sacononoco in 1643. If one can presume to speak for them, the Massachusett and Pawtucket sachems submitted to the government in 1644 because they wanted to secure their relationship to Massachusetts Bay in the event of Narragansett retaliation. Winthrop made this connection, even though he construed the course of events to the colony's credit rather than to its shame. He concluded that the Massachusetts and Pawtuckets had offered to submit to the colony because of "our kind dealing with Pomham and Sacononoco, protecting them against the Narragansetts, and righting them against Gorton, etc., who had taken away their land."[20]

The three remaining signatories of the act of submission—Passaconaway, Nashowanon, and Wossamegon—lived forty or more miles to the north and west of Boston. Their inland location apparently spared them the full fury of the epidemic of 1616–1619: Thomas Dudley reported in 1631 that Passaconaway had "under his command four or five hundred men." The three sachems and their bands had participated in the fur trade prior to the act of submission; however, they had little previous contact with permanent English settlement. The first Puritan towns in the area—Haverhill, Lancaster, and Andover—were not established until the mid-1640s. The distance of these Indians from the coastal center of the English population, as well as their inability to avoid the smallpox epidemic of the mid-1630s, left them vulnerable to the Mohawks and other marauders.[21]

Passaconaway, who is usually classified as a member of the Pennacook branch of the Pawtuckets, resided at various locations in the Merrimack Valley, including Pantucket (now Lowell) at the confluence of the Merrimack and Concord Rivers. He was not only a sachem but also a "powwow" (shaman), an unusual combination of functions in native society. Various legends grew up around this redoubtable figure, who died in the early 1660s. Daniel Gookin, the longtime Indian Superintendent in Massachusetts Bay, claimed that Passaconaway lived for more than 120 years; William Wood reported that he could "make the water burn, the rocks move, the trees dance, metamorphosize himself into a flaming man, . . . and make of a dead snake's skin a living snake"; and Thomas Morton heard that the sachem could "in the heat of all summer . . . make ice appear in a bowl of fair water." Passaconaway radiated his influence as far west as Mount Wachusett, one of the homes of his eldest son, Nanamaconcuk, and throughout much of the Merrimack Valley. The sachem and his two principal sons, Nanamaconcuk and Wannalancett, appear only four times in the Winthrop documents and the published General Court records before the act of submission. The most noteworthy of these occasions came in

September 1642, when the General Court, in response to the latest rumors of a Narragansett-inspired Indian conspiracy against the orthodox colonies, sent forty soldiers to Pantucket to disarm Passaconaway and to bring him to Boston for interrogation. The soldiers were unable to locate the sachem, and settled instead for one of his sons (whom the sources do not identify) and the son's wife and small child. On the way back to Boston, the son "slipped his line" and escaped into the woods. After firing once at the fleeing Indian—the bullet "missed him narrowly"—the heroes continued home with only his wife and child as their prize. The General Court then dispatched Cutshamekin, evidently without English supervision, to Pantucket to negotiate a settlement. The Massachusett sachem succeeded in this difficult embassy. Shortly thereafter, the court returned the wife and child, and Passaconaway sent Nanamaconcuk to Boston with the weapons. After receiving satisfactory answers to their questions, the magistrates dismissed Nanamaconcuk and restored the weapons.[22]

Little is known about Nashowanon and Wossamegon, who do not appear in the Winthrop sources or the General Court records until the act of submission. Both sachems were almost certainly Nipmuck Indians. Nashowanon, who died in 1654, lived at Nashaway (Lancaster) to the east of Mount Wachusett. Wossamegon, who resided near Quabag (Brookfield) to the south of the mountain, evidently adopted the alternative name of Matchippa, probably to distinguish himself from the famous Oussamegon (Massasoit) of the Pokanokets in Plymouth Colony. At the time of their submission, Winthrop knew so little about Nashowanon and Wossamegon that he called them simply "two sachems near the great hill to the west called Wachusett." Yet these two Indians journeyed to Boston in March 1644 and accepted the authority of the General Court. It is unlikely that either of them had ever been there before.[23]

Two sources illuminate the circumstances behind the submissions of Nashowanon and Wossamegon. The first is a letter that Eliot wrote to Endecott in 1661. Eliot reported that the Indians near Mount Wachusett had contributed to a collection of wampum for presentation to the General Court at the time of the submissions. He specified the amount of the tribute (200 fathoms, leaving someone with a tidy profit, since the sachems furnished a total of 56 fathoms in 1644); the names of three of the natives who contributed to it (Nashowanon, Wossamegon, and Wompontupont, another Nipmuck sachem near

Quabag); and the reason for the collection ("they crave[d] the benefit... of protection"). Eliot did not identify the person or persons who received the wampum for delivery to the court. The second is a letter that William Pynchon, the founder of Springfield, wrote to Winthrop in 1648 about two recent raids on Nipmuck Indians living near Quabag and Nashaway. This letter suggests that Cutshamekin was the person who had arranged the submissions and collected the wampum. Pynchon explained that soon after the second raid, the natives in question asked Cutshamekin to send English troops against the marauders. This request implies that the victims expected the sachem to deliver on a promise to provide protection. Pynchon's letter also offers a clue about Cutshamekin's possible reason for arranging the submissions. After receiving the request, the sachem went to Eliot and informed him that the Quabag and Nashaway Indians were entitled to protection because they were "his [Cutshamekin's] subjects." Cutshamekin's probable objective—if he was the person primarily or exclusively responsible for negotiating the submissions of the Quabag and Nashaway sachems—was to create a network of bands dependent on him for access to English power. The establishment of such a network would restore the hegemony that the Massachuset Indians had once enjoyed over these Nipmucks: Gookin said in 1674 that the "old men" of the Massachusetts reported that "in former times" their sachems controlled many of the Nipmucks from Nashaway to Pocumtuck (Deerfield).[24]

In February 1644 Cutshamekin, Josias Wompatuck, and Mascononomo made the aforementioned visit to Winthrop. The Indians not only offered their own submissions, but also disclosed that "all the sachems of Wachusett, and all the Indians from Merrimack to Titicut [near Taunton]," wished to "tender themselves to our government." The geographical extent of the proposal must have astonished Winthrop, since it extended to Indians whom he had apparently never met. The unidentified "sachems of Wachusett" surely included Nashowanon and Wossamegon. If the foregoing analysis is correct, Cutshamekin had convinced these two sachems to submit to the General Court. The "Indians from Merrimack" were clearly Passaconaway and his sons. The Massachuset sachem had traveled to Pantucket in the aftermath of the disarming in 1642, and on this or a later occasion may have persuaded Passaconaway to join in the submission. If so, Cutshamekin was probably trying to extend his influence to Indians who had never been under the control of the Massachusetts: Gookin reported that the natives in the Merrimack Valley had traditionally been on amicable terms with the Massachusett sachems but had not been subject to them. The Indians at Titicut, for their part, were or once had been under the Massachusett sachems. In 1650 a group of Massachusetts and Pawtuckets testified that "Chickataubut his bounds did extend" to Titicut. The Titicut Indians, however, did not submit to Massachusetts Bay, perhaps because the colony wished to avoid a jurisdictional dispute with Plymouth.[25]

Much of the subsequent history of Puritan-Indian relations in Massachusetts Bay derived from the act of submission. With the passage of time, as the colony clarified the terms of submission, the sachems and their bands reevaluated the meaning of the 1644 action. These later developments, however, should not obscure the circumstances under which the submissions occurred in 1644. Although there can be no certainty about the matter, the initiative seems to have originated with the sachems, particularly Cutshamekin. Massachusetts Bay had apparently not negotiated, let alone coerced, the submissions.

The submission of the sachems led the General Court to enact a series of missionary directives. On June 10, 1644, less than two weeks after Passaconaway and his sons accepted the colony's authority, the Court of Deputies "enjoined" natives "who have submitted themselves to this government" to receive instruction on Sundays from "those whose hearts God shall stir up to that work"; on November 13, 1644, the Court of Assistants asked the county courts to arrange for the instruction of the Indians in their jurisdictions; and in October 1645, the magistrates and deputies jointly encouraged the elders to begin the work of "bring[ing] the natives to the knowledge of God and his ways."[26] None of these three directives produced any immediate results, and the colony continued to search for a way to instruct the Indians until Eliot undertook the task in 1646.

Many scholars have recognized the connection between the submission of the sachems and the three missionary directives of 1644 and 1645. The standard argument is that the colony assumed that the establishment of legal jurisdiction over the Indians was the prerequisite for the Indian work.[27] The problem with this argument is that the pre-1644 Massachusetts Bay sources I have consulted contain no expression of the idea that the natives had to accept the General Court's authority before a mission could begin.

An alternative interpretation more in keeping with Puritan missionary theology is that the colony viewed the submissions through the affective model. It was not the act of submission per se but the sachems' putative reason for their action that convinced the saints that a mission was now possible. The only person who explicitly made this point was Edward Winslow, who observed in 1649 that "the justice, prudence, valor, temperance, and righteousness of the English . . . begat a good opinion of our persons, and caused them [the sachems] to affect our laws and government." Winslow was writing five years after the fact, and he was a Plymouth and not a Massachusetts man. The only contemporaneous evaluation of the sachems' action, Winthrop's February 1644 journal entry, suggests that Winslow's observation reflected a conclusion drawn in Massachusetts Bay at the time the submissions were made. After learning that "all the sachems [from] Wachusett to . . . Titicut" were prepared to submit to the General Court, Winthrop stated that "we now began to conceive hope that the Lord's time was at hand for opening a door of light and grace to those Indians." He then attributed the Indians' offer of submission to one special act of Puritan virtue, "our kind dealing with Pomham and Sacononoco."[28]

Eliot's First Two Missionary Sermons

John Eliot's first documented missionary lecture was delivered in September 1646 to Cutshamekin and other Massachusett Indians then residing at Neponset (near Dorchester), about four miles from Roxbury. An Indian interpreter and several Puritan ministers—probably Richard Mather of Dorchester and John Allin of Dedham—accompanied Eliot on this occasion. Cutshamekin was an appropriate choice. He lived near Eliot's Roxbury home and was "acquainted with the English language" in the event that the interpreter failed to meet the linguistic challenge; moreover, his preeminence among the sachems of 1644 probably led the colonists to assume that he was the one most eager to receive Christian instruction. The sermon was a disaster: the Indians "gave no heed unto it," Eliot explained a year later, "but were weary, and rather despised what I said." Cutshamekin may have hoped that an unenthusiastic response to the sermon would discourage future missionary visits; he may have also concluded that he could safely disregard the ministers because he no longer lived in fear of the

Narragansetts. In late August 1645, Cutshamekin and Josias Wompatuck witnessed a treaty between the United Colonies and the Narragansett and Eastern Niantic sachems. The treaty prohibited the Rhode Island Indians from molesting natives "in friendship with or subject to any of the English." Cutshamekin was explicitly identified as one of the Indians not to be harmed.[29]

The second sermon was preached on October 28, 1646, to Waban and other Massachusetts at Nonantum. Eliot's English companions on this occasion were Shepard and two other persons (a monument erected in nearby Newton in 1879 identifies them as Isaac Heath, a ruling elder in the Roxbury church, and Daniel Gookin; this claim does not rest on any seventeenth-century source known to me). The three-hour visit to Nonantum began with a prayer in English. With the assistance of the interpreter, Eliot then delivered a seventy-five-minute sermon and supervised a question and answer session with the Indians. In the sermon he concentrated on "all the principal matters" of Protestant theology. During the question and answer period, Eliot and his three colleagues explored the missionary potential of natural theology. "We asked them," Shepard recalled, "if they saw a great wigwam or a great house, would they think that raccoons or foxes that had no wisdom built it . . . or some wise workman made it though they did not see him?" The visitors were pleased by the Indians' responses. After the question and answer session, Eliot offered a second prayer and distributed apples to the children and tobacco to the men. He and the other Englishmen then returned to their homes.[30]

On November 4, 1646, one week after Eliot's visit to Nonantum, the assistants and deputies in Massachusetts Bay enacted five measures that took the two-sermon-old mission into account. Two of the measures were directed to the elders. The first created a rotation plan for the instruction of the Indians. The colony's ministers were asked to choose two of their number each year to "make known the heavenly counsel of God among the Indians . . . by the help of some able interpreter." The second enjoined Eliot, Shepard, and Allin to begin the work of civilizing the Indians at Nonantum by securing a place for them to "live in an orderly way among us" and by preparing a code of "wholesome laws . . . to reduce them to civility of life."[31]

The third and fourth measures pertained to "such pagan Indians as have submitted themselves to our government." One placed them under the jurisdiction of an existing law that sentenced colonists to death for blasphemy, and the other imposed fines, ranging from 20 shillings to £5, for acts of idolatry ("powwow[ing] or perform[ing] outward worship to their false gods and to the devil"). The purpose of the blasphemy and idolatry laws is open to debate. Jennings argues that the Bay Colony enacted the two statutes, particularly the former, in order to intimidate the Indians into obedience. "The permitted choice of range," he writes, "lay between perfunctory observation of accepted ritual, at minimum, and unqualified profession of faith, at optimum. To go outside that range was to commit the blasphemy for which death was mandatory."[32]

There are problems with Jennings's well-known interpretation of the two laws. To judge from the published records of the General Court, Massachusetts Bay never indicted, much less convicted and executed, any native for blasphemy or fined a pagan Indian for idolatry. The only enforcement of the two laws came in the case of nominally Christian Indians whom Gookin fined for powwowing in the late 1660s and early 1670s. Furthermore, Jennings's assumption that anything less than "perfunctory observance of accepted ritual" constituted "blasphemy" underestimates the heinousness of the offense. In 1646 the General Court defined blasphemy as "obstinate[ly] denying the true God" or "curs[ing] God" and considered it a more serious crime than idolatry. The Bay Colony later convicted three Englishmen of blasphemy; in all three cases the accused had made outrageous statements. In 1654 Benjamin Sawcer asserted that "Jehovah is the devil, and that he knew no god but his sword, and that would save him"; in 1681 William King claimed that "he was the eternal Son of God and that he was as holy and pure as God himself"; and three years later, Joseph Gatchell called Jesus "an imperfect savior and a fool" and also denied the existence of God, hell, and the Devil.[33]

The General Court apparently passed the blasphemy and idolatry laws in 1646 in order to placate God rather than to force the Indians to accept the missionary program. A decade earlier, Cotton had told a correspondent in England that the natives ought to be "severely punished" for blasphemy and for "the worship of devils or idols" because he feared that God would become provoked at Massachusetts Bay if the colony were "lawful[ly] openly to tolerate" such practices within its jurisdiction. The General Court did not enact the two laws at that time, probably because there was no legal basis for doing so. The act of submission in 1644 furnished Massachusetts Bay with the authority to enact the laws in question, and Cutshamekin's response to Eliot's inaugural sermon probably gave the General Court special reason to fear divine retribution should the colony continue "openly to tolerate" such behavior. Furthermore, Cotton later explained that the court passed the two statutes because the sachems had pledged in 1644 to obey the Ten Commandments, which prohibited blasphemy and idolatry, and that there was otherwise "no warrant from God or the law of nations" for enacting the statutes. He also claimed that the purpose of the laws was "the preservation of religion" rather than the "propagation of religion."[34]

The blasphemy and idolatry laws carry a tremendous weight in the secondary literature. They provide the sole or the primary documentary basis for the claim advanced by Jennings and others that the Indians in Massachusetts Bay were "forced" to accept Christian instruction and that Eliot's mission was not "voluntaristic." This claim is not necessarily false, even though it is less self-evident that these scholars assume. Pagan Indians who learned of the two laws may have accepted the mission because they feared the statutory penalties in question. These natives could not have known why the General Court passed the laws, whether the colony would enforce them, and how the colony construed "blasphemy." Nevertheless, the argument that the two laws coerced pagans into becoming Christians obscures the fact that Indians had reasons of their own for embracing the mission, as explained in the next chapter.[35]

The fifth and final step taken at the November 1646 court session was to appoint Edward Winslow as the colony's agent in London. Winslow replaced Thomas Weld and Hugh Peter, whom the colony had fired in 1645. The new agent's greatest achievement in England was his role in the creation of the New England Company. Missionary fund-raising, however, was not explicitly mentioned either in Winslow's public instructions or in what Winthrop called his "more secret ones." The General Court initially sent Winslow to England to convince the Warwick Commission to reverse the precedent-setting 1646 ruling that awarded Shawomet to the Gortonists, an action that compromised the Bay Colony's autonomy under the charter. To this end Winslow was given a letter, signed by Winthrop and Increase Nowell, the colony's secretary, to present to the commissioners. As Jennings observes, the letter tried to bolster the colony's case by creating the false impression that the infant Indian mission was located in

Rhode Island and not in Massachusetts Bay: "Mr. Eliot's hopeful beginnings are likely to be dashed, if Gorton, etc. shall be countenanced and upheld against them ['the poor Indians'] and us." By the time of his departure in mid-December 1646, Winslow's instructions had been broadened to include responding to "any other complaints" made against the colony by persons in England. This was clearly a reference to William Vassall and Thomas Fowle. These two men had recently sailed to London on behalf of Dr. Robert Child and other Massachusetts residents known as the "Remonstrants," who were disturbed by the colony's departures from English law, particularly the intolerance of Presbyterianism and the restriction of the franchise to full church members. Winslow met with mixed results in London. He was unable to defeat Gorton. In July 1647 the Warwick Commission reconfirmed Gorton's title and issued him a safe conduct to return to Shawomet through Boston harbor. Gorton arrived in Massachusetts in May 1648. The colony reluctantly permitted him to proceed to Shawomet, which he promptly renamed Warwick in honor of the Earl. Winslow did succeed in his anti-Remonstrant diplomacy, though this bears no direct relation to the birth of the mission. In the summer of 1647, the commission ruled that the Bay Colony had acted within its rights in the matters that disturbed the Remonstrants.[36]

Massachusetts Bay learned about the initial confirmation of Gorton's title to Shawomet in September 1646, when one of his associates, Randall Holden, disembarked in Boston with a safe conduct from the Warwick Commission and a warrant to occupy Shawomet. Jennings notes that Eliot preached his first missionary sermon shortly before or soon after Holden's arrival: Winthrop recorded in his journal that Holden entered Boston on September 13, and Shepard noted that Eliot delivered the sermon at Neponset "about six weeks" before he gave the one at Nonantum on October 28, 1646. Jennings acknowledges that the specific date of the first sermon is uncertain; nevertheless, he insists that chronological precision does not affect the "issue of substance"—the colony's need to stabilize relations with London after Holden's arrival.[37]

Jennings is certainly correct in concluding that Holden's arrival alarmed Massachusetts Bay. The General Court initially commissioned Winslow for no other purpose but responding to Gorton. Furthermore, Jennings is probably right about the timing of Eliot's inaugural sermon. In the absence of any alternative explanation in the sources, Holden's arrival in Boston must be viewed as the event that led the magistrates to encourage Eliot to begin the mission. The Apostle, for his part, would have needed little convincing. His Roxbury church records in the mid-1640s reveal that he despised Gorton's "heretical, blasphemous, and reproachful" opinions, and that he wanted Winslow to "dash the hopes" of "Gorton and his accomplices."[38] That Holden's arrival probably explains the timing of Eliot's first sermon, however, does not mean that he preached it merely for the sake of diplomatic expediency. Eliot's antipathy for Gorton scarcely accounts for his decision to begin the mission, and it manifestly fails to explain why he continued it for forty years after the Warwick Commission reconfirmed Gorton's title to Shawomet in July 1647.

Eliot's Decision to Undertake the Mission

The "Apostle to the Indians" began his mission fifteen years after he arrived in Massachusetts Bay. Little has been uncovered about his life in England. He came from the Lea Valley: born in Widford, Hertfordshire, in August 1604, and raised in Nazing, Essex. In 1618 he enrolled as a pensioner in Jesus College, Cambridge, and in 1622 received his baccalaureate. After graduation he returned to Essex, probably to Nazing. Eliot next surfaces in 1629, when he became Thomas Hooker's assistant in the Puritan academy at Little Baddow, near Chelmsford, in Essex. It was in Chelmsford, probably under Hooker's influence, that Eliot experienced conversion. "Here the Lord said to my dead soul, 'live'; and through the grace of God, I do live, and I shall live forever." In 1630 Archbishop William Laud's pursuivants drove Hooker to Holland. Shortly thereafter the academy closed, and Eliot resolved to sail to Massachusetts. He later explained, in an illustration of Dwight Bozeman's "primitivist dimension," that he emigrated in order to "enjoy the holy worship of God, not according to the fantasies of man, but according to the Word of God, without . . . human additions and novelties." Thus Eliot did not claim that he came to Massachusetts Bay for a missionary purpose. He never returned to England. Five of his siblings eventually joined him in Massachusetts Bay: sisters Mary and Sarah and older brother Philip settled in Roxbury, and younger brothers Jacob and Francis in Boston. Philip and Jacob became deacons in the churches in their respective towns; the latter temporarily lost his office when he fell under the influence of

Anne Hutchinson. John Eliot's fiancée, Anne Mumford (Mountfort), also followed him to the New World. They were married in October 1632.[39]

Eliot reached Boston in November 1631, bringing with him twenty-three barrels of books. His fellow passengers on the *Lyon* included Margaret Winthrop and her stepson, John Winthrop, Jr. Upon his arrival, Eliot took a temporary position as pastor in the Boston church. Roger Williams, a passenger on the *Lyon* on its previous voyage to New England, had already turned down the temporary position because he refused to minister to Non-Separatists. In the summer of 1632 the church's regular pastor, John Wilson, returned from England. The congregation then offered Eliot a permanent appointment as teaching elder. He declined the offer (which Cotton later accepted) in order to move to Roxbury, where many of his Nazing friends had settled and had established a church with Thomas Weld as its pastor. In November 1632 the members of the congregation ordained Eliot as their teacher. He was probably the first Massachusetts minister who had not been previously ordained by an Anglican bishop.[40]

Eliot remained the church's teaching elder until his retirement in 1688, two years before his death. He outlived nearly every prominent first-generation Massachusetts Puritan—the most notable exceptions were Edward Rawson and Simon Bradstreet. Shortly before his death, in the only intentionally witty statement he is known to have uttered, Eliot remarked that Cotton, Shepard, and other founders who had "got safe to heaven . . . would suspect him to be gone the wrong way, because he had stayed so long behind them." Eliot published four treatises in his capacity as the Roxbury teacher: *The Christian Commonwealth* (London, 1659), *The Communion of Churches* (Cambridge, 1665), *The Harmony of the Gospels* (Boston, 1678), and *A Brief Answer to a Small Book Written by John Norcot against Infant Baptism* (Boston, 1679). Eliot also served as the church's de facto pastor for two extended periods. The first began when Weld went to England in 1641 and ended in 1650, when Samuel Danforth, the man who later preached the famous election sermon "A Briefe Recognition of New-Englands Errand into the Wilderness," was hired as Weld's replacement. The second lasted from Danforth's death in 1674 until Nehemiah Walter took over as Eliot's successor in 1688. Eliot's parishioners included William Pynchon (until his removal to Springfield in 1636); governors Thomas and Joseph Dudley, father and son; two future military leaders in New England, the brothers Daniel and George Denison, who grew up in Roxbury and moved away as adults; and George Burroughs, who was later executed in Salem for witchcraft. Cotton Mather said that the members of the Roxbury church were as "well-instructed . . . as in any part of all the country," and that the Roxbury Latin School, which Eliot and Thomas Dudley founded in 1645, "had afforded more scholars first for the college, and then for the public, than any town of its bigness, or, if I mistake not, of twice its bigness in all New England." Eliot left a portion of his estate to create another grammar school, now the Eliot School in Jamaica Plain, for English, Indian, and African students.[41]

Like other seventeenth-century ministers, Eliot regularly participated in the larger affairs of the colony. In 1636 or 1637 he wrote a justification for Roger Williams's banishment. (This document is not extant.) In 1637 Eliot served as one of Anne Hutchinson's interrogators during her examinations before the General Court and the Boston church. In 1638 he was appointed to a committee of ministers and laypeople to study wages and prices. In 1640 he served on a committee with seven other ministers to define orthodoxy on the question of immediate revelation that Hutchinson had so forcefully raised. In 1640 Eliot participated in the translation of the "Bay-Psalm Book" along with Weld, Mather, and perhaps Cotton. Eliot's involvement in the non-Indian business of the colony receded after the birth of the mission. In 1659 he preached the annual election sermon, the only one he was ever asked to deliver. The General Court did not order the publication of the sermon. In 1669 he and Allin organized a synod to deal with the schism in the First Church, Boston, over the Half-Way Covenant, an innovation that Eliot enthusiastically supported and that the Roxbury church resisted until the 1670s. In 1679 he and Ipswich's Thomas Cobbet were chosen the moderators of the famous "Reform Synod." Their selection was probably a tribute to their age, since the work of running the synod fell to younger men.[42]

John and Anne Eliot's six children—Hannah, John, Joseph, Samuel, Aaron, and Benjamin—were born between September 1633 and January 1647. Hannah married the Reverend Habbakuk Glover of Boston in 1653; she was still alive in 1691 when Cotton Mather wrote his biography of the Apostle, *The Triumphs of the Reformed Religion in America*. In 1649 Eliot said that he had "dedicated all my sons" to missionary service. John, Jr., minister at Cambridge Village (later

Newton), was the most active in this respect. He began to visit the Indians in 1657 and had learned Massachusett by the time of his death in 1668. His first wife, Sarah, was the daughter of Thomas Willet, the first English mayor of New York City; his second was Elizabeth Gookin, the daughter of the Indian Superintendent. Joseph Eliot also studied the local dialect and occasionally helped with the mission in the late 1650s and early 1660s. In 1662 he became Eleazar Mather's assistant at Northampton and in 1664 the minister in Guilford, Connecticut, where he remained until his death thirty years later. Joseph was the father of the most famous person directly descended from the Apostle: Jared Eliot, the Connecticut minister, physician, and scientist (neither Charles William Eliot, the distinguished Harvard president, nor Samuel Eliot Morison could trace his ancestry back to the Roxbury minister). Samuel and Benjamin Eliot also helped with the mission from time to time. Samuel's career was cut short by his death in his early twenties. Benjamin worked as his father's nonordained assistant at Roxbury after losing out to Josiah Flint for the position as Richard Mather's successor at Dorchester; he may have served as the first minister at Mendon prior to interviewing for the Dorchester job. Benjamin eventually became mentally ill. Son Aaron died at age eleven.[43]

Eliot's extant sources contain only two allusions to the Native Americans prior to the start of the mission. In 1633 he wrote a lengthy letter to the famous antiquarian Sir Simonds d'Ewes. In the course of this letter, Eliot observed that the colony provided a wall of protection for the local Indians, and he also remarked, "I trust, in God's time they shall learn Christ." This brief expression of missionary hope can hardly be regarded as a foretaste of things to come thirteen years later. The second was a passing reference in Eliot's church records to the Narragansett-Mohegan war of 1645. The standard Massachusetts Bay sources tie Eliot to the Indians on only two other occasions before the birth of the mission. The first was in November 1634, when he challenged the Bay Colony's recent treaty with the Pequots because the magistrates, in consultation with several other elders, had negotiated it "without the consent of the people." The magistrates asked Cotton, Weld, and Hooker to make Eliot "see his error." They convinced him that the colony could sign a treaty without the approval of the freemen, and he soon apologized for his action. Eliot's protest against the treaty probably reflected a concern for proper procedure in the precedent-minded 1630s and not, as Jennings suggests, "hostility" toward the Indians. The second occasion came in May 1637, after the start of the Pequot War, when the elders "set apart" Eliot and Wilson as candidates for the military chaplaincy and then chose Wilson through the casting of lots. The sources do not indicate if the two ministers had volunteered for the assignment or if they had emerged as finalists through an earlier process of elimination.[44]

The fact that Eliot was the person who preached the first two missionary sermons might suggest that he stood apart from his clerical colleagues in some important way. Such was probably not the case at the time. The creation of the rotation plan for Indian instruction in November 1646 implies that Eliot was distinctive only in the sense that he was the first minister to take his turn. Many scholars report that he commenced his study of the Massachusett language three years before he delivered the two sermons. If it could be corroborated by seventeenth-century documentation, this point of chronology would establish that he had a special yearning to engage in missionary work. However, Gookin and Winthrop, the only colonists who commented on the matter, reported that the Apostle started his linguistic training in 1646; Gookin added that Eliot began his study "not long after" the birth of the mission.[45] Finally, there is no indication in the missionary sources that in 1646 Eliot had a higher opinion of the natives' aptitude for Christian civilization than did the other elders who accompanied him to Neponset and Nonantum, or that he had broken with Cotton's pessimistic missionary eschatology and concluded that it was possible for large numbers of Indians to experience conversion before the national redemption of the Jews.

Eliot dated the birth of the mission from his sermon at Nonantum. "I first began with the Indians at Nonantum," he wrote in September 1647, in his earliest extant missionary letter, "those at Dorchester Mill [Neponset] not regarding any such thing." He did not explain in this letter, or on any other occasion, why he preached the Neponset sermon. Eliot did indicate in the letter, however, why he persisted after the failure at Neponset. He stated that "a while after" the Neponset sermon, he heard that "God [had] stirred up in some of them [the Indians at Nonantum] a desire to come into the English fashions, and live after their manner, but [they] knew not how to attain unto it, yea despaired that ever it should come to pass in their days, but thought that in forty years more, some Indians would be all one English, and in a hundred years, all Indians here about, would be so: which when I heard (for some of them told me they thought so, and that some wise Indians said so) my heart moved within me." Cutshamekin's response to Eliot's inaugural sermon, however, made him wonder if "this motion in them [the Nonantum Indians] was of the Lord." But "abhorring that we should sit still and let that work alone," Eliot proceeded on the assumption that the Nonantum Indians were interested in Christian instruction and preached the sermon to them. "I never found [natives] so forward, attentive, and desirous to learn until this time," he explained, "and then I told them I would come to their wigwams and teach them, their wives and children, which they seemed very glad of." The Indians' response to the sermon sealed Eliot's commitment to the work and obviated the proposed rotation plan. "From that day forward I have not failed to do [my] poor little," he recalled.[46]

The Apostle probably began his language training shortly after the sermon at Nonantum in October 1646. His language teacher, who also served as his interpreter in the early years of the mission, was a Pequot War captive then "living with" Dorchester's Richard Calicott, the commissary in the war. The Indian's legal status at the time is unclear: Eliot called him a "servant" and Jennings claims he was a slave. In either case, this "pregnant-witted young man" was already able to speak and read English, and Eliot soon taught him to write it. The Indian was also well-schooled in Christian theology, for he was a candidate for full church membership in Dorchester in February 1649, when he appears for the final time in the New England sources. With his help the Apostle translated "the commandments, the Lord's Prayer, and many texts of Scripture" as well as several "exhortations and prayers." By July 1649 Eliot was evidently able to instruct the Indians without assistance.[47]

Eliot said little about the process through which he learned Massachusett, a language that Cotton Mather considered so difficult that demons who understood Hebrew, Greek, and Latin were unable to fathom it. This highly inflected Algonquian dialect lacked Indo-European grammatical conventions like prepositions, the verb "to be," comparative and superlative forms (degrees of comparison were indicated through the use of additional adjectives), and the future tense (suffixes were added to the present indicative to create the future). In 1666, in his only discussion of the matter, Eliot briefly explained that he first transcribed Massachusett phonemes into Roman characters;

he eventually had to create a non-Roman character to represent an additional vowel. After learning the phonology of the language, he turned to its morphology and discovered its many "new ways of grammar." "I diligently marked the difference of their grammar from ours," he wrote, "[and] when I found the way of them, I would pursue a word, a noun, a verb, through all variations I could think of. And thus I came at it."[48]

The circumstances that led to the birth of the mission cannot be reconstructed with precision, though the course of events probably unfolded in this manner. The colony's assumption that the submission of the sachems was a voluntary action led the saints to conclude that the local Indians had affected the English virtues. Between June 1644 and October 1645, the General Court tried on three occasions to convince the ministers to begin the work of instruction. These three directives attracted no volunteers, perhaps because missionary achievement did not hold a high priority in the minds of the colony's elders, or perhaps because Cotton's eschatology discouraged them. The mission languished until Holden's arrival in Boston in September 1646, when the magistrates convinced Eliot to deliver the sermon to Cutshamekin and the Neponset Indians. Eliot had not prepared for the occasion by studying Massachusett, and he may have anticipated a short term of public service before turning the work over to another elder. Cutshamekin's reaction to the sermon made Eliot skeptical about the Indians' interest in Christian civilization. His skepticism lasted until the sermon at Nonantum. The natives' response to this sermon led him to began his linguistic training. Eliot's commitment to the mission followed, rather than preceded, the sermon at Nonantum.

CHAPTER THREE

. . .

The Early Development of the Mission

Eliot and his English associates moved quickly to consolidate the Nonantum mission after the successful sermon on October 28, 1646, traveling to the settlement on November 11 and 26, and again on December 9. Shortly after the last of these visits, Thomas Shepard wrote a progress report, *The Day-Breaking, If Not the Sun-Rising of the Gospell with the Indians in New-England,* and sent it to London for publication.[1] By the end of the year, the ministers had also carried out two of the directives enacted by the General Court at the November 1646 session. The first was to find a place for the Nonantum Indians to "live in an orderly way among us." The elders chose a site at or near Nonantum that met with the proselytes' approval. Shepard said that this tract was "hundreds of acres" in size. The court promised to pay for the land and then to secure reimbursement "out of the first gift that shall be brought over [from England] . . . for the good of the Indians." Shepard reported that the colony purchased the land; he failed to indicate who sold it and whether the expense was later recouped. The second directive was to prepare a code of "wholesome laws" for the Indians. The Nonantum code, drafted with Waban's assistance at some point in November 1646, is perhaps best known for its attempt to regulate praying Indian hygiene: "if any shall kill their lice between their teeth, they shall pay five shillings." Most of the code's regulations, however, fell into three other categories of greater concern to Eliot and other Puritans.[2]

The first was domestic relations and work habits. One of the Nonantum laws stated that husbands who beat their wives were to be "severely punished." Eliot said in 1647 that this practice "was very usual" among the natives and that the Nonantum Indians had recently disciplined and fined Wamporas, a prominent resident of the settlement, for physically abusing his spouse. The code also fined husbands 5 shillings for idleness and required single men to build their own domiciles and work their own fields instead of "shifting up and down to other wigwams." The reason for these last two provisions is well known to students of the period. In traditional Indian society, women were responsible for horticulture, with the exception of the cultivation of tobacco. English observers were disturbed by the sight of males loitering in villages while females tilled the fields. One of the first lessons that Eliot taught the Nonantum men was that the English "labor and work in building, planting, clothing ourselves, etc. and they do not."[3]

The second concern was Indian sexuality. The Nonantum code fined single men 20 shillings for fornication and women 2 shillings and sixpence for publicly exposing their breasts. These provisions reflected Puritan suspicions about the Indians' undisciplined sexuality. Eliot wrote in 1647 that native "hearts are full of sin, and especially full of the sin of lust." In fact, he so emphasized the need for Indians to "bridle lust by the laws of chastity" that several of his proselytes rendered the seventh commandment as "thou shalt not lust." Shepard characterized unmarried braves as "young lustful men" who "committed filthiness" with "many Indian women," and Abraham Pierson, the missionary in New Haven Colony in the 1650s and 1660s, warned his protégés to avoid the example of "bad Indians" who "defiled" themselves "with unclean lusts" and squandered "their estates when they want whores." The colonists' suppositions about Indian sexual practices extended beyond heterosexual acts between consenting adults. At the time of their submissions in March 1644, the General Court asked Cutshamekin and the four other sachems to abstain not only from adultery and fornication, but also from "incest, rape, sodomy, buggery, [and] bestiality."[4]

The third area was hairstyle. The Nonantum code imposed penalties of 5 shillings on men who wore their hair long and on women who allowed their locks to hang loose or who cut them in the fashion of English males. Eliot objected to these native tonsorial practices because he considered them violations of gender identity as well as expressions of moral decadence. Like other colonists of the day, he associated unshorn Indian men with two other longhaired objects of Puritan contempt: lazy, self-indulgent Anglicans and unkempt, undisciplined frontiersmen. Eliot's conviction that proper grooming reflected the values of stability, chastity, sobriety, and industry led one of his early Massachusett proselytes, Monequasson, to include hair among the "members" to be "pluck[ed] out" lest the "whole body . . . be cast into hell" (Matthew 5:29–30).[5]

The enforcement of the Nonantum code of laws was largely the responsibility of Waban, whom Shepard termed the settlement's "chief minister of justice." The sources do not indicate if Waban was appointed to this position by the English or chosen for it by the Nonantum Indians. In either case, by assuming this responsibility he exercised a power traditionally assigned to sachems. As Francis Jennings observes, Winthrop revealingly called Waban a "new sachem" and Shepard described him as "a man of great gravity and chief prudence and counsel . . . although no sachem." Waban was probably amenable to being promoted to a position of power, for he stated in 1652 that he once "wished to be a sachem." His commission as "chief minister" of justice, however, apparently did not constitute a coup d'état within the ranks of the Massachusett Indians. There is no evidence that his judicial authority extended beyond Nonantum to Cutshamekin's village at Neponset.[6]

A Christian faction nevertheless formed at Neponset. By September 1647, Eliot was regularly preaching to the Neponset Indians and the settlement was operating under a code of laws similar if not identical to the one in use at Nonantum. By this time Cutshamekin was attending the sermons and professing that he "knew God." As Neal Salisbury suggests, the sachem had probably concluded that an acceptance of the mission was "the only means of retaining authority within his shattered community."[7]

Cutshamekin soon learned that discipline was an important part of the missionary program. In 1647 Eliot observed that the sachem's teenage son mumbled the fifth commandment ("Honor thy father and thy mother") when reciting his catechism and also "behaved . . . disobediently and rebelliously" toward his parents. Eliot and John Wilson investigated the matter. The youth refused to confess his sins until Cutshamekin had acknowledged his own "hardness of heart." The two ministers handled the situation in conventional pastoral fashion. After "in private prepar[ing] him thereunto," they brought Cutshamekin before the Neponset Indians, who confronted him about the acts of "drunkenness, filthiness [sexual impropriety], false dealing, lying, etc." that he had committed "before he knew God." The sachem then "confessed his main and principal sins, ... expressed himself sorrowful, and condemned himself for them."[8]

The Massachusett sachem also learned that the mission resulted in the reduction, though not the elimination, of tribute from the Nonantum and Neponset Indians. Eliot reported in 1650 that Cutshamekin had told him that "the Indians who pray to God ... do not pay him tribute as formerly they have done." The Apostle reminded the sachem that "once before when [he] heard of his complaint that way," he had preached a sermon on Matthew 22:21 ("Render therefore unto Caesar the things which are Caesar's") and Romans 13:1 ("Let every soul be subject unto the higher powers"). But in response to the renewed complaint, Eliot surveyed some of the Massachusetts to determine the extent of their tribute payments in the past two years. He learned that they had given Cutshamekin twenty-six bushels of corn, £2 worth of beaver fur, and fifteen deer carcasses; that they had plowed two acres of his land, fenced his garden, and built him "a great house or wigwam"; and that they had paid a fine of £3 10 for an undisclosed transgression he had committed. The investigation convinced Eliot that the Massachusetts were providing adequate tribute. "The bottom of it lieth here," he concluded, "he formerly had all or what he would; now he has but what they will." In his next sermon, Eliot switched texts to Matthew 4, where Jesus resists the "temptations of the world." This sermon changed Cutshamekin's "countenance and carriage," and Eliot never mentioned further complaints from the sachem about the matter.[9]

Cutshamekin's subordinates supported Eliot in the disputes over discipline and tribute. In the episode with the disobedient son, the Neponset Indians assisted Eliot and Wilson in punishing Cutshamekin because his "sundry vices" were a matter of public knowledge. In the case of tribute, Eliot observed that when Cutshamekin "rages and gives sharp and cruel language" about the matter, the Massachusetts "admonish him of his sin, [and] tell him that is not the right way to get money." The proselytes were also prepared to discipline the members of the sachem's family. After Cutshamekin's confession of sin in 1647, the Neponset Indians pressured his son until "at last he also did humble himself, confessed all, and entreated his father to forgive him"; and in 1647 Ahawton, a Neponset Indian, brought Cutshamekin's wife before a native assembly for speaking of "worldly matters" on the Sabbath. Such actions inevitably produced tensions. In 1649 Eliot reported that several Massachusett Indians had asked him "If a man be wise, and his sachem weak, must he yet obey him?" and "Is the sachem commanded to love us?" Cutshamekin, for his part, clearly resented the discipline and the reduced tribute. Nevertheless, his acceptance of the mission enabled him to retain the allegiance of the Massachusetts. In 1651, shortly before the sachem's death, Eliot characterized Cutshamekin as "constant in his profession, though doubtful in respect of the thoroughness of his heart"; and in his *Indian Dialogues* (1671), the Apostle explained that even though the sachem "waver[ed] in the matter of praying to God, he so carried the matter that they [the Massachusetts] forsook him not."[10]

The Massachusett Indians' desire to redefine Cutshamekin's power was one reason why Eliot was able to establish the missions at Nonantum and Neponset. The colony's policies in the early period of settlement had inflated the sachem's authority beyond traditional limits and curtailed the role of his counselors. The mission enabled the Massachusett Indians to diminish Cutshamekin's newly acquired power by subjecting him to a collectively administered discipline and by reducing their tribute to him. At the same time, the Massachusetts wanted him to remain their sachem. In 1651, after their removal to the central praying town of Natick, the Nonantum and Neponset Indians elected Cutshamekin as their ruler of one hundred, the highest existing office in Eliot's scriptural civil polity, the system of rulers of tens, rulers of fifties, and rulers of hundreds found in Exodus 18. As Eliot observed at the time, Cutshamekin was "the chief sachem, and therefore chosen the chief." The Indians selected Waban and another unidentified Indian as the two rulers of fifties who would share power with him. Thus the Massachusett Indians used the mission to return the office of sachem to a more consensual form.[11]

A second factor that contributed to the successful establishment of the mission was the Massachusett Indians' need to secure a place of residence in the wake of English expansion around Boston. Shepard noted that after Eliot's first sermon at Nonantum, Waban and other natives asked the elders for permission to "possess all the compass of that hill upon which their wigwams then stood." This phrasing suggests that the Nonantum Indians were confined to a small area. John Speene of Nonantum also testified to the importance of land, stating in 1659 that he initially accepted Eliot's program "because I saw the English took much ground, and I thought if I prayed, the English would not take away my ground." Security of residence was an issue at Neponset as well. Monequasson stated in 1652 that he "loved to dwell at that place [Neponset], I would not leave the place, and therefore I thought I will pray to God . . . not for the love of God but for love of the place I lived in." At the time the mission began, the Neponset Indians were apparently living on a forty-acre tract near Dorchester: in June 1649 Cutshamekin testified that in October 1636 he had sold all but forty acres "where I like best" to Dorchester for twenty-eight fathoms of wampum. There is reason to think, moreover, that the Nonantum and Neponset Indians blamed Cutshamekin as well as the English for the loss of coastal land. Eliot wrote in *Indian Dialogues* that the Massachusetts had been angry at Cutshamekin for selling "all our lands which lay by the sea side and salt water save only one field"—possibly the forty-acre tract in question.[12]

Another reason for the mission's early success was the Indians' desire for literacy. James Axtell has argued that the ability to read and write appealed to Indians in colonial North America because literacy preserved words that were otherwise "evanescent and irretrievable" and also "duplicated a spiritual feat that only the greatest shamans could perform, namely, that of reading the mind of a person at a distance." He also observes that natives viewed books as magical objects "invested with supernatural powers in their own right." This argument has been challenged by Peter Wogan, who contends that Indians in the Eastern Woodlands were not necessarily mesmerized by what Axtell calls "the novelty and magic of print." Wogan's argument notwithstanding, there is sufficient evidence in the New England sources to think that literacy attracted the interest of the Indians around Boston. In 1646 Waban sent his eldest son to Dedham for schooling, and shortly thereafter Wamporas sent his son and three other children to Roxbury for the same purpose; in 1647 the Nonantum and Neponset Indians asked the elders to establish schools in the two settlements; in 1647 or 1648 Henry Dunster observed that some of the local natives "for their own benefit . . . behoove it [English-language literacy] of their own accord"; and in 1650 Eliot remarked that

Indian children were reluctant to move to Natick unless their English teachers could "go with them."[13]

A final reason for the initial appeal of the mission was that the Massachuset Indians sought English goods such as finished clothing, copper pots, and iron tools, as well as English skills such as carpentry, spinning and weaving, and husbandry. Consumer goods were valued not simply for their utilitarian and decorative functions. As Elise Brenner, Constance Crosby, and other scholars have pointed out, natives prized these goods because they served as markers of status and because they were seen as expressions of *manit*, the animistic power inherent in objects. English skills were also valued by the proselytes. After the elders' visit on November 26, 1646, the Nonantum Indians asked to "learn to spin," and at about the same time, Wamporas and Totherswamp sent their younger brother Anthony to Roxbury to apprentice to a blacksmith, who refused to accept him lest he learn to make and repair guns. Anthony then remained in Roxbury for a year, probably as an apprentice carpenter, before returning to Nonantum.[14]

In the meantime Eliot's work among the Massachusetts had attracted the attention of some Pawtuckets. Shepard explained that in early 1647 Attawans, an "inferior prince" at Musketaquid, requested and obtained permission from the selectmen of nearby Concord to establish an English-style town. The Indians also asked that Waban and Concord's Simon Willard draw up "certain laws for their religious and civil government and behavior." The Musketaquid code, which was more comprehensive than its Nonantum counterpart, imposed fines for excessive drinking, lying, powwowing, sabbath-breaking, bad grooming, fornicating (the man had to pay twice as much as the woman), gambling, fighting, and wife-beating. Other provisions required thieves to make fourfold restitution to their victims; criminalized violations of English decency such as "howling" and entering Puritan homes without knocking; altered the penalty for pinching lice to a penny per louse; and banned the traditional practices of wearing "disguises" when mourning, having more than one wife, segregating women during menstruation, and greasing the skin (probably a form of insulation in the winter and insect repellent in the summer). The Musketaquid code designated as capital offenses bestiality, adultery, and murder. Blasphemy was not mentioned.[15]

The Musketaquid Indians had learned about the Massachuset mission through Waban, Attawan's son-in-law. They first began to attend

Eliot's lectures at Nonantum in late 1646 and continued to receive their religious instruction at Nonantum or at Natick until the creation of the praying town of Nashobah (now Littleton) in the mid-1650s. The Musketaquid Indians probably hoped that the mission could provide a secure place of residence for, like the Massachusetts at Nonantum, they requested a specific location for their settlement ("this side the Bear Swamp or the east side of Mr. [Thomas] Flint's farm"). The prior dispossession of the Pawtucket Indians around Concord was probably as extensive as that of the Massachusetts: the sources indicate that the Squaw Sachem, her husband Webbacowet, and Attawans authorized many land transactions before the Musketaquid mission began. In October 1647 Shepard noted that the Indians had received land for a town but had not yet "settl[ed] down." He also reported that the Musketaquid Indians wanted to escape "higher Indian sachems" who took away their "skins, . . . kettles, and wampum at their pleasure." He failed to identify the sachems in question.[16]

The mission was not successful everywhere in coastal Massachusetts. In 1649 Eliot wrote that the Pawtucket Indians at Saugus (Lynn) were "all naught save one," the principal reason being that their sachem, Sagamore George, "is naught, and cares not to pray to God." Masconomo, another Pawtucket, evidently resisted the mission as well, for in 1655 the Commissioners of the United Colonies sent him a suit "of the coarsest cloth" to "encourage him to learn to know God and to excite other Indians to do the like." The fact that these quotations contain allusions to subordinate non-Christian Indians suggests that Sagamore George and Masconomo were able to preserve control over their bands without acquiescing to the mission.[17]

The growth of the mission in the late 1640s led Eliot to bring three petitions before the General Court. The first came in 1647, when he asked the legislature to "order a way for exercising government" among the praying Indians. He explained that the idea originated with the Massachusett proselytes, who "desired that they might have a court of their own" to punish natives who had "broke[n] out of their services" to other Indians and to the English. In May 1647 the assistants and deputies authorized the "sachems"—a category that presumably included Waban and Attawans—to hear minor civil cases in monthly sessions, to appoint constables, and to rule on criminal cases referred to them by English magistrates. The extent to which the "sachems" carried out these instructions prior to the creation of Natick is not clear. At this session the court also specified that fines imposed upon the praying Indians "be bestowed toward their . . . public use." This provision apparently became the practice in the settlements. Finally, at the May session, the General Court directed "one or more of the magistrates" to adjudicate important civil and criminal cases in quarterly sessions and to use these occasions to "endeavor to make the Indians understand our most useful laws, and those principles of reason, justice, and equity whereupon they are grounded." I have found no evidence that "one or more of the magistrates" held any such sessions, let alone quarterly ones, before the colony established the Indian Superintendency in 1658. Eliot explained in 1651 that "the difference of language and paucity of interpreters prohibit [the magistrates from acting], and if their [the Indians'] causes come, they may be longsome and yet of small importance."[18]

Eliot returned to the General Court in the fall of 1648, when he petitioned the legislature to license "but one ordinary" to "sell wine or any strong drink" to the Indians in order to "prevent . . . those scandalous evils which greatly blemish and interrupt their entertainment of the Gospel." By this time he had direct knowledge of the baneful effects of alcohol on the mission. "Cutshamekin's drunken Indians" had disregarded his inaugural sermon in September 1646; a "malignant drunken Indian" called George, who on another occasion had stolen and butchered an English cow and sold it to Harvard as moose meat, interrupted a lecture in 1647 to ask if God made wine; and Eliot's Indian servant (about whom nothing else is known) had been censured that same year for intoxication. The General Court, which had attempted to control the sale of alcohol prior to the birth of the mission, granted the Apostle's request in October 1648. The third of Eliot's petitions came in 1649 on behalf of two Indians with grievances against other natives. "Bringing them to justice," Eliot told the General Court, will "cause them to honor and acknowledge God." One of the natives was Totherswamp, a Nonantum Indian who in 1647 had sold six furs to a Mohegan for eighteen fathoms of wampum. The purchaser, who bore the disreputable-sounding name of Cogeleys, refused to make payment. Totherswamp then took his complaint to Eliot, who brought the matter before the Commissioners, probably because the dispute crossed jurisdictional lines. The Commissioners did not settle the case, which led Eliot to seek redress from the General Court in 1649. The other native was Anongaich, from whom three

Mohegans had stolen seventeen fathoms of wampum near Saybrook in 1646. Apparently acting on his own initiative, Anongaich took his case to the Massachusetts General Court, which promised to investigate the matter but failed to do so. In 1649 this Indian (who is otherwise absent in the sources) asked Eliot to renew his complaint. The court's published records do not indicate how the cases of Totherswamp and Anongaich were resolved.[19]

All the while Eliot maintained a regular schedule of visitation, traveling to Neponset every other Thursday and to Nonantum on alternating Saturdays. During his absences from Roxbury, other local ministers assumed responsibility for his weekday and Sabbath lectures in the English church. Eliot's missionary sermons were attended not only by the Nonantum, Neponset, and Musketaquid Indians, but also by Nipmucks from the Massachusetts interior. Several of these Nipmucks later became leaders at Natick or other praying towns: William of Sudbury, Captain Tom, and Owussumag, who were from Okommakamesit (Marlborough); and Monotunkquanit, whose place of origin is not known. During his visits to Nonantum and Neponset, Eliot catechized children, offered advice on discipline, supervised question and answer sessions, and preached to adults "with all the plainness and brevity" he could muster. In his sermons he instructed the Indians in Calvinist and natural theology, and expounded texts in Genesis, Exodus, Psalms, Matthew, and John. He compared Christian teachings to objects and activities familiar to the proselytes, likening postmortem punishment to the torture of captives, the sacraments to a fort, regeneration to the cleansing of filthy pipes, and various other doctrines to baskets, bows and arrows, sunlight, and apples. The natives' response to this program of instruction pleased Eliot. "The Indians . . . which I constantly teach," he wrote late in 1648, "diligently and desirously attend [the lectures], and in a good measure practice . . . the outward part of religion, both in their families and sabbaths."[20]

The Growth of the Mission in Southern New England

In the late 1640s the mission expanded beyond coastal Massachusetts Bay. Most of the evangelical work was done by Waban, Totherswamp, and other Nonantum and Neponset proselytes rather than by Eliot himself. "The most effectual and general way of spreading the Gospel," the Apostle wrote in 1651, "will be by themselves." The saints had planned on using native missionaries from the outset of the work. As Shepard explained in *The Day-Breaking*, "God is wont ordinarily to convert nations and peoples by some of their own countrymen who are nearest to them and can best speak, and most of all pity, their brethren."[21]

By 1649 Eliot had interested two inland sachems in the mission. One was Nashowanon. The Apostle made four journeys to the sachem's Nashaway home in the summer of 1648, and during one of these poorly documented visits, Nashowanon chose to "embrace the Gospel and pray to God." The other was Passaconaway. Eliot made three known trips to Pantucket between 1647 and 1649. Passaconaway's reaction to the first visit indicates that he had not requested a mission. "Pretending fear of being killed," Shepard wrote, the sachem "fled the presence of the light." His absence did not deter Eliot from addressing "the rest of Passaconaway's men, [who] attended to the things which were spoken and asked diverse questions." Eliot returned to Pantucket in the spring of 1648, the season when large numbers of Indians gathered to fish from the banks of the Concord and Merrimack Rivers during the shad and alewife runs. On this occasion Passaconaway welcomed him and "purposed in his heart from thenceforth to pray to God, and . . . to persuade all his sons to do the same." The sachem also asked Eliot and one of his companions, Simon Willard, to move to Pantucket. After the third visit, in the spring of 1649, Passaconaway "exceedingly earnestly [and] importunately" invited Eliot "to come and live there and teach them." To judge from this body of evidence, Passaconaway accepted the mission because he feared that he would lose subjects through a Christian secessionist movement, and because he hoped that other colonists would follow Eliot and Willard to Pantucket and thus build a wall of protection against marauders.[22]

A third mission field established in the late 1640s was in the vicinity of Quabag. In 1649 Eliot learned that an "aged [Nipmuck] sachem" at Quobagud (East Brookfield) wanted him to "come thither and teach them, and live there." That summer Eliot and some English and Indian companions traveled to the area. They were accompanied by twenty warriors furnished by Nashowanon, who was worried about Eliot's safety because of "some stirs between the Narragansett and Mohegan Indians" (probably a reference to a recent alliance between the Narragansetts, the Pocumtucks, and the Mohawks against Uncas). The trip was evidently a success, for shortly thereafter Eliot reported that an unspecified "Nipmuck sachem ha[d] submitted himself to pray unto the Lord, and much desires one of our chief ones to live with him and teach him." Whether or not Eliot was able to supply a resident teacher at this time is unclear.[23]

Two raids reveal the likely circumstances behind the Quabag Indians' interest in the mission. In 1647 marauders from Norwottuck (Hadley) assaulted the Nipmuck village at Ashquoach (Brimfield) and killed three of its residents; and in the spring of 1648, raiders from an undisclosed location struck a Nipmuck settlement situated between Quabag and Nashaway and took five lives. The natives around Quabag were vulnerable to attack for two reasons. First, there was no local English presence: Brookfield, the first town in the vicinity of Quabag, was not created until the 1660s. Second, the Indians were disunited. As William Pynchon observed at the time, "there are several small factions of Quabag, and in all near places there are other small factions. No one faction does rule all." In 1648 one of the Quabag sachems, probably Quancunquasit, reported the two raids to Boston. In early June the magistrates dispatched twenty soldiers to protect Nashowanon because, in Winthrop's words, the 1644 act of submission obligated the colony to show its "readiness to protect them [Nashawanon and his band], and revenge their wrongs." Shortly thereafter Nashowanon accepted the mission in the manner already described. The Quabag Indians, who were apparently upset that Massachusetts Bay had sent the troops to Nashaway and not to Quabag, then asked Cutshamekin to intervene. The Massachuset sachem went to Eliot and explained that the Indians at Quabag were entitled to protection because they were "his [Cutshamekin's] subjects." Eliot asked the magistrates to send soldiers to Quabag and also wrote to Pynchon about the matter; the Massachusetts council contacted Pynchon as well. In his reply to the council, Pynchon asserted that the Quabag Indians "have dealt very subtilely in getting Cutshamekin to get Mr. Eliot to be their mediator" and that they "will stick no longer to him than the sun shines upon him." Pynchon also explained that the Nipmucks in question had not submitted to the General Court in 1644 and hence were not "your subjects," that the marauders were "not within your jurisdiction," and that intervention "would endanger a war." The colony's leaders were delighted to have an excuse to drop the matter. Their failure to intervene at Quabag probably led to the 1649 request that Eliot "come thither and teach them, and live there." In making this request, the Quabag Indians were apparently trying to secure through Eliot the protection that they had not obtained through Cutshamekin.[24]

As these cases show, Eliot centered his attention on the sachems. "I do endeavor to engage the sachems of greatest note to accept the Gospel," he wrote in November 1648, "because that does greatly animate and encourage such as are well-affected, and is a damping to those that are scoffers and opposers." By this time he had interested Cutshamekin, Passaconaway, and Nashowanon, as well as the "new sachem" Waban, the "inferior prince" Attawans, and the "aged sachem" at Quobagud, in the mission. Presently convinced of the sachems' receptiveness to his program, Eliot concluded that the powwows (shamans) were the major native obstacles to missionary success. The powwows were charismatic leaders whose status derived from the spiritual power they claimed to command. Their traditional responsibilities were healing the sick, casting spells for good or evil, and divining the future. An Indian became a powwow when Hobbamock, an Indian deity also known as Abbemacho, appeared in a dream or vision in the form of an animal, fish, serpent, or bird. These visionary experiences were often preceded by a period of preparation when the aspirant went without sleep or food. Puritans thought that the powwows were witches and that Hobbamock was one of Satan's agents. For example, Shepard said in 1647 that "powwows are witches or sorcerers that cure by the help of the devil," and Gookin wrote in 1674 that the powwows are "partly wizards and witches, holding familiarity with Satan, that evil one, and partly are physicians . . . for curing the sick and diseased."[25]

The Apostle soon learned that he had misjudged the sachems. He stated in 1650 that the "business of praying to God . . . has hitherto found opposition only from the powwows and profane spirits; but now the Lord has exercised us with another and a greater opposition, for the sachems of the country are generally set against us, and counter-work the Lord by keeping off their men from praying to God as much as they can." He had three sachems in mind: Ninigret of the Eastern Niantics, Massasoit of the Pokanokets, and Uncas of the Mohegans. Eliot tried and failed to evangelize Ninigret in 1649; whether his conclusion about Massasoit and Uncas was based on experience or hearsay is unclear. These three sachems were unlikely candidates for a mission. Neal Salisbury has observed that the "tribes most impervious to Christianity were those with the strongest leadership." Moreover, Massasoit and Uncas had signed alliances with the English prior to the start of Eliot's work, and for this reason did not need to accept a mission in order to receive protection. In 1621 Massasoit and the Plymouth magistrates pledged that "if any did unjustly war against him, we would aid him; if any did war against us, he should aid us"; and in 1639 the sachem and his son Moanam renewed the agreement. Uncas was allied with Connecticut through the Hartford treaty of 1638 and with the Commissioners through agreements reached in 1644 and 1645. Ninigret, for his part, had no fixed treaty with any of the orthodox colonies, apparently because he preferred to maximize his diplomatic freedom of action.[26]

In time Eliot tried, or tried again, to evangelize the Pokanokets and other pagan groups outside the Bay Colony. In the late 1640s, however, he was probably relieved to have an excuse for ignoring these Indians. He and his native co-workers already had more mission fields than they could handle. In addition to the Indians in the coastal and inland settlements in Massachusetts Bay, natives outside the colony were interested in the mission. In 1647 Eliot delivered a sermon to some "attentive" Nausets at Yarmouth and also spoke with a "Narragansett sachem," probably a minor one named Auquontis. He also learned that the Indians around Titicut wanted a teacher and that some Pennacooks in present-day New Hampshire "were desirous to pray to God."[27]

In the late 1640s, Eliot thought about constructing a single settlement for all the praying Indians in Massachusetts Bay. "A place must be found," he wrote in 1648, where his proselytes could have "the Word constantly taught, and government constantly exercised, means of good subsistence provided, encouragements for the industrious, means of instructing them in letters, trades, and labors, as building, fishing, flax and hemp dressing, planting orchards, etc." Logistical problems prevented this plan from coming to pass. Eliot could not build the town near Boston because there was insufficient land around the city and because the Indians at Pantucket and other interior locations had "neither tools, nor skill, nor heart to fence their grounds." He then considered the alternative possibility of constructing this single settlement at Pantucket. In order to provide regular instruction at this distant location, he was prepared to resign from the Roxbury church and move to Pantucket if benefactors in England could meet the needs of his family. The plan soon unraveled because the Nonantum and Neponset Indians were "loath to go northward."[28]

By 1650 Eliot had decided to build a central praying town near Boston for the Indians along the coast and one or more settlements for proselytes in the interior. In 1650 he founded Natick, located some eighteen miles to the southwest of Roxbury, for the Nonantum, Neponset, and Musketaquid Indians as well as for Nipmucks who had moved to the coast in the late 1640s. The creation of Natick, however, led to a fresh set of logistical problems. Most of the Nonantum Indians and a few of the Neponsets and Nipmucks liked the site; however, the remaining Boston-area proselytes were dissatisfied with it. In the early to mid-1650s, Eliot had to establish additional praying towns for those Neponset, Musketaquid, and Nipmuck Indians who did not wish to reside at Natick.[29] The growing number of praying towns increased the demands on Eliot's time and prevented him from pursuing the once promising inland missions at Pantucket, Nashaway, and Quabag.

Edward Winslow and the Creation of the New England Company

In the meantime Edward Winslow was putting the mission to good use in England. The Bay Colony's newly commissioned agent had taken with him the manuscript of Shepard's *Day-Breaking*. This work, which was published in London in April 1647, proved to be the first in a series of ten missionary progress reports now termed the "Eliot tracts." In March 1648 Winslow issued the second of these tracts, Shepard's *The Clear Sun-shine of the Gospel Breaking Forth upon the Indians in New-England,* which continued the story through October 1647. This work also contained Eliot's earliest extant missionary letter, addressed to Shepard and dated September 24, 1647, as well as two dedicatory epistles signed by a group of English Puritan ministers, including the Presbyterian Stephen Marshall and the Congregationalist Thomas Goodwin. In June 1649 Winslow published the third Eliot tract, *The Glorious Progress of the Gospel amongst the Indians in New England,* which consisted of a dedicatory epistle to Parliament, written by Winslow; three letters by Eliot, two of which were addressed to Winslow and one to the recently repatriated Herbert Pelham, the first treasurer of Harvard College; a letter written to Winslow in September 1647 by Thomas Mayhew, Jr., who had been preaching to the Wampanoag Indians on Martha's Vineyard since 1643; and an appendix by John Dury, the Scottish-born ecumenist then residing in England. Winslow's dedicatory epistle and Dury's appendix included endorsements of the lost tribes of Israel theory of the Indians' ancestry that was soon to play an important role in the formation of Eliot's distinctive millennial vision. The fourth and final tract of relevance for present purposes, *The Light appearing more and more towards the perfect Day,* contained five letters that Eliot wrote to Winslow between July 1649 and October 1650. At Winslow's request, this work was edited by Henry Whitfield, the Guilford, Connecticut, minister who had returned to England in late 1650. *The Light appearing,* published in February 1651, also included a preface and postscript written by Whitfield, a dedication by the Independent divine Joseph Caryl, and a letter from Mayhew to Whitfield, who had learned about the Vineyard mission in September 1650, when the ship carrying him from Guilford to Boston was forced by "contrary winds" to land on the island.[30]

One purpose of the early Eliot tracts was to answer criticism that had exposed the Bay Colony's neglect of the Indian work. In 1642 Thomas Lechford revealed in *Plaine Dealing: Or, Newes from New-England* that "there has not been any sent forth by any church [in Massachusetts Bay] to learn the Indians' language or to instruct them in the religion"; and three years later, Robert Baillie charged in *A Dissuasive from the Errours of the Time* that of "all that ever crossed the American seas," the Bay Puritans were the "most neglectful of the work of conversion." Baillie, who had seen Lechford's *Plaine Dealing* and Williams's *Christenings make not Christians,* added that he had "read none of them [in New England] that seem to have minded this matter; only Master Williams in the time of his banishment from among them did essay what could be done with those poor desolate souls, and by a little experience did find a wonderful great facility to gain thousands of them." The two polemicists blamed the Bay Colony's church polity for the absence of a mission. Lechford, who became an Anglican after his repatriation in 1641, doubted that Congregationalists "can or ever could" conduct a proper mission; and Baillie, a Scottish Presbyterian delegate to the Westminster Assembly, claimed that church polity was the reason why Williams proved unable to make good his boast in *Christenings* about bringing "many thousands of these natives, yea the whole country, to a far greater Antichristian conversion than ever was yet heard of in America."[31]

The colonists soon responded to this criticism. In *The Day-Breaking* Shepard stated that "we are oft upbraided by some of our countrymen that so little good is done by our professing planters upon the hearts of the natives," and in *The Clear Sun-shine* he explained that "some persons maligning the good of the country are apt . . . to aggravate to the utmost any evil thing against it" and added that "if any malignant eye shall question and vilify this work, they shall now speak too late." Eliot spoke briefly to the same effect in one of the letters published in *The Light appearing*, and Cotton included a lengthy defense of the colony's missionary record in *The Way of Congregational Churches Cleared* (London, 1648). Explicitly responding to Lechford and Baillie, Cotton argued that Eliot's work proved that the congregational polity did not "hinder (much less exceedingly hinder)" the instruction of the "poor pagans." The Boston preacher also noted that Baillie had provided the wrong explanation for Williams's failure to make good his boast in *Christenings make not Christians*. The reason was not polity but the Rhode Islander's eschatology, "his own corrupt principles, . . . not ours."[32]

The first four Eliot tracts also contained appeals for financial assistance from benefactors in England. In *The Day-Breaking*, Shepard asked well-wishers of the mission to send their contributions to Harvard, where their money will be "under many hands and eyes"; in one of their dedicatory epistles to *The Clear Sun-shine*, Marshall and the other English divines wrote that Massachusetts Bay was unable "to bear the [financial] burden" of the mission; and in his appendix to *The Glorious Progress*, Dury implored his readers to pay for the pious work because Massachusetts Bay was unable to do so. Eliot's lifelong habit of asking for contributions began with his first missionary letter in 1647. Over the next few years, this "master of the begging letter"—as William Kellaway, the historian of the New England Company, aptly dubs him—requested tools, clothing, and medicine from English patrons of the mission, and also asked for money to pay Puritan teachers of Indian children, to purchase the services of skilled English craftsmen to construct buildings for the praying Indians, and to underwrite the printing costs of his planned Massachusett translations. Like Dury and others, Eliot stated that the mission was "too costly an enterprise for New England." The claim that the colony could not fund the mission was true enough at the time: Winthrop noted in a different context that the Bay was £1,000 in debt in November 1646.[33]

Fund-raising was a sensitive subject in England because of the unfortunate legacy of Thomas Weld and Hugh Peter. In the early to mid-1640s, the Bay Colony's original agents had raised money for a variety of purposes, including the instruction of the Indians and the transportation of poor children from England and Ireland to New England. The latter project was particularly suspect. Weld and Peter collected some £875 in English money for this end. The number of children sent to Massachusetts Bay, however, fell far short of the revenue raised for the purpose. As Raymond Stearns explains, some children succumbed to disease before they were shipped to New England, and others fled from the docks at Gravesend. Moreover, the persons responsible for transmitting to Massachusetts Bay the money designated for the children—Emmanuel Downing, Winthrop's brother-in-law; and Nehemiah Bourne, a major in Colonel Thomas Rainsborough's regiment—pocketed some of the revenue. The funds that managed to arrive in Boston were diverted to other purposes, most notably the construction of a new home for Henry Dunster and the reimbursement of Winthrop, Jr., for expenses he incurred between 1641 and 1643, when he was traveling throughout Europe in search of persons willing to invest in Massachusetts Bay.[34]

There were also irregularities in the collection of money for Indian instruction. On two occasions Weld listed the contributions that had been received in England for this purpose. The first came in April 1647, when he informed Massachusetts Bay that he and Peter had collected approximately £191 for Indian instruction: £80 from the Lady Mary Armine, who in 1644 had established a £20 annuity for "the poor preacher to the Indians in New England," £10 from a "Mr. Cradock" (possibly Matthew Cradock), £2 10 from "another," £20 "paid Mr. Eliot" for unspecified uses, and roughly £79 "more for the instruction of the Indians." Weld's second statement, written in early 1650 for publication in London, was his "Innocency Cleared." In this document, which was not printed until the nineteenth century, he listed only the £80 from Lady Armine and the small gift from "another," thus leaving a discrepancy of some £109 between the two accounts.[35]

Stearns and Kellaway are unable to explain the £109 discrepancy or to determine how much money Weld and Peter sent to New England for the mission. The Massachusetts Bay sources list few missionary expenditures prior to the creation of the New England Company in July 1649. The largest was the assignment of the £20 Armine annuity to Eliot in 1647, 1648, and 1649; the disposition of the annuity for 1644–1646 is unknown. The only other documented allocations were a £10 award to Eliot in 1647 and the possible purchase of land for the Nonantum Indians. The colony may have used whatever other revenue it received from England for legitimate missionary purposes. It is difficult to draw this conclusion, however, in light of Stearns's discovery about the fate of the money that arrived in Massachusetts for the care of the poor children. In 1651 the Company asked the Commissioners of the United Colonies to account for the disposition of the missionary moneys sent over by Weld and Peter so that London could "publish it to the world." The Commissioners unconvincingly replied that "those ancient gifts and sums of money . . . were most (as we conceive) expended in foundation work," and that "the gentlemen [who] might in those times have given a satisfying answer to so just a demand" had either died or left Massachusetts Bay.[36]

Winslow's talents as a lobbyist and publicist overcame the legacy of Weld and Peter. In March 1648, shortly after the publication of *The Clear Sun-shine*, the House of Commons discussed the possibility of "affording some encouragement and charity" to the infant mission in Massachusetts Bay. In early July 1649, not long after the appearance of *The Glorious Progress*, the Rump Parliament debated a proposal for the creation of a corporation "for the maintaining of the university of Cambridge in New England, and other schools and nurseries of learning there, and for the preaching and propagating of the Gospel among the natives." Later in July the Rump chose to restrict the proposed corporation's domain to "the preaching and propagating of the Gospel of Jesus Christ amongst the natives, and . . . [the] maintaining of schools and nurseries of learning, for the better educating of the children of the natives." On July 27 the bill was passed in this restricted form, thereby creating the "Society for Propagation of the Gospel in New England" (the corporation's first official name). At Winslow's suggestion, the Company's charter designated the Commissioners of the United Colonies, the only intercolonial institution in existence, as the corporation's middlemen in New England.[37]

The creation of the New England Company ensured that Massachusetts Bay would not pay for the mission. Thereafter, the General Court contributed no money to the Indian work except for paying the expenses of the Commissioners whenever their meetings were held in Boston and for covering the costs of surveying the land for a praying town established at Wamesit (now Lowell) in 1653. Nor were there documented financial contributions from individual colonists other than Eliot. Robert Keayne, the famous merchant, surely spoke for others when he stated in the early 1650s that "God has been pleased to provide such a comfortable supply from larger and fuller purses to carry on this great and good work among the Indians . . . that they shall not need the help of particular persons to make any addition that way."[38]

An Evaluation of the Mission through 1650

In the late 1640s, Eliot's program of instruction in civility and Christianity was effectively confined to the coastal settlements of Nonantum, Neponset, and Musketaquid. The Indians in these locations were constructing interior partitions in their wigwams in order to segregate parents from children and family members from servants; fencing their fields and pastures (although in this case Eliot occasionally bought their compliance with bribes); and wearing their hair and dressing in Puritan fashion. Moreover, the proselytes were learning the English skills, such as carpentry and husbandry, taught them by laypeople from the local churches, particularly Isaac Heath and William Parke(s) of Roxbury, Edward Jackson of Cambridge, and Simon Willard of Concord. Finally, the praying Indians were beginning to labor "as the English do" by starting cottage industries in the manufacture of baskets, brooms, and weirs; by selling fish and fruit in local markets; by working as servants to settlers or to other natives; and by contracting with the English to harvest hay or to perform other tasks (Waban earned £8 in 1647 for tending Cambridge's livestock).[39]

The Indians in the coastal settlements were also advancing in Christian faith and practice. On Sundays the leading proselytes conducted worship services based on lessons that Eliot had prepared in advance. Parents catechized their children and sent them to the Massachusett-language schools at Nonantum and Neponset, or to dame schools and town schools in Roxbury, Dedham, Cambridge, and Dorchester—the respective homes of Eliot, Allin, Shepard, and Mather. The Indians also subjected sinners to discipline. Examples included Cutshamekin and his unruly son, Wamporas the wife-abuser, and Eliot's drunken servant. In some disciplinary matters, the Christian Indians were unable to determine the appropriate course of action and asked Eliot for advice. One such problem involved gambling debts incurred before the birth of the mission. The Apostle handled this case by telling creditors that gambling was a sinful practice, by reminding debtors about the importance of honoring promises, and by convincing the two parties to split the monetary difference. Other problems, the resolutions of which are not recorded in the sources, concerned acceptable behavior on the Sabbath. The Indians were uncertain if they could rekindle a fire on Sundays, if Cutshamekin's wife was permitted to speak of "worldly matters" on the Lord's day, and if Waban could fell a tree in order to catch a raccoon to serve to his sabbath dinner guests.[40]

The progress of the mission enabled ministers on both sides of the Atlantic to use the proselytes as object lessons for English degenerates. Shepard, for example, said in *The Day-Breaking* that "Indians shall weep to hear faith and repentance preached, when Englishmen shall mourn, too late, that they are weary of such truths," and he remarked in *The Clear Sun-shine* that "I wish the like hearts and ways were seen in many English who profess themselves Christians." Similarly, John Dury wrote in his appendix to *The Glorious Progress* that the "converted heathens in New England go beyond you, O ye apostate Christians in England!"; and Whitfield warned readers of *The Light appearing* that "these Indians will rise up in judgment against us and our children at the last day."[41]

Although they were pleased with the Indians' advances, the elders were less sanguine about the natives' progress toward conversion. "The day of grace is not yet come unto them," Eliot stated in November 1648. Shepard shared this judgment. "We know," he wrote, "that the profession of very many is but a mere paint, and their best graces nothing but mere flashes and pangs, which are suddenly kindled and as soon go out and are extinct again." Shepard gave two main reasons for the saints' skepticism about conversion. The first was the elders' lack of missionary experience: "we have not learned as yet that art of coining Christians, or putting Christ's name and image upon copper metal." The second was the Jews-then-Gentiles sequence. It would not be until the conversion of the Jews that "these western Indians will . . .

come in." Prior to that time, "the calling in of a few Indians to Christ is the gathering home of many hundreds in one."⁴²

The elders were nevertheless confident that a few Indians would soon experience conversion. Shepard wrote in September 1647 that "the power of the Word has taken place in some, and that inwardly and effectually, but how far savingly time will declare." He and Eliot were particularly impressed by the natives' "tears of repentance." Shepard observed proselytes "weeping abundantly" during prayers and sermons, and Eliot noticed that his servant, as well as Cutshamekin and Wamporas, cried when they were censured for their transgressions. "Indians are well-known," Shepard remarked, "not to be much subject to tears, no not when they come to feel the sorest torture, or are solemnly brought forth to die." In one poignant incident witnessed by Edward Jackson in 1647, Totherswamp and other Nonantum Indians abandoned "their old superstitious observances at such sad times" and buried a child in an English-style coffin. Before long "the woods rang out . . . with their sighs and prayers." "If the Word works these tears," Shepard concluded, "then surely there is some conquering power of Jesus Christ stirring among them."⁴³

The Indians' acceptance of the mission came at considerable cost to them. To begin with, Eliot's program created social problems for the Massachuset and Pawtucket proselytes. One was that "other Indians . . . did revile them." In 1647 Wamporas told Shepard that pagans "abroad in the country hate us and oppose us," and that same year Eliot noted that "mock[ing] and scoff[ing]" natives had called two of the praying Indians Jehovah and Jesus Christ. This problem persisted throughout the period prior to King Philip's War: Eliot wrote in *Indian Dialogues* that Waban had told some recently evangelized Nipmucks that "the carnal world will hate you, mock you, injure you, speak all evil against you, and it may be if they can they will kill you."⁴⁴

A second problem was that the mission ended polygamous marriages. The Massachusetts and Pawtuckets probably did not practice polygamy to the extent that many Puritans imagined: Roger Williams reported that the Narragansetts "generally have but one wife," and James Axtell has drawn the same conclusion from a larger cross-section of evidence in colonial North America. When the problem of plural marriage surfaced among the proselytes, the usual solution was to preserve the initial marriage and annul later ones, unless the first wife was, in Winthrop's phrasing, "an adulteress, etc." Wequash, for instance, "put away all his wives, saving the first, to whom he had most right," and Ponampam, a Neponset Indian, apparently did likewise. As George Tinker has noted, this practice meant that secondary wives and their children were left to fend for themselves. On at least one occasion, the standard policy created special difficulties. In 1647 Shepard reported a case in which the first wife had no children and the second one did. He failed to disclose how this case was resolved.[45]

A third social problem was that the mission sometimes divided families. In certain cases the mission pitted husband against wife. "If but one parent believe," an Indian asked in 1649, "what state are our children in?" Eliot had answered a similar question in 1647 by stating that "when God chooses a man or a woman to be his servant, he chooses all their children to be so also." The mission also divided siblings. Two prominent Nonantum families had this problem. Anthony initially resisted the mission even though his brothers Wamporas and Totherswamp had accepted it, and John Speene held out longer than his brothers Robin and Thomas. Eliot handled this problem by telling proselytes that love for a non-Christian brother was inferior in quality to love for a Christian stranger. There were also pagan parents with Christian children and Christian parents with pagan children. The elders dealt with the first problem by explaining that God would not visit the sins of parents on their children, and with the second by stressing the importance of forgiveness. Lastly, there was the case of a pagan wife who left her Christian husband, "commit[ed] adultery with . . . remote Indians," and then wanted to return to her spouse. Whether she was allowed to come back is left unsaid.[46]

A final social problem was the flight of nonproselytes from the Christian settlements into the interior. In 1657 Eliot recalled that "when the Lord had bowed the hearts of some, . . . such as bowed not fled farther off." Some of these centrifugal Indians eventually returned to the fold. Ponampam and John Speene left Neponset and Nonantum, respectively, because they disliked praying-town discipline, and came back because they missed their families and friends. Other Indians, like Monequasson and Anthony, thought about fleeing but decided to stay.[47]

The mission also created intellectual difficulties for the proselytes. Charles Cohen has observed that in traditional native religion, salvation "depended on 'works' (i.e., establishing proper relationships with other creatures) rather than on an infusion of supernatural grace," and that "prior to contact, Amerindians could not have developed Christian conceptions of sin, either as an original transgression corrupting the first couple's heirs or as a violation of an omnipotent Lord's decree." Several of the questions asked by the Indians in the late 1640s corroborate Cohen's judgments: "If a child die before he sin, whither goes his soul?" "May a good man sin sometimes?" "Why did God make hell before Adam sinned?" The proselytes had other intellectual difficulties as well. Several Indians initially wondered "whether Jesus Christ did understand, or God did understand, Indian prayers." Like the Narragansetts observed by Roger Williams, these natives probably assumed that "the Englishman's God made Englishmen, and the heavens and earth there, . . . [and that] their gods made them." Ponampam assumed that "all men die alike" and that he "sprang from my father and mother" and not from God; Magus believed that "the world was of itself, and all people grew up in the world of themselves"; Captain Tom "did not think . . . that the Bible was God's book, but that wise men made it"; and Anthony could not imagine that "there was but one God."[48]

This body of evidence shows that the early proselytes did not embrace the mission because they had become convinced of the merits of Calvinism. The natives had turned to Eliot's program for the benefits it promised, such as access to literacy and a guaranteed place of residence. Their participation in the mission, however, obliged them to come to terms with Puritan theology. As we shall see in Chapter 5, the leading proselytes developed a greater appreciation for Calvinism by the time of the Natick church examinations in the 1650s.

Eliot first articulated his plan to create a central praying town in 1648, at a time when he almost certainly subscribed to Cotton's eschatology, which provided no basis for thinking that the millennium was imminent among the natives. But by the time Natick was founded in 1650, the Apostle had concluded that the kingdom was nigh among the Indians. From that time until his conviction about the imminence of the millennium wavered in the mid-1650s, Eliot equated the process of establishing the town's civil and ecclesiastical institutions with the process of establishing the millennium among his proselytes.

CHAPTER FOUR

• • •

The Mission and the Millennium

Eliot's earliest extant discussions of the millennium appear in three letters he wrote to Edward Winslow between July and December 1649. These discussions were inspired by the events of the English Civil War, particularly by the execution of King Charles I on January 30, 1649. Eliot expanded the views expressed in these letters in later sources, most notably in his millennial blueprint for England, *The Christian Commonwealth, or the Civil Polity of the Rising Kingdom of Jesus Christ*. He wrote this treatise at some point between September 1651, when he installed the millennial civil polity at Natick on a "day of fasting and prayer," and July 1652, when he sent the manuscript to England for publication. For reasons that are no longer clear, *The Christian Commonwealth* did not appear in print until 1659, when someone who identified himself only as "a server of the season" saw the work through the London press.[1]

The Apostle's millennial views were clearly influenced by John Cotton's earlier lectures on Revelation and Canticles. As Dwight Bozeman explains, Eliot shared Cotton's contempt for human inventions, understood the millennium as the restoration of primitive institutions in their original splendor, equated the birth of the millennium with the Middle Advent, and located the second coming, the universal resurrection of the dead, and the last judgment in the distant future.[2] Bozeman, however, has a keener eye for the similarities rather than the differences between the two men. Despite his undeniable debt to Cotton, Eliot broke with the Boston preacher in important ways.

Eliot believed that the execution of Charles I was an event of world-historical significance. The regicide indicated that the institution of monarchy was to be "dashed in pieces" in "all places whatsoever." Eliot thought that the destruction of the universal dominion of kings would reverse a process of degeneration that stretched back to the age of the biblical patriarchs. He surmised that Nimrod, the shadowy figure of Genesis 10, had invented the institution of monarchy in defiance of God's will; from this impious foundation, the polity spread to other ancient peoples, including the Israelites, who, in a verse Eliot cited in *The Christian Commonwealth,* asked Samuel "to make us a king to judge us like all the nations" (1 Samuel 8:5). The conclusion that monarchy was a human contrivance is absent in the surviving texts of Cotton's lectures on Revelation and Canticles and in his other sources. For Eliot, the subsequent history of kingly rule in Israel, Europe, and elsewhere confirmed his judgment about the human provenience of the institution: monarchs were "terror[s] to men" because they governed with their own interests, and not those of God, in mind. Charles Stuart, "too high to stoop to the Lord Jesus, to be ruled by his command," was a case in point. Eliot anticipated that the destruction of monarchical government would be accompanied by the collapse of other man-made polities, particularly religious ones, that were sustained by "the strongest iron sinews of civil states." God had consigned all institutions "contrived by the wisdom of man" to obliteration in order to replace them with their millennial scriptural counterparts. "We wait for the coming of the kingdom of the Lord Jesus," he wrote in *The Christian Commonwealth,* "who . . . will reign over all the nations of the earth in his due time. I mean, the Lord Jesus will bring down all people, to be ruled by the institutions, laws, and directions of the Word of God, not only in church government and administration but also in the government and administration of all affairs in the commonwealth. And . . . when all things among men are done by the direction of the word of his mouth, his kingdom [the millennium] is then come among us."[3]

Eliot's choice for the millennial civil polity was the system of rulers of tens, fifties, hundreds, and thousands found in Exodus 18:21–22, where Jethro told Moses to "provide out of all the people able men, such as fear God, men of truth, hating covetousness; and place such over them, to be rulers of thousands, and rulers of hundreds, rulers of fifties, and rulers of tens." Eliot chose this polity because it was "that form of government which we find Israel was under at the first, and never quite lost." Its temporal priority among the Israelites' various civil polities—including monarchy—testified to its impeccable primitive credentials. He also explained in *The Light appearing* that he selected the system of tens through thousands after consulting with "Mr. Cotton and others." It is not clear if Cotton or another person suggested this civil order. Eliot indicated only that the consultation convinced him that his "general rule" should be to follow "the Scripture in all things both in church and state."[4]

The Apostle anticipated that once they were installed in power, the rulers of tens, fifties, and hundreds would preserve the other two institutional components of the millennium. The first was the ecclesiastical polity. Although he changed his mind about the matter after the Restoration, he believed during the Interregnum that Congregationalism was the millennial church order. The second was the judicial laws of Moses "in so far as they are moral and conscionable." Eliot's commitment to the restitution of ancient Israelite law sometimes reached such proportions that it seemingly entailed the total eradication of all man-made legal systems, including those in England. "Oh the blessed day in England," he told Winslow in 1649, "when the Word of God shall be their only Magna Carta and chief law book." Such statements, however, should probably be regarded as rhetorical flourishes. On other occasions during the early Interregnum, Eliot said that English law could be harmonized with biblical law, a common assumption at the time. He proposed in *The Christian Commonwealth*, for instance, that it "would be a work worthy of the labors of the best divines and the best of men, to demonstrate the equity of all the wholesome and wise laws of England by the Word of God."[5]

The most conspicuous structural feature of Eliot's millennial proposal was its multitude of officials. In order to accommodate the population of nation-states, he extended the biblical civil polity to include rulers of ten thousands through rulers of millions. A single ruler of one million presupposed over a hundred thousand subordinate officials, each holding courts of law at stated intervals. Eliot took delight in the arithmetic of his proposal, at one point trying—and failing—to accurately calculate the maximum number of men who could live under the jurisdiction of a ruler of one thousand. Eliot had two reasons for thinking that an abundance of rulers was necessary for the proper functioning of the millennium. The first was human iniquity: "sin will grow apace, like ill weeds, if it be not always watched and often weeded out." Thus he arranged for "every order [to] . . . cohabit together as near as may be because that does tend to facilitate both the watch and work of the Lord's government." The second was the slow course of justice in England, a situation he attributed to the complexity of English law and to the self-interest of lawyers. To provide for a "speedy and easy determination" of judgment, he established as many courts of law as the Word of God allowed; and to control the lawyers, he simply abolished the profession. No lawyer walks the pages of Eliot's *Christian Commonwealth*, where all cases were heard between the rulers, the defendant, the plaintiff, and the witnesses.[6]

The destruction of the Stuart regime convinced Eliot that England was ready for the millennium. "Behold, now Christ . . . gloriously breaks forth in the brightness of his coming," he told Winslow in July 1649, in a clear reference to the Middle Advent. With the traditional order in ruins, the saints were positioned to "set up the longed for, prayed for, and desired kingdom of the Lord Jesus." The purpose of Eliot's *Christian Commonwealth* was to convince the revolutionary leaders to establish the millennial civil polity throughout England. The treatise was accordingly addressed to "the chosen, and holy, and faithful, who manage the wars of the Lord against Antichrist in Great Britain." At the same time, Eliot hoped that all thoughtful Christians in England, Scotland, and Ireland would support his proposal because of its fidelity to the Scripture. "If there be a divine form of civil government," he explained in the preface to the work, "I doubt not but that all the godly . . . would chose that way of government before any other."[7]

At the time he wrote *The Christian Commonwealth*, Eliot believed that England was *the* inaugural location for the millennium. As Bozeman points out, the Apostle stated in the treatise that the island nation was the place where the Lord of the Middle Advent would "begin his blessed and waited-for reign over all the nations of the earth" and that "Christ is the only right heir of the Crown of England, and of all other nations also; and he is now come to take possession of his kingdom, making England first in that blessed work of setting up the kingdom of the Lord Jesus." This perspective so decentralized Jerusalem that Eliot's early Interregnum sources contain only two passing references to the City of David and none to the destruction of the Ottoman empire. Eliot's conclusion that England was the birthplace of the millennium rested on an unexpected foundation. His conclusion was not a straightforward deduction from the fact that England's Antichristian regime had been destroyed. This fact in itself did not explain why the Stuarts had been overthrown before the Bourbons or the Hapsburgs. Nor did Eliot base the conclusion on any patriotic profession that England was God's "elect nation." His sources for the period contain no suggestion that the mother country was the appropriate inaugural location for the millennium because the nation had a long history of special providential favor. His stated reason was that England stood at the "end of the earth" (Deuteronomy 28:64) westward from Mt. Ararat, the resting place of Noah's ark and the starting point for the peregrinations of Noah's son Japheth, the supposed ancestor of the European peoples. Eliot's surviving sources provide no explanation but this geographical one for the Lord's decision to begin the work of destruction and reconstruction in England.[8]

Eliot's interpretation of the regicide meant that Cotton's two preconditions for the millennium did not apply to England. The first was the destruction of Roman Catholicism by the "ten kings" in the Battle of Armageddon. For Eliot, the ruin of Rome was the necessary antecedent to the establishment of the millennium on the Continent but not to its birth in England. He also did not share Cotton's supposition that Catholic kings were to convert to Reformed Protestantism, destroy the Roman church, and exercise political power during the millennium. Eliot expected that the Catholic monarchs, like their Anglican counterpart, would prove so "loath to stoop to Christ" that only violence could end their reigns. So great was the contrast with Cotton's lectures in this respect that Eliot begged readers of *The Christian Commonwealth* for clues about the identities of the "ten kings which shall hate the whore" because he did not know who they could be. The second of Cotton's preconditions was the national conversion of the Jews following the destruction of Catholicism. Eliot anticipated that the restoration of ancient Israelite civil and legal institutions in England, as well as the elimination of Catholic images from the nation's churches, would convince the European Jews of the superiority of the Christian religion; however, he did not think that England's entrance into the kingdom had to await the conversion of the Jews or, for that matter, the readmission of the Jews into England and the redemption of the lost tribes of Israel. Eliot's early Interregnum eschatology required the physical presence of Japheth's descendants, not Shem's, in England.[9]

The execution of Charles I evidently did not dislodge Cotton from his conviction that the destruction of the papacy and the national conversion of the Jews were the preconditions to the birth of the millennium in England and on the Continent. The Boston preacher wrote little that survives from the period between the regicide and his own death in December 1652. His fullest discussion of the "last things" came in a 1651 sermon on the image of the "sea of glass mingled with fire" (Revelation 15:2–3). In the earlier lecture series on Revelation, he had interpreted this image as an allusion to the dissension that would remain within the Protestant ranks until the millennial restoration of the apostolic church, when "the sea of glass mingled with fire" would be transformed into "the sea of glass like unto crystal" (Revelation 4:6). Cotton viewed the image in the same way in the 1651 sermon. He explained that Protestants would continue to dispute matters of faith and practice "until God brings on his ancient people, [who] . . . will learn us much that we have not learned." Only "then [would] . . . Christian churches . . . see the purity of their members, and the amity of the purity." He listed as examples of these disagreements the conflicts over baptism, synodial authority, hymnody, and prophesying in Massachusetts Bay, and the controversies over church polity, predestination, and eucharistic doctrine on the Continent. Cotton centered his attention in the sermon, however, on the ecclesiastical quarrels between the Presbyterians and the Independents in England. He recommended that the two parties create a national church that would combine features of both polities. This expedient would resolve differences until the inevitable vindication of Congregationalism at the Middle Advent. Thus at a time when Eliot was encouraging the saints to establish the millennium in England, Cotton was proposing a caretaker measure that would keep the brotherhood intact until "God brings on his ancient people."[10]

In this sermon Cotton also addressed the political division between the English Presbyterians and the Independents over the regicide. The death of the king created a serious exegetical problem for Cotton: in the lectures on Revelation and Canticles, he had included the British monarch among the "ten kings" who would come to "hate the whore." The regicide had destroyed the Stuart dynasty before it could perform its latter-day duty. Cotton stated in his 1651 sermon that the Stuart's execution should not divide the Presbyterians and the Independents because the sentence of death had been just. In contrast to Eliot's, however, Cotton's defense of the regicide rested on constitutional and not eschatological grounds. The purposes of the Solemn League and Covenant had been to protect "the purity of religion" from "popery and prelacy" and to "preserve the liberty and safety of the people against tyranny"; Charles had committed "such acts as have been dangerous and destructive to the commonwealth"; the Rump Parliament "represented the whole kingdom" and hence possessed "lawful authority" to kill the king; and the regicides did not represent "a conspiracy of private men." Cotton repeated these same constitutional arguments in a July 1651 letter to Oliver Cromwell (as though Cromwell had not heard them before!). He then congratulated the future Lord Protector for having waged "the wars of the Lamb against the Beast" (Revelation 17:14) in England and Scotland, and added that "I am fully satisfied that you have all this while fought the Lord's battles." Cotton did not explain, however, how these battles fit into biblical prophecy. Cromwell's reply, written in October, suggests that Cotton's letter had not clarified the matter. Cromwell's haunting refrain—"What is the Lord a doing? What prophecies are now fulfilling?"—probably haunted Cotton as well.[11]

Eliot had much to say about the implications of his political radicalism and nothing to say about the origins of it. For this reason, any attempt to explain why he became a radical is necessarily speculative. His antimonarchicalism is probably best understood as an extension of the characteristic Puritan contempt for human inventions beyond conventional examples (such as the episcopal polity and stained-glass windows) to the forms of civil government. Once he had concluded that monarchy was a man-made polity, he was in a position to develop his views about the significance of the regicide in the manner outlined thus far in this chapter. Eliot's interpretation of the regicide, moreover, was not unprecedented at the time. His affinities with the Fifth Monarchy movement in contemporary England have been noted by James Maclear and others. The members of this movement, who included several repatriated Massachusetts men—most notably William Aspinwall, a merchant, and Thomas Venner, a cooper—advocated the establishment of a scriptural civil polity in England, the creation of a congregational state church, and the adoption of a biblically based code of laws. The effectiveness of the movement was compromised by its controversial agenda and by internal disagreements over the choice of a suitable scriptural alternative to monarchical government (the system of rulers of tens through thousands was by no means orthodox), over the place of infant baptism and charismatic preaching in local churches, and over the extent to which English law approximated Israelite law. The movement's influence in England peaked when the Barebones Parliament was convened in July 1653, and receded rapidly after Cromwell abolished the assembly in December and established the Protectorate.[12]

The Christian Commonwealth was not the only major eschatological statement that Eliot wrote during the early Interregnum. Early in 1653, some six months after he composed *The Christian Commonwealth*, he sent a lengthy letter to Thomas Thorowgood, a Presbyterian minister in Grimston, Norfolk and the person who later bestowed upon Eliot the epithet of "Apostle." This letter, which Thorowgood published under the title "The learned Conjectures of Reverend John Eliot touching the Americans," contains the missionary's only sustained discussion of the Indians' origins. Eliot argued in his "Learned Conjectures" that New England stood at the opposite end of the earth from the British Isles. This argument revised his earlier notion that England would be the birthplace of the millennium. There were now *two* inaugural locations for the coming kingdom: a western branch in England for the descendants of Japheth and an eastern one in New England for the Native American posterity of Shem.[13]

The "Learned Conjectures" and the Origins of the Indians

The chain of events that led to Eliot's "Learned Conjectures" began in England and Holland. In late 1648 or early 1649, John Dury read an unpublished manuscript by Thorowgood that argued that the Native Americans were the descendants of the ten lost tribes of Israel. Thorowgood had been interested in the lost tribes theory since the mid-1630s, when he exchanged letters with Roger Williams, who was intrigued by it at the time. The manuscript led Dury to recall a strange story that he had heard in 1644, when he was living in The Hague as chaplain to Mary, Princess of Orange. In order to refresh his memory about the details of the story, Dury contacted Menasseh ben Israel, a rabbi in Amsterdam, who soon provided him with the information he requested. Menasseh explained that in 1644 a Marrano calling himself Antonio deMontezinos had disembarked in Amsterdam, fresh from a voyage to South America. DeMontezinos reported that he had encountered in the mountains of present-day Colombia a group of Israelites who recited the Shema, practiced various Mosaic rites, and claimed to belong to the lost tribe of Reuben. Dury soon told Edward Winslow the story. Winslow then endorsed the lost tribes theory in his introduction to *The Glorious Progress* and appended to the work a similar endorsement from Dury. In this appendix Dury identified the Indians as the "dry bones" of Ezekiel 37. In 1650 two major statements of the lost tribes theory were published. One was Menasseh's *Esperança de Israel* (Amsterdam, 1650). Latin and English translations appeared later that year in Amsterdam and London, respectively. The other was Thorowgood's misleadingly entitled argument for the Israelite-origins view, *Iewes in America* (reissued in 1652 as *Digitus Dei: New Discoveries*). Thorowgood's book also included "An Epistolicall Discourse of Mr. John Dury" written in support of the theory.[14]

Dury, Thorowgood, and Menasseh were not in agreement about the nuances of the lost tribes theory (Winslow's discussion was confined to a single paragraph and does not permit a sustained comparison). Menasseh and Dury thought that some of the lost tribes had established permanent residence in Asia and that others of them had continued into the New World by crossing over the Straits of Anian. Thorowgood apparently assumed that all of the Israelites eventually passed through the Straits into America. In *Iewes in America*, he is silent on the subject of a permanent Asian residence.[15] Menasseh believed that vast numbers of Tartars had followed the lost tribes into the New World and that the Indians were descended from these Tartars and not from the lost tribes. According to Menasseh, the Israelites maintained a continuous and conscious tradition of observance in isolated locations like the Andes; in time the Indians borrowed features of the Mosaic Law from the lost tribes. Dury, Thorowgood, and Winslow, however, held that the lost tribes were the ancestors of the native Americans. The three Christians evidently did not think that there had been an ancient Gentile migration to the Americas. Aside from tiny groups like the one deMontezinos allegedly encountered, the lost tribes degenerated so deeply into paganism in the New World that they lost conscious memory of their religious heritage. Nevertheless, they retained elements of their Israelite past. These supposed vestiges included the practice of circumcision, the segregation of menstruating women, belief in divine providence and in the immortality of the soul, and legends about a primordial couple and about a flood.[16]

Menasseh and Dury anticipated that the Jews and the lost tribes would soon be restored in Palestine; Dury expected that the Karaites (Jews who rejected the authority of the Talmud) would join them. For Menasseh, the return of Jacob's descendants to their ancestral homeland was the precondition to the advent of the messiah; for Dury, it was the precondition to the birth of the millennium following the Battle of Armageddon and the conversion of Jacob's posterity. As Dury wrote in *The Glorious Progress,* "it is the expectation of some of the wisest Jews now living, that about the year 1650, either we Christians shall be Mosaic, or else that themselves Jews shall be Christians." Thorowgood, for his part, did not discuss a possible restoration in Palestine or advance any millennial claims in *Iewes in America.*[17]

In late 1648 or early 1649, Winslow wrote to Eliot about the growing interest in the lost tribes theory. Although it has not survived, Winslow's letter surely characterized the theory as holding that the Indians were degenerate Israelites rather than Tartars or some other Gentile people. Eliot replied in the same July 1649 letter that contains his earliest extant discussion of the millennial reconstruction of England. He explained that he had already started to examine "the original of this people" in order to "find under what covenant and promise their forefathers have been." Eliot then told Winslow that it was "clear in the Scripture" that the Indians "are the children of Shem," the eldest son of Noah and the eponymous ancestor of the Semitic peoples (Genesis 5–11). Eliot next briefly evaluated two Semitic-origins views. The first, which he attributed to Hugh Broughton, a late Elizabethan Hebraist, was that the Indians were the Gentile [sic] descendants of Joktan, the son of Eber. Eliot said that Broughton was "probably" correct about the matter. The second was the lost tribes theory. Eliot stated in the July 1649 letter that he believed that the lost tribes had established permanent residence among the Asian peoples. He then explained that he was presently unable to accept the proposition that "some of the Israelites were brought into America and scattered here." Nevertheless, he wanted to learn more about the lost tribes' possible dispersion into the New World, and he importuned

Winslow to provide more information about it: "for that opinion of Rabbi ben Israel which you mention, I would entreat you to request the same godly minister [Dury] . . . to send to him to know his grounds, and how he came to that intelligence, when it was done, which way they were transported to America, by whom, and what occasion, how many, and to what parts first, or what steps of intimation of such a thing there may be."[18]

Eliot soon received another (missing) letter from Winslow as well as a copy of *The Glorious Progress*. In his reply to Winslow's second letter, Eliot explained that he was fascinated by Dury's appendix to *The Glorious Progress*, which identified the Indians as Ezekiel's "dry bones." The Apostle had preached one or more of his early sermons at Nonantum on this text, although at the time he did not construe it as a reference to the lost tribes (otherwise his reluctance to endorse an American diaspora in the July 1649 letter to Winslow would be difficult to explain). Eliot then disclosed that he had come across some corroborative evidence of his own for the Israelite-origins view: Thomas Cromwell, a buccaneer commissioned by the Earl of Warwick to hunt Spanish ships in the West Indies, had recently reported in Boston that there were "many Indians to the southward circumcised." Eliot termed Cromwell's report "one of the most probable arguments ever I yet heard of" for the lost tribes theory. He then asked Winslow to send him Thorowgood's forthcoming book. Eliot did not request a copy of Menasseh's *Hope of Israel*, and there is no evidence that he ever read it.[19]

Thorowgood's *Iewes in America* reached Eliot shortly after its publication in early May 1650. The two men then began to correspond. In October 1650 Eliot told Thorowgood that the arguments for the lost tribes theory, "though they be not so weighty considered singly, yet laid together and remembered, they are observable." Thorowgood soon encouraged Eliot to disclose his views about the Indians' ancestry. The Apostle obliged early in 1653, sending Thorowgood a long letter with "liberty to print or suppress" it. Thorowgood chose to publish this letter—"The learned Conjectures"—in the revised edition of his own work, entitled *Jews in America* (1660). Eliot based his "Conjectures" almost entirely on his reading of the Hebrew Bible rather than on alleged vestiges of the Indians' Israelite past. "The surest thread to guide us in this dark enquiry," he explained, "is to follow the line of the Scriptures, for Scripture notes and marks will be the best evidences to move God's people to believe whether this, or that people be of the remnant of lost Israel, or not." Eliot's decision to "follow the line of the Scriptures" must have disappointed Thorowgood, who surely hoped that the Apostle had discovered additional remnants of the Law among the Indians. By relying on the Scriptures, Eliot authored a statement that he could have written almost as easily in Thorowgood's armchair in Norfolk as in the wilderness of New England.[20]

Eliot argued in his "Learned Conjectures" that the earliest and the predominant inhabitants of America were descendants of Eber's Gentile son Joktan. The Apostle proposed that roughly a century after the Flood, the Hebrews in question had moved into the then "deserted eastern part of the world." Some of them remained in Asia and eventually populated the continent, and the rest continued eastward and filled the vacant New World. "Hence therefore we may say," he wrote, "that fruitful India are Hebrews [that is, Joktanites] of Eber, that that famous civil (though idolatrous) nation of China are Hebrews, so Japan, and these naked Americans are Hebrews." Eliot offered two pieces of evidence for this conclusion: first, he surmised that the Joktanites had been obliged to migrate into Asia because Europe, the Middle East, and Africa were "already taken up and possessed" by other descendants of Noah; and second, he detected "footsteps of the Hebrew language" in the Indians' speech.[21]

Having established to his satisfaction the Indians' Joktanite ancestry, Eliot turned to the matter closer to Thorowgood's heart, the location of the ten lost tribes of Israel. The Apostle stated that the Bible supported Thorowgood's conclusion that the lost tribes had migrated into the New World. Eliot explained that following their subjugation by the Assyrians, the Israelites had made an eastward journey of their own (see 1 Kings 14:15). Like the Joktanites before them, some of them remained in Asia and others of them continued into America, eventually reaching the Atlantic coast (Eliot did not speculate about their point of entry into the New World). The two Hebrew peoples were able to interact because of their similar "language and spirit." In time the American Israelites lapsed into paganism and ceased to be distinguishable to human observers from the Joktanites. Eliot based his conclusions about the dispersal and degeneration of the lost tribes on a single biblical verse, Deuteronomy 28:64, where Moses warns the posterity of Jacob—the future Houses of Israel and Judah—that "the

Lord shall scatter thee among all people, from the one end of the earth even unto the other; and there thou shalt serve other gods, which neither thou nor thy fathers have known, even wood and stone." Eliot's uncritical acceptance of the Bible led him to assume that this ancient warning must have come to pass in history. Hence he was able to argue in "The learned Conjectures" that the lost tribes had reached the shores of the Atlantic, the "utmost ends of the earth eastward" from the Promised Land, and that the lost tribes had abandoned their ancestral faith for deities "of wood and stone."[22]

Thus Eliot maintained in his "Learned Conjectures" that the American Indians, as well as the Asian peoples, were of two distinct though no longer distinguishable lineages, Joktanite and Israelite. The quaintness of his argument must not obscure the significance that it held for him. The two Semitic-origins views served different purposes in his early Interregnum eschatology.

The Joktanite theory provided Eliot with a basis for thinking that New England was to be the birthplace of the eastern branch of the millennium. There were two steps to this conclusion. First, Eliot surmised from his reconstruction of the Joktanites' migrations that America was "part of the eastern world" because it had been "peopled by eastern inhabitants." This idea broke with an article of orthodoxy on both sides of the Atlantic. Early modern English sources routinely placed America in the western world and termed its native inhabitants "western Indians," presumably because the New World lay to the west of Europe and had been colonized by Europeans. As we shall see later in this chapter, Eliot followed orthodox opinion about this matter until he wrote "The learned Conjectures." Second, the Apostle reasoned that New England stood at the easternmost end of the earth and was thus the appropriate starting place for "Christ his expected kingdom" in "the vast eastern world, the huge posterity of Shem." Eliot interpreted the figure of the temple in Ezekiel 40–47 as a reference to the branch of the millennium that was to begin among the Indians in New England and then spread westward across America and Asia: "when Ezekiel's gospel-temple . . . shall be measured, the eastern gate is first measured, Ezekiel 40.6, [and] when the glory of the Lord comes into that glorious temple, he is upon his western progress, and first enters that temple at the eastern gate." Although there is no explicit assertion to this effect in his "Learned Conjectures," Eliot's conclusion that New England was the "eastern gate" of "Christ his expected kingdom" clearly meant that England was no longer the only inaugural location for the millennium.[23]

The lost tribes theory had a different function from the Joktanite theory in "The learned Conjectures." Eliot assumed that the "glory of the Lord" could not enter Ezekiel's temple at its "eastern gate" until God had "open[ed] the door of grace" and that the Joktanites' Gentile ancestry placed them at the end of the Jews-then-Gentiles sequence. The Israelite-origins view solved these two problems. Eliot believed that despite their long alienation from God, the lost tribes of Israel remained entitled to the biblical promises of eschatological redemption given to the posterity of Jacob. As he wrote in his "Learned Conjectures," in a statement that also shows that he had come to identify the lost tribes as Ezekiel's "dry bones": "though the Lord has scattered the ten tribes into corners, and made their remembrance to cease among men, as he threatened, Deuteronomy 32.21, insomuch as that they are lost, and no one knows where to find them up again; yet the Lord has promised to bind them up again, and to gather together those dry and scattered bones, and to bring them to know the Lord, and to be known and acknowledged among men again." Eliot then argued that the migration of the lost tribes into their midst gave the Joktanites a secondhand stake in the biblical promises. When God poured forth his grace upon the Israelites, he would simultaneously deliver the Gentiles among whom they had settled. Eliot had first articulated this doctrine of simultaneous conversion, which he based on Genesis 48:19 and Zechariah 8:23, in his July 1649 letter to Winslow:

> Our God who can and will gather the scattered and lost dust of our bodies at the resurrection, can and will find out these lost and scattered Israelites, and in finding them, bring in with them the [Gentile] nations among whom they were scattered, and so shall Jacob's promise extend to a multitude of nations indeed; and this is a great ground of faith for the conversion of the eastern [in this case, the Asian] nations, and may be of help to our faith for these Indians, especially if Rabbi ben Israel can make it appear that some of the Israelites were brought into America and scattered here.

At the time he wrote this letter, the Apostle was not prepared to accept the notion of an Israelite dispersion from Asia into America. His reservations about the matter had disappeared by the time of "The learned

Conjectures." Eliot's next step was to argue that the ten lost tribes deserved to be redeemed before the Jews: the former had lived in ignorance of Christian teaching and the latter in contempt of it. The temporal priority of Israel over Judah, in conjunction with the doctrine of simultaneous conversion, meant that the eschatological redemption of the Gentiles in America and Asia no longer had to await the national conversion of the Jews. Eliot completed his argument by appealing to the conviction in England, "of late more stirring than in former times," that the conversion of the lost tribes was imminent. "Now the time is even at hand," he announced, "wherein the people of God do hope for the accomplishment of that great work."[24]

Eliot's argument in "The learned Conjectures" immensely appealed to him. The doctrine of simultaneous conversion created the exhilarating prospect of massive eschatological conversions among the American and Asian peoples, as the lost tribes of Israel and the Joktanites along with them received the blessings of God's grace. New England's location at the easternmost end of the world meant that the spectacle would begin there, and the contemporary supposition that "the time is even at hand" for the redemption of the lost tribes meant that it would begin soon. Once it started to unfold, this spectacle would not only end the laborious process of instructing the local Indians in Christianity in the hope that a few of their number might experience conversion in advance of the redemption of the Jews, but also inaugurate the eastern branch of the millennium.

"The learned Conjectures" was Eliot's most mature statement about the Indians' place in biblical prophecy. To judge from his surviving sources, it was not until he wrote the work that he realized that there could be a second inaugural location for the millennium at the opposite end of the earth from England. Prior to this time, he assumed that the island nation would be *the* birthplace for the Lord's millennial reign over the entire world, and not simply over its western portion. Eliot's views about Natick during the early Interregnum cannot be assessed properly without an awareness of this chronology.

The Rise and Fall of the Indian Millennium

Eliot first disclosed his millennial objectives for the mission in the three 1649 letters that included his earliest discussions of the reconstruction of England and the natives' ancestry. He told Winslow in the first of these letters that "the Lord Jesus is about to set up his blessed kingdom among these poor Indians," in the second that "my work is to endeavor the setting up Christ's kingdom among the Indians," and in the third that "I intend to direct them . . . to set up the kingdom of Christ fully, so that Christ shall reign both in church and commonwealth, both in civil and spiritual matters. And when everything both civil and spiritual is done by the direction of the word of Christ, then does Christ reign, and the great kingdom of Jesus Christ which we do wait for, is even this that I do now mention."[25]

These remarks were shaped by Eliot's interpretation of the regicide and not by his still inchoate views about the natives' origins. Like the Puritan revolutionaries across the Atlantic, the Boston-area Indians had dismantled their traditional political order by ending the "former tyranny" and "usurpations" of their sachems. Cutshamekin and other local rulers, or so Eliot said in 1650, "used to hold their people in an absolute servitude . . . [T]heir former manner was that if they wanted money, or if they desire[d] anything from a man, they would take occasion to rage and be in great anger; which when they ['the people'] did perceive, they would give him all they had to pacify him." This statement vastly exaggerated the traditional authority of the sachems. There was no "former tyranny" for Indians to escape, and sachems had never held "their people in an absolute servitude." Cutshamekin was not Charles Stuart and tribute was not ship money. For Eliot, the destruction of the power of the sachems meant that the proselytes were ready for millennial reorganization. As he explained elsewhere, the Christian Indians resembled an "abrasa rasa, scraped board" on which he could "write and imprint" the appropriate "Scripture form[s] of civil government . . . and church government."[26]

Thus, Eliot concluded in the immediate aftermath of the regicide that the Indians were poised to enter the millennium. At the time, however, he did not think that he could inaugurate the millennium; this was an honor he assigned exclusively to the saints in England, who were to be "first in that blessed work of setting up the kingdom of the Lord Jesus Christ." Prior to writing "The learned Conjectures," he believed that the best he could do was to prepare the Indians for the millennium by installing its institutional forms. Once England had established these same forms, he would be able to state that the natives had entered the kingdom. In Eliot's estimation, the Indians were not only ready for the millennium but also well-suited for it. Unlike European Christians, who were reluctant to "lay down their own imperfect starlight . . . for the perfect sunlight of the Scripture," natives did not "cavil at divine wisdom." "These poor Indians . . . have no principles of their own, nor yet wisdom of their own (I mean as other [European] nations have) wherein to stick," he told Winslow in 1649; "therefore they do most readily yield to any direction from the Lord, so that there will be no such opposition against the rising kingdom of Jesus Christ among them."[27]

Having articulated in 1649 his goal of "set[ting] up the kingdom of Christ fully . . . both in civil and spiritual matters," Eliot tried to achieve it at Natick. In September 1651, he installed the millennial civil polity at Natick up through a single ruler of one hundred. With the millennial civil order in place, Eliot turned his attention to its ecclesiastical counterpart, the Congregationalist church order. In October 1652, he invited representatives from the local English churches to Natick to evaluate the conversion narratives of a group of Indians hoping to form a church of their own. Although they were impressed with the natives' progress since the birth of the mission, the referees rejected the narratives, thus denying the Indians the authorization to establish a church.[28]

The referees' verdict did not diminish Eliot's conviction about the imminence of the millennium at Natick. The quality of the conversion narratives indicated to him that the Indians were on the verge of gathering a church. Later in 1652 he sent transcripts of the conversion narratives to London for publication by the New England Company. He also wrote and forwarded two prefaces, one addressed to Oliver Crowmell and the other to the reading public, as well as a statement by Richard Mather that explained why the referees rejected the Indians' confessions. These materials, along with a recent letter from Thomas Mayhew, Jr., to the corporation, were published in May 1653 as the sixth Eliot tract, *Tears of Repentance*.

Eliot told Cromwell in the first preface that "the design of Christ in these days is double, namely, first, to overthrow Antichrist by the wars of the lamb, and second, to raise up his own kingdom in the room of all earthly powers which he does cast down, and to bring all the world subject to be ruled in all things by the word of his mouth." After congratulating him for achieving the first part of this design in England, Eliot encouraged Cromwell to accomplish the second part "by promoting Scripture government and laws, so that the word of Christ might rule all." Eliot then announced, as he began his account of the Indians' conversion narratives, that the millennium was "rising up" at Natick: "I doubt not, but it will be some comfort to your heart, to see the kingdom of Christ rising up in these western parts of the world; and some confirmation it will be, that the Lord's time is come to advance and spread his blessed kingdom, which shall (in his season) fill all the earth." In the second preface, Eliot wrote that the Indians' narratives showed that "the words of prophecy . . . for the conversion both of the Jews (yea all Israel) and of the Gentiles . . . are in part begun to be accomplished."[29]

These statements must be located within the chronology of Eliot's early Interregnum sources. By this time, he had written *The Christian Commonwealth* but not "The learned Conjectures." His appeal to Cromwell about establishing the millennium in England was consistent with the purpose of the former work. What was new was the claim (soon to be evaluated) that Natick was "confirmation that the Lord's time is come to advance and spread his blessed kingdom" in England. Eliot's declaration in the second preface about the fulfillment of "the words of prophecy . . . for the conversion both of the Jews (yea all Israel) and of the Gentiles" strongly suggests that he had already accepted the lost tribes theory, although explicit evidence to this effect did not surface until "The learned Conjectures." Even at this point, however, an acceptance of the theory would have been an important conclusion for Eliot. The start of the redemption of the Israelites meant that the time of isolated Indian conversions was nearing its end, in keeping with the doctrine of simultaneous conversion that he had first articulated in 1649. But to judge from his use of the phrase "the western parts of the world" in the preface to Cromwell, Eliot had not yet realized that Natick could be the inaugural location for an eastern branch of the millennium.

The basis for Eliot's statement to Cromwell that the "kingdom of Christ [was] rising up" at Natick also requires clarification. The reason for his assertion was neither the settlement's size, for there were barely enough adult male Indians for a single ruler of one hundred, nor its efficiency, for the residents were new to his missionary program. Nor was the reason a matter of geographical location, for he had not yet invested the New England landscape with a special status. Moreover, Eliot's conviction was not based merely on formal organization, as though the millennium would automatically exist among the Indians once the correct institutional forms were in place. Proper timing was necessary in addition to proper organization: the kingdom had to have the right forms, and it had to appear at the right moment in history. At this point, the millennium was imminent at Natick because it was imminent in England.

No more than four months elapsed between the time Eliot wrote the prefaces to *Tears of Repentance* and the composition of "The learned Conjectures." The circumstances that led to his insight that New England stood at the eastern end of the earth are unclear. The act of sitting down and writing a lengthy discussion of the Indians' origins—"The learned Conjectures" is ten thousand words long—probably forced him to think systematically about the geography of the millennium. What is clear was the significance of his insight: Eliot's argument in "The learned Conjectures" transfigured Natick. The settlement ceased to be an outpost on the fringes of the "western parts of the world" and became instead the staging area for the millennial reconstruction of America and Asia. Moreover, his argument enabled him to conclude that the Indians' entrance into the kingdom no longer had to await the establishment of the millennium in England. The supposition that "the time is even at hand" for the national conversion of the lost tribes meant that the "glory of the Lord" was soon to enter Ezekiel's "gospel-temple" at its "eastern gate," regardless of the delayed "kingdom work" across the Atlantic.

Students of Eliot's early Interregnum eschatology differ in their assessments of it. Timothy Sehr is reluctant to advance any claim beyond stating that Natick was a "sign of the approaching reign of Christ." James Holstun sees Eliot's *Christian Commonwealth,* as well as James Harrington's *Commonwealth of Oceana* (1656), John Milton's *The Ready and Easy Way to Establish a Free Commonwealth* (1660), and several other seventeenth-century utopian works, as harbingers of modern forms of organizational discipline. The standard scholarly approach, however, is to interpret Natick within the framework of the Bay Colony's alleged millennial errand into the wilderness. "Eliot believed," James Maclear wrote in 1975, "that his own humble Indian flock . . . was destined to take the first step toward the millennium" and that Natick would "serve as a model" for England; and Philip Gura stated in 1984 that Eliot "hoped that his accomplishments with the unlettered Indians in Natick would provide the beacon for another, greater city on a hill" in England. In 1988 Dwight Bozeman challenged the majority view, asserting that Eliot "never claimed" that

Natick was "the exemplary model guiding England toward millennial transformation." Bozeman supported his contention by accurately observing that in *The Christian Commonwealth*, Eliot "nowhere ... advance[d] Natick as such as the model for European imitation" and that in the treatise he mentioned the praying town only to explain that the Indians' need for a civil polity was the "occasion [that] did first put me upon this study."[30]

Bozeman rightly rejects the conventional wisdom. First of all, the errand thesis wrongly assumes that Eliot subordinated Natick to his plans for England, when in fact the eschatological purpose of the settlement was to bring the Indians, not the wayward saints across the Atlantic, into the millennium. Natick was the "pattern and model" for future praying towns rather than for England. Furthermore, there is insufficient evidence in Eliot's early Interregnum sources to support the standard thesis. The only passage that could possibly be construed in this manner was his statement to Cromwell that Natick was "confirmation ... that the Lord's time is come to advance and spread his blessed kingdom" in England. This statement does not offer the praying town's institutional order as a model for emulation. In this respect, the passage in question contrasts with what most scholars (including Bozeman) would surely consider a clear contemporary expression of the millennial errand thesis, Edward Johnson's "Wonder-Working Providence of Sions Saviour in New England," completed in 1650 or early 1651. Like Eliot, Johnson concluded from the destruction of the Stuart regime that "all other new upstart kingdoms, dukedoms, or what else can be named, shall fall before him [the Lord of the Middle Advent]; not that he shall come personally to reign upon earth (as some vainly imagine), but his powerful presence and glorious brightness of his Gospel ... shall not only spiritually cause the churches of Christ to grow beyond number, but also the whole civil government of people upon earth shall be his." Johnson explicitly claimed that the Bay Colony's institutional order, which he construed primarily in ecclesiastical terms, was "the porch of the glorious building" destined to appear in England, and that the Lord of the Middle Advent had "set up his standard of resort" in New England. Johnson, in fact, so emphasized the colony's exemplary role that he designated Massachusetts Bay "the western end [sic] of the world," as though the Atlantic were a river and not an ocean. Eliot's modest appeal to Natick's "confirmatory" role pales in comparison to statements like these.[31]

"The learned Conjectures" proved to be the last documented occasion when Eliot claimed that the millennium was imminent at Natick. By the early 1660s, the twin foundations of his conviction about the matter—his interpretation of the regicide and his support for the lost tribes theory—had crumbled.

The evidence that Eliot revised his judgment about the regicide postdates the restoration of the Stuart monarchy in May 1660. His sources contain no discussions of English political affairs between late 1652, when he wrote the preface to Cromwell in *Tears of Repentance*, and the Restoration. Eliot's views in the mid- to late 1650s were probably similar to those of the Fifth Monarchists in England. The creation of the Protectorate in December 1653 led many Fifth Monarchists to oppose the Cromwellian government. After Cromwell's death in 1658, many members of the movement intensified their efforts to rally the nation to their program. Eliot's *Christian Commonwealth* was published in October 1659 by Livewell Chapman, the proprietor of a Fifth Monarchy press in London. The "server of the season" who saw the work through the press explained on the title page that the treatise was "now published (after his [Eliot's] consent given)." This phrasing suggests that the Apostle had approved the belated publication of the work, possibly because he hoped that its appearance would stem the royalist tide in England. The return of Charles II convinced most members of the movement to revise their eschatologies. A notable exception was Thomas Venner, who organized a small but bloody rebellion against the restored Stuart monarchy. Venner was executed in January 1661 as an object lesson for all Fifth Monarchists who refused to accept the Restoration. This was a mistake that Eliot did not make. In December 1660, he was one of a group of ten Massachusetts elders who advised the General Court about how best to acknowledge the "king's majesty" and "most rightful" claim to the throne; and after the Restoration (as we shall soon see) he incorporated the institution of monarchy into his revised doctrine of the millennium.[32]

Eliot had withdrawn his endorsement of the lost tribes theory by October 1656, when he told Thorowgood that "your labors and letters have drawn me further that way than otherwise I would have gone." Eliot explained that he retreated from the theory because he had "some reasons in my breast, which to me seem weighty," but he never indicated what they were. One possible reason was that he had reevaluated the biblical evidence for the Israelite-origins view. In this respect, he may have learned of Hamon l'Estrange's reply to Thorowgood, *Americans No Jews, or Improbabilities that the Americans Are of that Race* (London, 1652), or he may have come to concur with contemporary opinion in Massachusetts Bay. Despite several scholarly claims to the contrary, there is no evidence known to me that anyone in the colony at the time accepted the lost tribes theory or, for that matter, the Joktanite one. The Tartarian-origins view seems to have been the orthodox perspective throughout the seventeenth century.[33] A second possible explanation was the Indians' uneven progress toward church estate. For reasons explained in the next chapter, Eliot was less certain in the mid-1650s about the advent of the natives' day of grace than he had been in late 1652 and early 1653. His discussions in *Tears of Repentance* and "The learned Conjectures" indicate that for him there was a strong connection between the imminence of the Indians' conversion and the viability of the lost tribes theory. When his confidence about the former began to falter in the mid-1650s, his conviction about the latter may have wavered as well.

In 1659 Eliot tried a second time to gather a church at Natick. On this occasion, the referees approved the candidates' conversion narratives; and in 1660, the Indians signed the covenant that formally created the first native congregation in Massachusetts Bay. With the ecclesiastical order now in place, Eliot had seemingly reached his goal of "set[ting] up the kingdom of Christ fully . . . both in civil and spiritual matters." Yet in his lengthy report about the 1659 church examinations, *A further Account of the progress of the Gospel Amongst the Indians in New England* (London, 1660), he did not claim that the "kingdom of Christ was rising up" at Natick or announce that the "glory of the Lord" had passed through the millennium's "eastern gate." The Apostle had failed to "set up the kingdom of Christ fully" in the early 1650s, when he thought that it was possible to do so. By decade's end, the historical moment had passed.

The Communion of Churches: Eliot's New Vision of the Millennium

After the Restoration Eliot continued to believe in the Middle Advent and in a terrestrial millennium. Nevertheless, his eschatology during this period differed in two major respects from its early Interregnum counterpart. First, he did not state or imply that the millennium was imminent among the Indians. Second, he redefined the institutional components of the kingdom in response to recent events in New and particularly in Old England. Eliot first disclosed his new understanding of the millennium in a July 1663 letter to Richard Baxter, the leader of Restoration Nonconformity. In this letter Eliot outlined the component parts of his revised eschatology: a "divine form of church government," a "universal character and language," an "advancement of learning," and a "divine form of civil government." He centered his attention on the first of these components, the subject matter of his *Communion of Churches* (1665).[34]

The Communion of Churches offered a model for "Christ his ecclesiastical kingdom." Eliot chose to have the treatise printed in Cambridge in a limited edition so that copies could be "committed privately to some godly and able hands, to be viewed, corrected, amended, or rejected" by them. He planned to revise the work for publication in England after the readers had evaluated it. Although he prepared a revised version in late 1667, Eliot never sent *The Communion of Churches* to the London press. The reason was surely the poor reception given the plan by the preliminary readers. Baxter, who had received copies of the 1665 and 1667 versions of the work, registered many objections to the proposal. The response in New England was apparently no better. In February 1670 Baxter asked John Woodbridge, Jr., of Killingworth, Connecticut, about the local reception of *The Communion of Churches*. Woodbridge replied that Eliot's treatise "better took with himself than with any of his brethren, not because of his pride, I suppose you know him better, but the peculiar cut of his genius."[35]

Eliot's proposal in his *Communion of Churches* combined Congregationalist and Presbyterian features; hence, the work broke with his earlier conviction that Congregationalism was the millennial ecclesiastical polity. Eliot's starting point in *The Communion of Churches* was the individual congregation, to which he assigned the power to select and ordain officers and the right to control access to the sacraments of baptism and communion. He then placed above the individual congregation a Presbyterian-like system of councils based on the number twelve, which he called "the foundation number" of the "New Jerusalem" (Revelation 21:14). In the 1665 version of the work, Eliot directed each local church to send its teaching elder and one of its ruling elders to a "first council" with jurisdiction over twelve congregations, and he instructed each first council to chose two elders as representatives to a "provincial council" that had authority over twelve first councils. This pattern continued through "national councils" and "ecumenical councils" for Christian nations, and it climaxed with a "great ecumenical council" that was to meet in Jerusalem and govern the universal millennial church. In the revised version of the plan, Eliot proposed that magistrates as well as elders should serve as delegates to the various councils. The first councils were to supervise the formation of new congregations, make emergency appointments to ecclesiastical office, and hear appeals from the local churches. The provincial and national councils, which ordinarily would work in tandem, had broader concerns, such as the adjudication of appeals and the formulation of a standard of faith and order for use in the local churches. The duties of the various ecumenical assemblies were left unspecified until "those glorious times when such councils shall be called."[36]

The Apostle had three reasons for thinking that a system of councils was necessary. One was his experience in New England. "After thirty or forty years' experience in the way of Congregational churches in fullness of liberty," he wrote in *The Communion of Churches,* "we find more and more need to insist upon . . . that men may be tied to attend unto counsel." Another was the missionary limitations of Congregationalism. Eliot proposed that any duly constituted council could designate persons for full-time missionary service to pagan peoples, to persons who lived in the "dark corners" of "professing nations," and to Roman Catholics. These missionaries would be ordained by their home congregations and then promptly released from future pastoral obligations to them. The third was the need for ecclesiastical union between Presbyterians and Congregationalists in England. In 1657 Baxter had tried and failed to interest Eliot in developing a proposal for alliance. In the 1660s, however, the Apostle decided that his Reformed brethren in England had to make a united stand against their Anglican oppressors.[37]

Accompanying Eliot's revised ecclesiology was a new attitude toward monarchical government. In a striking reversal of his early Interregnum position, Eliot restored the European monarchs, including England's, to the ranks of the ten kings destined to "hate the whore, . . . make her desolate and naked, . . . eat her flesh, and burn her with fire" (Revelation 17:16). Like Cotton before him, the Apostle anticipated that these monarchs would embrace Reformed Protestantism and dismantle the Antichristian state churches in their respective domains. "If the supreme powers command the parishes to be reformed in their church estate and ordered into communion of churches, there would presently be councils in . . . the proposed form and order," he wrote in 1668. The "supreme civil authority" would then enforce conciliar rulings at the local church level and also punish—and, if necessary, execute—individuals who "presumptuously" rejected the authority of the councils. "Kings and queens . . . shall be as nursing fathers and mothers to the churches of Christ" (Isaiah 49:23), Eliot told Henry Ashurst, the corporation's treasurer, in 1670.[38]

The Apostle never explained why he changed his mind about the institution of monarchy. The major reason was surely the Restoration itself: the return of the House of Stuart was a sign that kings ruled with God's blessing. The conduct of Charles II probably contributed to Eliot's altered judgment as well. The new king had authorized the reestablishment of the New England Company, which had been dissolved in 1660 by the Convention Parliament's Act of Oblivion and Indemnity. He was also more amenable to constitutional rule than his father had been.[39]

Eliot had less to say about the other institutional components of his revised eschatology. In *The Communion of Churches,* he advocated the modernization of the Hebrew language so that delegates to the "great ecumenical council" in Jerusalem, as well as educated persons throughout the world, could have a common tongue. The Apostle had first proposed the use of Hebrew as a universal language in his July 1663 letter to Baxter. "I lately met with an excellent book of Dr. Charleton's," he told Baxter in reference to Walter Charleton's *The Immortality of the Human Soul* (London, 1657), "where . . . he, speaking of other excellent matters, speaks of that long talked about and desired design of a universal character and language." In contrast to Charleton, a royalist physician who was publicizing a recent proposal for the creation of a universal set of characters patterned on Egyptian hieroglyphs and Chinese ideograms, Eliot argued that Hebrew was a better choice for the honor. He thought that Hebrew had been the only language in existence from the time of Adam and Eve through the destruction of the Tower of Babel, a common assumption in the seventeenth century; and that the universal restoration of Hebrew would fulfill Zephaniah 3:9 ("For then will I turn to the people a pure language, that they may all call upon the name of the Lord, to serve him with one consent"). Moreover, Eliot was attracted to Hebrew because it was the only language "of God's making," because Jesus had used it when he converted Saul on the road to Damascus, and because it was "the purest language on earth, not as yet defiled with the scurrilous froth and foam of the carnal wits in writing." Finally, the Apostle was impressed with the "trigrammical foundation" of the language: nearly all words in biblical Hebrew have three-letter roots that can be construed as nouns, verbs, or adjectives depending on vocalization. This structural feature made it "capable of a regular expatiation into millions of words, no language like it."[40]

Charleton's *Immortality of the Human Soul* intrigued Eliot in another respect as well. The book contained a lengthy survey of recent achievements in medicine, optics, astronomy, and geometry by British and continental scientists and mathematicians. These achievements indicated to Eliot that "an admirable advancement of learning" (see Daniel 12:4) had begun "in these late days." He had revealed no previous awareness of the revival of learning tradition in seventeenth-century English Protestant eschatology, which, in the judgment of most scholars, began with the posthumous publication of Francis Bacon's *The New Atlantis* in late 1626. For Eliot, as for others, the improvements in medical treatment suggested that God planned to restore the long lives of the biblical patriarchs. The Apostle also thought that the use of a universal language would accelerate the transmission of wholesome knowledge. As he explained to Baxter in 1663, "all arts and sciences in the whole encyclopedia would soon be translated into it [Hebrew]; and all paganish and profane trash would be left out . . . [and] all schools would teach this language, and all the world, especially the commonwealth of learning, would be of one."[41]

This "admirable advancement of learning" led Eliot to revise his understanding of the millennial civil order. He told Baxter in 1663 that "if it may please the Lord to direct his people into a divine form of civil government, of such a constitution, as that the godly learned in all places may be in all places of power and rule, this would so much the more advance all learning and religion, and good government; so that all the world would become a divine college." Eliot never clarified the details of this "divine form of civil government" except by briefly noting in *The Communion of Churches* that "holy and righteous kings, princes, and chief rulers" could share political power in it with the "godly learned." The reference to "holy and righteous kings" was not surprising in light of Eliot's newfound respect for the institution of monarchy; the meaning of "princes" is in this case obscure; and the expression "chief rulers" was one of his designations for the rulers at Natick and in other praying towns.[42]

The larger patterns in Eliot's eschatology after the Restoration are much less distinct than their early Interregnum counterparts. He almost certainly continued to assume that the two "ends of the earth" were the inaugural locations for the millennium. There are three reasons for thinking that this was the case. First, he clearly did not adopt the alternative view that the kingdom would begin in Palestine. The "great ecumenical council" in Jerusalem was the end point, not the starting place, of the millennial ecclesiastical order. He assumed that the establishment of this council lay well in the future; even the subordinate ecumenical councils for Christian nations were "somewhat higher than we can well descry." Second, Eliot's post-1660 sources presuppose that England was to be the first European nation that would implement his *Communion of Churches*. He thought that the persecution of the English Presbyterians and the Congregationalists indicated that God planned to end their suffering and reward their fortitude with the millennium. "The faith and patience of the saints . . . under these present pressures and calamities," he told Baxter in 1668, "are no small beam of the glorious coming of Christ . . . in power and great glory." Third, the Apostle continued to think that his mission fields were situated at one of the "ends of the earth." The October 1656 letter to Thorowgood is the last known occasion when Eliot discussed the question of the Indians' ancestry. In this letter he distanced himself from the lost tribes theory; however, he betrayed no uneasiness in the letter about the Joktanite-origins view, his basis for thinking that America stood at the eastern end of the world.[43]

Eliot did not claim that the Restoration-era praying towns exemplified or anticipated the millennium, even though he evidently thought that the settlements stood in a propitious location. He was unable to establish the millennial ecclesiastical polity because the creation of a "first council" required at least twelve local congregations. By the time of King Philip's War, there were only two native churches in Massachusetts Bay, the one at Natick and the other, gathered in 1673, at Hassanamesit. By this time many of the praying towns had native teachers and rulers. Nevertheless, the Apostle never equated these officials with the "godly learned" and "chief rulers" of the millennial civil polity.

After the Restoration Eliot probably pinned his hope for the Indian millennium on the lost tribes theory. His October 1656 letter to Thorowgood was not a repudiation of the Israelite-origins view but only a retreat from it: "I desire you to spare me in this, and give me leave to hear and observe in silence what the Lord will teach others to say in this matter." If Thorowgood or another person could supply him with proof for the lost tribes theory, then Eliot would have reason to think that the time of the natives' mass conversion was nigh. Once it began, the eschatological redemption of the Indians would yield a multitude of churches from which to construct a system of ecclesiastical councils. Eliot remained intrigued by the lost tribes theory for the duration of his life. Cotton Mather, who knew the aged Apostle well, noted that the possibility of an Israelite migration into the New World enabled Eliot to continue "his [missionary] travails ... the more cheerfully, or at least, the more hopefully"; and in June 1691, thirteen months after the Apostle's passing at age eighty-five, Samuel Sewall learned of "a small paraphrase of Mr. Eliot's upon Ezekiel 37, written about half a year before his death." The famous diarist did not disclose the contents of the "paraphrase."[44] But since Ezekiel 37 was the vision of the revivification of the "dry bones" by the Spirit of the Lord, a text that Eliot had come to associate with the conversion of the lost tribes, one suspects that the Apostle went to his death dreaming about a spectacle that he had not lived to witness.

An assessment of the bearing of Eliot's eschatology—and particularly the early Interregnum version of it—on his missionary program requires the kind of detailed discussion better provided at later points in the narrative. We shall see that his millennial views gave the praying Indians a semipermanent form of political organization, distanced him from mainstream opinion in Massachusetts Bay, created diplomatic problems for the colony in its relations with the restored Stuart government, and had significant implications for what is now known as "American exceptionalism." But although it was an important part of the story of the mission, Eliot's quest for the Indian millennium was not the main story line. His commitment to the Indian work, as well as his plans to create the central settlement that became Natick, predated the initial expression of his millennial vision in the 1649 letters to

Winslow. At no subsequent point, not even in the early 1650s, did Eliot's mission cease to be a program for providing instruction in civility and Christian doctrine so that some natives could receive saving grace and settle into full church membership. The millennium fascinated the Apostle because it bore the promise of miraculous transformation. The kingdom did not come during the early Interregnum, nor did it arrive after the Restoration. Yet throughout it all, Eliot continued to pursue his conventional missionary objectives, come what conversions may.

CHAPTER FIVE

. . .

The Natick Mission

In the spring and summer of 1650, Eliot and several proselytes began to search for a suitable site for the planned central settlement. By October they had selected Natick (now South Natick), an unimproved area along the Charles River in the northwestern portion of the massive 200-square-mile grant that the General Court had awarded to Dedham in 1636. Representatives from Dedham immediately tried and failed to convince Eliot to choose a location outside the town's grant. In October 1651 the General Court assigned Natick 2,000 acres of land to the north of the river. Dedham reluctantly consented to the action, provided that the natives "lay down all claims in that town elsewhere."[1]

The Nonantum Indians were pleased with the location. Eliot explained in 1650 that "a great part" of Natick was the "inheritance of John Speene and his brethren and kindred," and that the Speenes were "very willing" to live there and to accept no greater an allotment in land than other residents. Wamporas, another prominent Nonantum Indian, also approved of the location. Most if not all of the Nonantums soon moved to Natick. They were joined in the early to mid-1650s by various Nipmuck Indians, including Captain Tom, William of Sudbury, Monotunkquanit, and Owussumag. The site was less satisfactory to the Neponsets, who preferred another location—Punkapoag near Dorchester—because they perceived the choice of Natick as a special favor to the Nonantum Indians. Eliot attempted to persuade the Neponsets to relocate to Natick by preaching sermons on Matthew 4:19 ("Follow me and I will make you fishers of men") and Matthew 19:29 ("And every one that hath forsaken . . . lands, for my name's sake, . . . shall inherit everlasting life"). Some Neponset Indians, such as Monequasson and Cutshamekin, moved to Natick in the early 1650s; others, like Josias Wompatuck and the Ahawtons, chose to await the creation of Punkapoag in 1654.[2]

Construction on the north side of the Charles River had commenced by the time the General Court awarded the land in October 1651. In early autumn 1650, the Indians built a "fair house . . . after the English manner high and large, . . . with chimneys in it," as well as an eighty-foot-long bridge over the river that soon proved sturdy enough to survive a flood that destroyed a bridge built in Medfield five miles away. By late October 1651 the natives had fashioned a small room, with a bed, in a loft above the main floor of the "fair house." Eliot used the room during his visits to the settlement; the residents also stored their valuables in it. Between April and October 1651, the Indians erected a fort that stood ten to twelve feet high and filled a quarter acre of land. Eliot explained that this "strong palizado" was for "security against an invasion of the wilder Indians." Construction of a meetinghouse and a schoolhouse began after the completion of the fort. The meetinghouse, twelve feet high, fifty feet long, and twenty-five feet wide, was completed by mid-October 1652; the schoolhouse was under construction in 1652 and was finished by 1662 at the latest. Eliot's original plan was to place these two buildings within the fort. Nineteenth-century evidence suggests that the meetinghouse was inside the fort, and that the fort stood on what is now the site of the Eliot Church in South Natick. The location of the schoolhouse is unknown. Seventeenth-century sources indicate that the "fair house" was outside the fort. A sawmill was in the planning stages in 1651, and by the early 1660s one had been built along the Charles about a mile east of the town's central buildings.[3]

The settlement expanded in size in the 1650s. In 1651 the Indians fenced in two common fields to the south of the Charles and also laid out streets on both sides of the river. The land to the south, which had not been part of the 1651 grant, was used for agriculture. Over the course of the decade, the residents planted apples, hay, maize, beans, squash, and hemp; raised pigs, cows, goats, and oxen; and built several barns and laid additional fence. Keeping swine and particularly cattle was a noteworthy achievement. As Virginia Anderson has explained, Indians in southern New England had trouble incorporating these two creatures into their traditional social and spiritual worlds. She also observes that when given a choice, natives strongly preferred hogs to cows because the former behaved like dogs, the only domesticated animals prior to contact, and in contrast to the latter, required little supervision.[4]

Eliot was proud of the Natick Indians' early achievements, for the importance of hard work was a consistent theme in his missionary preaching. As John Speene remarked in 1652, "God does make my body strong to labor." The town's residents constructed the central buildings with minimal help from English craftsmen, refused to eat food that they had not produced, and declined New England Company compensation for work done on the settlement's behalf. The natives initially used tools supplied by private benefactors in England or purchased in Massachusetts Bay against corporation credit; the first shipments of Company goods did not arrive until the summer and fall of 1651. Eliot was also pleased with the Indians' conformity to English gender roles: the men tilled the fields and raised the livestock, and the women learned to spin and weave once the men had grown enough hemp for the purpose in the mid-1650s. Eliot had placed many orders for clothing and cloth prior to this time; he seldom did so thereafter. He distributed clothing, tools, and other English goods in small quantities because he wanted to discourage residents from "embezzl[ing] them away" and vagrants from "loitering and filching" in the town, and also because the Commissioners of the United Colonies had warned him that excessive generosity would teach Indians to "follow Christ [only] for loaves and outward advantages."[5]

The construction of the central buildings and the practice of plant and animal husbandry were Eliot's two main strategies for creating a sedentary community at Natick. As he wrote in *Tears of Repentance,* Indians would be more inclined to maintain "a fixed condition of life" if they had "some means of livelihood to lose." To further the same end, he urged the natives to build English-style houses, and by 1654 fifty lots had been laid out for homes. The Apostle achieved his overall objective, but not in the manner he desired. Natick was a residential community throughout the prewar period; however, most of the proselytes lived in wigwams. Gookin explained in 1674 that the

Natick Indians preferred wigwams because houses were expensive to build, harder to heat, impossible to move during invasions of insects, and difficult to decorate in traditional fashion. The fact that Gookin did not condemn the continued use of wigwams suggests that Eliot became reconciled to the practice as well. The Indians also pursued traditional hunting and fishing activities in addition to developing English forms of husbandry. Gookin noted but did not criticize these traditional subsistence activities, and Eliot clearly learned to condone them as well. In 1662 he and John, Jr., approved the sale of a tract of land near Mendon to two men from Braintree. The Natick and Punkapoag Indians who sold the land retained easements to "fish, fowl, and hunt" on it.[6]

The expansion of the settlement to the south of the Charles, which was done with Eliot's authorization, precipitated a boundary dispute with the town of Dedham. The Dedhamites wanted the Indians to remain in the area to the river's north that had been assigned them in 1651 (see Map 2). In the early summer of 1653, the General Court created a committee to investigate the matter; and in May 1655, Dedham petitioned the court for "relief in respect of several [unspecified] affronts offered them by the Indians, as also some difference in relation to land between them." The colony's published records contain no evidence that the committee met or that the court responded to the

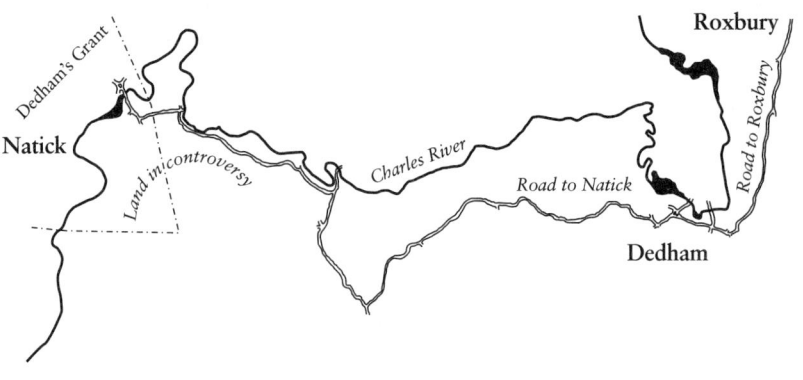

Map 2   Natick and Dedham. Adapted by Matthew Offield from map in Frank Smith, "Controversy over Dedham's Grant to the Natick Indians," *Dedham Historical Register* 9 (1898): 37–41.

petition. The dispute apparently languished for several years before resuming in the late 1650s, probably because, as Dane Morrison has suggested, the second generation at Dedham needed the land to the river's south.[7]

Two attempts to resolve the dispute took place in 1660, but neither satified both parties. First, in May a committee created by the General Court recommended that the natives return the land to the south, expand further toward Sudbury to the north, and receive 80 acres of meadow at a place of their own choosing. This recommendation was unacceptable to Natick. Eliot explained that the Indians had already improved the land to the south, and that "the best of those lands" toward Sudbury had been awarded to Richard Russell of Charlestown several years earlier. Second, in September 1660 a group of unidentified "Christian friends and neighbors" from outside Roxbury and Dedham proposed that Dedham "lovingly . . . grant unto the Indians the lands now possessed by them on the south side of the river" in exchange for lands elsewhere, and that the proselytes surrender any future claim to land within Dedham's boundaries as well as acknowledge that their victory in the dispute was due to the "love and Christian condescendence of the English at Dedham and not from the right of any Indian title." The arbiters also scolded Eliot for permitting Natick to expand to the south and for resisting "such reasonable motions as were made by the brethren of Dedham for a peaceable and righteous resolution of so great a controversy." This recommendation was unacceptable to Dedham.[8]

Dedham then resorted to a less neighborly course of action. Between October 1661 and January 1662, residents of the town sued Waban, John Speene, and other Natick Indians for illegally occupying the land south of the river. On each occasion, the Suffolk County Court ruled in favor of Dedham and the Bay Colony's magistrates "refused the verdict." Eliot prepared a lengthy statement, "Natik case drawen up in defence of the pore Indians," for the last of the Suffolk Court sessions. He argued that the Indians deserved the cultivated land to the river's south because a General Court directive in 1652 had guaranteed right of possession to territory improved by natives within the colony, because the Dedhamites "had never procured unto themselves the Indians' right" to the land in question, because a Dedham victory would make proselytes "wonder . . . [about] the actings of the English . . . to take away their lands at such a distance," and because pagan Indians would be alienated from the mission if Natick lost the land. In this document he also challenged a recent statement made by Dedham minister John Allin, who claimed that Chickataubut, Cutshamekin's brother, had given the land south of the river to Dedham. Eliot contended that Chickataubut lacked the authority to cede the land in question because it had belonged to his wife, and that she had given it to their son, Josias Wompatuck, who in 1650 had transferred to Natick "his right in these lands, unto God, to make a town, gather a church, and live in civil order in this place." What this last statement meant for Eliot's 1650 claim that the Speene family held the land at Natick is not clear.[9]

In May 1662 the General Court vindicated Natick by rendering the "final issue of the controversy." The body ruled that "although the legal right of Dedham thereunto cannot in justice be denied, yet such had been the encouragement of the Indians in their improvements thereof, the which, added to their native right, which cannot, in strict justice, be utterly extinct, [the colony] does therefore order that the Indians be not dispossessed of such lands as they are at present possessed of there." This ruling gave the Indians approximately 2,000 acres on the south side of the river to go with the 2,000 acres to its north. At the same session, the court awarded a compensatory grant to Dedham. Representatives of the town promptly requested and received title to a tract of land just to the west of Medfield. In May 1663 the General Court also awarded Dedham a grant of 8,000 acres; two years later, the town chose land near Pocumtuck (Deerfield). The General Court's resolution of the Dedham-Natick dispute, however, did not end the ill will between the two towns. The animosity over the boundary lingered into the eighteenth century.[10]

Three other boundary disputes surfaced in the prewar period. In 1650 or 1651, Eliot permitted Natick to expand into an unspecified portion of a 1,700-acre tract near Medfield that Robert Keayne and several partners had received from the General Court in 1649. Keayne wanted the Indians to return the land but dropped the matter after learning that the Apostle "would not be taken off nor persuaded by any . . . that spoke with him about it." Annoyed by Eliot's "unkind carriage," the famous merchant altered a provision in his will, assigning money originally designated for the mission to Harvard College for the purchase of cows. The second dispute was over 800 acres of land adjacent to Keayne's property. This land had been assigned to

Simon Bradstreet in 1650 and surveyed in 1656. Eliot initially approved of the award, probably because he and Bradstreet were friends. For reasons no longer clear, the Apostle petitioned the General Court in 1658 to give the land to the Natick Indians because the award to Bradstreet had been to their "prejudice." The petition was apparently rejected, for Bradstreet was still in possession of the land in 1662. The third dispute concerned the boundary between Natick and Sherborn. In May 1675 the two towns amicably agreed to exchange some land. This transaction, approved by Eliot and Gookin, was delayed by King Philip's War and was not finalized until 1685.[11]

The Apostle initially assumed that Natick would become the home for all praying Indians then living along the coast. In 1651, when he supervised the election of civil officers in the town, he optimistically instructed the male voters to choose a ruler of one hundred men, two rulers of fifty men, and ten rulers of ten. Many voters lived outside Natick and "came together from diverse places" for the purpose of electing officials. Eliot's assumption that most of these Indians and their families would move to Natick proved unjustified. The available population figures indicate that there were never as many as one hundred adult male residents in prewar Natick. In 1651 John Wilson and John Endecott observed that there were approximately one hundred adults at a lecture day service in the settlement; in 1654 Eliot noted that there were "no less than two hundred" adults and children living in the town; and in 1662 a committee appointed by the General Court to investigate the boundary dispute with Dedham reported that there were "about sixty families" at Natick. More recently, Daniel Mandell has estimated that roughly two hundred men, women, and children were living in the town in 1675.[12]

The Civil Polity

The election of rulers took place on August 6, 1651. Eliot had prepared the Indians for the occasion by reading to them "several times before" the passage in Exodus 18 where Jethro told Moses to establish rulers of tens through thousands. As James Holstun notes, Eliot ignored or overlooked the fact that Jethro instructed Moses to appoint the rulers. After the votes were cast, each adult male not elected to office lined up behind the person he wanted to be the ruler of ten for him and his family. The natives chose Cutshamekin as their ruler of one hundred. Eliot was able to approve the selection of Cutshamekin because he assumed that "religion . . . [would] put a bridle" upon any reappearance of the sachem's "former tyranny." Waban was elected one of the two rulers of fifty. The other original ruler of fifty cannot be named with certainty. In 1670 Eliot stated that the recently deceased Attawans had been "a ruler of fifty in our civil order" but failed to specify the place (Attawans was living in the praying town at Nashobah in the 1660s; whether he had moved from Musketaquid to Natick in the early 1650s is unclear). Another possibility was Totherswamp, who had sufficient prestige to warrant election as a ruler of fifty. In 1654 Eliot identified him as a "ruler" at Natick. Several of the early rulers of tens are named in the sources. One was Peter, who was probably a Neponset; another was Piumbuhhou, a Nonantum Indian and "the second man next Waban that received the Gospel"; and a third was Thomas Speene, Sr. Peter and Thomas died shortly after the election. Nishohkou, a Neponset, was chosen a ruler of ten but declined the office because he considered himself unworthy of it.[13]

The polity was formally installed on September 24, 1651, when the Natick Indians fasted and entered into civil covenant with God. Eliot had prohibited the proselytes from fasting until this time because they had not covenanted before the Lord. Much of the day was devoted to sermons and prayers by the Apostle and by six Indian speakers. At the end of the day, the rulers and then the remaining men assented to the following civil covenant:

> We are the sons of Adam. We and our forefathers have a long time been lost in our sins, but now the mercy of God begins to find us out again. Therefore, the grace of Christ helping us, we do give ourselves and our children unto God to be his people; he shall rule us in all affairs, not only in our religion and affairs of the church (these we desire as soon as we can, if God will) but also in all our works and affairs in this world; God shall rule over us. [Isaiah 33:22] The Lord is our judge, the Lord is our lawgiver, the Lord is our king. He will save us; the wisdom which God has taught us in his books, that shall guide and direct us in the way. Oh Jehovah, teach us wisdom to find out thy wisdom in thy Scriptures, let the grace of Christ help us, because Christ is the wisdom of God, send thy spirit into our hearts, and let it teach us; Lord take us to be thy people, and let us take thee to be our Lord.

The opening confession of sin was included at Cotton's suggestion after he had learned from Eliot that Cutshamekin had recently become inebriated at Samuel Gorton's Warwick plantation while in the Narragansett Country on diplomatic business. Otherwise, the Natick civil covenant was entirely Eliot's creation. The central section contains phrases similar or identical to ones found in his discussions of the millennium in the 1649 letters to Winslow and in *The Christian Commonwealth*. The extent to which Eliot had informed the Natick Indians about their place in the millennium is uncertain. He clearly had instructed them about the three final "last things"—the second coming, the universal resurrection of the dead, and the last judgment—and about the importance of present-day preparation for these distant events. This fact does not mean that he also told his proselytes about the Middle Advent and the millennium; after all, the second coming, the resurrection of the dead, and the last judgment were staples of Puritan theology, whether millennial or not. There is no explicit evidence that Eliot briefed the praying Indians about his contemporary millennial views, even though it is reasonable to assume that he did.[14]

On October 8, 1651, two weeks after the covenanting ceremony, Eliot held an open house for Puritan visitors. Ten or twelve persons, including John Wilson, John Allin, John Endecott, and Edward Rawson, the colony's secretary, traveled to Natick for the occasion. They were accompanied by twenty soldiers for protection from marauders. The dignitaries toured the settlement and then sat through a two-hour worship service conducted in Massachusett. Several weeks later, Wilson and Endecott wrote accounts of the visit for publication in the fifth Eliot tract, *Strength out of Weaknesse*, which appeared in London in August 1652. The two men were impressed by the Indians' progress in civility and in Christian knowledge, by the unidentified native who had delivered a forty-five-minute exposition of the parables of the kingdom in Matthew 13:44-46, and by the quality of the fort, the "fair house," and the bridge.[15]

Neither Wilson nor Endecott mentioned Natick's form of civil organization. Assuming they knew about the town's political order, their silence about the matter is not difficult to explain. There were probably few and possibly no Puritans in contemporary Massachusetts Bay who shared Eliot's current conviction that he had established the civil portion of the millennium at Natick. The reason was not simply that colonists were unwilling to take their eschatology from Indians, for Eliot's millennial experiment would have been controversial even if he had pioneered it in an English town. Current scholarship has identified only a handful of colonists—Edward Johnson, William Aspinwall, Thomas Venner, and several others—who agreed with the Apostle that the regicide was a sign of an imminent millennium. With the exception of Johnson, the others returned to England in the early 1650s. None of the repatriates is known to have designated the system of rulers of tens through thousands as the millennial civil polity, and Johnson assumed that the Bay Colony's existing political system was an acceptable form of millennial organization. Natick's civil order was controversial for other reasons as well. James Holstun notes that the settlement's nearly universal adult male suffrage departed from the Bay Colony's current practice of restricting the vote to communicant men, and Dwight Bozeman observes that Eliot's *Christian Commonwealth* "not only ignored New England institutions, but also implied a severe critique" of them. Thus, the implications of Eliot's political program at Natick were that Massachusetts Bay should broaden its franchise and also replace selectmen, deputies, and assistants with rulers of tens, fifties, and hundreds. His extant sources, however, contain no explicit evidence that he hoped that such would become the case. The closest he came to expressing this hope was in a wistful passage in "The learned Conjectures." "God grant that the old bottles of the western world," he wrote in a likely reference to the saints in New England no less than to those in Old, "would not be so uncapable of the new wine of Christ his expected kingdom, that the eastern bottles be not the only entertainers thereof for a season."[16]

The civil authorities in Massachusetts Bay apparently tolerated Eliot's Fifth Monarchy radicalism in the 1650s, when it passed for respectable opinion across the Atlantic. But once the Restoration had thrown the status of the royal charter of 1629 into question, the colony's leaders could no longer afford to overlook Eliot. In May 1661 the General Court condemned his *Christian Commonwealth* "for being justly offensive . . . to kingly government in England," ordered the destruction or defacement of all copies of the incendiary treatise in the colony—there were probably few of them around—and directed Eliot to affirm that monarchy was a scriptural form of government. Shortly thereafter, the Apostle appeared before the court and "freely and fully acknowledged" that monarchy was "not only a lawful but an eminent form of government," testified that "all forms of civil government deduced from Scripture, either expressly or by just consequence, . . .

[are] of God and to be subjected unto for conscience sake," and "once [and] for all cordially disown[ed]" any statements in *The Christian Commonwealth* that were "inconsist[ent]" with these assertions.[17]

The 1661 censure of Eliot was an internal procedure probably undertaken so that the General Court could have a disciplinary action on record in the event that the restored government accused the colony of condoning Eliot's Fifth Monarchy views. In their direct dealings with London, however, the local authorities did their best to conceal the Apostle's identity. He was a prominent minister and the supervisor of a diplomatically useful mission, and he could not be disowned as easily as his fellow radical Thomas Venner. "Diabolical Venner . . . went out from us," the General Court told Charles II in August 1661, after receiving news of the repatriate's attempt to overthrow the Stuart government, "because he was not of us." On two occasions in 1660 and on a third in 1665, the court included accounts of the mission in letters respectively addressed to Charles, to the Parliament, and to the four royal commissioners sent by the Crown to investigate the New England colonies, particularly Massachusetts Bay. Eliot was not mentioned by name in any of these letters. The Commissioners of the United Colonies had to walk the same fine line. They chose for diplomatic reasons to dedicate the 1661 and 1663 editions of Eliot's Indian Bible to the restored monarch. In the dedicatory prefaces to the two editions, the Apostle was identified only as a "painful laborer" among the Indians.[18]

Eliot's recantation of *The Christian Commonwealth* in 1661 was not a repudiation of Jethro's system of tens through hundreds. What he disavowed—sincerely, as explained in Chapter 4—was his antimonarchical radicalism. In the 1650s, Eliot thought that monarchy was an unscriptural form of government destined to be replaced by the Jethroan polity. In 1661 he acknowledged what he had refused to concede in the 1650s, namely, that monarchy was "a form of government deduced from Scripture." After the Restoration, Eliot continued to think that the numerical polity was a legitimate form of government, and he kept it intact at Natick. One reason he retained the system was that he had vowed before God in the early 1650s that he would never dismantle it, and another was that he remained attracted to its primitive allure. "We are expressly conformed to the Scriptures," he wrote in 1673, in an explicit reference to Jethro's polity, "and to that form of government which we find Israel was under at the first."[19]

Eliot and Gookin never identified Natick's Restoration-era rulers by their numerical rank. Both men called Waban simply the "chief ruler" of the town. He had presumably been the "chief ruler" since Cutshamekin's death in late 1651 or early 1652, and remained such until his own passing in the mid-1680s. Waban probably retained Cutshamekin's title of ruler of one hundred even though there were never one hundred adult male residents in prewar Natick. Eliot and Gookin referred to the subordinate officials in the town as "rulers" and "constables." The former were evidently rulers of fifties, and the latter rulers of tens. Persons who served as "rulers" at various times between the Restoration and King Philip's War were Captain Tom, Piumbuhhou, and Moshosinan (who is otherwise absent in the missionary sources). No prewar Natick constable is named in the documentation.[20]

The Apostle considered Waban an able ruler, stating in *Tears of Repentance* that his "gift [lies] in ruling, judging of cases, wherein he is patient, constant, and prudent, in so much as he is much respected among them." Eliot's assessment is borne out by the way Waban handled the only documented case of justice that came under his purview. In 1668 Sarah Ahawton, the wife of William Ahawton, was observed "speak[ing] alone" with Joseph, a married man. The matter was brought to Waban's attention, even though the two natives lived at Punkapoag and not at Natick, because he sometimes exercised authority at Punkapoag. Waban initially concluded—correctly, it seems—that the two Indians had not committed adultery, and he prudently instructed them to avoid each other's company. Sarah and Joseph, however, disobeyed him and soon broke the seventh commandment. Waban then turned Sarah over to Gookin. The Indian Superintendent brought her before the General Court, which ordered her to stand on the gallows in Boston for a hour with a noose around her neck, receive thirty stripes at Natick, and pay court costs. Joseph managed to escape punishment, apparently by fleeing to the Pokanokets.[21]

There is only one other well-documented example of Natick justice prior to King Philip's War. In the spring of 1654, three drunken Natick Indians forcibly intoxicated Totherswamp's eleven-year-old son, telling the child that "now we will see whether your father will punish us for drunkenness, . . . seeing you are drunk with us for company." Totherswamp and his fellow rulers sentenced the three men to twenty lashes and time in the stocks. The boy, whom the rulers punished for association with evildoers rather than for intoxication, was briefly placed in the stocks and then whipped in front of his classmates at Natick. Eliot was present at the sentencing of the four natives but did not advise the rulers about how to handle the case.[22]

Little else is known about the conduct of Natick rulers before or after the Restoration. In 1653 or 1654 Eliot wrote "a relation of such judgments as the rulers have executed upon sinners" and sent it to London for publication. This document has left no traces upon the sands of time. The rulers at Natick handled minor infractions like drunkenness, fighting, sabbath-breaking, truancy, idleness, and disobedience to parents. Civil cases over 20 shillings and serious criminal cases were heard by the Indian Superintendent; thus Waban acted correctly in turning Sarah Ahawton over to Gookin. The Superintendent sometimes sent these cases to the Assistants or, as was done with Sarah, to the General Court. The special duties of rulers of tens included supervising work details and collecting tithes of grains and vegetables at harvest time. These tithes were then distributed to the town's rulers and teachers "proportionably."[23]

The installation of Jethro's polity in the early 1650s was the first step in Eliot's stated agenda of "set[ting] up the kingdom of Christ fully . . . both in civil and spiritual matters." He also had a conventional missionary reason for establishing the polity. As he explained in *Tears of Repentance,* the Indians could not properly administer church discipline unless they had an appropriate system of government and a sedentary way of life: "until they [had] . . . come unto civil cohabitation, government, and labor, . . . they were not so capable to be betrusted with that treasure of Christ [the sacraments], lest they should scandalize the same, and make it of no effect, because if any should through temptation, fall under censure, he could easily run away (as some have done) and would be tempted to do so."[24] The creation of an Indian church, however, required more than a form of civil government and fixed residence. Candidates for church membership also had to undergo instruction in Christian teaching and deliver satisfactory conversion narratives.

The Educational Program

The Natick school was a native-run institution that used Massachusett as the language of instruction throughout the prewar period. Men and women were taught to read phonetically, and boys and girls learned (as Eliot put it) "by rote and custom, as . . . [Puritan] children do." In 1650 the school followed the standard English practice of teaching males to read, write, and cypher, and females only to read; the assumption was that women did not need the additional skills in order to run households. There is no evidence that Natick altered this practice at any time before the war. In 1660 the Commissioners reported that "about one hundred of Mr. Eliot's Indians" could read Massachuset (this figure surely included natives resident in other towns); and in 1981 Kathleen Bragdon estimated that about 30 percent of Natick adults were literate in Massachuset by the time of King Philip's War. In 1674, Eliot, Gookin, and leading proselytes approved a plan for making English the language of instruction at Natick and in the other praying towns. Gookin explained the rationale for the proposed change: natives would be able to "converse with the English familiarly, . . . read any English book, . . . [and] understand our English ministers, who are better fitted to instruct them in substantial and orthodox divinity." He also observed that "the changing of the language of a barbarous people into the speech of a more civil and potent nation . . . [will] reduce such a people unto the civility and religion of the prevailing nation." The transition to English-language education, however, did not take place until after the war.[25]

In the early 1650s, the Natick curriculum consisted of training in literacy and instruction from a manuscript "short catechism" prepared by Eliot. "We aspire to no higher learning yet," the Apostle explained. There were two schoolteachers in the town at this time. One was Monequasson, whom Endecott observed in 1651 writing English "true and very legibl[y]." Monequasson evidently died in 1656, the year he last appears in the missionary sources. The other teacher in the early 1650s was probably either John Sassamon or Job Nesutan. Eliot described the bilingual Sassamon as "a man of eminent parts and wit," and Gookin characterized Nesutan as "a very good linguist in the English tongue." Like Monequasson, these two Indians were Neponsets. Sassamon's controversial career is evaluated in Chapter 7. Nesutan, who died on the English side in King Philip's War, was apparently one of the Indians who had intoxicated Totherswamp's son in 1654. By 1656 all three Neponsets were serving as schoolteachers, presumably at Natick.[26]

The primary purpose of Massachusett-language literacy was to enable Indians to read the various translations and original works that the Apostle and his native associates began preparing in the 1650s. These writings were published at New England Company expense but printed in Cambridge because Eliot's presence was required for proofreading. His chief colleague in the production of these Massachusett works was Job Nesutan. Sassamon also participated in the translations. Two other Indians probably helped as well, even though there is no evidence to this effect. One was Monequasson and the other was James the Printer, a Nipmuck apprenticed to Samuel Green, the Harvard printer, in 1660. The extent to which Eliot relied on the proselytes is difficult to determine. In 1974 Neal Salisbury reported without further comment that he had learned from Frank T. Siebert that "the Indian assistants, rather than Eliot himself, did the actual translating." The natives surely contributed heavily to the work; that they "did the actual translating" is unlikely. First of all, rendering the Bible and other texts into Massachusett required a command of English and a theological erudition that no native at the time possessed. Furthermore, the Apostle was sufficiently familiar with various technical problems in translation to discuss them in a 1663 letter to Richard Baxter. Finally, four present-day authorities—Ives Goddard, Kathleen Bragdon, Stephen Guice, and Kenneth Miner—have shown that Eliot's command of Massachusett was more than adequate for the task. Miner, in fact, calls Eliot "the true founder of American linguistics."[27]

Eliot's initial Massachusett publication was a "primer and catechism" based on the manuscript "short catechism" in use at Natick by 1651. The first edition appeared in 1654, and later ones in 1662, 1669, and 1686 or 1687. Only the third edition is extant in its entirety, under the title *The Indian Primer*. Its central sections are a "Large Catechism" for adults and a "Short Catechism" for children, both organized on the question and answer format. These catechisms were original works of Eliot's and not, as is often suggested, translations of the Westminster Assembly's longer and shorter catechisms. The 1669 *Indian Primer* also contains a series of Massachusett expositions of biblical texts that address the obligations of children to parents, wives to husbands, servants to masters, and superiors to inferiors; translations and expositions of the Lord's Prayer and the Apostles' Creed; the

English alphabet and syllabary; the Roman and Arabic systems of numerical notation; and the names and order of the books of the Protestant Bible.[28]

The Apostle then published translations of three biblical books. He had been planning to translate some of the Scriptures since July 1649 if not earlier. Over the winter of 1652–53, Eliot and his native associates finished a metrical rendition of "the whole book of the Psalms." For unknown reasons, the work did not appear in print until 1658 or 1659. Massachusett versions of Genesis and Matthew were published in 1655. The former contained an English interlinear for the first nineteen chapters, a practice abruptly terminated as a cost-cutting measure.[29]

The Commissioners of the United Colonies were perturbed that Eliot had completed "the primer and catechism" and the biblical translations without the assistance of Thomas Stanton, Sr., of Stonington, Connecticut, whose knowledge of the Narragansett dialect might have broadened the works' appeal. The Apostle probably did not consider the rough-hewn Stanton, the Commissioners' official interpreter, suitable for the task. Hezekiah Usher of Boston observed that Stanton was not "godly" enough "for . . . spiritual work." Instead of approaching Stanton, Eliot asked several other bilingual Englishmen, probably Thomas Mayhew, Jr., and Abraham Pierson, to evaluate the translations of Genesis and Matthew. "I heard not of any faults they found," he reported in 1658. This gesture failed to satisfy the Commissioners, who probably hoped that a successful mission to the Narragansetts would facilitate English expansion into the area. Eliot's refusal to use Stanton's services remained a source of annoyance for several years thereafter.[30]

Eliot was initially pessimistic about the chances of finishing the entire Bible. "I have no hope to see the Bible translated, much less printed, in my days," he told the corporation in 1651. Yet he lived to see the publication of two separate editions of the Bible. The original translation of the two testaments was finished in late December 1658. The reason why Eliot and his native colleagues had been able to make such rapid progress is not explained in the sources. They probably took advantage of the Apostle's lengthy convalescence from a bout of sciatica. The malady first afflicted him in August 1656, kept him in bed until November, and restricted his mobility for nearly a year thereafter.[31]

The printing of 1,500 copies of the New Testament began in July 1660 and ended in the spring of 1661; and the printing of 1,000 copies of the Old Testament ran from September 1660 until May 1663. The simultaneous production of the two testaments was possible because (as explained more fully in Chapter 8) there were two presses and two skilled printers located in the same room in the so-called "Indian College" at Harvard. Five hundred copies of the New Testament were separately published in 1661; the rest were left unbound until the publication of the full Bible in 1663. Placed between the Old and New Testaments in the 1663 edition were a metrical Psalter (a nonmetrical translation was included in the Old Testament section) and two short expositions entitled "How can I walk with God all the day long?" and "What should a Christian do, to keep perfectly holy the Sabbath day?" This translation was the first Bible printed in any language in the New World. The revised versions of the Old and New Testaments were published in 1681 and 1685, respectively.[32]

Various language experts have praised the Indian Bible. Roger Williams, who had once asserted that Eliot was insufficiently skilled "to open the mysteries of Christ Jesus in . . . [the Indians'] speech or language," commended him for having "gain[ed] their language" well enough to translate the Scriptures. James Hammond Trumbull, the nineteenth-century authority on Massachusett, stated that the translation "was probably as good as any *first* version that has been made, from his time to ours, in a previously unwritten and so-called 'barbarous' language." Goddard, Bragdon, Guice, and Miner admire the achievement as well. The translation, of course, contains curiosities. Eliot rendered Exodus 3:14 ("I am that I am") as "I exist, I exist" because the Indians' language did not have the verb "to be," and he used English words with Massachusett affixes for terms with no native counterparts. Examples include "book," "horse," "elder," "Gentiles," "Bible," "brass," "Psalm," and "lattice." The last noun bears mention because of a legend that Eliot translated the word "lattice" in Judges 5:28 ("The mother of Sisera looked out at a window and cried through the lattice") as "eelpot" because such was the closest Massachusett equivalent. Trumbull, who exposed the legend's falsity by the simple expedient of consulting the Massachusett text, notes that the translation's "most curious mistake" was to transform the ten wise and foolish virgins of Matthew 25:1–13 into men because "chastity was a masculine virtue" among the Indians.[33]

After overseeing the publication of the Indian Bible, the Apostle translated devotional works by Richard Baxter, Thomas Shepard, and Lewis Bayly. Baxter's writings had intrigued Eliot since at least 1656, when he told the famous divine how much he had enjoyed *The Saints Everlasting Rest* (London, 1650). In this letter he encouraged Baxter to "spend the rest of your life in writing practical meditations" because the "world is full of polemical books and doctrinal," and also suggested that he prepare "a practical meditation upon all the chief steps and operations of spirit through the whole work of conversion." Although he did not say so in the letter, Eliot probably wanted Baxter to author a work of this sort so that it could be translated for the Indians. The suggestion came at a time when Baxter was planning to write such a book, which proved to be *A Call to the Unconverted* (London, 1658). Eliot and his associates were at work on Baxter's *Call* in July 1663, and they had finished it by the end of the year. The translation was published in 1664 and reprinted in 1688. By August 1664 Eliot and his partners had "almost translated" Shepard's *The Sincere Convert* (London, 1640) and *The Sound Believer* (London, 1645). Eliot interrupted the two-part Shepard project in order to undertake an abridged translation of Lewis Bayly's *The Practice of Piety* (3rd ed. London, 1613). The Massachusett edition of Bayly's masterpiece, which Eliot had "intended to be the last," was published in 1665 and reprinted in 1686 (with a 1685 date on the title page). Eliot had changed his schedule because Robert Boyle, the corporation's governor after the Restoration, had advised that he translate *The Practice of Piety* before finishing the Shepard works. Boyle probably made this recommendation because Bayly had been an Anglican bishop and not a Puritan minister. Eliot had ignored Boyle's earlier suggestion that he translate Bayly's book before he published Baxter's *Call*. The translation of Shepard's *The Sound Believer* was never printed and perhaps never finished; *The Sincere Convert* was not published until 1689, after the original translation had been revised by Grindal Rawson, the Mendon minister and son of the colony's longtime secretary.[34]

Bayly's *Practice of Piety* was the last translation published before King Philip's War (see Appendix 5). Although an abridgment, the Massachusett version of the work was nearly 400 pages in length. Eliot and his Indian associates had been a prolific team. Since finishing the Psalms in the winter of 1652–53, they produced approximately 1,400 densely worded pages of printed translations.

The Apostle undertook a different type of project after completing *The Practice of Piety*. Boyle had suggested in 1664 that he prepare a Massachusett grammar for the benefit of Englishmen with missionary aspirations. Eliot replied that he had long wanted to "reduc[e] this language unto rule," and he promised to do so after finishing the Bayly translation. He kept his word and wrote a manual for English speakers "who have a heart to study and learn" Massachusett, publishing it in 1666 under the title *The Indian Grammar Begun: Or, An Essay to bring the Indian Language into Rules*. Eliot disparaged the quality of the work, stating that it was "not worthy [of] the name of a grammar" and only represented "some bones and ribs preparatory at least for such a work." Dismissing the Apostle's modest claims, Kenneth Miner concludes that *The Indian Grammar Begun* is "the first published attempt, to my knowledge, at a description of an 'exotic' language which can justifiably be called scientific." Miner and the other authorities on the language explain that Eliot recognized and accepted the many affixes and augments of non–Indo-European types that he encountered in Massachusett, and that he was particularly adept at describing the larger structures of the language, such as its basic nominal and verbal paradigms. He was less skilled at describing smaller patterns of nuance at more complex morphological levels. He also had a sophisticated knowledge of phonology, even though he was sometimes inconsistent at representing consonants. His understanding of euphonics—how sounds transmute and coalesce under certain speech conditions—was poor; however, he was clearly sensitive to these changes, and his inconsistencies in representing consonant clusters were probably indicative of his struggles with the problems of phonetic change and consonantal coalescence.[35]

Eliot also wrote three original works in Massachusett. Two were minor pieces. One was the Natick church covenant, published as a bilingual broadside entitled *A Christian Covenanting Confession*. The other, apparently a hornbook for children that contained woodcuts, was a work known only as "Our Indians' A B C." The former was printed shortly after the creation of the Natick church in 1660 and reissued, with slight variations, around 1670; the latter publication, which is no longer extant, appeared in 1671. The third of Eliot's works written in Massachusett was the ambitious *Logick Primer*, published in 1672. Miner and Guice have explained that Eliot's *Logick Primer* was an original composition and not, as Perry Miller claimed, an abridged translation of one of Peter Ramus's writings; the two linguists disagree as to how Ramist in influence the work is. The *Logick Primer* is Eliot's only Massachusett publication with English interlinear throughout the text. He designed the work for the native preachers, in order to "lead my readings to them, and to guide them ... to understand, open, and improve the plain things ... revealed in the Scriptures." As Miner observes, the Apostle tried to find Massachusett equivalents for abstract philosophical terms like "logic" (a term that for Eliot included what we would call syntax), "syllogism," and "single notions," instead of using English loanwords. Miner suggests that this "curious practice may reflect a belief on Eliot's part that logical concepts are of universal applicability" in contrast to "culture-specific concrete terms." The *Logick Primer* grew out of the semimonthly summer lectures on theology and logic that Eliot began delivering at Natick in 1670. The purposes of these lectures, which were partly funded with gifts from Boyle and Lady Armine, were to instruct the preachers and rulers at Natick and other praying towns "how to analyze, and lay out into particulars both the works and Word of God; and how to communicate knowledge to others methodically and skillfully, and especially the method of divinity."[36]

The religious instruction of the rank and file took place in the Natick meetinghouse, where sermons (normally termed "lectures") were delivered three times each week, twice on Sunday and once during the week. In the early 1650s, Eliot lectured at Natick on alternating weeks and spent the intervening occasions in other Indian settlements. There is no evidence that he altered this schedule in the prewar period except when incapacitated by sciatica. Eliot's early lectures, which can be partly reconstructed from the numerous references to them in the native conversion narratives, were evidently expositions of scriptural passages reduced to a doctrinal or moral point. The texts were initially taken almost exclusively from the three books first translated (Genesis, Psalms, and Matthew) and from the Ten Commandments. Most of the lecturing at Natick, however, was done by Indians whom Eliot had briefed in advance. These unordained preachers were usually called "teachers." Natives known to have served in this capacity in the 1650s were Totherswamp, Nishohkou, Ponampam, and Monotunkquanit's son Samuel; Monequasson, Job Nesutan, and John Sassamon probably did so as well. The regular teachers in the 1660s were John

Speene and Anthony, both of whom turned to drink after King Philip's War and lost their jobs. In the early 1650s, the teachers did not follow the Puritan "method of preaching . . . by way of doctrine, reason, and use" because they lacked the training to do so. Eliot's lectures on theology and logic, however, honed the homiletical skills of the native teachers, for Gookin observed in 1674 that they could "speak methodologically and profitabl[y] unto any plain text of Scripture." By this time Eliot had also established a regular "exercise of prophesying, . . . wherein four of them [Indian teachers] exercise in one day, and I moderate and order them."[37]

Sunday devotions were the focal points of the proselytes' religious lives. "When Christ shall judge the world," Eliot wrote in *Indian Dialogues,* "he will examine all men how they spent every sabbath." Preparation for the Sunday morning and afternoon worship services began at sundown on Saturday, when families ceased all worldly activities. The Sunday services, which were announced by the beating of drums, consisted of Scripture reading, Psalm singing, catechism, prayer, and a lecture. Men and women sat separately "according to their age, quality, and degree." In keeping with Puritan practice, the Psalms were sung line by line to an English tune without instrumental accompaniment. Eliot noted that the Indians were "much pleased to have their language and words in meter and rhyme," and that their traditional manner of singing, which to his ear sounded like "ululation, howling, yelling, or mourning," had been in harmony but not in rhyme and meter. The Indians observed fast and thanksgiving days in the same manner they kept the sabbath. Some of these fast and thanksgiving days were for Natick-specific occasions; others were colony-wide observances decreed by the General Court.[38]

Prayer was not restricted to formal worship services but was a crucial part of the Indians' devotional lives. Eliot encouraged individuals to pray when they rose from bed, when they paused during the day, and when they retired at night; and he instructed families to pray in the mornings and evenings as well as before meals. The natives prayed with "eyes and hands to heaven" in the early years of the mission, and with bowed heads later on. The Indians clearly had a predilection for prayer: Eliot noted in 1647 that they "call[ed] all religion . . . praying to God," and he stated in 1651 that "in prayer . . . they exceed my expectations." Robert James Naeher suggests that praying appealed to the Indians because it gave everyone a chance to encounter the divine, much like the visionary experiences pursued by all natives in traditional culture.[39]

Although they had a regular worship service since 1651, the Natick Indians did not have an official church until 1660. The formation of a congregation of visible saints required evidence of conversion in the Puritan sense of the word. In the early 1650s, Eliot concluded that the leading proselytes were approaching conversion. He informed Winslow in October 1650 that "there is grace in their hearts, a spark kindled by the Word and Spirit of God that shall never be quenched," and he told him the following April that the natives were continuing to improve "in the practice and power of grace, both in constant care in attendance on the worship of God on sabbath days and lecture days, especially profiting in the gift of prayer, and also in the exercise of love to such as be in affliction."[40] By 1652 the Apostle was ready to begin formal preparations for gathering a church at Natick.

The Church

The first step took place in the summer of 1652, when fifteen Natick Indians delivered trial-run conversion narratives to their fellow proselytes. Five of the speakers were from Nonantum (Waban, Robin and John Speene, Totherswamp, and Anthony), four or five were Neponsets (Nookau, Monequasson, Nishohkou, Ponampam, and possibly Peter, the short-lived ruler of ten), three were Nipmucks (William of Sudbury, Captain Tom, and Owussumag), and two (Magus and Ephraim) came from unspecified locations. Nishohkou and four other proselytes gave two trial narratives each, and Robin Speene presented three. Only in Nishohkou's case was the reason given: Eliot explained that there had been "many things he spoke that I missed, for want of a thorough understanding of some words and sentences." The Apostle translated the narratives and then published them—with the exception of Waban's, excluded for an undisclosed reason—in *Tears of Repentance;* he also read the translations to some unidentified Puritan elders in order to learn if "there might be fit matter for a church" at Natick. The elders could see "no impediment for our proceeding thereunto," and Eliot began to plan for a public evaluation of a fresh set of conversion narratives.[41]

This evaluation took place at Natick in October 1652. In keeping with the practice in Massachusetts Bay, the local churches sent delegates to conduct the examination. Teaching and ruling elders, as well as magistrates and other "grave men," were in attendance. John Allin, Richard Mather, and John Wilson are the only English visitors named in the documentation. John Cotton, already suffering from the "distemper" that contributed to his death two months later, declined an invitation. Eliot also asked Thomas Mayhew, Jr., and William Leverich, a missionary in Plymouth Colony, to help him translate the conversion narratives; neither was able to attend. Eliot's only assistant during the proceedings was his Indian "interpreter," presumably Job Nesutan. Five of the Indian candidates for church membership are identified in the sources: Totherswamp, Waban, William of Sudbury, Monequasson, and Ponampam. There were at least two more proselytes in attendance, since seven was the minimum number of men needed to gather a church in early Massachusetts Bay.[42]

The day began with prayers and with sermons by Eliot and by two of the Indian candidates for church estate. The Apostle then asked the referees if they wished to examine the natives in their knowledge of Christian doctrine—a normal procedure—before hearing the conversion narratives. The evaluators chose to begin with the narratives and to conduct a doctrinal examination later in the day if the narratives proved satisfactory. By the end of the afternoon, only the five aforementioned Indians had spoken. The visitors then decided to adjourn, and for reasons given shortly, ruled that "as for the gathering of a church among them that day, it could not be."[43]

English versions of the five narratives were also published in *Tears of Repentance*. These translations were not pristine renditions of the Massachusett originals: Eliot confessed that he had "oft [been] forced to inquire of my interpreter" during the examination because he "did not perfectly understand some sentences." Nevertheless, he claimed that he had "not knowingly or willingly" changed the narratives when rendering them into English, and there are several reasons for thinking that his translations were reasonably accurate.[44]

For one thing, the conversion narratives delivered at the official examination contain the same biographical details and the same armature as the trial narratives in the four cases for which comparison is possible (Totherswamp, Monequasson, William of Sudbury, and Ponampam). Moreover, the official narratives contain damaging statements that show that the translations were not concocted to impress benefactors in England, a charge brought against the narratives by scholars who question Eliot's integrity. Waban, for example, ended his confession by saying that he "cannot repent," and William of Sudbury concluded his with the astonishing assertion that "I do not believe the Word of God and Gospel of Jesus Christ." In addition, the variations in quality in the narratives are consistent with the biographies of the speakers. Monequasson, the schoolteacher, displayed a greater knowledge of Scripture and theology than the other four Indians. Waban's incoherent narrative contains no scriptural quotations or paraphrases. Eliot said at the time that Waban was unskilled "in expressing himself this way," and Shepard had noted several years earlier that "many others far exceed him in the light and life of the things of God." Finally, there are no anachronistic statements in the narratives. Five of the Indians in the trial or the official narratives explained that they had learned something by hearing the catechism, which was in use by 1651 even though it was not published until 1654. Eleven Indians included quotations or paraphrases of biblical passages. Only the literate Monequasson claimed to have read these passages, doubtless in the lesson plans that Eliot prepared for him; the others stated that they had heard the texts preached in sermons. There was nothing unusual about the ability of an illiterate person to quote or paraphrase the Bible, as George Selement has shown in an analysis of the narratives offered by candidates for communion in Shepard's Cambridge congregation. Moreover, the Indians had a special aptitude in this respect, perhaps because of their long experience at preserving oral material. Eliot observed in 1651 that there was "a good measure of ability in them, . . . in memory to rehearse such Scriptures as I have read unto them and expounded," and he later remarked that Old Jacob, a Nipmuck proselyte, "had so good a memory that he could rehearse the whole catechism."[45]

The trial and the official narratives contain recurring themes that clearly came from common sources, particularly the catechism and the lectures delivered by Eliot and the native teachers. First, the speakers confessed to the types of sins that Puritans routinely accused Indians of committing: lusting, gambling, wearing long hair, desecrating the sabbath, and neglecting labor. Second, many of the Indians made a distinction between praying "outwardly" with one's "mouth" and "with words" and praying "inwardly" with one's "heart" and "soul," and condemned themselves for doing only the former. Third, they often confessed in good Reformed Protestant fashion that they deserved damnation and yet were unable to save themselves. "I cannot redeem myself, nor deliver myself, because of all these my many sins," Nishohkou said in a representative passage. Fourth, the native speakers testified that they could choose to believe, in contradiction to their many professions of the inability of humans to contribute to salvation. Ponampam, for instance, claimed that a person could "repent and believe, and be saved." As Holstun notes, Eliot was "almost Arminian" in his "assumption that the Indians . . . can choose grace without ever worrying about the election or nonelection of individuals." Holstun's judgment is confirmed by the absence in Eliot's missionary sources of any discussion of predestination.[46]

In December 1652 Richard Mather wrote an account of the examination for inclusion in *Tears of Repentance*. He explained that the referees were impressed by the Indians' "clear sight and sense of sin, . . . not only of gross and external sins, but also of such as are more inward in the heart and soul," and also by the "tears trickling down the cheeks of some of them," which indicated that "they spake with much good affection and holy fear of God." Nevertheless, the natives had not reached "a full and thorough conversion yet" but only "a hopeful beginning and preparation thereto." Negative verdicts were not unprecedented in the colony: Mather's flock at Dorchester and John Fiske's at Wenham initially failed to receive authorization to gather a church. Mather then explained that the "principal, if not the only, reasons" for rejecting the Indians' narratives were the lateness of the day, the absence of a sufficient number of corroborating translations, and the lack of "an able pastor and elder" for overseeing "all the affairs of the church and administrations of the House of God."[47]

The negative verdict did not diminish Eliot's conclusion that the "wheel of conversion of these Indians is turning." He explained in *Tears of Repentance* that there were "evident demonstrations that God's spirit by his Word has taught them, because their expressions, both in prayer and in the confessions . . . are far more, and more full and spiritual and various, than ever I was able to express unto them." For Eliot, the impending establishment of a native congregation of visible saints was a significant event in its own right—he had planned for the day since the birth of the mission in 1646—and also within the framework of his contemporary eschatology. *Tears of Repentance* contains Eliot's statement about "the kingdom of Christ . . . rising up in these western parts of the world" as well as his statement that the "words of prophecy . . . for the conversion both of the Jews (yea all Israel) and of the Gentiles . . . are in part begun to be accomplished."[48]

After the examination of the conversion narratives in October 1652, Eliot decided to hold a public evaluation of the Indians' "knowledge in the doctrinal part of religion." He initially planned to schedule this evaluation for 1653 but postponed it until 1654. One reason for the delay was that copies of *Tears of Repentance* were slow to return from Old to New England. He wanted the printed copies of the work to circulate in Massachusetts Bay so that knowledge of the Indians' narratives could reach colonists who had not attended the 1652 examination. A second reason was an "utterly groundless" report in 1653 that the Christian Indians "were in a conspiracy with others, and with the Dutch, to do mischief against the English." This report, based on rumors that Ninigret was forming an alliance with the Dutch and the Mohawks against the orthodox colonies, indicated that "it was no season for me to stir or move in this matter, when the waters were so troubled." Eliot's concern about the matter was doubtless heightened by the fact that England was presently at war with Holland. The doctrinal examination, which took place at Roxbury in June 1654, was open to "any Christian man who thought good to propound any question" to the Indians. The only mainland Englishmen besides Eliot known to have been present for the occasion were Ezekiel Rogers of Rowley, William Walton of Marblehead, and members of the Roxbury church, including Samuel Danforth and Isaac Heath. Assisting Eliot in the work of translation were an unidentified praying Indian as well as Mayhew, Jr., and one of his proselytes. The Apostle almost postponed the examination because of the incident with Totherswamp's inebriated son, which had occurred shortly before the scheduled date. Heath persuaded him that this incident was "but a transient act" and that the punishment meted out by the rulers "was an ordinance of God and would remain."[49]

"About eight" Indians—none identified by name—answered questions during the doctrinal examination. The referees did not follow "the catechetical method strictly, in which way children might answer"; instead, they asked questions in random order in order to "try whether they [the proselytes] understood what they said." Eliot translated the questions into Massachusett and the answers into English;

Mayhew and the two native interpreters then confirmed or refined the translations. The examiners did not have time to interrogate the Indians on all points of doctrine; nevertheless, they "found considerable satisfaction" in the "taste which they had" and "spake words of acceptance" that the proselytes possessed sufficient doctrinal knowledge to form a church once they had delivered satisfactory conversion narratives. Eliot then sent the questions and translations of the answers, along with a narrative introduction, to London for publication in September 1655 as the seventh Eliot tract, *A Late and Further Manifestation of the Progress of the Gospel amongst the Indians in New-England*.[50]

Four years passed before Eliot took another formal step toward the creation of an Indian church. In *A Late and Further Manifestation*, he gave three reasons why he was "well content to make slow haste" about the matter: the importance of establishing a proper "pattern and precedent" for future Indian churches, the "danger of polluting and defiling the name of Christ" by the admission of unworthy persons to the sacraments, and the absence of a native pastor for the proposed church. Other complications appeared later in the decade: Eliot's sciatica prevented him from making regular visits to the settlement for over a year, and the death of Monequasson around 1656 stripped the mission of one of its leading lights. Furthermore, by 1656 Eliot had distanced himself from the lost tribes theory, with its likely implications for his conviction about the imminence of the Indians' conversion.[51]

The step Eliot took was a daylong fast at Natick in November 1658. The observance was undertaken "partly in preparation for gathering a church" (fasting was a common step in the process of church formation) and partly in response to recent afflictions. As John Speene explained in Eliot's translation of the proceedings: "great rain and great floods and unseasonable weather . . . spoil our labors; our corn is much spoiled with the wet, so that the Lord does threaten us with want of food; also our hay is much spoiled, so that God threatens to starve and kill our cattle; also we have great sickness among us; so that many are dead: the burying place of this town has many graves, and so it is in all our towns among the praying Indians. Also in our houses are many sick, and a great many are crazy, and weak, and not well." During the fast-day observance, Speene and five other Indians—

Waban, Nishohkou, Anthony, Piumbuhhou, and Captain Tom—gave exhortations from texts in Genesis and Matthew to their fellow proselytes and to Eliot and Eliot, Jr., the only Englishmen present for the occasion. The Apostle included translations of these exhortations, "clothed . . . [in] our English idiom," in the eighth tract, *A further Accompt of the Progresse of the Gospel amongst the Indians in New-England,* published in April or May 1659.[52]

The "great sickness" of 1657–58 was not the proselytes' first or last encounter with infectious disease. Some of the future Natick Indians had suffered through the epidemics of 1616–1619 and 1633–34, as well as through an unspecified "epidemic" in 1647 that left "whole families sick, young and old." Between 1648 and 1650, the praying Indians apparently escaped serious brushes with European disease. In 1649 the smallpox spared the proselytes but visited some "profane [Massachusett] Indians" near Weymouth. In the winter of 1650–51, however, smallpox struck Natick, killing three; and in the spring of 1652, the "bloody flux" (dysentery) ravaged the settlement. The Indians also suffered from "consumption" (tuberculosis) throughout the prewar period. Many prominent Natick residents had a personal experience with death or severe illness. In the spring and summer of 1652, Robin Speene lost three children, Monequasson his wife and son, and Nishohkou his wife and a child; and later in the decade, Anthony lost his brothers Wamporas and Totherswamp, Ponampam two children, John Speene several children as well as his brothers Robin and Thomas, Captain Tom his wife and children and then his new wife, and Piumbuhhou his wife and children.[53]

The missionary sources indicate that the Natick Indians often viewed disease and death in the manner of contemporary Puritans—as acts of divine judgment on the sins committed by individuals and by the group. The proselytes' ability to do so is a measure of the progress they were making in mastering Eliot's theological perspective. But at the same time, the praying Indians also interpreted physical affliction and healing through a Christianized traditional orientation. Harold van Lonkhuyzen observes that they saw Jesus as a shaman because several fast-day speakers used the figure of "Christ the physician" (Matthew 9:12) in their exhortations. Charles Cohen also notes this point, adding that the natives extended Christ's healing powers beyond sick bodies to sick souls as well.[54]

Up to this time, Eliot's objective had been to create an Indian church of visible saints rather than to permit qualified proselytes to join an English church. But in early 1659, he agreed to a compromise proposal that reflected "the general inclination of the saints, both magistrates, elders, and others." According to the terms of the proposal, Indians who offered acceptable conversion narratives would receive the sacraments of baptism and the Lord's Supper, as well as participate in "any special exercise of discipline," in an English congregation. After a period of "season[ing]" among Puritan saints, these natives would form a church of their own. In the meantime, they would continue to keep "their usual sabbath conversations . . . among their own people" in the worship services at Natick. The same "magistrates, elders, and others" also suggested "with one mouth" that Roxbury should be the congregation, even though Dedham was ten miles closer to Natick. Roxbury was doubtless chosen because it was Eliot's church and because Dedham was disinclined to admit their Natick antagonists into Christian fellowship.[55]

This decision changed the category of evaluation from the authorization of Indians to form a church to the admission of Indians into an existing congregation. In April 1659, seven natives assembled before the full members of the Roxbury church and delivered trial conversion narratives, which Eliot called "private preparatory confessions." An ailing Waban was unable to attend the event; he soon traveled alone to Roxbury and gave a narrative. Seven of the eight natives (John Speene, Anthony, Nishohkou, Captain Tom, Ponampam, Piumbuhhou, and Waban) had presented a conversion narrative in 1652 and/or delivered a fast-day exhortation in 1658; one of them (Monotunkquanit) had not spoken in either 1652 or 1658. Eliot and Eliot, Jr., translated the eight "preparatory confessions" for the benefit of the Roxbury church members, who were encouraged by the quality of the Indians' statements. The translations were printed in the ninth Eliot tract, *A further Account of the progress of the Gospel Amongst the Indians in New England,* published in London in March 1660.[56]

The Roxbury church members then asked the "neighbor churches" if "any among them . . . had any just offense against any of these eight Indians." No negative testimonies were submitted. To this point the saints at Roxbury had followed standard procedures for admitting persons into a congregation: prospective communicants delivered trial conversion narratives to the full church members, who then welcomed outside comment about persons who had given promising narratives.

Roxbury next asked ten unspecified local churches to send "messengers" to Roxbury for an official evaluation of the fitness of the eight Indians for church estate. This was a procedural irregularity; the admission of members into an existing church was normally an internal decision. Eliot may have insisted upon the variation in procedure because he did not want outsiders to say that Roxbury had admitted the Indians only as a courtesy to him.[57]

The examination took place at Roxbury on July 5, 1659. The eight Indians arrived in town several days earlier, in order to give conversion narratives to Eliot and Abraham Pierson, who then prepared written translations, which were also printed in *A further Account*. Eliot took these translations to the public evaluation on July 5. The referees consisted of the Roxbury church members and the representatives from the local congregations; John Wilson and John Allin are the only "messengers" mentioned in the sources. Also in attendance were various language experts: Pierson and Eliot, Jr.; Peter Folger, the Martha's Vineyard schoolteacher who was Benjamin Franklin's maternal grandfather, and one of Folger's native pupils; two other Vineyard Indians, Joel Hiacoomes and Caleb Cheeschaumuck, then attending grammar school in Cambridge; and Thomas Stanton, Jr., and his brother John, who left without permission shortly after the proceedings commenced. Six of the eight proselytes spoke during the examination. Their narratives were not translated on the spot. In order to save time, Eliot read the translations prepared several days earlier to the assembled language experts, who then confirmed that the orally delivered Massachusett testimonies they had just heard were substantially the same as the written translations. The referees permitted the remaining two Indians, Piumbuhhou and Waban, to allow the translations of their narratives to speak for them.[58]

Many themes found in the 1652 narratives were also present in the 1659 statements. The Indians again condemned themselves for having lusted after women, distinguished between internal and external praying, confessed that they deserved damnation, explained that they were unable to save themselves, and paradoxically affirmed (in Nishohkou's words) that "if you repent and believe, you shall have pardon and be saved." New themes and new emphases appeared as well. In 1659 the natives confessed to other sins that they had committed prior to their acceptance of the mission: worshipping many gods, consorting with powwows, and "running wild." Over the intervening seven years, the proselytes had clearly become more familiar with the Puritan critique of their traditional way of life. Professions of a desire to receive the sacraments of baptism and communion were present in most of the 1659 narratives and absent in all the 1652 ones. Another innovation was a consistent acknowledgment of the doctrine of original sin. All eight Indians noted the doctrine in 1659; only three of the speakers had done so in the trial and official narratives of 1652. Finally, there were many more scriptural references in the 1659 statements.[59]

The 1659 narratives can also be compared to their English counterparts. Over a hundred contemporaneous Puritan conversion narratives exist in printed form today, many of them from Shepard's Cambridge church. Cohen has observed that the chief difference between the two bodies of narratives was that "Amerindians both truncated and muted the affective cycle Puritans underwent, lopping off the joys of sanctification and mitigating the horrors of humiliation." He explains that the emotional lives of the Indians were specifically lacking in three respects. First, the proselytes did not reach the same depths of despair: "their rhetoric of abnegation pales beside the magnificient self-disgust Puritans display." Second, they were not liberated by the conversion experience, which released the "strength engendered by the new birth to perform God's will" and "suffused saints with a sense of God's love for them." The natives lacked "a psychological counterpart to the new birth." Third, none of the eight native speakers expressed any sense of assurance about salvation, in contrast to some of the fifty-one persons who offered narratives for admission into the Cambridge church between 1638 and 1645. As Selement notes, "eighteen [of these] candidates expressed in twenty-two statements reasonable certainty about closing with Christ." Other points of contrast with the Puritan narratives stemmed from the Indians' special circumstances. According to Selement's count, the Cambridge narratives contained 106 references to clergymen besides Shepard. The Natick Indians were almost exclusively dependent on Eliot and on their native teachers. Furthermore, the proselytes owned up to certain sins that Puritans could not or would not confess: polytheism and powwowing (the closest English analogues were Catholicism and Anglicanism), "wildness," and laziness.[60]

The examiners found the eight conversion narratives satisfactory. Wilson then "desired further to hear how they [the Indians] were instructed in the knowledge of Christ." The natives "readily answered" a series of "catechetical questions, . . . which would be too long to rehearse." This doctrinal exam was probably perfunctory because the Natick Indians had passed a more thorough test in 1654. The referees then unanimously agreed that the eight Indians were "fit matter for church estate." This decision authorized the natives in question to receive the sacraments of baptism and communion at Roxbury and to present their young children for baptism. These actions presumably took place shortly thereafter.[61] The eight Indians did not long remain in the Roxbury congregation, however, and may not have attended it at all. A native church with its own sacraments and covenant was formed at Natick in 1660 (see Table 1). The sources provide no explanation for the short duration of the seasoning process at Roxbury. The eight individuals may have objected to making the eighteen-mile journey to the English town: the proposal of early 1659 to send them to Roxbury for the sacraments had been made by unspecified "magistrates, elders, and others" and not by them. Furthermore, Eliot had not been enthusiastic about the proposal in the first place. He explained that he had "yielded" to the recommendation to admit qualified natives into the Roxbury congregation. His preference was for an independent church. "Let them [the Indians] keep sabbath and worship together," he told Richard Baxter in 1657, so that "the strong [can] help the weak."[62]

The public examination of 1659 was the last occasion when Natick Indians delivered conversion narratives to Puritan referees. After the creation of the church in 1660, the native saints controlled their own membership. Eliot explained in 1673 that prospective members of the Natick congregation "are diligently instructed and examined both publicly and privately in the catechism; their blameless and pious conversation are publicly testified; their names are publicly exposed as desiring to make confession and join unto the church. The teachers and chief brethren do first hear their preparatory confessions, and when they judge them meet, they are called publicly to confess, confederate, and be baptized, both themselves and their children, if not grown up." Indian saints were rigorously disciplined after their admission into church estate. "They are so severe [in this respect] that I am put to bridle them to moderation and forbearance," Eliot noted. By 1669 there were between thirty and forty communicants at Natick as well as "sundry . . . upon preparatory confession to be received";

Table 1 Formal steps in the creation of the Natick church

Date	Location	Event
Summer 1652	Natick	Delivery of trial conversion narratives to an Indian audience
Oct. 13, 1652	Natick	Evaluation of official conversion narratives by Puritan referees
June 13, 1654	Roxbury	Examination in Christian doctrine by Puritan referees
Nov. 15, 1658	Natick	Fast-day exhortations before an Indian audience
April 15, 1659	Roxbury	Evaluation of trial conversion narratives by Roxbury church members
Ca. July 2, 1659	Roxbury	Translation of official conversion narratives by Eliot and Pierson
July 5, 1659	Roxbury	Evaluation of official conversion narratives and examination in doctrine by Puritan referees
[Month?] 1659	Roxbury	Admission of Indians into full membership in the Roxbury church[a]
[Month?] 1660	Natick	Creation of the Indian church

a. Presumed event; no documentation exists in the missionary sources or in the Roxbury church records.

by 1670 the congregation had between forty and fifty full members. The membership included nonresident Indians who traveled to Natick from other praying towns in order to receive the sacraments.[63]

Eliot administered the sacraments at Natick until the ordination of Daniel Tokkohwompait in July 1683. The Apostle explained in 1673 that the Natick Indians did not want a native minister "because so long as I live, they say, there is no need but we propose (God willing) not always to rest in this answer." The Apostle occasionally thought about resigning his Roxbury charge and becoming a full-time minister to the Indians. He had broached this possibility in the late 1640s but rejected it for fear of impoverishing his family. He was apparently still considering the idea in the late 1660s, for Baxter told him in 1670, in response to a missing letter, that "were I your neighbor, and did believe that forsaking your church would enable you to do much more service to the poor Indians than your church service comes to, I should cast in my judgment that it were your duty so to do, and to be only the apostle to the Indians."[64]

Scholars are in no position to know whether or not the Natick Indians ever experienced conversion in the Puritan sense of the word. The proposition that divine grace had transformed the souls of the Native Americans cannot be confirmed or disconfirmed by any historical-critical or social-scientific method. Students of the period, however, are able to evaluate the extent to which the elite praying Indians grasped Christian doctrine. By this measure, native conversion narratives compared favorably with their English counterparts. As Charles Cohen, an authority on Puritan spirituality, has written, Indian saints were "at least as conversant with essential doctrines as . . . the goodmen and goodwives of Puritan Massachusetts."[65]

The leading proselytes' knowledge of Puritan doctrine shows how far they had traveled since the birth of the mission. "It is . . . to be wondered at," Mather wrote in his account of the 1652 church examination, "that in so short a time, the thing is in so much forwardness as it is."[66] The future Natick Indians had originally turned to the mission in the 1640s for the material advantages it promised. By the time the town was settled in the early 1650s, the proselytes had secured a place of residence, gained access to English goods and to literacy and other skills, and (at least in the case of the Massachusetts) reformed their band structure. There was no material incentive for any of the Christian Indians to master Puritan doctrines well enough to qualify for full church membership. A material explanation probably accounts for the leading proselytes' initial attraction to Eliot's program; however, it fails to explain the quality of their participation in it.

Natick was initially the place of residence for natives from various locations. The original civil rulers who are known by name consisted of four Nonantum Indians (Waban, Totherswamp, Piumbuhhou, and Thomas Speene, Sr.) and one Neponset (Cutshamekin); the schoolteachers were three Neponsets (Monequasson, Job Nesutan, and John Sassamon); the lecturers in the worship services were a Nonantum Indian (Totherswamp), two Neponsets (Nishohkou and Ponampam), and a Nipmuck (Monotunkquanit's son Samuel); the original eight church members included two Nipmucks (Captain Tom and Monotunkquanit), four Nonantum Indians (Waban, Piumbuhhou, John

Speene, and Anthony) and two Neponsets (Nishohkou and Ponampam); and the rank and file was comprised of Neponsets, Nipmucks, and Pawtuckets in addition to the Nonantum majority. The town became more exclusively a Nonantum settlement in the 1660s and early 1670s, when Eliot dispersed many of the residents to other praying towns, normally to ones of their own choosing.

CHAPTER SIX

· · ·

The Remaining Praying Towns

The creation of Natick set a precedent for the establishment of other praying towns. In October 1652, the General Court ruled that "if, upon good experience, there shall be a competent number of the Indians brought on to civility, so as to be capable of a township, upon their request to the General Court, they shall have grant of lands undisposed of for a plantation, as the English have." Daniel Gookin explained in his *Historical Collections of the Indians in New England* (1674) that this ruling had been made for three reasons: first, to "prevent differences and contention" between Indians and colonists over boundaries; second, to "secure unto them [the proselytes] and their posterity places of habitation"; and third, to enable the praying Indians "to cohabit together, without which neither religion nor civility can well prosper." By the time he wrote the work, Gookin was able to identify fourteen praying towns in Massachusetts Bay. He termed Natick and six others the "old praying towns," and he called seven settlements recently established among the Nipmuck Indians the "new praying towns" (see Map 1).[1]

Punkapoag (now parts of Canton and Stoughton) was the first old praying town created after Natick. Settlement of this town, the place of residence for Neponset Indians reluctant to live at Natick, was under way by October 1653. In June 1657 Eliot asked Humphrey Atherton and other inhabitants of nearby Dorchester to formally assign land to Punkapoag, and in December the selectmen awarded a grant "not exceeding" 6,000 acres to the natives with the provision that they "shall not alienate or sell their plantation, or any part thereof, unto any English, upon the loss or forfeiture, of the plantation." The Indians evidently retained this land throughout the prewar period, for Gookin said that Punkapoag was 6,000 acres in size in 1674. By this time twelve families were living in the town.[2]

The settlement had several rulers during the prewar period. The residents initially chose Josias Wompatuck as their ruler but only after he "had promised before the governor and the magistrates . . . to pray unto God . . . all the days of his life." Josias did not keep this promise. He was catechized and "profess[ed] the Christian religion for a while" in the early 1650s but "turned apostate" in the mid-1650s. Thereafter he and an unspecified number of followers moved to Matakesset (now Pembroke) in Plymouth Colony, in a portion of the Bridgewater-Taunton-Middleboro triangle claimed by the Massachusett sachems. In 1668 John Cotton, Jr., made several unsuccessful attempts to renew Josias's interest in Christianity. The sachem died in a 1669 battle with the Mohawks discussed later in this chapter. In the meantime he had been succeeded as the ruler of Punkapoag by his brother Squamaug, who governed on behalf of Josias's young son Jeremy. Squamaug remained the ruler of Punkapoag at least through 1668. He apostatized in 1669 or 1670 and was replaced by Ahawton, a venerable Neponset Indian. Jeremy was alive at the time; whether he had also renounced the Christian religion is unclear. Ahawton proved to be an ineffective ruler. As Eliot explained in 1670, he was "more loved than feared; the reins of his bridle are too long. Waban is sometimes necessarily called to keep court here."[3]

The Punkapoag Indians occasionally sold land beyond the town's boundaries. In some cases the transactions were retroactive payments for Boston-area lands occupied by the English in the early settlement period. Many sales of this type took place in the mid-1660s, when the royal commissioners were challenging Puritan titles. In 1665, for example, Josias, the Ahawtons, Squamaug, and other present or former Punkapoag residents received payments from Hingham and Braintree, towns settled in the 1630s. In other cases the transactions transferred land to Englishmen in Massachusetts and Plymouth or to natives in the latter colony. These sales were for territory located in Plymouth, particularly in the Bridgewater-Taunton-Middleboro area, rather than in the Boston vicinity, where there was no fresh land to sell. The

Punkapoag proselytes rarely benefited from the transactions in Plymouth; Josias usually made them on his own authority or in conjunction with other apostates.[4]

The residents of Punkapoag received regular religious instruction in the period prior to King Philip's War. The native teachers were William Awinian, a bilingual Indian who died in 1670, and Ahawton's son William, who continued in the position until his death in 1717. Eliot, Jr., lectured in Massachusett twice a month, and the Apostle's son-in-law, Habbakuk Glover of Boston, preached through an interpreter after the younger Eliot's death in October 1668. There were plans to form a church in 1669, but one was not gathered until after the war.[5]

Eliot established three more settlements shortly after the creation of Punkapoag in 1653. In May 1654 he asked the General Court to award land "free from any just challenge of an English interest" for Nipmuck Indians at Hassanamesit and Okommakamesit and for Pawtuckets at Nashobah. Later that month the court granted his request and also prohibited the residents from selling their allocations without permission.[6]

Hassanamesit (now Grafton) was located about forty miles to the southwest of Boston. English travelers sometimes lodged in the Indian settlement as they made their way to and from the Connecticut River. Twelve families lived on Hassanamesit's 8,000 acres of land in 1674. Two of the civil rulers are known by name, Anaweakin and Petavit. Anaweakin was one of the four sons of William of Sudbury. Two of William's other sons also lived at Hassanamesit: James the Printer, who moved there after his work on Eliot's Massachusett works had been completed; and Joseph Tuckawillipin, who served as the town's teacher. In 1670 Monotunkquanit began to share the teaching duties. In 1674 the other ruler, Petavit, died from the "stone" (kidney stones), an affliction to which the natives had long been immune. Eliot noted that the "first Indian that was ever known to have that disease" died at Natick in 1670. Winthrop, Jr., attributed the natives' long resistance to the malady to their fondness for corn, "easy of digestion and very diuretic." Petavit's two sons, Joseph and Sampson, also lived in the settlement, as did Captain Tom, the ruler of the new praying towns.[7]

Natick and Hassanamesit were the only praying towns with churches prior to King Philip's War. Many of the full members of the Hassanamesit congregation were transplanted members of the Natick church. Plans for forming a congregation at Hassanamesit had surfaced by the fall of 1671; the church was gathered in September 1673. Joseph Tuckawillipin, who had been conducting worship services—as opposed to official church services—at Hassanamesit prior to this time, was the pastor; William of Sudbury, who had been admitted into the Natick church in 1669, was the deacon; and Piumbuhhou, one of the original eight Natick church members, was the ruling elder. In 1674 Gookin stated that the Hassanamesit church had sixteen communicant members and thirty baptized persons. (He did not explain if the latter figure included the communicant members.) Several of the full members of the congregation were residents of other praying towns.[8]

Okommakamesit, the second town established by the court in 1654, was 6,000 acres in size in 1674. William of Sudbury, Captain Tom, and Owussumag came from this area, although only the latter resided in the praying town. Owussumag served as ruler until his death in 1674. By that time ten families were living in the settlement. The teacher until his retirement in 1669 was Nausquonit, about whom little is known. Job Kattananit, the fourth son of William of Sudbury, and Sampson, the son of Petavit, were slated to share the teaching duties as Nausquonit's replacements. It is unlikely that either man did so. In 1670 the town's teacher was Solomon, who had lived at Okommakamesit since 1657; and in 1674 Job Kattananit and Sampson were teachers in other praying towns.[9]

Okommakamesit was adjacent to the English town of Marlborough, which had been created in May 1656, when the General Court awarded six square miles to younger men from Sudbury who had been demanding in vain that the selectmen grant them strips of land as well as greater power in town affairs. The court's carelessly researched award to Marlborough included some land already occupied by the Okommakamesit Indians. In May 1657 Eliot petitioned the legislature for redress; in October, in response to this petition, the General Court authorized surveyors to lay out 6,000 acres of land for the Indians; and in October 1658, the court formally awarded the land for the praying town. The grant to Okommakamesit was prejudicial to Marlborough in the sense that it assigned "part of the nearest and best of the planting land" and "the nearest and most considerable meadow" to the Indians.[10]

The court's 1658 action created tension between the Marlborough planters, who were a fractious lot to begin with, and the proselytes.

The "contiguity and cohabitation are not barren in producing matters of interfering," Eliot wrote in 1670, and Gookin observed four years later that the Okommakamesit Indians "do not much rejoice under the Englishmen's shadow, who do so overtop them in their number of people, stocks of cattle, etc." King Philip's War provided the town of Marlborough with a dreadful opportunity for revenge. In August 1675 Samuel Moseley, captain of a band of volunteers that included Dutch and English pirates pardoned to participate in the war, twice brutalized the Okommakamesits along with James the Printer and other Indians who had taken refuge in the praying town. Gookin explained that the perpetrators had been "instigated thereunto by some people of those parts, no lovers of Christian Indians," and that the "occult and main reason" for their action was a desire for praying town land.[11]

Eliot tried to solve the dispute between the towns on two occasions before the war. The first was in May 1663, when he told the General Court that because of "the inconveniences of so near neighbors," the Okommakamesit Indians were "willing to remove their township" to a site "about halfway from them to the Nipmuck [Blackstone] River," provided Marlborough gave them £20 for surrendering their plowed fields. The court granted Eliot's request, but for some reason the Indians remained at Okommakamesit. The second attempt was made in 1674, when Eliot and Gookin proposed to the Commissioners that a biracial school be constructed at Okommakamesit on a tract of disputed land. Marlborough, which had a church but not a school by this time, was to pay the salary of an English schoolteacher as well as build a house and lay out a farm for him. Indian children were to receive their books and uniforms from the New England Company and attend the school for free. The proposal was intended to facilitate the curricular transition from Massachusett to English, promote cooperation between Okommakamesit and Marlborough, and remove two common objections raised by potential Puritan schoolteachers to the Indians by providing competent maintenance and an English place of worship. Eliot and Gookin told the Commissioners that the plan had been accepted by the "principal [Indian] rulers and teachers" but had not been broached to the "most prudent" residents of Marlborough. Whether or not the local settlers learned of the idea before the war is not known.[12]

The third settlement created in 1654 was Nashobah (now Littleton), the home for Pawtucket Indians who had once lived in Musketaquid, some ten miles to the southeast. The teacher of the town was John Thomas, and the original ruler was his father-in-law, Attawans, the Musketaquid sachem who had embraced the mission in 1647. Attawans was succeeded by his son, John Attawans, Sr. By 1670, both father and son had died. The position of ruler was then assigned to Captain Josiah, who also served in the undefined capacity of "marshall-general belonging to all the praying Indian towns." In 1669 many of the town's inhabitants temporarily fled in fear of Mohawk marauders. Eliot explained that the residents of Nashobah were innocent victims in the feud between the Mohawks and several New England Indian groups because the settlement lay "on the roadway which the Mohawks hunted." Resettlement of the town began in 1670. By the time of King Philip's War, Nashobah's 8,000 acres of land were home to ten Indian families.[13]

In contrast to Punkapoag and the three settlements established in 1654, the old praying town at Magunkog hardly qualified as "old." Created at Eliot's request in October 1669, Magunkog was located between Natick and Hassanamesit, in parts of modern Ashland and Hopkinton. The settlement was home for "some Nipmuck Indians who [had] left their own places." In October 1670 the General Court enlarged the town because the original grant had been "grievous to the poor Indians" and had "disappointed . . . their hopes." In 1674 the settlement was 3,000 acres in size. The ruler of Magunkog's eleven families was Pomham (not the Narragansett sachem of the same name). The town's teachers in 1669 and 1670 were Wohwohquoshadt and Simon, two natives about whom nothing else is known. By 1674 Job Kattananit had assumed the teaching duties.[14]

These five praying towns stood within twenty-five miles of Natick. Eliot's habit in the prewar period was to visit Natick twice a month and to travel to another settlement in the intervening weeks. The specifics of his visitation schedule are otherwise unclarified in the sources. He probably went to Punkapoag and Magunkog more frequently than to Hassanamesit, Okommakamesit, and Nashobah because the former two towns were closer to Roxbury. The remaining old praying town, Wamesit, was a special case for three reasons. First, Eliot and his native assistants seldom visited this settlement, which was located about forty miles from Roxbury and Natick at the confluence of the Concord and Merrimack Rivers, near present-day Wamesit Falls. Second, the Wamesits were Pennacook (Penawog, Pennywoof) Indians in contrast to the Massachusetts and Nipmucks, who dominated the other towns. Third, the Indians at Wamesit, as well as those at the nearby pagan settlement of Pantucket located several miles up the Merrimack near Pawtucket Falls, were the leading participants from southern New England in a disastrous raid against the Mohawks in the summer of 1669.[15]

Wamesit, Pantucket, and the Expedition against the Mohawks

In the late 1640s, Eliot made at least three trips to the juncture of the Concord and Merrimack Rivers. He was planning to return in the spring of 1651; whether he did so is unclear. The Apostle traveled to the area in the summer of 1652, in the company of Simon Willard and others whom the General Court had recently appointed to explore the Merrimack Valley up through Lake Winnepesaukee. During this visit Passaconaway and "sundry other sachems and people did solemnly give up themselves unto praying to God" and asked for "somebody to travail in those parts to teach them." The sachem had made similar requests in 1648 and 1649. But once again, Eliot was unable to provide regular instruction. He returned to the area in the spring of 1653 and discovered the price of neglect: the local wigwams were filled with Catholic images of saints and angels secured from Indians to the north. "I marvelled," he explained, "having never seen the like before at any place I ever came to." He promptly convinced several unidentified sachems to "demolish the idols."[16]

In May 1653 Eliot asked the General Court to create a praying town on the west bank of the Concord just south of the Merrimack. The request was granted, and Wamesit came into being. At the same session, the court established the English town of Chelmsford and directed the planters to "break up" land for the Wamesit Indians at the designated location. In May 1656 Eliot convinced the General Court to expand Wamesit to the east bank of the Concord, and in May 1664 he persuaded the court to further extend the settlement's eastern boundary. The second extension required some maneuvering because the land in question had already been granted to Margaret Winthrop. Eliot had tried and failed to secure this land for Wamesit in 1661; he succeeded in 1664 because the Winthrop estate was willing to accept a compensatory grant near Billerica. The two eastern expansions notwithstanding, Wamesit remained the smallest of the old towns. The settlement was 2,500 acres in size in 1674.[17]

Fifteen families lived at Wamesit on the eve of King Philip's War. In 1669 Numphow was the town's "chief ruler" and Mystic George the teacher. Both men continued in these capacities until the war. Numphow, who had resided in the settlement since at least 1660, was Passaconaway's son-in-law. By 1674 John Lyne, possibly the Wamesit Indian known as "Sagamore John," was sharing the ruling duties with Numphow; and Samuel Numphow (the ruler's son) and Simon Beckom, both of whom were able to read and write English, were serving as Mystic George's colleagues. Numphow and Mystic George died from exposure during King Philip's War; Samuel and Simon survived the conflict; John Lyne's fate is not known.[18]

The General Court apparently did not award land to Pantucket, which by all accounts remained a pagan enclave until the early 1670s. The settlement's most notable residents were Passaconaway and his son Wannalancett, both of whom also lived at other locations in the lower Merrimack Valley, including Pennacook (Concord, New Hampshire) and Naticot (Dunstable, Massachusetts). Passaconaway, who died around 1662, apparently never received Christian instruction. Eliot was unable to provide it, and the sachem probably lost any use for it. As I argued in Chapter 3, Passaconaway initially had two reasons for being interested in the mission. The first was to prevent the loss of subjects through a Christian secessionist movement. Eliot's inability to make regular visits to the area diminished the likelihood of any such secession; furthermore, Passaconaway may have been able to retain his influence over the Wamesit Indians through his daughter's marriage to Numphow. The second was to increase English settlement in the area as a way of discouraging marauders. The nearby towns of Chelmsford and Billerica were settled in the mid-1650s. The English presence in the area angered some of the Pennacooks, who were reportedly "up in arms" about the matter in 1660. Passaconaway warned the belligerent natives to "take heed how you quarrel with the English, for though you may do them much mischief, yet assuredly you will all be destroyed." Wannalancett, for his part, accepted the mission on the eve of King Philip's War. He survived the carnage by fleeing shortly after it began, and died around 1697 in the care of Jonathan Tyng of Dunstable.[19]

Eliot and Gookin traveled to Wamesit and Pantucket in the spring of 1669. There is no conclusive evidence that either man, or that native missionaries from other praying towns, had been there since the Apostle's trip in 1653. During the 1669 visit, Eliot and Gookin discovered that the local Indians were in a state of agitation about the Mohawks. The Wamesits had recently built a fort for protection, and Gookin arranged for an English garrison to be temporarily stationed nearby. Eliot and Gookin prohibited the Pantucket Indians from moving into the Wamesit fort because they "refused to desist from powwowing." They soon constructed a fort of their own near Wamesit, in the future Belvidere. By the time the two men returned to the area in the spring of 1670, the Wamesit and Pantucket Indians had been devastated by their participation in the expedition into the Mohawk Country in August 1669.[20]

The origins of Pennacook-Mohawk friction can be traced back to the early 1650s. In the fall of 1650, the leaders of New France forged an anti-Mohawk alliance with the Eastern Abenakis along the Penobscot and Kennebec Rivers, and with the Sokokis, who inhabited the Connecticut River Valley between Northfield, Massachusetts and Hinsdale, New Hampshire. These native groups had recent histories of trouble with the Mohawks. In early December 1650 Gabriel Druillettes, a Jesuit missionary to the Eastern Abenakis on the Kennebec, came to Boston in the hope of persuading the English to join this "league offensive and defensive" against the Mohawks. He appealed both to the colonists' Christian concerns, for the Mohawks were harassing his mission to the Abenakis, and to their economic interests, for Mohawk aggression was jeopardizing the French and English fur trade in Maine. Druillettes was told that his proposal could be heard only by the Commissioners, who had concluded their annual meeting several months earlier. The Jesuit remained in southern New England for a month, meeting notables and lobbying for his plan. William Bradford of Plymouth served him a fish dinner on Friday, and Eliot hosted him for a night. The two missionaries spent the evening discussing native languages, probably in Latin. "He treated me with respect and kindness," Druillettes recalled, "and begged me to spend the winter with him."[21]

Druillettes returned to southern New England in September 1651 for the Commissioners' scheduled meeting in New Haven. He was accompanied by Jean Godefroy, a member of the Council of Quebec. By then the Sokokis had brought the Pennacooks, the Pocumtucks, and the Mahicans (who lived along the Hudson River near Albany) into the alliance. The Commissioners refused the Frenchmen's request to join the alliance because the Mohawks had done nothing to the orthodox colonies and in fact had assisted them in the Pequot War, because participation in the alliance would endanger exposed English towns as well as "our neighbor Indians . . . which profess Christianity and . . . expect just protection from us," and because (as Neal Salisbury has noted, although the Commissioners concealed the fact from the French), the Pynchons and other fur traders needed the pelts supplied by the Mohawks through the Beaver Wars of the 1640s and 1650s.[22]

The French and Indian alliance against the Mohawks stayed intact even though the orthodox colonies did not join it. During the remainder of the 1650s, there were minor skirmishes but no major confrontations between the Mohawks and the allied Indian groups. At the time the Mohawks were more concerned with other matters, such as dispersing the Neutrals and the Eries, who lived around Lake Erie. In the 1660s, however, the Mohawks made four major raids on native settlements in New England, attacking the Penobscot Abenakis in May 1662, the Sokokis in November 1663, the Pocumtucks in the winter of 1664–65, and the Pennacooks near the future Concord, New Hampshire, at some point in mid-decade (Gordon Day suggests in the fall of 1666). Smaller Mohawk raiding parties were also active in New England at the time. In early September 1665 five Mohawks were captured outside Cambridge. "The English had heard much," Gookin recalled, "but never saw any of those Mohawks until now." The Massachusetts council examined the five Iroquois, scolded them for their "secret, skulking manner," denied a request to execute them made by natives whom Gookin called only "our neighbor Indians," released them because they had harmed no one, and sent with them a letter that warned their sachems not to harm natives "within a day's journey of Boston." In 1668, in ignorance or in defiance of this admonition, Mohawk raiders killed the brother of Numphow and the father of John Thomas of Nashobah. Each victim was fishing at the time of his death.[23]

The escalation of hostilities prompted the Commissioners and the General Court to make modest distributions of firearms and ammunition to the Christian Indians. Several days after the capture of the five Mohawks, the Commissioners spent roughly £5 of New England

Company money on "powder and shot delivered Mr. Eliot" for the proselytes' "necessary defense against the Mohawks"; in October 1666 the court authorized Gookin to purchase, presumably at corporation expense, a hundredweight of powder "with liberty to dispose thereof to the Indians"; two years later the Commissioners used Company funds to cover an unitemized debt of £20 that Eliot had incurred for ammunition given to the natives for "defense against the Mohawks" and for spinning supplies for squaws; and in 1669 the Commissioners spent £10 of Company money for powder for proselytes "greatly distressed by the Mohawks." The distribution of firepower to praying Indians was controversial. The corporation, which heretofore had assigned only a donated "musket and fowling piece" to the natives, wondered why the proselytes were responsible for their own defense. "We . . . are of the opinion," Robert Boyle told the Commissioners in a 1669 letter that he apparently never sent, "that the colony in which those Indians are is . . . bound to protect them."[24]

The modesty of firearms allocations in the mid- to late 1660s indicates that the magistrates also had reservations about the practice. On several earlier occasions, the Commissioners and the General Court had tried (with little evidence of success) to control the flow of arms and ammunition to natives, whether Christian or not. From time to time the authorities made exceptions. Prior to the act of submission, Massachusetts Bay gave Cutshamekin, Masconononomo, and the Squaw Sachem permission to possess firearms; and in 1648 and 1649, the court and the Commissioners issued Eliot two marked guns, plus two pounds of powder and six pounds of shot, for distribution to Christian Indians as he saw fit. The magistrates otherwise took a firm stand against the Indians and against Eliot, a strong advocate of arming the proselytes, most of whom lived in exposed locations. At some point in the late 1640s or early 1650s, Massachusetts Bay sent soldiers to Neponset to disarm the residents. In 1654 and 1655 Eliot asked the United Colonies to allocate powder and shot to the praying Indians. The Commissioners told him that "many Indian professors" were "loose and false," and they turned his requests over to the Bay Colony. The court's published records contain no mention of action on the matter.[25]

In the mid-1660s, the alliance against the Mohawks lost several of its members. In 1666 the Mahicans made peace with the Mohawks at a New York–brokered conference at Hartford. Pennacook,

Pocumtuck, and Sokoki delegates to the conference refused to join the Mahicans in the treaty. In 1667 the Mohawks negotiated a peace with New France, which had twice sent regiments into their territory in 1666. The soldiers did little damage but convinced the Iroquois of French power. The French withdrawal from the alliance, however, did not end the resolve of the remaining Indians.

The number and identity of the Algonquian participants in the expedition against the Mohawks in 1669 are difficult to determine. Gookin said that "about six or seven hundred men ... marched into the Mohawks' country," whereas Jean Pierron, a Jesuit missionary who witnessed some of the hostilities, estimated that the attacking party consisted of 300 natives, including 25 women. If these two sets of numbers are accurate, and if Gookin's figure represents the size of the force that left New England, then there were significant defections during the long march into Iroquoia. The participants in the raid surely included Sokokis, Eastern Abenakis, and Pocumtucks. Eliot stated that "many ... non-praying" Pennacooks, including the Pantucket Indians, were involved in the "imprudent expedition"; and that Numphow and an unspecified number of Wamesits also took part because they wanted to avenge the murder of Numphow's brother and because they had been "stirred up" by the "northern sachems," who were evidently the Eastern Abenakis because the Apostle explicitly distinguished these "northern sachems" from the pagan Pennacooks. Eliot and Gookin tried and failed to discourage the Wamesits and Pantuckets from participating in the raid. The Wamesits fared better on the expedition than the Pantuckets. Eliot reported that Numphow "had such about him, and was so circumspect, that he came off well, though he lost one principal man," and that the Pantuckets and other pagan Pennacooks lost "many sachems and men of note."[26]

The participants in the expedition were not limited to longtime partners in the anti-Mohawk alliance. In March 1669, five months before the attack, Springfield's John Pynchon reported that the Pocumtucks and other Indians in the Connecticut Valley were "contriving to get strength to go against the Mohawks" and that they had sent delegates to various southern New England groups, including the praying Indians in the Bay Colony. As Salisbury explains, this diplomatic initiative was undertaken because the bands in the Valley were alarmed by a growing bond between the Mohawks and the Mohegans. The delegations met with mixed results. No Narragansetts, Eastern Niantics, or

Pokanokets are known to have taken part in the expedition, but Josias Wompatuck and an unspecified number of followers clearly did take part. Whether these Massachusetts had responded to the March initiative, or to a similar one, is uncertain. The sachem's role in the venture remains mysterious. Gookin called Josias "the chiefest general" of the expedition, while Eliot said that he went on it "rashly . . . and without due attendants and assistance." It is difficult to imagine that Sokokis, Eastern Abenakis, Pocumtucks, and Pennacooks marched forth from New England under the command of Josias, who was almost certainly a latecomer to the alliance. The most plausible way of harmonizing Gookin and Eliot is to say that Josias was not "the chiefest general" when he embarked on the expedition, but became such once the fighting began. By all accounts, the sachem fought bravely until his death.[27]

The extent to which praying Indians—other than the ones at Wamesit—were involved in the raid is an open question. The Apostle never commented on the matter, and Gookin claimed that he and Eliot had so "cautioned" the proselytes "that not above five of them went." Gookin did not specify the place of residence of the five or fewer exceptions. His claim is manifestly false if he intended it to include Wamesit, and it is probably false even if he meant it to refer to Christian Indians in other locations. Most and probably all of the old praying towns and the future new ones were alarmed by the Mohawks, even though Wamesit was apparently the only settlement with a long-standing involvement in the alliance. The Pawtuckets at Nashobah had suffered the loss of John Thomas's father. Gookin noted that prior to the expedition, the Mohawks had been "in hostility" with the Nipmucks, including those at Quabag and Nashaway, and had also been "at some other [unidentified] praying towns" but had "never shot a bullet or arrow at any person near those towns." He explicitly excluded Natick and Hassanamesit, explaining that the Iroquois had "never [been] seen" near the two settlements before the 1669 expedition. The fact that the Mohawks attacked Natick and Hassanamesit after King Philip's War, however, may indicate that there were tensions in the 1660s that Gookin failed to detect. Although the sources permit no conclusive judgment about the matter, it seems likely that persons from at least some of these settlements chose to strike at the Mohawks when the opportunity for concerted action arose in 1669. Evidence to this effect surfaced in 1675, when Monoco of Nashaway remarked that James Rumney Marsh, a Nipmuck proselyte, was a "valiant man" who had "been with me in the war with the Mohawks."[28]

The destination of the expedition was the easternmost fortified Mohawk village, Caughnawaga (Gandaouague), located on the Mohawk River northeast of Schenectady, some 200 miles from the Massachusetts coast. Gookin, Eliot, and Pierron wrote accounts of the attack, which took place at dawn on August 18, 1669. Gookin said that the New England Indians conducted their westward march poorly: they had no carriages for their ammunition and food, they lingered in native villages along the way, and they wasted ammunition in displays of bravado. The siege of Caughnawaga lasted for several days; the fort held fast and few persons died on either side. The Algonquians, short on food and ammunition and suffering from illness, then retreated toward the coast. The Mohawks left the fort, took a detour, and ambushed the Indians twenty or thirty miles away. Josias lost his life in the ensuing battle. Eliot reported that the sachem fought "valiantly and . . . fell alone" after "being deserted by all (some knowingly say through treason)." He also stated, surely inaccurately, that if Josias had been supported by "ten men, yea five in good order with him, he would have driven all his enemies before him." Pierron said that the victorious Mohawks returned to the fort with nineteen scalps and ten prisoners. The Iroquois claimed to have killed "nearly a hundred warriors" in the battle; Algonquian survivors interviewed by Gookin said that "about fifty of their chief men . . . were slain in this fight." Pierron catechized and baptized the Mohawks' prisoners before they were executed.[29]

The expedition's outcome invigorated the missions at Wamesit and Pantucket. Eliot and Gookin visited the settlements each spring from 1670 until King Philip's War. During the first of these visits, the Apostle told the surviving Pennacooks to "take notice of" the "over-ruling hand of God" in their defeat. That same year, as if to reinforce Eliot's point, Mohawks attacked a small party of Wamesits outside the town, killing several and scalping a girl who managed to survive through the ministrations of "an ancient and skillful woman" at Woburn. The Pantuckets "bow[ed] their ears to hear and submit to pray unto God" in 1670, and Eliot promptly sent Peter Jethro, a Nipmuck Indian and occasional Natick resident, to be their teacher. Wamesit also added two teachers, Samuel Numphow and Simon Beckom, and a second ruler, John Lyne. Wannalancett, whose role in the expedition against the Mohawks is unknown, began attending Eliot's annual lectures in 1670. In 1674 the sachem promised to forsake his "old canoe and embark in a new canoe" and to attend the regular worship services conducted by the native teachers at Wamesit.[30]

Eliot revived the dormant mission to the Pennacooks at about the same time that he and his native associates resumed their work among the Nipmuck bands in central Massachusetts. By the time of King Philip's War, seven new praying towns and two semiofficial ones had been established among these Nipmucks.

The New Praying Towns and the Settlements at Quabag and Nashaway

The Apostle made four known trips into the heart of the "Nipmuck Country" between the late 1640s and the mid-1650s. The first came in 1649, when he traveled to Quobagud (now East Brookfield) to visit an "aged sachem" who had asked him to "come thither . . . and live there." Three years later Eliot set out for the Quinebaug (Mohegan) River to meet with a Nipmuck sachem, Pummakummin, who had come to Boston in October 1651 and "offered himself and his men to worship God." Although heavy rains prevented him from reaching the Quinebaug, the Apostle was pleased by the results of the journey. "All the Indians we met with and came among," he explained, "had some savor of the Gospel and had sometimes come and heard the word [at Nonantum, Neponset, and Natick], and our coming unto them was very gladly accepted." Eliot returned to the area in 1655, on this occasion traveling through to the Connecticut River, and again in 1656, in a trip cut short by "wars of the Indians" (probably between the Narragansetts and the Mohegans).[31]

By the mid-1650s two old praying towns, Hassanamesit and Okommakamesit, had been created in the Nipmuck Country. The mission elsewhere in the region languished until the late 1660s. The reasons for the neglect are not spelled out in the sources. In the interim, Eliot was devoting much of his attention to his Massachusett translations. Moreover, native missionaries were probably hesitant to venture deep into the Nipmuck Country because of its well-deserved reputation for danger. Narragansetts and Mohegans raided various Nipmuck villages in the late 1650s and the 1660s, and Mohawk marauders were active as well.[32] The same or similar factors doubtless help to explain why the missions at Wamesit and Pantucket were neglected during the same period.

The event that renewed the Nipmuck mission was the submission of eight sachems to the General Court in May 1668. This action, which has received little scholarly attention because many of the pertinent sources are unpublished, came about because the Indians wanted protection from raiding parties and release from tribute payments. An acceptance of the mission and a submission to the General Court was the price the natives paid for obtaining these objectives.

The submissions of 1668 directly resulted from a Narragansett raid. In August 1667 Quaiapen, sister of Ninigret and widow of Canonicus's son Mixan, sent her men to attack a Nipmuck village at Quantisset (now Pomfret, Connecticut). The Narragansetts killed several persons, destroyed cornfields, and carried off guns, powder and shot, and wampum. Delegates from the Quantissets then went to Eliot and offered to "submit to God" and to the General Court so that the colony could "protect them" like "the other praying Indians." The Apostle soon informed Governor Richard Bellingham and the Massachusetts council about the matter. In October the colony arranged a meeting in Boston between the rival parties. The Narragansett representatives claimed that they launched the raid because the Quantisset Nipmucks had failed to pay them tribute and also "named their deceased sachem [Mixan], which is a great crime with them, and ... sent scurrilous messages to their sachem, and robbed some of their people." The Quantissets denied that they had done any of these things; insisted that they were not subject to the Narragansetts, suggesting that an "uninterested" sachem, Metacom (King Philip) of the Pokanokets, be asked if they were Narragansett tributaries; and repeated the offer to accept the mission and submit to the General Court. The Massachusetts Bay magistrates then told the Narragansetts that if they could prove that the Quantisset Indians were their subjects, the colony would determine "how much tribute the Nipmucks ... shall pay ... from time to time in the future." The magistrates also promised to arrange another hearing about the matter.[33]

The Bay Colony scheduled the second meeting for May 8, 1668, and sent notification to both parties about the date. Captain Tom and Job Kattananit brought eight Nipmuck sachems to Boston for the occasion. The sachems represented four future new praying towns (Quantisset, Chabanakongkomun, Wabquisset, and Manchage) and two other settlements (Asukodnoeog and Resepusqus) that I am unable to identify. Shortly before the scheduled date, the Narragansetts asked Roger Williams to furnish the proof requested by Massachusetts Bay. In a letter dated May 7, 1668, Williams told the General Court that the Quantissets were "unquestionably subject to the Narragansett sachems" and that he had "abundant and daily proof of it." This letter was written too late to have any bearing on the proceedings, however, and besides, the Narragansetts failed to show up on the appointed date. On May 9 the eight Nipmuck sachems formally pledged to "give up ourselves . . . to God" and to "submit ourselves to the government of the Massachusetts." The Narragansetts did not arrive until May 13, explaining that the colony's written notice about the meeting had been delayed in the delivery. By this time the Nipmucks had returned to their villages. Thus confronted with a fait accompli, the Narragansetts agreed to surrender their jurisdictional claim and to return the stolen goods, provided the Nipmucks demonstrated "the reality [of] . . . their profession to pray to God and be in subjection unto . . . Massachusetts Bay."[34]

The consolidation of the Nipmuck mission was primarily the work of Natick and Hassanamesit Indians. The Apostle apparently went into the Nipmuck Country on only three occasions between the 1668 act of submission and the start of King Philip's War. In the spring of 1669, he traveled through the area en route to the Connecticut River. Eliot failed to explain what he accomplished during the trip. In the summer of 1673, he and Gookin appointed Captain Tom the ruler, and Black James the constable, over "five or six or seven [unspecified new] towns." Gookin authorized Black James to "suppress drunkenness, sabbath-breaking, [and] especially powwowing and idolatry" and instructed him to bring persons who had committed "smaller faults" to Captain Tom at Hassanamesit. Cases of "idolatry and powwowing" were to be sent directly to Gookin for adjudication. The two Puritans returned to the area in September 1674, when they assigned teachers or approved existing ones for all seven settlements.[35]

Little is known about the seven new towns. Quantisset, the leader in the submissions of 1668, was appropriately the first one formed. In the fall of 1669, Eliot told Boyle that the Quantisset Indians were "newly come in to pray unto God" and that Joseph Tuckawillipin and Monotunkquanit, the teachers at Hassanamesit some twenty-five miles away, had agreed to provide them with occasional instruction.

The Remaining Praying Towns · 157

These two men remained the town's nonresident teachers at least through 1670. In 1674 a Natick Indian, Daniel, began to serve as the teacher to Quantisset's twenty families. This "sober and pious young man" was probably Daniel Tokkohwompait, the future pastor of the Natick church. Eliot and Gookin did not stop at Quantisset, which was located about seventy-five miles from Boston, during their 1674 journey into the Nipmuck Country. Their lifelong silence about the settlement's physical features suggests that neither man ever went there. Pakachoog and Chabanakongkomun were the next new towns to be created, in both cases around 1672. The former was situated some seven miles northwest of Hassanamesit, in present-day Auburn; and the latter twenty miles northeast of Quantisset, near modern Webster and Dudley. Twenty families were living at Pakachoog, and nine at Chabanakongkomun, when Eliot and Gookin visited the two settlements in 1674. The nonresident teacher at Pakachoog was James Speene of Hassanamesit; the "rulers . . . coordinate in power" were two local sagamores, John and Solomon; and the constable was Matoonas, whose son the colony had executed in 1671 for murdering an Englishman near Dedham in April of that year. The teacher at Chabanakongkomun was a transplanted Hassanamesit Indian, Joseph (the brother of Sampson). Black James also lived in this settlement.[36]

The order of creation of the four remaining new towns cannot be specified. Wabquisset (near North Woodstock, Connecticut) was located some four or five miles north of Quantisset. Eliot and Gookin stopped by the settlement in 1674. A large boulder called "Eliot's Rock," from which the Apostle is said to have preached, still stands in the area. At the time thirty families were living at Wabquisset. Gookin reported that the resident teacher, Sampson, had been "a few years since, a dissolute person" but was now "sober and pious" and that the town's unidentified sagamore "inclines to religion, and keeps the meeting on sabbath days at his house." The establishment of the Wabquisset mission alarmed Uncas. During the 1674 visit, Eliot and Gookin were accosted by an "agent for Uncas," who challenged the colony's "right to, and dominion over, the people of Wabquisset." Gookin replied that the settlement was "within the jurisdiction" of Massachusetts—a claim the Bay Colony advanced until 1749, when it conceded the area to Connecticut—and that the local Indians had submitted to the General Court. The Superintendent then explained that he and Eliot "did not meddle with civil right or jurisdiction" or "intend . . . to abridge the Indian sachems of their just and ancient rights over the Indians, in respect of paying tribute or any other dues." The latter statement probably dismayed the Wabquissets, who surely viewed their submission to the government as a way of escaping tribute payments to Uncas. Manchage, another of the new towns, now Sutton, was about midway between Chabanakongkomun and Hassanamesit. Most of the town's twelve families were away when Eliot and Gookin dropped by in 1674. An obscure Indian, Waabesktamin, served as the town's teacher. Maanexit (now Thompson, Connecticut) was about seven miles south of Chabanakongkomun. During their 1674 visit, the two Puritans appointed John Moqua, who became a prominent Natick resident after the war, the town's teacher. At this time there were twenty families in the settlement. Waeuntug (Mendon, Uxbridge) stood on the west bank of the Blackstone (Nipmuck) River ten miles south of Hassanamesit, across from the recently settled English town of Mendon. The town's nonresident teachers were two Hassanamesit Indians, James the Printer and Sasomet. Gookin stated that he had never been to Waeuntug and provided no population figures for it.[37]

In his *Historical Collections,* Gookin debated whether or not to list two other Nipmuck areas, Nashaway (Lancaster) and Quabag (Brookfield), as praying towns. He chose to exclude them, even though the local Indians were "coming on to receive the Gospel," because they were "not fully settled." Gookin failed to explain how he defined "settled." The official new towns were not settled in the sense that they had received grants of land from the General Court. Gookin wrote that the court "intended shortly" to do so; the colony's published records contain no evidence that any such awards were made before King Philip's War.[38] In any event, Nashaway and Quabag had longer missionary pedigrees than any of the new praying towns. Nashowanon of Nashaway and Wossamegon of Quabag had submitted to the General Court in 1644; in addition, Eliot had made four trips to Nashaway in the summer of 1648, and he had visited Quobagud, one of the villages around Quabag, to speak to the "aged sachem" in 1649.

Missionary activity in and around Quabag was virtually nonexistent. There is no conclusive evidence that Eliot returned to the area after he visited the "aged sachem" in 1649, and his native evangelists were probably reluctant to travel there. A mission field was established at the Quabag village of Putikookuppog (now Fiskdale), although the underlying circumstances are not clear. According to two sources written in 1715, two Putikookuppog sachems, Wattalloowkin and Nakin, gave or sold 1,000 acres of land to the Apostle in September 1655. Nine years later Eliot asked for and received from the General Court a grant "not exceeding" 4,000 acres for the Putikookuppog Indians. The court dispatched surveyors, but nothing more appears in the published sources.[39]

Otherwise the Quabag Nipmucks appear in the missionary record only when they appealed to Eliot or to Massachusetts Bay for protection against Uncas. The best-documented episode occurred in early March 1661, when the Mohegans killed three natives around Quabag, carried off five captives, and stole the Indians' valuables. One of the local sachems went to Eliot, who was at Natick at the time, and explained to him that he was among the five sachems who had submitted to the General Court in March 1644 under the "name of Ousamequin [Wossamegon], though now his name be changed to Matchippa." Eliot decided to intervene in the matter, even though he did not know if the sachem was being truthful about his identity—a telling indication of the Apostle's unfamiliarity with the Quabag Indians. Eliot wrote a letter to Governor John Endecott and asked the alleged Wossamegon to deliver it. The letter explained that the victims "crave[d] the benefit of your promise which you made them at the time of their submission, viz., protection."[40]

Eliot's letter led to two actions, one by Massachusetts Bay and the other by the Commissioners of the United Colonies. In May 1661 the General Court sent Uncas a letter demanding the return of the captives and the restitution of the stolen property, warning him that the colony would "war upon him" if he refused to comply. The court also directed Simon Willard and several soldiers to go to Quabag, remain there for several days, and discharge their weapons at regular intervals to "terrify the enemies of Wossamegon." In September 1661 the confederation informed Uncas in a letter that they supported the Bay Colony's threatened aggression. Shortly thereafter, the Commissioners learned from Connecticut's John Mason that Uncas "was altogether ignorant that they were subjects belonging to the Massachusetts and further that they were none of Wossamegon's men but belonging to ... his deadly enemy" Onopequin, a Pocumtuck sachem later killed by the Mohawks. Mason also reported that Uncas had returned the captives; he said nothing about the stolen goods. The matter evidently came to rest at this point.[41]

Like the Quabag villages, Nashaway and its sister settlement at nearby Weshakim (now Sterling) were neglected during the prewar period. Whether or not the Apostle returned to the area after the four 1648 visits to Nashowanon is uncertain. The only evidence that he may have done so was in 1654, when the Assistants and Deputies asked him to go with Increase Nowell to Nashaway and Weshakim:

> Whereas Nashowanon . . . is lately dead, and another is suddenly to be chosen in his room, they being a great people who have submitted to this jurisdiction [in 1644], this court does order that [Eliot and Nowell] . . . direct them in their choice, their eyes being upon two or three which are of the blood, one whereof is a very debauched, drunken fellow, and no friend to the English; another of them is very hopeful to learn the things of Christ. If, therefore, these gentlemen may, by way of persuasion or counsel, not by compulsion, prevail with them for the choice of such a one as may be most fit, it would be a good service to the country.

It is unclear whether Eliot and Nowell made the journey.[42]

Eliot's proselytes made one or two attempts to instruct the Nashaway and Weshakim Nipmucks. In August 1664 the Apostle reported that the local Indians had recently asked Natick to provide a teacher. The request was almost certainly the result of a missionary visit that Piumbuhhou had made to "his kindred and friends" at Nashaway. Whether a teacher was sent at the time is not known. Ten years later Eliot and Gookin asked Peter Jethro to instruct the Nashaway and Weshakim Indians. To prepare the way for him, Gookin sent a letter to the local sachem, Sagamore Sam, that stressed the evils of sabbath-breaking, drunkenness, and "whoredom and powwowing." Sam had recently succeeded Nashowanon's late nephew Sagamore Matthew; the former may have been the "debauched, drunken" candidate in 1654 and the latter the "hopeful" one. At this time Gookin also appointed a Nashaway Indian to the office of constable and authorized him to "apprehend drunkards, and take away their strong drink, and bring the delinquents before me to receive punishment." This unidentified native accepted the office on the condition that the Nashaway and Weshakim Indians approved his commission.[43]

The Nashaway area was one of the centers of anti-English militance during King Philip's War: Sagamore Sam and Monoco were two of the Nipmuck leaders during the conflict; Peter Jethro, who was presumably at Nashaway when the war began, likewise joined the native cause. The Nipmuck leadership also included Matoonas and Sagamore John of Pakachoog as well as Mattaumpe of the Quabag-area town of Wekabaug (now West Brookfield). Matoonas commanded the first known Nipmuck attack on an English town, the raid on Mendon on July 14, 1675.[44] Peter Jethro, Matoonas, and Sagamore John appear in the prewar missionary sources; Monoco, Sagamore Sam, and Mattaumpe do not.

In time the hostile Nipmuck bands contained (as Gookin put it) "most" of the natives in the new towns as well as prominent residents of several old ones. Many of the defections in the old towns took place in early November 1675, when Mattaumpe, Sagamores Sam and John, Matoonas, Monoco, and about 300 other bellicose Indians confronted 200 proselytes—50 of whom were men, "for the most part unarmed"—outside Hassanamesit and pressured them into joining their ranks. The praying Indians, who came primarily from Hassanamesit and Magunkog, included Captain Tom and his son Nehemiah, James the Printer, Joseph Tuckawillipin, William of Sudbury, the brothers Sampson and Joseph, and Pomham. Job Kattananit and James Speene, who were standing off to the side at the time, managed to escape. How willingly Captain Tom and the others defected to the Nipmuck side, and how actively they fought against the English, were debated questions at the time and remain so today. Gookin provided a spirited defense of the defectors in his *Historical Account of the Doings and Sufferings of the Christian Indians in New England* (1677).[45]

These individuals met various fates during and after the war. Massachusetts Bay executed Sagamore Sam, Monoco, Mattaumpe, and Captain Tom (the latter over the protests of Eliot, Gookin, and leading praying Indians). Sagamore John brought Matoonas to Boston in July 1676 and shot him to death with the colony's permission. John was then assigned as a slave to Thomas Prentice of Cambridge; the Indian escaped during the following winter. Peter Jethro was pardoned, but his pagan father, Old Jethro, whom he had turned over to the authorities, was executed. Sampson was killed in battle by Christian Indians, and his brother Joseph was captured by Plymouth, sold into slavery in Jamaica, and retrieved by Eliot. James the Printer received a pardon; after the war, he helped set the type for the second edition of the Indian Bible and also preached at Hassanamesit. Joseph Tuckawillipin, William of Sudbury, and Captain Tom's son Nehemiah were also pardoned. Pomham's fate is unknown.[46]

The problem of Nipmuck bellicosity has received little scholarly attention, probably because of the paucity of relevant sources. Philip Ranlet does not address the problem in his article "Another Look at the Causes of King Philip's War." Salisbury and Jennings evaluate the matter only in passing: the former attributes the Nipmucks' militance to "economic, political, and cultural pressures on Indian autonomy," and the latter blames the mission. "If further proof is needed that Eliot's proselytizing had been forcible and resented," Jennings writes, "the rising of the Nipmuck 'converts' should be evidence enough."[47]

Salisbury's "economic, political, and cultural pressures" on Nipmuck autonomy were probably not strong enough to provoke armed aggression. This point can be illustrated by comparing the Nipmuck Country with Plymouth Colony, where the pressures on Metacom and the Pokanokets were severe. First of all, there was little prewar English settlement in the extensive Nipmuck territories in central Massachusetts. Sudbury was created in the late 1630s, Lancaster in the mid-1640s, Marlborough in the mid-1650s, Brookfield and Mendon in the mid-1660s, and Worcester on the eve of the war. All of these towns were small settlements with large numbers of nonresident shareholders. Thus in contrast to Plymouth, there was no rising tide of English expansion in the Nipmuck Country. Second, the Massachusetts General Court showed little inclination to restrict the Nipmucks' political autonomy. There were no known counterparts to the disarmings and interrogations by magistrates that helped drive the Pokanokets to violence. Gookin, the court's representative to the praying Indians, seldom set foot in the Nipmuck settlements: he evidently visited five of the new towns only once or twice, and Quantisset, Waeuntug, Quabag, and Nashaway never at all. He preferred to exercise his authority through native officials—Captain Tom and Black James in the new towns and the unidentified constable at Nashaway. The former two were commissioned only in 1673, and the latter not until 1674. Moreover, it is unlikely that these three natives aggressively asserted the court's authority: they were not accompanied by English troops, and they could not assume that the colony would send soldiers to protect them from refractory Indians.[48]

Jennings's explanation for his assertion is also unconvincing. His conclusion that "Eliot's proselytizing" was "forcible" rests on his dubious supposition that the Nipmucks were evangelized at gunpoint by native missionaries whom Eliot had armed for this purpose.[49] Moreover, the Nipmucks were hardly engaging in a collective act of apostasy, if this is what Jennings means by placing the word "converts" in quotation marks. These Indians had barely been Christianized at the time the war began: Quantisset, Wabquisset, Manchage, Maanexit, Nashaway, and Chabanakongkomun were without resident teachers until 1674, and Pakachoog, Waeuntug, and the Quabag-area villages had none at all. Nevertheless, Jennings may be right that the Nipmucks "resented" the mission, even if he is wrong about the reason for the resentment. The Indians in the seven new towns probably did not wish to be evangelized. There is no evidence that they had asked for the resident and nonresident teachers assigned them between 1669 and 1674, that they had invited Eliot and Gookin to visit their homeland in 1673 and 1674, and that they had requested the appointment of Captain Tom and Black James in 1673. Eliot and Gookin presumably justified these actions on the basis of the 1668 submission, which obliged the signatories and their bands to receive instruction in exchange for protection from Quaiapen's Narragansetts. But no sachems from three of the new towns—Pakachoog, Maanexit, and Waeuntug—signed the act of submission, and the signatories from the other four towns may have seen no need for a mission once the problem with Quaiapen had been solved. Eliot and Gookin, moreover, did nothing to sweeten the pot: there is no evidence that they distributed English consumer goods to the Indians in the new towns.

With some adjustments the same argument applies to Nashaway and Weshakim (the Quabag Indians were apparently never assigned a teacher or constable). Nashowanon submitted to the government in 1644 in order to receive protection from marauders, and he accepted the mission in 1648 after Massachusetts Bay had sent soldiers to protect him in the aftermath of a raid (discussed in Chapter 3). Eliot's inability to sustain the Nashaway mission after 1648 probably pleased Nashowanon and his successors because the colony had already demonstrated its readiness to protect them. The attempt to revive the mission at Nashaway in 1674 may have been unwelcome: Gookin did not indicate that the natives had requested the teacher and constable assigned them in 1674, or that any English goods were given to the Indians.

It is also possible that the mission had little to do with the Nip-

164 · *The Remaining Praying Towns*

mucks' belligerence. The Indians had other grievances against the English. Two obvious cases in point were Matoonas, whose son the colony had executed in 1671, and the Okommakamesits, whose quarrels with Marlborough have already been noted. Furthermore, there is evidence of native displeasure about the land transactions that created the English towns in the Nipmuck Country. In 1643 or 1644 an unidentified Nashaway "sagamore" (surely Nashowanon) sold the land for Lancaster, and in 1667 the General Court authorized the town to buy additional acreage from the "sagamore of Nashaway," evidently Matthew. The bellicose Sagamore Sam may not have profited from the English acquisition of this territory. In 1648 the Sudbury settlers paid £5 to a local sachem for the town's land. The sachem, who was probably Old Jethro, could scarcely have been satisfied with such paltry compensation. In 1662 four Indians, two from Punkapoag and two from Natick, sold some or all of the future Mendon to two Braintree men for £24 (the speculators transferred their interest to residents of Mendon in 1670). The Nipmucks at nearby Waeuntug apparently did not benefit from this transaction. In 1665 a Wekabaug sachem, Shattoockquis, sold the land for Brookfield to a Springfield man for 300 fathoms of wampum; eight years later the purchaser assigned the title to residents of Brookfield. Mattaumpe, another Wekabaug sachem, may have felt cheated. The deed for Brookfield states that he "challeng[ed] some interest in the land above sold" but "consented to the sale" after receiving "part of the pay." In July 1674 Gookin and several other proprietors bought the land for Worcester from Sagamores John and Solomon of Pakachoog. The deed called for the purchasers to surrender 26 shillings in cloth and £12 in cash. The cloth was delivered at the time the sale took place; "full payment" of the money, however, was not made until after the war.[50]

An alternative explanation centers on the Nipmucks' well-known contempt for Uncas, who after flirting with the Pokanokets decided to join the English cause in King Philip's War. On June 28, 1675, about a week after the war began in Plymouth, the Massachusetts magistrates reported that they had recently sent delegates to Pakachoog, Maanexit, Wabquisset, Quantisset, Chabanakongkomun, Quabag, Hassanamesit, and Manchage. The local sachems promised to be "faithful to the English" and "not [to] assist Philip." Uncas committed to the Puritan side on or about July 9, when he sent six braves to Boston "to assure his friendship and offer his service against Philip." The Nipmuck attack on Mendon occurred less than a week later.[51]

Any attempt to explain the problem of Nipmuck belligerency is highly speculative. Based on the evidence presented above, the following reconstruction is the most plausible. The natives feared that the birth of an unwelcome mission meant that stronger assertions of magisterial authority and increased English settlement would soon follow. Their past grievances against the colony gave them special reason to dread this prospect. The Nipmucks vacillated until Uncas entered the conflict. They did not become bellicose because the English had already stripped them of their political autonomy and seized much of their land, or because Eliot's native evangelists had intimidated them into accepting the mission.

An Overview of the Praying Towns

By the time of King Philip's War, the mission had reached many of the native groups in the coastal and south central portions of the colony. Eliot wrote in 1671 that "all the Massachusetts pray" to God. Most of them resided at Natick or at Punkapoag; the rest lived in other praying towns or in English communities. Eliot also indicated at the time that "a large part" of the Nipmucks were participating in his program. Three of the old towns (Hassanamesit, Okommakamesit, and Magunkog) and all seven of the new ones, as well as Quabag and Nashaway, were Nipmuck settlements. The mission was less well established among the Pawtuckets, who lived to the north and east of Boston, and among the Pennacooks in the Merrimack Valley. "To the north and east I have not conversed far, not above thirty or forty miles," Eliot wrote in 1669. His successes among the Pawtuckets and Pennacooks were apparently limited to the Indians at Nashobah, Wamesit, and Pantucket.[52]

There were approximately seventy people living in each of the old towns in 1674, and roughly ninety in each of the six new ones for which Gookin supplied figures. Most if not all of the fourteen praying towns were located in sites chosen by the residents. Natick and Punkapoag were the desired locations for the Nonantum and Neponset Indians, respectively; the Hassanamesits lived at "the place of their desires"; Nashobah was a "chief place of residence" for Pawtucket

Indians; and Wamesit was "an ancient and capital seat" for the Pennacooks. Okommakamesit was doubtless on or near a traditional Nipmuck village because Owussumag, William of Sudbury, and Captain Tom were from the area. The new towns were clearly the places where the Indians were living when they were missionized, rather than places to which they had been relocated.[53]

Many of the settlements were located on or near major Indian trails (see Map 1). Natick, Magunkog, Hassananamesit, Manchage, Chabanakongkomun, Maanexit, Wabquisset, and Quantisset lay on or within a few miles of the Great Trail (the "Old Connecticut Path"). The Bay Path ("Springfield Bay Path") branched off from the Great Trail west of Chabanakongkomun and then continued through the Quabag area to Springfield. The Nipmuck Trail began in New London, crossed the Great Trail west of Quantisset and Wabquisset, and eventually joined the Bay Path. The Narragansett Trail ("Providence Path") started in Providence, intersected the Nipmuck Trail south of Quantisset, and continued westward to the Great Trail. Okommakamesit, Nashaway, Weshakim, and several Quabag villages were located on what John Winthrop, Sr., called "the new way" to Connecticut, as opposed to the old one, the Great Trail. Punkapoag, Nashobah, Wamesit, Pakachoog, and Waeuntug were the only old or new towns that lay six or more miles from one of these thoroughfares.[54]

The General Court awarded land to the seven old towns. These grants ranged in size from 2,500 acres (Wamesit) to 8,000 (Hassanamesit and Nashobah). None of the new towns had received awards by the time the war began. Gookin said that the land at Punkapoag was "not generally as good as in other [old] towns," which he variously characterized as "very fertile" (Magunkog), "good" (Okommakamesit), "well-tempered and watered" (Hassanamesit), "well stored with meadows and woods" (Nashobah), and "fertile" (Wamesit). He also praised the quality of the land at Manchage, Chabanakongkomun, Maanexit, Wabquisset, and Pakachoog; he was silent about Waeuntug and Quantisset, two towns he never visited.[55] Prewar English settlements were located within seven or eight miles of seven of the official praying towns—Natick (Dedham, Medfield, Sherborn, Sudbury), Okommakamesit (Marlborough), Wamesit (Chelmsford, Billerica, Dunstable), Punkapoag (Dorchester, Weymouth, Milton, Dedham, Braintree), Nashobah (Groton), Waeuntug

(Mendon), and Pakachoog (Worcester)—as well as Nashaway and Weshakim (Lancaster) and Quabag (Brookfield).

The proselytes in all fourteen settlements followed the traditional pursuits of "planting corn, fishing, [and] hunting." The Nipmucks in the new towns probably relied exclusively on these time-honored subsistence activities, while the residents of most of the old ones also developed nontraditional forms of plant and animal husbandry. The Natick, Punkapoag, Hassanamesit, and Magunkog Indians kept cattle and swine; Natick also had goats and oxen, and Magunkog horses; Natick, Hassanamesit, Nashobah, and Okommakamesit maintained orchards; and Natick, Hassanamesit, and Nashobah grew other crops besides corn. Gookin praised the Hassanamesit Indians for their diligence, stating that they even surpassed Natick in this respect. Hassanamesit and Natick were the only two settlements known to have constructed English-style buildings prior to the war (in Hassanamesit's case, a meetinghouse and several homes). Gookin was particularly disturbed by the Wamesits, whom he considered the most indolent of the old-town Indians. His account of the town mentions no livestock or European forms of agriculture. But Wamesit differed from Natick and Hassanamesit only in degree, not in kind. Gookin lamented that all the old-town Indians "fall very short of the English both in diligence and providence."[56]

The residents of the old towns participated in the English economy in three ways. First, they sold products of their labor. The Punkapoag and possibly the Magunkog Indians marketed cedar shingles and clapboards to the English, who "chose rather to buy [from] . . . the Indians than make them themselves"; the Natick Indians received seed money to begin cottage industries in "spinning or other manufactory" in 1662; and John Josselyn noted later in the decade that the hogs raised by praying Indians "are counted the best in New England." Second, the proselytes worked as laborers for the English, particularly during the 1660s, when the Mohawk threat drove them closer to the colonists. As Gookin wrote, "necessity forced them to labor with the English in hoeing, reaping, picking hops, cutting wood, making hay, and making stone fences, and like necessary employments." Third, the natives served as apprentices, though not to the extent that the saints desired. Gookin explained that Indian parents were "generally so indulgent of their children that they are not easily persuaded to put them forth to the English." In 1660 the Commissioners offered parents various material inducements "to put their children apprentices"; the following year, the General Court encouraged the self-proclaimed Wossamegon and the other beleaguered Quabag Indians to surrender some of their children "as an assured token of their hearty love and fidelity to the English" for solving their problem with Uncas; and in 1674 Gookin devised a scheme that combined apprenticeships for boys and girls with education in English schools. It was not until after the war, however, that appreciable numbers of children began to serve in the desired capacity.[57]

By the time of King Philip's War, Eliot had introduced Natick's numerical system of civil government into an unspecified number of praying towns. He wrote in a 1673 letter that "we are expressly conformed to the Scriptures . . . to have rulers of ten, of fifty, of a hundred; we have yet gone no higher." He also explained in this letter that Gookin's duties included "ordain[ing] rulers of ten, of fifty, etc." Surviving sources, however, do not correlate specific Indian rulers with their numerical ranks except in the case of Natick in the early to mid-1650s. Gookin never used the numerical terms in *The Historical Collections* and *An Historical Account*, and Eliot's occasional allusions to the biblical polity after the mid-1650s are not illuminating. Gookin invariably referred to the native civil officials as "chief rulers" or "rulers" and as "constables," and Eliot usually did so as well. By 1674 the seven old towns had one or more rulers and constables, and the new town at Pakachoog had two rulers, Sagamores John and Solomon, as well as a constable, Matoonas. There is no evidence of Indians serving in either official capacity in the remaining new towns. None of the fourteen towns had one hundred men, and at least eight of them did not even have one hundred residents. The ruler of "a hundred" whom Eliot mentioned in the 1673 letter was probably Waban (if he inherited Cutshamekin's original title at Natick) or possibly Captain Tom, who had recently been appointed the ruler of the new towns.[58]

By 1675 all fourteen praying towns had resident or nonresident teachers conducting worship services on a regular or occasional basis. Natick and Hassanamesit, however, were the only towns with official churches before the war. The two native churches had full members who resided at Punkapoag, Nashobah, Okommakamesit, and Magunkog; these Indian saints were obliged to travel to Natick or Hassanamesit in order to partake of the Lord's Supper and to present their children for baptism. This arrangement bothered Eliot, who "moved and argued among the elders" in 1673 that qualified natives should be permitted to receive the sacraments in more conveniently located English churches. The elders rejected the argument, apparently because they questioned the proselytes' ability to understand English. No Wamesit Indians (including the teachers) or new-town Indians (save for the teachers) were known to have belonged to either native church. Eliot observed in 1670 that the Wamesits "have not much esteem for religion"; Gookin wrote after the war that the new-town Nipmucks had been "raw and lately initiated into the Christian profession." The Superintendent made a partial exception in the case of the Chabanakongkomun Indians, who were "better instructed in the worship of God, than [in] any of the other new praying towns."[59]

Instruction in the old and new towns was almost entirely the responsibility of Indians whom Eliot had educated for the purpose. "Their own nation trained up and schooled unto ability for the work," he wrote in 1673, "are the most likely instruments to carry on this work." This practice was both a virtue and a necessity. On the one hand, Eliot recognized that Indians were better suited for the task than colonists because the former knew the "language and ... manners" of natives.[60] On the other, he knew that few English ministers were willing to join him in the work of Indian instruction. Eliot did not expect his clerical colleagues to serve as resident teachers in the praying towns. He had considered doing so himself and rejected the idea for financial reasons. "The work is full of hardship, hard labor, and chargeable also, and the Indians not yet capable to give considerable support and maintenance," he explained in 1670, in a letter published in London in 1671 as the tenth and final Eliot tract, *A Brief Narrative of the Progress of the Gospel amongst the Indians in New England*. The Apostle had in mind three less demanding forms of missionary service. The first was for saints to follow his lead by learning an Algonquian dialect and instructing Indians on a part-time basis. Eliot, Jr., was probably the only other Bay Puritan in the prewar period who learned Massachusett well enough to deliver sermons in it. Two other Bay colonists started language training but never attained sufficient proficiency to do any preaching in it. One was Jonathan Ince, a 1650 graduate of Harvard (Eliot noted after Ince's premature death in 1657 that he had "a singular facility to learn and pronounce the Indian tongue, far better than I have"); the other was Joseph Eliot. The second type of service was to preach through one of the ever-growing number of English-speaking natives. Edmund Brown, minister at Sudbury, and Habbakuk Glover, Eliot's son-in-law, clearly preached to Indians in this manner, and Ince and several of the Apostle's sons probably did so as well. The missionary sources contain no other evidence of this form of activity in the prewar period. The third form of service was for ministers to take in bilingual Indian students and educate them for the ministry. Eliot made such a suggestion to the colony's clergy in 1670, apparently to no avail.[61]

The elders' overall lack of participation in the Indian work bothered Eliot. In a 1651 letter to Edward Winslow not written for publication in England, he lamented that "it is one discouragement to me . . . that so few look after what we do, or so much as ask me about it." In the early 1650s, however, the Apostle concealed the truth in his public sources. In *Tears of Repentance,* for instance, he praised the colonists for "the godly counsels and examples" that they had given the Christian Indians; and in "The learned Conjectures," he wrote that "I do perceive that the work of preaching to the Indians is generally accepted among the people of God." But by the early 1670s, he had become more outspoken about the absence of consistent clerical involvement in the mission, complaining about the matter in *A Brief Narrative* and in *Indian Dialogues* as well as in letters to the corporation and to the senior Thomas Mayhew.[62]

The Apostle should not have been surprised by this state of affairs. From the outset of the Indian work, the clergy had envisioned a native-run program of instruction. "God is wont ordinarily," Shepard wrote in 1646, "to convert nations and peoples by some of their own countrymen who are nearest to them and can best speak, and most of all pity, their brethren."[63] The colony's ministers were willing to help Eliot establish the mission by accompanying him on his journeys to Nonantum and Neponset, by assuming some of his pastoral duties at Roxbury, and by refereeing the Natick church examinations. But the elders were otherwise removed from the work. As explained in Chapter 1, the saints did not consider the evangelization of the Indians to be a "principal end" of colonization, only an incidental one. The lofty pronouncements about the centrality of missionary work that appeared in the Massachusetts charter and other official symbols of purpose were commonplaces in promotional literature, not views characteristically expressed by the founders in their personal statements of purpose. It was once no different with Eliot. As indicated in Chapter 2, he did not claim in his account of his reasons for emigration that he had come to New England in order to proselytize the natives. The mission became important for Eliot because he came to know the Indians as individuals and to sympathize with their problems. He was the colonist whose values had changed.

Prior to King Philip's War, Eliot and his Indian associates tried to carry the mission to the Podunks and possibly the Mohegans in Connecticut, the Narragansetts and Eastern Niantics in Rhode Island, and the Nausets and Pokanokets in Plymouth. None of his attempts to expand his work beyond Massachusetts Bay produced any lasting results, either because the natives in question resisted him or because Englishmen in these colonies took up the task of instructing the local Indians. In the meantime other missionaries in southern New England, most notably the Mayhews on Martha's Vineyard and Nantucket and Abraham Pierson in the New Haven colony, began missions among groups whom Eliot had never tried to evangelize.

CHAPTER SEVEN

· · ·

Missionary Work outside Massachusetts Bay

Thomas Mayhew, Jr., Congregationalist minister at Great Harbor (Edgartown) on Martha's Vineyard, began the first sustained mission in southern New England. His work commenced shortly after English settlement of the island. In 1641 Mayhew, Sr., obtained permission from the Council of New England to colonize Martha's Vineyard, Nantucket, and the adjacent islands; in 1642 the two Mayhews and their families, along with approximately fifty other English settlers, moved onto the Vineyard, then home to 2,000 or perhaps 3,000 Wampanoag Indians; and in 1643 a native named Hiacoomes, "thinking there might be better ways and means among the English," came to Mayhew, Jr., and asked to learn about the Christian religion. The minister provided the instruction Hiacoomes requested, and the Indian in turn offered training in the local Algonquian dialect. The two men were soon preaching regularly to the Wampanoags living at the east end of Martha's Vineyard and on Chappaquiddick.[1]

The younger Mayhew was a more successful missionary than Eliot. As William Simmons has written, the former surpassed the latter "in the thoroughness and permanence of his conversions, and in the number of converts and the longevity of the Christian Indian communities which he helped create." An important reason for Mayhew's greater success was that he had a different point of focus. He and Eliot recognized that the powwows and the sachems were the leading guardians of the traditional native order. Mayhew determined that the powwows were "the strongest cord[s]" tying Indians "to their own way," and he devoted his energies to evangelizing the powwows. Eliot concluded that the sachems were "a greater opposition" and tried to win them to his missionary program, with uneven results. The reasons why the two men adopted these contrasting strategies are easily enough surmised. Mayhew lived in greater proximity to natives and was a more perceptive student of their culture. Eliot was shaped by the Bay Colony's practice of conducting diplomacy through sachems, and also—at least during the early Interregnum—by his Fifth Monarchicalism, which led him to exaggerate the power of the sachems over native institutions. Mayhew's writings are silent on the subject of eschatology.[2]

An examination of Mayhew's work through 1652, the year when his last extant source was written, shows the effectiveness of his powwow-oriented approach. In 1645 a "universal sickness" ravaged Martha's Vineyard. The disease was surely European in origin because the powwows were unable to counteract it. Mayhew and Hiacoomes, who until this time had achieved little missionary success, took advantage of the situation. As Mayhew wrote several years later:

> There was one [Indian] about sixty years of age, who was sick of a consuming disease, insomuch as the Indian powwows gave him over for a dead man. Upon which resolution of all the powwows on the island, the sick distressed heathen upon a Lord's day came unto me (the rest of the English being then present) to desire me to pray unto God for him. And so when I had by reasoning with him convinced him of the weakness of the powwows' power; and that if health were to be found, it must be had from him that gave life, and breath, and all things; I commended his case unto the Lord, whereof he rejoiced, gave me thanks, and he speedily recovered unto his former strength.

Mayhew's ability to cure an Indian whom the powwows had pronounced beyond remedy, as well as the fact that the epidemic had spared Hiacoomes and his family, attracted the attention of two sachems, Myoxeo and Towanquattick, who soon asked Mayhew to provide regular instruction. In 1647 Towanquattick faced two major challenges to his newly adopted faith. The first came when he survived an assassination attempt by an Indian angry at him for "walking with the English." The sachem "prais[ed] God for his great deliverance." The second came when his son contracted a fever. The sachem refused to seek treatment from the powwows, who told him that his son "should die, because he sought not to them," and instead took the child to Mayhew. "I bound his arm, and with my penknife let him bleed, . . . and in a short time he began to be very cheerful," the missionary explained.³

Many of the local natives were soon convinced that the powwows had lost their ability to cure disease. It was "an observation of the Indians of this island," Mayhew noted, "that since the Word of God has been taught unto them in this place, the powwows have been much foiled in their devilish tasks, and that instead of curing have rather killed many." From a pragmatic point of view, Mayhew had been blessed with good fortune. The surviving sources contain no evidence that he failed to cure any of the Indians who came to him for treatment, or that the powwows healed any of the natives who sought traditional remedies in the early years of the mission. Furthermore, no Christian Indian family on the Vineyard encountered death until 1650, when Hiacoomes lost a five-day-old baby to disease. The Wampanoag set an example of Christian fortitude by refusing to follow native burial practices: "there were no black faces, . . . nor goods buried with it [the body], nor hellish howlings over the dead." Finally, the epidemic of 1645 occurred at a time when Mayhew and Hiacoomes were ready to exploit it. In contrast, the major epidemics on the mainland—the "plague" in 1616–1619 and the smallpox of 1633–34—preceded the birth of the Eliot work by nine or more years.⁴

Mayhew nevertheless recognized that he had destroyed only one aspect of the powwows' hold over the native population. He observed in 1650 that "many" Indians remained fearful of the powwows' "power to kill men." As Simmons points out, Mayhew promptly resolved to challenge the powwows' putative ability to work sorcery by having Hiacoomes stand "in the midst of all the powwows of the island" to prove that "the worst of their witchcrafts" could do him no harm. The powwows accepted the challenge but failed to win it. Shortly thereafter two powwows came forward, "with their joints shaking, and their bowels trembling, their spirits troubled, and their voices with much fervency," renounced "their diabolical craft," and pledged to follow "the ways of God."⁵

The surrender of these two powwows in 1650 was the key that unlocked the island to Mayhew and Hiacoomes. "Not long after the two powwows had forsaken their old way," Mayhew explained, "diverse Indians desired to become the servants of the Lord." This group of proselytes included a powwow named Tequanonim "of great esteem and very notorious." Shortly thereafter fifty more natives accepted the mission. Thus, the Vineyard Indians did not embrace the Christian religion in large numbers until Mayhew and Hiacoomes had evangelized the powwows after successfully challenging their powers of healing and sorcery. The fact that the sachems Myoxeo and Towanquattick had supported the mission since 1646 was of little consequence. There were apparently only twenty-two adult proselytes in early 1650; later that year, soon after Hiacoomes had dared the powwows to injure him, there were thirty-nine male proselytes and a greater though unspecified number of women; by the fall of 1651, nearly 200 Indian men, women, and children had accepted the mission; and in the fall of 1652, the total approached 300 persons "not counting young children," as well as eight evangelized powwows. That same year a school was established, plans were made to create a praying town, and the Christian Indians publicly confessed their sins and covenanted together to "serve Jehovah." Nothing in the Eliot mission can match this record of rapid achievement.[6]

Eliot did not evangelize many powwows. There are only four or five known cases in the period prior to King Philip's War: the Squaw Sachem's husband, Webbacowet; a husband and wife at Nonantum; Robin Speene; and Black James (who was, Eliot wrote, "in former times reputed by the English to be a powwow, but I cannot tell this"). The paucity of Christianized powwows was partly the result of Eliot's practice of concentrating on the sachems, and partly because of other considerations. To begin with, Eliot knew little about the powwows. His occasional discussions of them show that he recognized that healing was one of their responsibilities. As he wrote in 1647, "there is another great question that has been several times propounded, namely, if they leave off powwowing, and pray unto God, what shall they do when they are sick?" Eliot never indicated, however, that he was aware of the shamans' presumed expertise in sorcery or, for that matter, in divination. His habit was to dismiss their nonmedical functions as "praying to the Devil" and "diabolical exercise[s]." Second, the Apostle acknowledged that native medicine was effective. To judge from his sources, Mayhew refused to make this concession to the enemy camp. In 1647 Eliot proposed that the Christian Indians receive compensation for sharing with the English traditional native remedies "virtuous in the way of physic," and in 1671 he wrote in *Indian Dialogues* that when "powwows use physic by roots, and such other things which God has made for that purpose, that is no sin." The powwows' "great sin," he explained, was "praying to, and worshipping the Devil."[7]

The extent to which powwowing continued in the mainland settlements is difficult to determine because the Massachusetts Bay sources contain little discussion of the matter. The practice clearly survived in the new praying towns and at Pantucket and Nashaway. Whether or not it lingered in the older Christian settlements is uncertain. On the one hand, Eliot was convinced that shamanism had disappeared along the coast. He claimed in 1647 that the Nonantum Indians "have utterly forsaken all their powwows, and given over that diabolical exercise," and he noted in 1673 that powwowing was "abandoned, exploded, and abolished," presumably in the old praying towns.[8] Furthermore, the leading proselytes often said in their conversion narratives in the 1650s that they had renounced "powwowing" and "praying to the Devil." On the other hand, it is difficult to imagine that the practice had disappeared entirely in the old towns. The early history of the Mayhew mission indicates that the eradication of shamanism required a successful challenge to the powwows' healing abilities (Eliot was willing to make compromises in this case) as well as the destruction of their power of sorcery (the Massachusetts sources provide no evidence that there were any overt attempts to achieve this goal).

The difference in orientation was not the only point of contrast between the two missionaries. First of all, with the exception of his views about Indian medicine, Mayhew was more tolerant of native culture. His sources contain no denunciations of Indian lustfulness, grooming habits, laziness, and government. He focused his attention on changing the natives' religion; he did not try to restructure their overall way of life. Mayhew also had two advantages that Eliot lacked. He operated in a less politically complicated setting than the Apostle, who had to contend with many often competitive colonial and native governments; and he was not handicapped by the presence of a large English population. There were fewer than 200 settlers on the Vineyard in 1675, as opposed to the 25,000 or more colonists in Massachusetts Bay; the English did not outnumber the Wampanoags on the island until 1720.[9] While they certainly contributed to Mayhew's success, these three factors were probably not decisive because they were present throughout the period between 1643 and 1652. The crucial factor was the evangelization of the powwows in 1650.

Mayhew, Jr., died in November 1657 when the ship carrying him to

England sank before reaching its destination. "The Lord has given us this amazing blow," Eliot lamented, "to take away my brother Mayhew." Among the other passengers were Jonathan Ince, the promising student of Massachusett, and Herbert Pelham's son Nathaniel. Mayhew's father, who was not a minister, then took over the mission and continued to supervise it until his death in 1682. Several persons assisted him. John Cotton, Jr., learned the local dialect and preached to the Indians between 1665 and 1667, while he was serving as minister in the Edgartown church. (No one else wanted the pulpit; Cotton was forced to take it because he had been accused of adultery in Wethersfield and received no other job offers.) In the late 1660s and early 1670s, the younger Mayhew's sons Matthew and John began to participate in the Indian work. When King Philip's War broke out, there were nearly 300 Christian Indian families on Martha's Vineyard and Chappaquiddick as well as two churches with around 50 communicant members. By this time the mission had also spread to Nantucket, where there were roughly 300 proselytes plus a church with 30 in communion. After the war, John's son Experience and Experience's son Zachariah sustained the work into the early nineteenth century. Kathleen Bragdon suggests that several of the later Mayhews may have been native speakers of Massachusett.[10]

The Apostle apparently did not travel to Martha's Vineyard during the younger Mayhew's lifetime; however, he visited the island at least twice after Mayhew's death. In 1662 Eliot went to Edgartown to administer the sacraments to the members of the English church (Cotton had not yet been hired) and to the Christian Indians, who had formed a congregation of their own three years earlier. Eliot returned to the Vineyard in 1670, when he and Cotton participated in the ordination of Hiacoomes and John Tackanash to the ministry (the former as pastor and the latter as teacher) and then partook of the Lord's Supper in the native church, which had "no officers" until this time. Visiting members of the Edgartown congregation, who were once again without a pastor of their own, also received the sacrament on this occasion. Hiacoomes and Tackanash were surely the first natives ordained to the ministry in the New World. The Catholic Church did not ordain any Indians until the nineteenth century; the first native minister in Massachusetts Bay, Joseph Tuckawillipin of Hassanamesit, was not ordained until 1673; and to the best of my knowledge, there were no earlier ordinations in the other English colonies or in New Netherland.[11]

The Mayhews were less well known in England than Eliot. They labored outside the orthodox colonies and beyond their web of connections in London. Nevertheless, the Apostle's preeminence was not simply a matter of geographical location and political influence in England. On one occasion he enhanced his own reputation at the younger Mayhew's expense. In November 1648 the Apostle told Edward Winslow in a letter published in *The Glorious Progress,* "Our Cutshamekin has some subjects on Martha's Vineyard, and they hearing of his praying to God, some of them do the like there, with some other ingenious Indians, and I have entreated Mr. Mayhew (the young scholar, son to old Mr. Mayhew), who preaches to the English there, to teach them; and he does take pains with their language, and teaches them not without success." As Francis Jennings observes, this statement created the false impression that Eliot had inspired the Vineyard mission, which had commenced three years before his own. The Apostle soon apologized for his inaccurate claim, explaining in a 1649 letter printed in *The Light appearing* that the syntax of his remark had made its "sense untrue." He then used his influence on Mayhew's behalf: he praised him in subsequent letters to the New England Company, and he persuaded the corporation to buy him a library left behind in Massachusetts Bay by the repatriate Thomas Jenner, former minister at Weymouth and Saco. Mayhew, for his part, was willing to overlook Eliot's false claim in *The Glorious Progress,* assuming he knew about it. He visited Eliot's settlements on several later occasions, including the doctrinal examination at Natick in 1654.[12]

The reputations of Eliot and the Mayhews were often reflected in the Commissioners' prewar allocations of New England Company moneys and goods. In most cases, the confederation gave preferential treatment to the Eliot mission. The Apostle first received a New England Company salary (of £20) in 1652. The award was increased to £40 in 1654 and to £50 in 1656, where it remained through 1672, the last prewar year for which good financial records exist. His salary came in addition to the £20 Armine annuity, which he received from 1647 through at least 1654, the final time it is mentioned in the sources. The Commissioners contacted Mayhew, Jr., for the first known occasion in September 1651, informing him that he was to receive the Jenner library as well as some of the tools and articles of clothing that the New England Company had recently shipped to Boston. According to the Commissioners' records, goods worth £43 were sent to him later in the month. It was not until 1654, however, that

Mayhew was given a corporation salary (£40). His stipend was renewed at the same amount in 1655 and increased to £50 in 1656 and 1657. Eliot and Mayhew received identical New England Company salaries from 1654 through 1657; but the Apostle had drawn a corporation paycheck since 1652 and received the Armine annuity between 1647 and 1654. Mayhew, Sr., was first given a New England Company stipend (of £10) in 1657; his salary was increased to £20 the following year; and between 1659 and 1672, he received either £30 or £40 per annum. He justly complained about his compensation. He was probably shortchanged because he was not an ordained minister.[13]

The Commissioners also made payments to family members of the missionaries; in these cases, the awards seem to have been equitable. Eliot's brother Francis, who instructed the Indian men in the construction of fences and buildings as well as in the care of livestock, received a New England Company salary ranging from £10 to £30 between 1651 and 1657, when the Commissioners terminated payments to him, to the Apostle's irritation. Eliot, Jr., received a stipend of £20 or £25 from 1657 until his death in 1668; Joseph Eliot, who was less active than his brother, was given £10 from 1659 to 1661. The Commissioners supported the widow of Mayhew, Jr., from 1658 through 1667. Her award began at £20 a year and had shrunk to £6 by 1667. In the interim the corporation tried to eliminate payments to her, but Winthrop, Jr., and the Commissioners intervened on her behalf. Between 1658 and 1663, the New England Company also funded the education of her son Matthew at Elijah Corlet's grammar school in Cambridge, at a cost of £15 to £20 a year.[14]

The corporation paid teachers and rulers as well. Eliot's native teachers received stipends from 1651 through 1672, and the Mayhews' from 1654 until the same time. Payments were typically £5 or £10 for mainland teachers, and £3 or £6 for their island counterparts—a clear inequity. Rulers in both locations were also compensated, usually £1 per annum (£3 a year in Waban's case). Roughly equivalent numbers of native teachers and rulers received awards. Peter Folger, the bilingual schoolmaster on Martha's Vineyard, was given a stipend ranging from £10 to £30 between 1654 and 1661. The Commissioners terminated his salary after he turned Baptist and moved to Nantucket. There were no bilingual English schoolteachers in prewar Massachusetts Bay.[15]

The Eliot mission received many more allocations for specific purposes than the Mayhew one. The Commissioners, for example, paid £28 for medical expenses sustained by Anthony after he fractured his skull during the construction of the Natick meetinghouse in 1652; that same year they awarded Eliot an unspecified amount of money for the rain-shortened trip to the Quinebaug River; in 1657 the Commissioners purchased £15 worth of corn for the Natick Indians during the famine caused by flooding and sickness; and in 1659 the language experts who evaluated the Natick Indians' conversion narratives divided the sum of £10. Another such instance occurred in or around 1672, when the Commissioners spent some £30 to £40 to outfit a party of six or seven Christian Indians, who then set out from Massachusetts Bay on a missionary journey to a "great lake or sea" located some 300–400 miles from the coast. Gookin, the source of information about this ambitious undertaking, supposed that the natives who lived near this "sea"—surely one of the Great Lakes—were Massawomacks, an Iroquois group now known to have inhabited the upper reaches of the Potomac and Susquehanna Rivers and to have controlled the beaver trade in the region until the mid-seventeenth century. The trip was aborted in the Connecticut Valley; why it was undertaken is not explained. Far fewer miscellaneous allocations were made to the Mayhews. In August 1654 Thomas, Jr., asked for materials and tools to construct a meetinghouse and also for a boat to sail to the mainland. The Commissioners gave him £40 worth of building supplies and £15 to purchase a vessel. Three years later he and Eliot received £80—presumably divided in two—for "two new towns now to begin" (Punkapoag in the latter's case). Otherwise there were apparently no purpose-specific awards made to the Mayhew mission prior to King Philip's War.[16]

The Commissioners of the United Colonies never explained why they were more generous toward Eliot. The two Thomas Mayhews were more effective missionaries than he was, and by this measure they deserved a greater portion of the pie. The New England Company, however, did not instruct the United Colonies to make awards that correlated to missionary success, and the confederation was not necessarily aware of the superiority of the Mayhews' achievement. The Commissioners probably favored Eliot because he produced many Algonquian language works and the first two Mayhews authored none, because he lived in one of the confederation's constituent colonies, and because (as we shall see in the next chapter) he constantly asked them for financial support. In any case, the Eliot and

Mayhew missions were the primary beneficiaries of the corporation's revenue. Margaret Connell Szasz has determined from the Commissioners' published records that these two missions received 75 to 80 percent of the prewar allocations of New England Company goods and moneys.¹⁷

At the time of the corporation's creation in 1649, Mayhew, Jr., and Eliot were the only active Puritan missionaries in southern New England. Colonists in Connecticut, Plymouth, and other locations eventually took up the Indian work with varying degrees of success and commitment. Little is known about these missions, making comparisons with Eliot's program difficult. The only colony that did not produce its own evangelists prior to King Philip's War was Rhode Island. The missionary history of Rhode Island was largely the history of Eliot's sporadic attempts to evangelize the Narragansetts and Eastern Niantics.

Connecticut, New Haven, and Long Island

The missionary section of Connecticut's 1662 royal charter was clearly taken from its Massachusetts Bay counterpart of 1629. The Connecticut charter instructed the colonists to use "their good life and orderly conversation" to "win and invite [sic] the natives of the country to the . . . Christian faith, which in our royal intention, and the adventurers' free profession, is the only and principal end of this plantation."¹⁸ The residents of the colony had achieved no discernible missionary success by the time the charter was granted, and they accomplished little in the remaining years before King Philip's War.

The colony's first documented step to begin a mission occurred in 1650, when the Connecticut General Court directed the ministers to choose one of their number to preach two or more missionary sermons a year with the assistance of Thomas Stanton, Sr. Stanton had the language skills for the task but lacked the inclination and the Christian knowledge necessary to perform it properly. Four years later the General Court, admitting that "little has hitherto been attended through want of an able interpreter," asked John Minor of New London to study divinity with Hartford's Samuel Stone in order to replace Stanton. By this time Minor had acquired some knowledge of the Mohegan-Pequot dialect. Acting on Connecticut's advice, the Commissioners agreed to pay for Minor's education. He soon moved to Hartford and began his studies. At their meeting the following September, the Commissioners offered Minor a seven-year contract as Connecticut's missionary interpreter. He evidently rejected the offer, for he promptly vanishes from the sources.[19]

There were apparently no further attempts to find a suitable interpreter. Connecticut then relied on volunteers willing to study an Indian language and to do their own preaching. Four colonists in the prewar period are known to have started, or at least considered, language training in preparation for missionary careers. With the exception of Norwich's James Fitch, the individuals in question soon lost their enthusiasm for the idea.

Two of these irresolute missionaries planned to evangelize the Western Pequots, who lived at Noank under the rule of Robin Cassasinamon during much of the period between the Pequot War and King Philip's War. The first was Richard Blinman (Blindman), a minister in New London. In 1651 the Commissioners reported that he was "studying the [Mohegan-Pequot] language." Blinman next surfaces in the missionary sources in 1657, when the Commissioners awarded him £20 to hire a bilingual native teacher and promised him an annual stipend if he persisted in his studies. He soon moved to New Haven, and in 1659 he returned to England, apparently for good. Blinman's successor in the Western Pequot mission, William Tompson of New London, had slightly more staying power. He began to learn Mohegan-Pequot in 1659, and he was preaching in it by 1661. Winthrop, Jr., reported at about this time that he "speaks their language very well." Tompson received allocations of £10 or £20 from 1659 through 1662. In 1663, however, the Commissioners informed the corporation that Tompson had "desisted [from] the work."[20]

Connecticut made plans to revive the Pequot mission in late May 1675, when the General Court issued a set of laws for both the Western Pequots—some of whom were now living in the area around present-day Ledyard—and the Eastern Pequots, who then resided on the west shore of the Pawcatuck River near what is now North Stonington, under their governor Harmon Garrett (Caushawashott). These "Laws for the Pequots," which were in several respects more stringent than any of the missionary directives passed in Massachusetts Bay, required the Indians to accept Christian instruction from "any minister . . . sent among them" and sentenced natives who failed to attend the lectures or who misbehaved during them "to be punished with a fine of five shillings or be corporally punished." The code also specified that Pequots who "spoke against the only living and true God" were to be penalized "as the nature of the offense may require," and that sabbath-breakers had to "pay a fine of ten shillings . . . or be sharply whipped for every such offense." These directives proved of little consequence, for only three weeks elapsed between their enactment and the start of King Philip's War.[21]

Another halfhearted Connecticut missionary was John Blackleech, Sr., a merchant who lived in Salem, Boston, New Haven, Stratford, Hartford, and Wethersfield at various times between 1634 and his death in 1683. In April 1657 the New England Company wrote to the Commissioners of the United Colonies to recommend him for the Indian work. The Commissioners replied that although "most of us [are] strangers to Mr. Blackleech," they would support him if he offered his services. He evidently did not volunteer until May 1669, when the Connecticut General Court gave its "approbation" to his profession "to make known to the Indians (in the best way that he can) something of the knowledge of God according as he shall have opportunity." By November of that year, Eliot had sent him a copy of the Indian Bible as well as other Massachusett-language works. Blackleech soon abandoned his missionary aspirations, perhaps because Eliot's writings had convinced him of the magnitude of the linguistic challenge.[22]

Blackleech probably intended to work among the Podunks and other bands in the Connecticut Valley. This area was the location of Eliot's only known missionary preaching in Connecticut, aside from his work in that portion of the Nipmuck Country that became part of Connecticut in the mid-eighteenth century. In 1657 the Apostle traveled to Hartford as a member of a Massachusetts delegation that tried and failed to end the long-standing rift between Samuel Stone and elder William Goodwin over the choice of a successor to Thomas Hooker, who had died a decade earlier. While in Hartford, Eliot did some exploratory preaching among the Podunks, who told him that his mission was an excuse to "get away their lands and . . . make servants of them." Eliot blamed the Marlborough planters for his poor reception, explaining in 1662 that "profane Indians . . . at Connecticut" had "laugh[ed] at the praying Indians and at praying to God" because they knew about the English attempts to seize the Okommakamesit land.[23]

Connecticut's most powerful Indians were Uncas and the Mohegans. In October 1650 the Apostle reported that Uncas had informed the Commissioners during their recent meeting at Hartford of his "great unwillingness" to receive a mission. It is uncertain if Eliot and his proselytes had tried to evangelize the Mohegans by this time. The only known instance of prior contact came in 1647, when the sachem's counselor Foxun, "accounted the wisest Indian in the country," was in Boston to meet with the Commissioners, who were then investigating reports of Mohegan depredations against certain Pequots and Nipmucks. Eliot brought Foxun before a group of proselytes and then exposed his ignorance of the Christian religion. "He was a fool in comparison to you," the Apostle told his protégés; "he had not one word to say, [except] . . . about such poor things as hunting, wars, etc., [and] you could speak of God and Christ." Eliot did not say whether he then tried to interest Foxun in his missionary program. With the possible exception of this incident, there is no evidence that Eliot and his Indians attempted to proselytize the Mohegans prior to King Philip's War. In December 1652 Eliot told William Steele, the president of the New England Company, that Connecticut and not Massachusetts Bay was responsible for instructing Uncas and his people.[24]

No one in Connecticut took up Eliot's challenge until the spring of 1671, when James Fitch began to preach through an interpreter to Uncas, the sachem's son Oneiko (Owaneco), and other Mohegans. The Apostle was excited by the news because he thought that the establishment of a Mohegan mission "in that end of the country" might led to the creation of a Mohawk one. In 1672, at Eliot's request, the Commissioners began to pay Fitch a stipend (of £31, the interest from the Mouche benefaction discussed in Chapter 8); his Indian assistants were also given a total of £10 at this time. Fitch later reported that Uncas had "at first carried it teachably and tractably" but soon refused to "throw down [his] . . . heathenish idols and . . . tyrannical monarchy," and that he "would not suffer them [the Mohegans] to give so much as an outward attendance to the ministry of the Word of God." Despite the sachem's opposition to a mission, Fitch achieved a measure of success by the time of King Philip's War. He told Gookin in 1674 that he had some thirty adult proselytes among the Mohegans and that he had secured 300 acres of land for a praying town. By this time Fitch had "gained some understanding in the Indian language."[25]

Connecticut inherited the work of Abraham Pierson with the absorption of the New Haven colony in late 1664. Pierson served as the minister at Branford from 1644 until 1667, when he and others, disgruntled by the annexation, left the area and founded Newark, New Jersey. By September 1651 he was studying the Quiripi dialect in order to preach to the Quinnipiac Indians on the north shore of Long Island Sound, and in 1662 the Commissioners tried unsuccessfully to convince him to move to Stonington in order to replace Tompson as missionary to the Pequots. Pierson received a salary, normally £20 or £30, from 1653 through 1667. The fact that the Commissioners made no recorded allocations to any Indian assistants suggests that he had none. In September 1654 Pierson was preparing a Quiripi catechism, and two years later the Commissioners asked Stanton, Sr., to help him render the work "into the Narragansett or Pequot language [so] that it may be the better understood by the Indians in all parts of the country." The catechism was finished in 1657 and printed in Cambridge in late 1659 under the title *Some Helps for the Indians Shewing them How to improve their natural Reason, to know the True God, and the True Christian Religion*. The title page, which bears the erroneous date of 1658, states that Stanton had "examined and approved" the translation. Pierson's catechism was the only Algonquian-language work published in New England during Eliot's lifetime in which he had no part.[26]

Pierson had little success in evangelizing the Quinnipiacs, even though he preached to them twice a week. Fitch told Gookin in 1674 that "when Mr. Pierson did frequently try . . . [to instruct them], they did generally show an averseness, yea a perverse contempt for the Word of God; and at present they will not yield to any settled hearing or attendance upon the ministry of the Word." Pierson's lack of progress is not difficult to explain if his missionary lectures resembled the interlinear in his catechism. The work provides the following three answers to the question, "How do you prove that there is but one true God?":

[1.] Because the reason why singular things of the same kind are multiplied is not to be found in the nature of God; for the reason why such like things are multiplied is from the fruitfulness of their causes, but God has no cause of his being but is of himself; therefore he is one. 2. Because singular things of the same kind when they are multiplied, are differenced among themselves by their singular properties; but there cannot be found another God differenced from this by any such like properties. 3. Because it is proper to God to do whatsoever he wills; if there were many

186 · *Missionary Work outside Massachusetts Bay*

gods, they might will contrary things and one might be hindered by another for that he could not do what he would, which cannot stand with the omnipotence and nature of God.

The author of this passage blamed the Indians for his missionary failures. "I find them very slow and slight-spirited," Pierson wrote in 1664, in one of the least self-critical assessments of native intelligence in Puritan sources.[27]

Connecticut could perhaps also take credit, by virtue of its controversial claim over eastern and central Long Island, for the modest missionary achievements of Thomas James, Congregationalist minister at East Hampton from 1650 until his death in 1696. In 1660 the Commissioners, after learning from Eliot and Pierson that James was "willing to apply himself to instruct the Indians," awarded the minister £10 to hire a Montauk language instructor. James was known to be preaching to the natives in 1662, and by 1668 he was skilled enough in the dialect to prepare a catechism in it. James, however, was unable to pursue serious missionary work, even though he drew a corporation paycheck through 1672. He told Winthrop, Jr., in 1667 that his pastoral responsibilities to the English, as well as his duties as interpreter in disputes between Indians and Europeans "from one end of the island to the other," prevented him from "attend[ing] to the Indian work."[28]

The Indians in Connecticut did not embrace Christianity in appreciable numbers until the First Great Awakening, when New Light revivalists developed a homiletical style that had more emotional power than traditional missionary preaching, and when they offered natives a vision of a more egalitarian society than the one that had existed in southern New England since the end of King Philip's War. The First Great Awakening was also the time when, for the same reasons, the Narragansetts and Eastern Niantics in Rhode Island and the Pokanokets in the former Plymouth Colony ended their long resistance to Christianity.[29]

Rhode Island

The Rhode Island colony's 1663 charter contained the familiar injunction to "win and invite the native Indians of the country to the knowledge and obedience of the only true God" through a "good life and orderly conversation." Although nowhere asserting that missionary work was Rhode Island's "principal end," the charter claimed that twenty-four colonists—including Roger Williams, Samuel Gorton, and John Clarke, the Baptist physician who negotiated the 1663 charter—had professed "their sober, serious, and religious intentions" of seeking the "conversion of the poor ignorant Indian natives, in those parts of America." This collective profession of missionary purpose surely had no basis in fact. Gookin wrote in his *Historical Collections,* in a statement contested by no historian, that "God has not yet honored . . . any [Englishman] in that colony that I can hear of, with being instrumental to convert any of those Indians."[30] Eliot and his native associates may have been the only ones who attempted to evangelize Rhode Island's two major Indian groups, the Narragansetts and the Eastern Niantics, in the period before King Philip's War. Their missionary activity in the area is difficult to reconstruct and was probably minimal.

There are only two known occasions when Eliot came into personal contact with Rhode Island Indians. In 1647 he met with a "Narragansett sachem" (probably Auquontis, who lived at Chaubatick near Shawomet) at an undisclosed location and probed his knowledge of the Christian religion. Shepard, who reported the meeting in *The Clear Sun-shine,* noted without further comment that the sachem told Eliot he had not sought instruction from Williams because he was "no good man who goes out and works upon the Sabbath." The other instance took place some twenty years later, when Eliot intervened in an acrimonious dispute between Pomham and the Gortonists. In April 1665 the royal commissioners ordered Pomham and his people to leave their home on Shawomet Neck in exchange for compensation from the Gortonists. The sachem accepted the money and then refused to move; in fact, he never left. In January 1666 Pomham visited Eliot, who wrote a letter on his behalf and asked him to give it to Sir Robert Carr, one of the royal commissioners. Eliot told Carr that the Gortonists had used "both force and fraud . . . to drive them or deceive them [Pomham and his people] out of their lands," and then asked him to permit the Indians to retain "that little which they still hold." The sachem delivered the letter to Carr and tried unsuccessfully to convince him that it came from the governor of Massachusetts Bay. Carr wrote back to Eliot, scolding him for thinking that the commissioners "were not able to order the King's affairs in these parts, without your advice and direction." Eliot's involvement in the dispute evidently ended at this point.[31]

The Apostle sent proselytes into the Narragansett Country on three documented occasions in the late 1640s and early 1650s. The first was in April 1649, when he dispatched two unidentified Indians to Ninigret and the Eastern Niantics, who lived in the southwestern portion of the Narragansett Country, "to stir them up to call upon God." He sent along a letter of introduction to the sachem as well as a jacket for him. Eliot had undertaken this mission at the suggestion of the younger John Winthrop, who had proposed it in late March or early April, when he was in Boston for his father's funeral. Winthrop, Jr., probably hoped that a mission to the Eastern Niantics would open up territory for English expansion: his designs on the Narragansett Country are well known. The native evangelists met with mixed results. Eliot explained in *Strength out of Weaknesse* that Ninigret "did little less than despise the offer [of the Gospel], although he took the present," and that the two proselytes had been "received . . . with great gladness" by Indians who were "a little more remote from the great and proud ones."[32]

The other two visits took place in the early 1650s, and neither was clearly missionary in purpose. In July 1650 two Christian Indian brothers, at least one of whom understood English, traveled to Warwick and Providence on unspecified business and attended a Gortonist worship service. The Indians later told Eliot that the lecturer had denied the existence of heaven and hell, disclosed that infant baptism was "very foolish" and that ministers and magistrates were "needless thing[s]," and then made a confusing remark about "the Parliament in England." Next, in August or September 1651, Cutshamekin went to the Narragansett Country in order to "appeas[e] . . . some strife among some sachems." This "strife" was probably the "provocations" that Williams discussed in a letter written to Winthrop, Jr., at about this time. Williams explained that Auquontis had alienated Ninigret and the major Narragansett sachems by claiming to be subject to Pomham and not to any of them. Pomham came to Auquontis's defense. He told Ninigret and the others that "he was as great a sachem as they," a claim that soon led to a fight in which there was "no blood spilled." Auquontis then asked the Bay Colony to intervene; this request evidently led to Cutshamekin's embassy. The trip ended in disaster when Cutshamekin became intoxicated at Warwick in the incident that led to the altered wording in the Natick civil covenant.[33]

There is no additional evidence in the Massachusetts Bay sources that Eliot's Indians went to the Narragansett Country or were in contact with the Narragansetts or Eastern Niantics at any time before King Philip's War. Williams stated, however, that proselytes from the Bay Colony had repeatedly tried to evangelize the Rhode Island Indians prior to November 1651, when he sailed to England on his second diplomatic voyage on Rhode Island's behalf. In the course of a lengthy letter written to the Massachusetts General Court on October 5, 1654, several months after his return to Rhode Island, Williams recalled that "at my last departure for England, I was importuned by the Narragansett sachems and especially by Ninigret, to present their petition to the high sachems of England that they might not be forced from their religion, and for not changing their religion be invaded by war. For they said that they were daily visited with threatenings by Indians that came from about the Massachusetts, that if they would not pray they should be destroyed by war." Williams then explained that he was disturbed that "the Narragansett chief sachems . . . [were] publicly branded for refusing to pray and be converted" in the Eliot tracts that he had examined in England. He presumably had in mind Shepard's report in *The Clear Sun-shine* about Eliot's 1647 encounter with the "Narragansett sachem"; a passing remark that the Apostle made in *The Light appearing* about his prayers for "the Mohegans, Narragansetts, etc."; and Eliot's account in *Strength out of Weaknesse* of the failed mission to Ninigret in 1649. Later in the letter Williams reminded the General Court that "the glorious conversion of the Indians in New England" and "unnecessary wars and cruel destruction of the Indians in New England" were antithetical ends and that "prudent and pious Mr. Winthrop deceased" had been an advocate of missionary work.[34]

The aim of Williams's letter was not to scold the Bay Colony about Eliot's mission but rather to prevent an expedition against Ninigret that the Commissioners of the United Colonies had authorized in September 1654. The pretext for the action was that Ninigret had failed to make required tribute payments to the confederation, and its purpose was to control the sachem, whom the Commissioners had long suspected of conspiring with the Dutch and the Mohawks against the orthodox colonies and the Mohegans. The expedition commenced on October 9, when Simon Willard and eighty soldiers left Dedham for the Narragansett Country. Whether or not Williams's letter had arrived by this time is uncertain. Willard marched under what Glenn LaFantasie terms "ambivalent instructions that failed to clarify whether he was to battle Ninigret to the death or win a peace at all costs." Willard chose the latter course of action and negotiated an agreement with Ninigret. The commander and his troops then returned to Boston no worse for wear.[35]

Williams's statement about the "threatenings by Indians that came from about the Massachusetts" requires careful evaluation. He was surely incorrect in reporting that praying Indians had "daily visited" the Narragansetts and Eastern Niantics in the late 1640s and early 1650s. The only known encounters are the three mentioned earlier in this chapter; and unless one wishes to assume that Eliot and other Bay Puritans deliberately concealed the extent of the activity in the Narragansett Country, there is no reason to assume that Williams was right, even if "daily" is taken to mean "regularly" or "frequently." His more significant claim, that Eliot's proselytes had told the Narragansetts and Eastern Niantics that "if they would not pray they should be destroyed by war," cannot be so easily dismissed. There are two ways of interpreting this statement.

The first is to presuppose that the "threatenings" were made. The question then becomes whether they originated with Eliot or with his proselytes. There is some basis for thinking that the Apostle deserves the blame: his then-pronounced Fifth Monarchy millennialism countenanced violence. He remarked without further elaboration in *The Christian Commonwealth* that tyrants could be overthrown "by councils or wars or otherwise," and in other contemporary sources he placed the sachems of southern New England in this category. In *The Light appearing,* for instance, he spoke of Cutshamekin's "former tyranny," and in the December 1652 letter to Steele, he wrote that "there be two great sachems in the country that are open and professed enemies against praying to God . . . , and whenever the Lord removes them, there will be a door open for the preaching of the Gospel in those parts where they live." The sachems in question were the "rag[ing]" Ninigret and the "tyranniz[ing]" Uncas. The alternative in this case is that Eliot's Indian evangelists issued the "threatenings" on their own authority, perhaps to warn the Narragansetts and Eastern Niantics that their refusal to accept a mission would provide the

Bay with a justification for an invasion. At least one proselyte believed for a time that Massachusetts Bay was capable of destroying natives who resisted Eliot. In his 1659 conversion narrative, Waban recalled that in the early years of the mission, he "sometimes ... thought if we did not pray, the English might kill us."[36]

The second interpretation assumes that neither the Apostle nor the praying Indians issued any "threatenings." If so, why did Williams report that Eliot's Indians had done so? There are at least three ways of answering this question. First, Williams's native informants may have misunderstood something told them by the proselytes. Philip Ranlet suggests that the Rhode Island Indians misconstrued a reference to the Battle of Armageddon. While the possibility that they misheard this or some other statement cannot be ruled out, Ranlet's specific suggestion is difficult to accept because the word "Armageddon" does not appear in Eliot's extant sources. Second, the natives may have misinformed Williams. This is not to say that they deliberately lied to him in order to win his support for their cause. These Indians already knew that Williams would champion them against any threatened aggression from Massachusetts Bay. Rather, the natives may have been convinced by an external party that the Bay Puritans were capable of invading the lands of their religious enemies. Gorton, for instance, represented the Bay Colony's 1643 expedition into his Shawomet plantation in similar terms, telling the royal commissioners that Massachusetts was prepared at the time to "put us to the sword" if "we would not relinquish our religion." Third, Williams may have been expressing through the Indians his worst suspicions about Eliot. Williams probably feared that Eliot's Fifth Monarchy millennialism sanctioned military action against sachems whom he had "publicly branded for refusing to pray and be converted." During his stay in England between 1651 and 1654, Williams would have encountered expressions of the Apostle's antimonarchical radicalism in letters printed in various Eliot tracts (*The Christian Commonwealth* was not published until 1659) and also observed the violent carriage of Fifth Monarchists.[37]

Although there is no way to resolve the issue conclusively, several points are clear. First of all, the alleged "threatenings" were made during the early Interregnum, the only period in Eliot's missionary career when he could have countenanced a use of military force for a missionary purpose. After the Restoration, he concluded that the destruction of antichristian regimes would come about through royal decree and not through warfare; and as we shall see in the next chapter, he was appalled by the slaughter of obdurate pagans during King Philip's War. Second, the planned invasion did take place in October 1654, when Willard led the eighty soldiers into the Narragansett Country. The expedition was not justified on the grounds that Ninigret had refused "to pray and be converted," however, and it resulted in no loss of blood. Finally, the Apostle's missionary activity in the Narragansett Country had ended by December 1652, when he told Steele in the aforementioned letter that he and his proselytes were too "much taken up with the attendance of our work at Natick" to evangelize the Eastern Niantics and the Mohegans.[38]

In the 1652 letter to Steele, Eliot assigned responsibility for an Eastern Niantic mission to "the English at Pequot [New London]," which is to say, to Winthrop, Jr., who had proposed it in the first place. Winthrop apparently took no steps in this direction until the early 1660s, when he went to England in order to secure a charter for Connecticut. At some point between September 1661 and May 1662, he presented to the New England Company a document that he endorsed as a "Rough draft of proposals to the corporation for Ninecraft's Indian business." In it Winthrop suggested that the missionary foundation invest £5,000 in English money on an ambitious plan to instruct natives in Christianity and train them to produce "hemp, flax, . . . pitch, tar, wheat, [and] prairie grass" for English and American markets. The proposal extended to the Indians who lived between Narragansett Bay and the Thames River, an expanse of territory that included the Narragansetts, the Eastern Niantics, and the Eastern and Western Pequots. Winthrop's endorsement to the document, however, indicates that his design centered on Ninigret. Winthrop told the corporation that its investment would be repaid within five years and that the plan was likely to succeed because the Indians in "those western parts of New England" were "more civil and active and industrious than any other of the adjacent parts." The New England Company liked the idea, for Robert Boyle asked the Commissioners in May 1662 to "consider of some employment in the way of trade and manufacturing to employ the Indians." The proposal was well received in London because Boyle and other contemporary scientists wanted to integrate the Indians in New England, as well as the poor in England, into the social and economic order, and because the corporation was troubled by the absence of a mission to the natives in Rhode Island. In 1657 the officers wondered if Roger Williams and "Mr. Blackstone" (presumably William Blackstone, an eccentric Rhode Island Anglican) might be "fit persons to preach to the Indians." But as it turned out, the New England Company lacked the funds to implement Winthrop's proposal. Besides, the man he had in mind for the task, William Tompson, lost his interest in missionary work at about this time.[39]

It is difficult to imagine that Tompson would have succeeded even if he had undertaken the work Winthrop assigned to him. Gookin stated that the natives in Rhode Island were "more indisposed to embrace religion than any Indians in the country." The Superintendent was probably right about the matter—neither of the other major pagan groups in southern New England, the Mohegans and the Pokanokets, were as implacably opposed to a mission as the Narragansetts and the Eastern Niantics. A small number of Mohegans participated in Fitch's mission, and the Pokanokets, as we shall soon see, permitted a Christian Indian teacher to live among them in the 1660s, even though the teacher achieved no discernible results. Gookin attributed the uncompromising paganism of the Narragansetts and the Eastern Niantics to the lethargy of Williams and other Rhode Islanders and to the "averseness" of the sachems to a mission.[40] The responsibility for creating this "averseness" must rest on the Apostle's shoulders. Eliot and his native associates were the only persons known to have tried to evangelize the Rhode Island Indians in the period before the war. Moreover, they annoyed the paramount Narragansett sachems by establishing a mission among their tributaries at Quantisett, and they may have issued the "threatenings" that Williams reported to Massachusetts Bay.

Plymouth Colony

On the eve of King Philip's War, there were slightly more than 500 Christian Indian men, women, and children in the unchartered colony of Plymouth. Most of these proselytes were Nausets on Cape Cod. Eliot probably preached the first missionary sermon to the Nausets, although the task of evangelizing them fell to residents of Plymouth. In 1647, with Thomas Shepard and John Wilson, Eliot went to Yarmouth in order to heal a "bruised church." On the return trip, he preached to some Nauset Indians through "one or two interpreters who were then present." Although he encountered resistance from a local sachem whose "fierce, strong, and furious spirit" had already led the local English to call him "Jehu" (see 2 Kings 9:1–10:36), Eliot was pleased with the results of the sermon because many of the auditors were "attentive and knowing what was said."[41]

The Apostle apparently made no follow-up efforts in the area until 1650 or 1651, when he sent some proselytes to visit the Nausets at Mashpee. The native evangelists reported that the local Indians wanted him to ask William Leveritch, the minister at Sandwich since 1639, to provide them with instruction. Eliot soon wrote to Leveritch, who agreed to undertake the task. By September 1651 Leveritch was studying the language. That same year Eliot sent him some New England Company tools and advised him to "put the Indians upon labor." Leveritch's missionary career, however, proved to be short-lived. He moved to Oyster Bay, Long Island, around 1653; the Commissioners gave him £5 for his "former service" in 1655; two years later they offered him a £20 stipend if he would resume his language work in preparation for Indian work on Long Island; and in 1658 they sent him £5 "for his pains and encouragement." He then disappears from the sources.[42]

Leveritch's departure for Long Island left the Mashpee Indians to Richard Bourne, a wealthy man who had settled in Sandwich around 1640 and then become a lay minister to the English. He began to preach to the Mashpees through an interpreter at some point in the mid-1650s. He eventually attained what Gookin called "a competent knowledge and ability . . . in the Indian language." Bourne's New England Company salary went from £15 in 1658 to £35 in 1672; a raise from £25 to £30 in 1664 came about through Eliot's intervention. Several of Bourne's native teachers also received stipends of £3 or £6 between 1663 and 1672. In 1660 he created the praying town of Mashpee, using £15 of his own money to purchase the land from a local sachem. In 1670 Eliot and Cotton, Jr., participated in Bourne's ordination as pastor of the Mashpee church. Bourne was probably the first Englishman ordained for a native congregation in colonial America. By 1674 the church had twenty-seven communicant and ninety more baptized members. Bourne continued to pastor the congregation until his death in 1682. His grandson and great-grandson sustained the Mashpee mission; his granddaughter, Remember, married Experience Mayhew.[43]

In time other persons preached to the Nausets. Thomas Tupper, Sr., of Sandwich began to instruct the Indians at Herring Ponds (near present-day Bourne) in 1658 and continued to do so, apparently without compensation, until his death in 1676. His son of the same name (who married the daughter of Mayhew, Sr., by his second marriage), his grandson, and his great-grandson continued the work through the late eighteenth century. Samuel Treat, minister at Eastham and one of future Connecticut governor Robert Treat's twenty-one children, instructed the local Nausets from shortly before King Philip's War until his death in 1717. He became highly skilled in the language. After the war Samuel Danforth, Jr., who was the minister at Taunton, learned Algonquian and preached to the Indians into the eighteenth century. Tupper, Jr., Treat, and Danforth all received stipends from the New England Company.[44]

The last notable missionary in the Old Colony was John Cotton, Jr., who moved from Martha's Vineyard to Plymouth town in 1667. By the time of King Philip's War, he had preached with varying degrees of success to the Nausets and to the Sakonnets (Sogkonates) near present-day Little Compton, Rhode Island, and also to Josias Wompatuck and other Indians in the Bridgewater-Taunton-Middleboro triangle. Cotton received a corporation salary of £20 by 1667; his award reached £30 in 1672. There is no record of any payments to Indian assistants. In 1697 Cotton left Plymouth for Charleston, South Carolina, after rumors of another extramarital affair surfaced. He died of yellow fever two years later, having founded the first Congregationalist church in that city. His wife and sons Josiah and Rowland remained behind in New England. Both sons became missionaries in the Plymouth area; the former compiled an Algonquian dictionary in 1707 or 1708.[45]

Before leaving for Charleston, Cotton helped Eliot prepare the revised edition of the Indian Bible. The Apostle explained that Cotton "read over the whole [first edition of the] Bible, and whatever doubts he had, he wrote them down in order, and gave them to me," adding that Cotton's suggestions "afforded me more help in that work of translation, than ever I had before from any Englishman." The revised New Testament was printed in 1681. Some of the copies were immediately published (with a 1680 date on the title page), but most were left unbound until the completion of the Old Testament in 1685. The Apostle had several reasons for wanting to publish another edition of the Bible even though the transition from Algonquian to English had begun in the Indian schools in Massachusetts Bay. First, many of the older proselytes had lost their Bibles during the traumatic relocations of King Philip's War; second, Eliot hoped to carry the mission to pagan bands in the distant reaches of New England; and third, he knew that the Indians on Martha's Vineyard and Nantucket needed additional copies of the Bible. Eliot's Massachusett-language works, in fact, brought the island's dialect into conformity with Natick's. As Experience Mayhew noted in 1722, the "difference [between the dialects] was something greater than it is now is, before our Indians had the use of the Bible and other books translated by Mr. Eliot; but since that [time] most of the little differences that were between them, have been happily lost, and our Indians speak, but especially write, much as those of Natick do."[46]

Plymouth Colony was the site of Eliot's only sustained attempt to establish his missionary program outside Massachusetts Bay. In the 1660s he endeavored in three different ways to interest Metacom (King Philip) and the Pokanokets in a mission. Whether or not these were the Apostle's first efforts to proselytize the Pokanokets is unclear. He wrote in *The Glorious Progress* that Massasoit was "too wise" to receive Christian instruction. Eliot did not explain, however, if he had learned of the sachem's resistance from firsthand experience or secondhand reports. In either case, Massasoit remained opposed to the Gospel until his dying day. William Hubbard recalled that the sachem had asked Plymouth shortly before his death in 1662 "never to attempt to draw away any of his people from their old pagan superstition and devilish idolatry to the Christian religion."[47]

Eliot's first documented attempt to evangelize Metacom and the Pokanokets took place in the early 1660s, when he sent them a resident teacher. The Apostle later explained that he had done so at the request of "Philip and his people," who wanted to "learn to read, in order to praying unto God." Eliot chose John Sassamon to serve as the teacher. This Neponset Indian had been part of the mission since at least 1651, when he was given two New England Company axes. He was a student at Harvard in the fall of 1653; he appears in the college records at no other time. In the 1650s Sassamon helped Eliot with his Massachusett translations and also worked as a schoolteacher, probably at Natick; and in the summer of 1659, he served as an interpreter in the suspect sale of two tracts of Narragansett land to Winthrop, Jr., and Humphrey Atherton.[48]

Sassamon was living with the Pokanokets by August 1664, when Eliot asked the Commissioners to "give encouragement [money] to John Sassamon, who teaches Philip and his men to read." The Neponset had probably arrived in the Pokanoket camp several years earlier. In 1662 he doubled as translator and witness during the negotiations that led to a treaty between Wamsutta (Metacom's short-lived predecessor) and Rhode Island; later that year, after Wamsutta's death, he witnessed Metacom's renewal of the Pokanokets' 1621 mutual assistance pact with Plymouth; and in 1662 or 1663, he was surely the native who wrote to Plymouth Governor Thomas Prince, in English, to explain that Philip remembered that "this last sumer" he had promised the Pilgrim Colony magistrates that he would "not sell no land in 7 years time," and that the sachem "would have no english trouble him before that time." Sassamon continued to perform similar duties into the mid-1660s. In 1664 and 1665 he witnessed two of the various land transactions that Metacom made in defiance of his promise to "sell no land in 7 years time"; in 1666 he wrote from Philip's seat at Mount Hope to the "Chief Officer of the town of Long Island" about the sachem's quarrel with Ninigret over native jurisdiction on the island; and later in the year he witnessed and probably wrote a document in which Philip assigned to two Indians the right to sell a piece of land on his behalf. The latter transaction is apparently the last occasion when Sassamon can be placed among the Pokanokets.[49]

There is no evidence that Sassamon persuaded any of the Pokanokets to accept a mission. His lack of missionary success probably means that "Philip and his people" had asked Eliot for a teacher because they wished to acquire literacy for its own sake, and not because they wanted to "learn to read, in order to praying unto God." After leaving the Pokanokets, Sassamon went to Natick, where he was admitted into full church membership and baptized. Eliot did not explain why the teacher returned to Massachusetts Bay. John Easton, the deputy governor of Rhode Island, said in 1675 that Sassamon left the Pokanokets after Philip discovered that the Neponset had rewritten the sachem's will to his own considerable advantage. Hubbard and Increase Mather provided a different explanation, claiming that Sassamon had originally gone to the Pokanokets because he had renounced Christianity and needed a place of refuge, and that he returned to Natick after repenting for the sin of apostasy. But, as Jennings points out, Sassamon had probably not apostatized because

Eliot's 1664 letter to the Commissioners indicates that the Indian was "teach[ing] Philip and his men to read" with the Apostle's blessing. In any case, Sassamon did not remain long at Natick. At some point in the early 1670s, he moved back to Plymouth Colony, to the north shore of Assawampsett Pond, near present-day Lakeville and Middleboro, to preach to Metacom's brother-in-law Tuspequin (Watuspequin, the Black Sachem) and his band. Sassamon was still living at Assawampsett—on land given him in 1673 by Tuspequin and his son William—when he was murdered in January 1675, in the event that triggered King Philip's War. "Since his death," Eliot wrote five months later, "we hear by some of the godly English of Taunton, that he so approved himself in their neighborhood, as that he had the esteem of a good Christian, and his death was much bewailed."[50]

Eliot's second way of approaching Metacom was through personal contact. The Apostle disclosed in his 1664 letter to the Commissioners that Eliot, Jr., had made several recent visits to the Pokanokets and that the two of them planned to return in the near future. Eliot later provided two brief accounts of his own visit or visits to Philip. In *Indian Dialogues*, he noted that when he had tried to stimulate interest in the mission, the sachem "neglect[ed] and despise[d] the offer" because he was engrossed in athletic contests; and in 1675, he recalled that "when I exhorted them [the sachem and his men] to keep the sabbath and pray unto God, . . . they answered me, why do you speak so to us, why do you not so speak to your own countrymen? We do but as they do."[51]

The third was to send two proselytes, William Ahawton and Anthony, to Metacom. Their attempt to evangelize the sachem is the subject of one of Eliot's "Indian Dialogues." Internal evidence in the dialogue indicates that the meeting of the three men occurred around 1670.[52] In this dialogue, Metacom registered three objections to a mission and the two native evangelists responded to them. The Apostle was not present during the conversation; for this reason, the statements attributed to Metacom probably represented views that Eliot had encountered in discussions with Cutshamekin or with other sachems.

According to Eliot, one of Philip's objections was that "you praying Indians do reject your sachems, and refuse to pay them tribute." Cutshamekin had regarded the missions at Nonantum and Neponset as secessionist movements, and he had also complained about the loss of tribute from the Christian Massachusetts. Eliot replied through William and Anthony that "the Word of God commands all to be subject to the higher powers and to pay them tribute, Romans 13:1–7" and that "all the time that Cutshamekin lived, . . . [the praying Indians] did always honor, obey, and pay tribute unto him." The Apostle was not deliberately misrepresenting the matter: he believed that the Massachusett proselytes had paid Cutshamekin an appropriate amount of tribute and that his election as ruler of one hundred at Natick had enabled him to remain in power.

Metacom's second objection was that if he embraced the mission, some of his people would defect "unto other sachems that pray not to God. And so it will come to pass that if I be a praying sachem, I shall be a poor and weak one, and easily trod upon by others." The Apostle acknowledged in the dialogue that Cutshamekin's "praying to God did make such of his people as loved not that way waver in subjection to him" (this was possibly a reference to the "profane Indians" at Weymouth). Nevertheless, Eliot insisted that these defectors were "wicked men" of little value to a sachem. He also explained that if he were to accept a mission, Metacom would become "friends" with the orthodox magistrates and the praying Indians in southern New England, and that the sachem would be more likely to lose subjects if he followed the examples of Cutshamekin and Josias Wompatuck and sold away land.

Metacom's final objection was that "sachems and people . . . are all fellow brethren in your churches. . . The vote of the lowest of the people has as much weight as the vote of the sachem . . . I am a sinful man as well as others, but if I must be admonished by the church, who are my subjects, I know not how I shall like that." Like the first two, this objection probably originated with Cutshamekin, who had learned about congregational discipline in the 1647 incident involving his disobedient son. Eliot replied that there was an "equality of vote" among church members regardless of their status. He then tried to assuage Metacom's fears about the matter by saying that discipline was administered "with all reverence, gentleness, meekness, tenderness, and love" and that sachems retained their power in the civil realm.[53]

The dialogue ends with Metacom "accept[ing] the Word of God and resol[ving] to keep the sabbath" and also asking for a teacher to provide further instruction in religion. This optimistic conclusion was not a statement of fact but rather a literary necessity given the fact that *Indian Dialogues* was written as a manual for native evangelists. The sachem's subsequent opposition to a mission is well established in the sources. Eliot indicated in letters written in 1671 and 1675 that the Pokanokets had not "open[ed] their hearts to the Word of God" and that they "pray[ed] not to God." Furthermore, Metacom and his counselors told John Easton in June 1675, in a statement evaluated later in the chapter, that "they had a great fear . . . [that] any of their Indians should be called or forced to be Christian Indians. They said that such were in every thing more mischievous, only dissemblers, and then the English made them not subject to their kings, and by their lying to wrong their kings."[54]

In August 1671 Eliot sent William and Anthony back to Metacom, on this occasion to mediate the intensifying quarrel between the Pokanokets and Plymouth. Historians have overlooked the Apostle's attempt to negotiate a settlement between the two peoples, and for this reason have failed to see that his peace initiative inadvertently helped provoke the Pokanokets to violence four years later.[55]

The spring and summer of 1671 were a tense period in the Old Colony. In early March a Plymouth ranger, Hugh Cole, reported to the General Court that he had recently seen some Shawomets in the Pokanoket camp "employed in making bows and arrows and half-pikes, and fixing up of guns." He also claimed that "Indians of several places" were in the vicinity and that Philip and sixty armed natives had marched up the Mount Hope peninsula toward the English settlements and then turned back. Plymouth reacted to Cole's testimony by summoning Metacom to a meeting at Taunton on April 10, 1671. According to contemporary accounts, the sachem admitted that he had "of late through my indiscretion, and the naughtiness of my heart" conspired against the colonists "by taking up arms, with evil intent against them, and that groundlessly." He then "freely engage[d] to resign up [to the magistrates] . . . all my English arms, to be kept by them for their security, so long as they shall see reason."[56]

The provision about weapons soon led to a series of subordinate disputes: Were the firearms surrendered at Taunton assigned permanently or temporarily to the colony's custody? Had Philip and his retinue turned over all or only some of the rifles that they had brought with them to Taunton? Did the Pokanokets also have to give up the weapons left behind on Mount Hope? Were the Sakonnets and the sachem's other presumed confederates in the colony also expected to relinquish their arms? Eliot knew of these disputes by June 16, 1671, when he wrote to Thomas Prince about them. The Apostle began the letter by apologizing for his "boldness in meddling with your state matters" and then advised Prince to approach the Pokanokets "with speed and vigor until they stoop and quake, and give up (at least) some" of the weapons that remained in their possession. The purpose of this show of force was to demonstrate that Plymouth was not "afraid of them and their guns." After making the point, the colony should "immediately" return the confiscated weaponry to the Pokanokets in an act of generosity that might "open an effectual door to their entertainment of the Gospel." There is no evidence that the Plymouth magistrates took Eliot's advice, probably because they considered it too lenient. The colony's leaders decided that the situation called for sterner action, and in early July they created a council of war, which promptly ordered the impressment of soldiers.[57]

Eliot formulated his plan for peace in response to this order for impressment. On August 1, 1671, he wrote a document entitled "Instructions from the Church at Natick to William and Anthony." The Apostle explained in the document that he was alarmed by Plymouth's preparations for war because he feared that the Pokanokets would "be destroyed" once fighting began, because he did not think that Metacom and his people had "done anything worthy of death," and because he knew that a mission to the Pokanokets could not be established in a climate of strife. The aim of Eliot's plan was to avert war by convincing the Pokanokets and Plymouth to allow Massachusetts Bay to arbitrate their dispute. His "Instructions" directed William and Anthony to join with John Sassamon and then visit the Pokanokets and any other Indians "concerned in the quarrel." If they persuaded the natives to accept his plan for arbitration, the three emissaries were to inform Prince of that fact, "beseech him and the rest of the magistrates . . . to cease pressing and arming of soldiers . . . against them that are desirous of peace," and ask him to abide by the proposed "way of making and establishing . . . peace."[58]

The "Instructions" briefed William and his companions about what they should say to the Pokanokets in order to induce them to agree to arbitration. The three intermediaries were to tell the Indians about two biblical passages and then "entreat them to obey" these texts. One was 1 Corinthians 6:1–6, where Paul scolds the faithful for suing one another in pagan courts of law and directs them to take their internal legal disputes to other Christians for adjudication. Eliot doubtless recognized that the specific circumstances in Corinth did not fit the case at hand: Philip and his people were not Christians, and their quarrel with Plymouth was more serious than a lawsuit. The Apostle was interested only in the larger principle that the passage established; he instructed his emissaries to explain to the Pokanokets that "God commands that when differences arise among people, they ought to put their differences to the arbitration of others."

The other text was Deuteronomy 20:10–11, where God tells the Israelites that when they "comest nigh unto a city to fight against it, then proclaim peace unto it. [11] And it shall be, if it make thee answer of peace, and open unto thee, then it shall be, that all the people that is found therein shall be tributaries unto thee, and they shall serve thee." Eliot's "Instructions" commented only on verse ten, which served his reconciliatory purpose well enough. He asked his native diplomats to inform the Pokanokets that the Bible teaches that "as it is the duty of Plymouth to offer you peace before they war against you, so it is your duty to offer, accept, and desire peace." He did not indicate whether or not the Indians had to become "tributaries" of Plymouth if they accepted the offer of peace. Eliot surely hoped that King Philip would follow the lead of Cutshamekin and other sachems in Massachusetts Bay and accept colonial jurisdiction. It is most unlikely, however, that he wanted Philip to submit to Plymouth under the coercive condition specified in verse eleven. The sachems who submitted to the Massachusetts General Court in 1644 and 1668 had not done so because the Bay Colony had threatened them with an invasion.

William, Anthony, and Sassamon approached Philip in early to mid-August 1671 and persuaded him to travel to Boston when Eliot sent word to do so. It is unclear if they told the sachem about the two biblical texts, and if they later spoke with Prince. The evidence that the three Indians contacted Metacom appears in a letter that James Walker, a Plymouth magistrate, wrote to Prince on September 1. Eight days earlier the Plymouth magistrates had instructed Walker and James Brown of Swansea to inform the sachem that he was to appear in Plymouth on September 13 in order to explain his refusal to surrender his arms, and also to answer fresh charges that he was plotting with the Sakonnets and others against the colony. Walker and Brown were instructed to invite Roger Williams to accompany them as an interpreter. The magistrates also resolved at this time "to endeavor his [Philip's] reducement by force" if he refused to come to Plymouth. Walker explained in the letter that his brother Harvey had gone with Brown to visit the sachem, who greeted them by knocking Brown's hat off his head. The next day the two delegates returned with Williams. Walker reported that the three Englishmen "could get no positive answer" from the sachem "because Mr. Eliot had sent for him to Boston, and he looked for another messenger that day; which messenger they met about two miles from Philip's house; which messenger told them that his message was to desire Philip to be at Punkapoag the last day of this week, and at Boston the Tuesday following."[59]

Philip duly arrived in Boston in early September, "made complaint" against Plymouth, and received for the time being a favorable judgment. The Bay magistrates determined that the Pokanokets' "covenants and agreements" with the Pilgrim colony constituted "a neighborly and friendly correspondency" and not a submission, and that Massachusetts "resented not his offense so deeply" as Plymouth did. Governor Prince, probably convinced that the magistrates in Boston had not been properly informed about the facts of the dispute, then invited the Massachusetts and Connecticut Commissioners to meet with Metacom at Plymouth on September 24. The sachem made the fateful decision to attend the meeting. The Commissioners made common cause against him, accusing him of committing "a great deal of wrong and injury" against Plymouth, and warning him "that if he went on in his refractory way, he must expect to smart for it." On September 29 Philip signed a statement in which he promised to make various indemnities to Plymouth, to sell no land or wage war without the colony's permission, and to take future disputes to Plymouth and not to Massachusetts Bay. He then unambiguously "subject[ed]" himself and his people to the authority of the Plymouth General Court.[60]

The peace initiative thus resulted in Philip's submission to Plymouth under threat of invasion. Eliot surely had not intended for this to happen. His objective in encouraging the sachem to seek arbitration in Boston was to avert war through a negotiated settlement, not to lure him into Plymouth's hands. The Apostle did not disclose in his "Instructions" what he wanted the terms of the settlement to be; nevertheless, his fear that the Pokanokets would "be destroyed" in a war, his conviction that they had not done anything "worthy of death," and his hope that the establishment of peace would create an environment conducive to a mission indicate that he sought a settlement that was fair to the Indians. Eliot's plan for peace failed because he misjudged Massachusetts Bay. Although the colony's leaders were sympathetic to King Philip when he visited Boston in early September, they ultimately sided with Plymouth in the action that led to his submission later in the month.

John Easton's 1675 statement about Metacom's contempt for Christian Indians is best evaluated in light of Eliot's peace initiative. Easton failed to clarify two important points. First, he did not identify the mission or missions that bothered the sachem. Eliot's work among the Pokanokets is the most likely but not the only candidate. Cotton, Jr., apparently tried to evangelize the Pokanokets, and Sassamon was active among the Assawampsetts under Metacom's brother-in-law, the Black Sachem. The Mayhew mission was another possibility because the Pokanoket sachems claimed jurisdiction over the island Wampanoags. In September 1654, presumably in response to complaints from Massasoit, the Commissioners advised the younger Mayhew to "be slow in withdrawing Indian professors from paying accustomed tribute and performing other lawful services to their sagamores"; and in 1665 Metacom went to Nantucket in order to kill a native preacher, John Gibbs (Assasamoogh), who had dishonored the name of the sachem's father. Gibbs was not harmed because the local English paid a ransom for his life. Second, Easton did not explain the phrase "called or forced to be Christian Indians." Francis Jennings interprets the phrase to mean "at gunpoint." This interpretation rests on his dubious conclusion that Eliot's native missionaries had already evangelized the Nipmucks in this manner. A more plausible way of construing Easton's statement is that Metacom feared that a missionary provision might be added to the existing act of submission or included in a future one.[61]

Metacom also informed Easton that "the English made them [praying Indians] not subject to their kings, and by their lying to wrong their kings." This or a similar charge had been levied against Eliot's mission on other occasions. In September 1654, for instance, the Commissioners gave Eliot the same advice given to Mayhew: "be slow in withdrawing Indian professors from paying accustomed tribute and performing other lawful services to their sagamores." The Commissioners did not explain why they offered this recommendation to the two missionaries. The likely reason was that sachems whose concerns the Commissioners had to respect were grumbling about the loss of tribute. The obvious sachem in Mayhew's case was Massasoit. The Eliot counterpart was probably Uncas, who had complained in the spring of 1654 about his diminished control over the Quinebaug Indians under Pummakummin. Similar charges against Eliot surfaced later in time. In 1665 the royal commissioners claimed that the Apostle taught his proselytes "not to obey their heathen princes." This claim probably originated with the English or the Indians in Rhode Island, the commissioners' main sources of information about Massachusetts Bay. In 1674 Eliot and Gookin told the "agent for Uncas" who accosted them at Wabquisset that they wished to honor the sachem's "just and ancient rights over the Indians, in respect of paying tribute or any other dues." As James Axtell notes, the fact that the two Puritans "anticipated the sachem's complaints of loss of tribute before they were ever raised" reflected the mission's reputation among the pagan sachems in southern New England.[62]

Easton also reported that Metacom had disclosed that praying Indians were "in every thing more mischievous, only dissemblers." Jill Lepore, observing that elsewhere in the document Easton told the story of the sachem's rewritten will, suggests that Metacom was speaking about Sassamon.[63] Her suggestion may not be relevant to the problem at hand because Easton did not indicate that he had heard the story from Philip. The sachem had other reasons for considering Sassamon a dissembler. Walker stated in his letter to Prince that "Philip and [his counselor] Tom Sancsuik [had] exclaimed much against Sassamon for reporting that any of the Narragansett sachems were there" during the peace embassy in August 1671. Walker provided no further details. More to the point, however, was the embassy itself. Metacom surely felt betrayed by Sassamon, William, and Anthony, who had encouraged him to take his grievances to Massachusetts Bay. The eventual outcome of the sachem's trip to Boston was the meeting at Plymouth in late September, when he agreed to a set of humiliating terms after learning that the three orthodox colonies, and not simply Plymouth, were aligned against him.

Easton's discussion with Metacom took place about a week before the start of the war. The sachem's complaints about native evangelists, whether made exclusively or largely in reference to Eliot's proselytes, indicate that resentment of missionaries contributed to Pokanoket belligerence. Many historians have drawn this conclusion from Easton's testimony, even though they rightly place more causal weight on other factors that surfaced in Easton's conversation with Philip, such as expansion, dishonest business practices, inequities in civil and criminal justice, and trespassing English livestock. Insofar as they speak as one, these scholars argue that Philip resented missionaries because he feared the formation of a Christian secessionist movement that would undermine his authority and because he did not want his people to be localized in praying towns. This is a valid argument, but it does not go far enough. None of the historians perceives the role that Eliot's well-intentioned attempt at mediation in 1671 played in intensifying Pokanoket anger against native missionaries.[64]

Eliot apparently never recognized that his peace initiative strengthened Metacom's resolve to prevent his people from being "called or forced to be Christian Indians" and that the initiative helped drive the sachem to violence in 1675. Although he was insufficiently self-critical to grasp his own role in bringing about these two eventualities, the Apostle was perceptive enough to see Plymouth's responsibility for them. As will be seen in the next chapter, Eliot blamed Plymouth's expansionist policies both for the failure of the Pokanoket mission and for King Philip's War. His conviction that the colonial governments had to do Indians "justice about their lands" is one of the least appreciated aspects of his character.

CHAPTER EIGHT

· · ·

The Supervision of the Mission

Shortly after its creation in July 1649, the New England Company asked the clergymen of England to read the act of incorporation to their congregations and to collect donations for the instruction of the Indians. The Company's fund-raising efforts also benefited from some free publicity that soon appeared in London. In 1650 Thomas Thorowgood published *Iewes in America,* and that same year the Baptist divine Henry Jessey produced a translation of Casparus Sibelius's account of Dutch missionary activity, *Of the Conversion of Five Thousand and Nine Hundred East-Indians.* Thorowgood and Jessey included summaries of the first three Eliot tracts in their works. In 1651 Henry Whitfield issued the fourth tract, *The Light appearing more and more towards the perfect Day.* The New England Company then funded its own publicity campaign, publishing the next five Eliot tracts and securing endorsements for most of them from prominent Presbyterian and Independent clergymen.[1]

The corporation's ability to raise money was impaired by the legacy of the Thomas Weld–Hugh Peter agency in the 1640s. In 1649 Edward Winslow told Weld that some ministers in London were reluctant to raise revenue for the Indian work because they suspected (rightly) that the "moneys they had formerly collected for transporting children to New England" had not been used for that purpose. Similar accusations soon surfaced against the mission. Whitfield observed in *The Light appearing* that persons in England were "either apt, or do believe" that the Indian work was a "device or engine . . . to cheat good people of their money"; Thomas Allen, the Charlestown minister who repatriated in late 1650 or early 1651, noted in *Strength out of Weaknesse* that "some of late have . . . publicly affirm[ed] that there was no such thing as the preaching and dispersing of the Gospel in New England"; Richard Mather wrote in *Tears of Repentance* that "some have thought . . . that this whole business of the Indians . . . is but a politic device and design to get money, and that there is indeed no such matter as any work of God's grace amongst that people"; and Eliot lamented in his "Learned Conjectures" that "some express their fears of some corruption to be the latent springs that move in the work of preaching to the Indians." Furthermore, the Company told the Commissioners in February 1654 that Hugh Peter had recently "heard [that] the work was but a plain cheat and that there was no such thing as gospel conversion among the Indians." Shortly thereafter, Peter suggested that the money available for the mission be given to the poor in New England.[2]

The Company published the five Eliot tracts in order to counteract these allegations. The strategy proved effective, for by 1660 nearly £16,000 had been donated to the Indian work. Roughly three-quarters of this money was promptly invested in England, primarily in real estate. The investments netted only £22 in 1653 but returned approximately £800 in 1656. The income receded in the late 1650s as tenants used the chaotic political situation as an excuse to withhold payments. Between 1650 and 1660, the New England Company spent approximately £1,500 on operating expenses and £4,700 on the various New England missions.[3]

The corporation was dissolved in 1660 by the Act of Oblivion and Indemnity. The Company's officers then faced the challenge of convincing the Stuart government to reestablish an organization founded by Puritans. The officers prudently purged their ranks of persons who had served on the Interregnum courts of justice and enlisted Richard Baxter and Robert Boyle to support the plan for reviving the missionary society. Baxter soon persuaded the Lord Chancellor, the Earl of Clarendon, to back the plan at court. The corporation was restored in February 1662 as the Company for Propagation of the Gospel in New England and the Parts Adjacent in America. The 1662 charter, like its 1649 counterpart, stated that England had to fund the missions because New England was too impoverished to do so. Although it was perhaps true in the 1640s, the assumption that the colonists could not pay for the Indian work was manifestly false in the 1660s. Francis Jennings has observed that "the wampum tribute extorted . . . from various tribes would have financed a considerable missionary effort," and Lynn Ceci has determined that by 1664 the Commissioners of the United Colonies had received from the natives in southern New England and on Long Island wampum indemnities worth approximately £5,000. Why the restored corporation did not demand that the orthodox colonies share or assume the financial burden is a matter for speculation. The Company's officers evidently did not know about the indemnities, and the confederation was unwilling to tell London about them.[4]

Boyle was the governor of the New England Company from 1662 until his death in 1689. He replaced William Steele, who had served as the corporation's president (the title was changed to governor in 1662) since 1649. Henry Ashurst became the treasurer following the death of Richard Floyd (or Lloyd) in 1659 and remained such until his passing in 1680. The governing body also included officers called "assistants," many of whom were Presbyterian or Independent merchants in London. Edward Winslow, Herbert Pelham, Edward Hopkins (the former governor of Connecticut), and Thomas Bell (a onetime Roxbury resident) served as assistants at various times during the prewar period.[5]

In April 1662 the New England Company had approximately £500 in available cash. Revenue declined in the 1660s and early 1670s because benefactors were not as generous as they had been during the Interregnum and because the Great Fire of 1666 destroyed many of the Company's landed investments. Furthermore, the royalist Colonel Thomas Bedingfield sued the corporation over valuable properties it had acquired in the 1650s; the Company was vindicated in 1669 but at great expense in legal fees. Annual income from investments averaged £440 between 1662 and 1690; additional expenses were covered by noninvested contributions.[6]

Both before and after the Restoration, the Commissioners of the United Colonies served as the intermediaries between the corporation and the missionaries. The Commissioners consisted of two magistrates from the four—after New Haven's absorption by Connecticut in 1664, the three—orthodox colonies. The representatives from Massachusetts Bay were usually Simon Bradstreet of Cambridge and either

Daniel Denison of Ipswich or Thomas Danforth of Cambridge. The Commissioners began to transact Company business in September 1650 and continued to do so at every annual session through 1664. The confederation then adopted what was for the most part a triennial schedule of meetings and instructed the delegates from Massachusetts and Plymouth, or any three of their number, to meet once a year between full sessions to administer the various missions. The latter provision was slightly modified in 1670, when the Massachusetts representatives were authorized to supervise the Indian work "with such others as shall be present or any three of the Commissioners." The confederation held its last regular meeting in 1684. The next year the New England Company created a body of magistrates and ministers called the "Commissioners for Indian Affairs." These commissioners, who were appointed by the corporation, included Samuel Sewall and Increase and Cotton Mather.[7]

The arrangements between the New England Company and the United Colonies changed over time. From 1651 through 1656, the corporation purchased goods in England and sent them to the Commissioners, who distributed some of the materials to the Indians and sold the rest in order to pay the missionaries and to cover other expenses. At their September 1650 meeting, the Commissioners asked the Company to ship clothing, cloth, and tools worth £1,000 in English money. The officers in London replied that "we are not in a capacity to send so much at present." Between April 1651 and May 1652, the corporation sent four shipments of merchandise worth about £500 in England. These shipments, for which detailed inventories exist, consisted of tools and utensils, clothing and cloth, spindles and needles, medicine, seeds, and many English-language works, including 200 Bibles. The boat carrying the second shipment ran aground off Scituate; the damaged cargo was recovered at a salvage cost to the corporation of approximately £14. The first two shipments were addressed to John Cotton and John Wilson, who had not asked for the responsibility of distributing the contents. In September 1651 the confederation directed Edward Rawson to receive the goods and to distribute or sell them as instructed. Rawson served in this capacity until procedures were changed in 1657; he was paid a corporation salary of £20 to £30 per annum for his trouble.[8]

The goods shipped from England in the early to mid-1650s were normally those requested by the Commissioners. The most commonly requested items were clothing and cloth, tools, and guns and ammunition. In 1654, 1655, and 1656 the Commissioners asked for merchandise valued at £468, £500, and £1,000, respectively, in English money. The corporation responded to the first request by sending materials that exceeded the proposed figure, to the second by shipping goods worth less than 10 percent of the requested amount, and to the third by altering procedures in a manner shortly explained.[9]

The arms and ammunition were for sale to colonists and not for allocation to Indians. The confederation and the corporation recognized that these items commanded a high price in New England markets. In 1652 the Commissioners placed their first known order for weaponry; later that year, the Company sent a shipment of goods that included 60 barrels of powder, 20 barrels of shot, 2 barrels of flints, 80 muskets, and 100 snaphance locks. Instead of putting them all up for public auction, the Commissioners distributed "one half at least" of the guns, powder, and shot to the Massachusetts, Plymouth, Connecticut, and New Haven troops in the event of war with the Dutch and their alleged Eastern Niantic allies. The confederation then wrote to London about what they had done. This letter explained that the weapons were for use against the Dutch; the Eastern Niantics were not mentioned. In September 1654 the Commissioners informed the Company that the four colonies had reimbursed Rawson for the weaponry. A suspicious corporation never again sent guns and ammunition for sale in New England. In 1655 the Commissioners asked for 20 barrels of gunpowder valued at £80, and in 1656 they ordered £100 worth of powder, promising on the latter occasion that "we shall not divide it among the colonies." The New England Company ignored both requests.[10]

In 1657 the corporation changed existing policy by instructing the Commissioners to send bills of exchange to England for goods purchased in New England and for moneys paid to the missionaries and to others. The change was made to eliminate the risk of loss of goods at sea and to give the Commissioners the benefit of the rate of exchange. The Commissioners were expected to furnish London with an itemized lists of expenditures that did not exceed a specified annual figure, initially £500 in English money. Hezekiah Usher, a Boston merchant and the first bookseller in Massachusetts Bay, was responsible for purchasing the goods in New England and also for negotiating the rate of exchange. The corporation hoped for an exchange rate of 25 percent and was willing to settle for 14 or 15 percent. Usher initially offered a 6 percent rate and eventually raised it to 12 percent.[11]

In 1659 the corporation neglected to set a ceiling figure on expenditures. The Commissioners promptly sent a bill for £800, which London managed to pay. In 1661 John Hooper, the secretary of the temporarily defunct corporation, asked the United Colonies to refrain from sending any more bills. The Commissioners nevertheless charged another £800 because the Indian Bible was in press and "require[d] speedy supply." The Company paid these charges "for the most part" after its reestablishment in 1662. Once the Bible was finished in 1663, the two parties negotiated more modest annual figures of £300 to £500.[12]

From the mid-1650s on, the Commissioners wanted the corporation to invest some of its money in New England. They did not get their way until 1669, when London sent a £360 gift from a Parisian lawyer, variously identified as "Mouche," "Mowchee," and "Montrye," whom Boyle had persuaded to contribute to the mission. Boyle pointedly reminded the Commissioners that £360 in England "makes £450 with you." In 1673 the Company wondered why the confederation found "it difficult to make a good improvement of Mr. Mowchee's gift," which to this point had apparently returned only the £31 given to James Fitch in 1672. The corporation nonetheless continued to make investments in New England. By 1683 approximately £3,400 had been invested locally; the return the previous year was only £156.[13]

Eliot's relations with the Commissioners were often strained. In the early to mid-1650s, he complained to Weld and others in England that the Commissioners were not adequately compensating him. His remarks reached the ears of the corporation's officers, who informed the Commissioners in February 1654 about "the many complaints made by Mr. Eliot to sundry of his friends here that you allow him but twenty pounds per annum" (his corporation salary at the time, as distinct from the Armine annuity). The London officers then recommended a pay increase, telling the United Colonies that "we are far from justifying Mr. Eliot in his turbulent and clamorous proceedings, but the best of God's servants have their failings, and as such so we look upon him." The Commissioners dutifully raised Eliot's stipend to £40 and then scolded him for criticizing them behind their backs. The following year, the corporation heard fresh complaints and informed the confederation about them. The Commissioners sent Eliot another scolding letter but nevertheless raised his 1656 salary to £50, where it stayed at least through 1672. Eliot remained dissatisfied with his compensation. In 1671 he told the Commissioners that "in all the public meetings, motions, journeys, translations, attendances on the press, and other occasions, I have never had (to my knowledge and remembrance) the least acknowledgment from yourselves, or one penny supply, save my bare salary."[14]

The Apostle was not as mercenary as these complaints make him seem. He may have been the only seventeenth-century Bay Puritan who contributed money to the mission. In 1651 he sent Winslow a list of goods he needed and explained that "if the things I desire, should a little exceed my £20 [the Armine annuity, which by this time was sent to him directly by the corporation] ... it will be acceptable [to me]"; in 1670 he told the New England Company that his stipend was "expended only upon the work"; and in 1671 he informed the Commissioners that his £50 salary "is bound before it comes" because he had incurred debts for various missionary expenses. Eliot also used some of his Company salary to help pay the printing costs for the second edition of the Indian Bible. He was also generous to others. In 1666 he asked the New England Company to assign his "whole year's salary ... unto such as Mr. Ashurst and Mr. [Thomas] Bell ... shall think fit." William Kellaway suggests that the beneficiaries were ejected ministers in England; in any event, the corporation honored the Apostle's wishes. There is also a legend that Eliot once gave his Roxbury salary to an impoverished family in Massachusetts Bay.[15]

Another area of friction concerned the goods shipped directly to Eliot by private benefactors in England. Between 1651 and 1657 Thomas Thorowgood and Henry Jessey, as well as Ferdinando Nicolls of Exeter and Jonathan Hanmer of Barnstaple, sent him merchandise worth approximately £200 in English money. In 1653 Eliot promised the Commissioners that he would "rest satisfied with a smaller allowance ... from corporation stock" in exchange for an exemption from giving them accounts of private benefactions. That Eliot agreed to these terms and then complained about his allocations understandably nettled the Commissioners. Fortunately for both parties, this problem eventually solved itself. The last known occasion when Eliot received goods from private benefactors in England was a shipment sent by Jessey in 1657.[16]

The Apostle was also prepared to circumvent the Commissioners and ask the New England Company directly for goods or funds. In April 1651 he instructed Edward Winslow to send "Bibles for the Indians, and also paper, inkhorns, [and] primers"; six months later, he made the same request in another letter to Winslow. These items were included in the two shipments of goods transported from London in 1652. In 1653 Winslow sent Eliot some "kettles, glass, tools, etc." that he had requested; and in 1655 the corporation shipped merchandise worth £34 to him. In 1670 and 1671 Eliot received directly from London cash awards of £40 and £80 to cover missionary debts. He wrote the 1671 letter because the Commissioners had refused to cover the £80 debt; whether they also refused the £40 one is not known. In 1675 Boyle also sent a gift of £30, which Eliot eventually divided between Cotton, Jr., and Gookin's widow and son, Daniel.[17]

Eliot frustrated the Commissioners in another respect as well. They expected him to keep records about how he distributed the New England Company goods they gave to him. In July 1652 Eliot furnished an itemized list of the distributions that he had made to the Indians since the spring of 1651, when the first shipments arrived; in this document he also accounted for the whereabouts of £20 worth of materials that he and Roxbury deacon William Parke had purchased in 1649 and 1650 against Company credit. Eliot provided another such list (now lost) in 1654. There is no conclusive evidence that he ever did so again.[18]

Eliot was also annoyed whenever the confederation turned down his purpose-specific requests. His habit was to send lists of requests to the Commissioners in advance of their meetings. Only two of these letters survive. In the first of them, written in August 1664, he asked for and received a £10 allowance for an Indian interpreter (presumably Job Nesutan) who was helping him with his current translation projects. At this time, the Commissioners also granted Eliot's request to give £5 stipends to eight native schoolteachers in Massachusetts Bay; in 1663 they had rejected a similar plea and instructed Indian parents to pay for the education of their children. In 1664 the Apostle also tried and failed to convince the Commissioners to extend the contract of Marmaduke Johnson, a local printer under contract to the New England Company, for an additional year; in 1663 he had persuaded them to keep Johnson through 1664. Eliot also asked in the 1664 letter that Gookin receive a raise (the confederation turned him down because the corporation had so advised) and that John Sassamon be compensated for teaching "Philip and his men to read" (there is no recorded action in this case). Finally, Eliot informed the Commissioners that he had told his native missionaries that they were to receive "shoes, stockings, a coat and neckcloth provided for them . . . by the rent of a farm in the hands of the worshipful [Thomas] Danforth, and I thank him he has ordered supply in the matter." According to James Hammond Trumbull, the manuscript copy of Eliot's letter in the Connecticut archives has a marginal note, apparently in Danforth's hand, that reads "a great mistake so to affirm."[19]

Eliot's second letter was written in September 1671. On this occasion he asked the Commissioners to pay the printing costs for *Indian Dialogues* and "Our Indians' A B C" and to honor a debt of "£100 at least" that he had incurred for his lectures on logic at Natick, for missionaries to the Nipmucks, and for powder and shot distributed to the Wamesit Indians for their "necessary defense in these times of danger." He explained, "A bill of £80 [£100 in New English money] to England would discharge me." The Commissioners paid the publishing costs but did not accept the £100 debt. On December 1, 1671, Eliot sent Ashurst a copy of his letter to the Commissioners and told him that they had refused to honor the debt. For good measure, he wrote to Boyle the same day and repeated the complaint. In March 1672 the officers of the corporation paid the debt and told the Commissioners that they had done so because they were "unwilling to discourage so worthy an instrument of the Gospel as Mr. Eliot."[20]

The Commissioners of the United Colonies were reluctant participants in the mission. As Eliot lamented in 1652, the Commissioners were "not so well informed or persuaded" about the Indian work. The supervision of the mission took time away from their primary responsibility, intercolonial defense against native or European aggressors. In 1656 the Company considered and rejected a proposal by Weld and Peter for creating a seven-man committee that would administer the mission for the Commissioners. Kellaway suggests that the plan was turned down because the corporation's charter did not give it the power to force co-opted members upon the Commissioners and because the proposal was too costly (each committee member was to receive an annual stipend of £20 in English money). For their part, the Commissioners were displeased that they themselves were not compensated by the corporation. In 1655, in an unsuccessful attempt to change this situation, they reminded London that they received not "one penny recompense either for time, pains, or charge expended therein." In 1658 the Massachusetts General Court instructed its current representatives to the United Colonies, Simon Bradstreet and John Endecott, to convince their fellow Commissioners that a "proportionable allowance" of corporation funds should be given to the colonies for supervising the various missions. Nothing came of the notion, and the Commissioners found other ways of obtaining rewards from the Indian work.[21]

Missionary Expenditures

The Commissioners spent most of the corporation's money in three areas. One, discussed earlier, was allocations to the missionaries and their English and Indian co-workers. The other two were the publication of Eliot's Massachusett works and his related writings, and the English-language education of natives in grammar schools and at the Indian College at Harvard.

Publication Costs

There were three printing presses in prewar New England, and Eliot made use of each of them. The first had been shipped to Massachusetts Bay in 1638 by the Reverend Jose Glover. This press was operated by Stephen Day and his son Matthew in the 1640s, and by Samuel Green thereafter. It became the property of Harvard in 1654—in all likelihood as a gift from Henry Dunster, who had married Glover's widow in 1641—and by 1656 was located on the ground floor of the Indian College. In late 1659 or early 1660, the New England Company sent over another press that was soon housed in the Indian College as well. The corporation also furnished a journeyman printer, Marmaduke Johnson, and gave him a three-year contract. Johnson's annual salary was £40 in English money, plus room and board; he was expected to work six twelve-hour days. In 1662 he was convicted, fined, and briefly jailed by the Middlesex County Court for proposing to one of Green's daughters even though he had a wife in England. Johnson went back to England in 1664, after the expiration of the grace year on his contract. By this time his wife had died and the engagement had ended. He returned to Massachusetts in 1665 with a new press and new type. Johnson operated this press elsewhere in Cambridge and later moved it to Boston. After Johnson's death in 1674, the press was managed by John Foster and later by several of Green's sons.[22]

The printers in Massachusetts Bay coveted Eliot's business. Samuel Green remarked in 1675 that producing the missionary writings was "the most considerable of any work in the country because of the pay for it." The two editions of the Bible were the most expensive publications. The actual cost of producing 1,500 copies of the New Testament in 1661 and 1,000 copies of the Old in 1663, however, cannot be determined. An estimate can be formed from the fact that Marmaduke Johnson spent approximately £170 on supplies between October 1660 and June 1661. The publication of 2,000 copies of the second edition of the Bible, which required resetting the type, cost roughly £900.[23] Table 2 summarizes the costs and print runs of Eliot's other New England Company publications.

Ever since its arrival in 1659 or 1660, the Company press was used for printing works unrelated to the mission. A survey of Charles Evans's *American Bibliography* and its supplements reveals that eleven nonmissionary books and various broadsides were produced by "Samuel Green and Marmaduke Johnson" (the standard designation for works printed on the corporation press) between 1660 and 1664, the year Green and Johnson ended their association. The Commissioners did not inform the Company about this questionable use of its property. In 1668 Charles Chauncy, Dunster's successor as Harvard president, asked the missionary society to give its press to the college for general printing purposes. The corporation agreed instead to loan the press to Harvard for use "upon necessary occasions." Whether the officers in London knew it or not, their decision made official what was already the case.[24]

By 1665 the Commissioners were eager to end the production of Massachusett-language works, telling London that the planned publication of Eliot's translations of Bayly's *Practice of Piety* and Shepard's *Sincere Convert* and *Sound Believer* "will cost nearly £200" and that these three works and those "already printed will be sufficient for the natives for many years." The Commissioners, however, stopped short of offering to ship the Company's press back to London after the Bayly and Shepard translations were printed. The corporation's immediate response to the proposed cessation of Massachusett publications is unknown because its correspondence from the mid-1660s does not survive. The Company clearly supported the idea by June 1668, when Boyle told the confederation that it was "necessary and seasonable to abate all charge that is not essential" and specifically instanced the "printing and binding of books." But by this time, the situation had

Table 2 Publication costs and press runs of Eliot's Cambridge imprints, exclusive of the Indian Bible

Work	No. of copies	Approximate cost
"Primer and catechism" (1st ed., 1654)	500	£10
"Primer and catechism" (2nd ed., 1662)	1,500	£15
"Primer and catechism" (3rd ed., 1669)	2,000	£20
"Primer and catechism" (4th ed., 1686 or 1687)	N/A	N/A
Genesis (1655)	N/A	N/A
Matthew (1655)	N/A	N/A
Metrical psalter (1st ed., 1658 or 1659)	N/A	N/A
Metrical psalter (2nd ed., 1663 or 1664)	500	£9
Metrical psalter (3rd ed., 1682)	N/A	N/A
Covenanting Confession (1st ed., 1660 or 1661)	N/A	N/A
Covenanting Confession (2nd ed., ca. 1670)	N/A	N/A
Call to the Unconverted (1st ed., 1664)	1,000	£20
Call to the Unconverted (2nd ed., 1688)	N/A	N/A
The Practice of Piety (1st ed., 1665)	200	£55
The Practice of Piety (2nd ed., 1685)	N/A	£20
The Indian Grammar Begun (1666)	450	N/A
Indian Dialogues (1671)	N/A	£8
"Our Indians' A B C" (1671)	N/A	£3
The Logick Primer (1672)	1,000	£26
The Sincere Convert (1689)	N/A	N/A

Sources: William Kellaway, *The New England Company, 1649–1776: Missionary Society to the American Indians* (New York: Barnes and Noble, 1962), pp. 134–146; and George Parker Winship, *The Cambridge Press, 1638–1692* (Philadelphia: University of Pennsylvania Press, 1945), pp. 159–274.

changed in New England. The Commissioners wrote back the following September to explain that they had authorized the publication of another edition of the "primer and catechism" because Eliot and Richard Bourne had said that "the instruction of the Indians is greatly obstructed for want of [it]." In the early 1670s the Commissioners also approved the printing of *Indian Dialogues, The Logick Primer,* and "Our Indians' A B C."[25]

English-Language Education

The emphasis throughout the prewar period was on conducting Massachusett-language training in native-run schools in the praying towns. But at the same time Eliot, the Commissioners, and the corporation advocated the education of selected Indian children in the colony's dame and grammar schools, and at Harvard. The proselytes also supported the idea because they considered literacy in English a mark of erudition. "He is a learned man among them," Eliot wrote in 1666, "who can speak, read, and write the English tongue."[26]

The grammar school education of Indian children was normally provided in Cambridge by Elijah Corlet or in Roxbury by Daniel Weld, the older brother of Eliot's former clerical colleague. James Axtell has determined that between 1658 and 1672, approximately twenty natives attended grammar school at Company expense. At least three of them came from Martha's Vineyard, one or more was a Pequot, and at least one was a girl. No fewer than eight of the students died while in school; Gookin noted that the leading cause of death was a "hectic fever issuing in a consumption." William Kellaway has calculated that it cost the corporation about £19 a year to feed, clothe, house, and educate a grammar school Indian.[27]

Three or possibly four natives attended Harvard prior to the construction of the Indian College in the mid-1650s. One was John Sassamon. Two others, called James (possibly James the Printer) and Jonathan, were enrolled between August 1645 and October 1646. Dunster complained that the boys were "so small as that they are incapable of the benefit of such learning as was my desire to impart to them, and therefore they being a hindrance to me and I no furtherance to them, I desire they being somewhere else disposed of with all convenient speed." The education of the two youths cost the General Court approximately £22; the expenses included a charge for "washing" them. Whether or not there was a fourth native at Harvard depends on how one reads John Cotton's ambiguous 1647 statement that "an Indian from Plymouth side was received into some employment at the college, that he might be trained up to knowledge for the help of his countrymen."[28]

The Indian College was not a separate institution with its own curriculum but a dormitory used primarily by regular Harvard undergraduates and secondarily by English and Indian students involved in the mission. The steps that led to the construction of the college began in 1651, when the corporation suggested that the United Colonies educate "English and Indian together for the better obtaining [of] each other's language" and when Dunster informed the Commissioners that the "decaying condition" of the existing Harvard dormitory (the "old college") forced "scholars . . . to lodge in the town." In September 1651 the Commissioners wrote a letter to Winslow, asking him to ascertain if the New England Company was willing to pay for "the enlargement of the college at Cambridge whereof there is great need and furtherance of learning not so much immediately respecting the Indian design." At the same time, the Commissioners told Dunster that if Winslow failed to convince his fellow officers in London to fund the construction of a dormitory, they would order the orthodox colonies to contribute "pecks, half bushels, and bushels of wheat" for the enlargement of Harvard. What Winslow did with the Commissioners' request is not known, but if he tried to convince the corporation to pay for the education and housing of Harvard undergraduates, he surely failed. In early 1649 the Parliament had rejected a proposal to make the missionary corporation's primary purpose the general education of colonists. The Commissioners were not optimistic about their chances of success, telling Dunster in 1651 that the 1649 act of incorporation did not grant "any such liberty."[29]

The matter rested quietly until May 1653, when Winslow informed the confederation that London wanted to educate six natives at Harvard so that they could master English and "disperse the Indian tongue" to their classmates. The Commissioners now saw an opportunity to enlarge Harvard at Company expense. During their meeting in September 1653, they wrote Winslow a letter explaining that in order to fulfill the corporation's wishes for the six natives, "we shall be forced to raise some building there for the conveniency of the Indians, wherein probably we shall be forced to expend at least one hundred pounds." At the same session, without waiting for approval from London, the Commissioners directed Massachusett Bay to erect a "building of one entire room at the college for the conveniency of six hopeful Indians to be trained up there according to the advice received this year from the corporation in London; which room may be two stories high and built plain but strong and durable, the charge not to exceed £120 [presumably in New English money] besides glass, which may be allowed out of the parcel the corporation has lately sent over upon the Indian account." Construction began within the year. In 1654 the Commissioners told the Bay Colony to "alter the form" of the building so that it "exceed not thirty feet in length and twenty in breadth." By September 1656 the edifice was complete. The cost of construction far exceeded the original estimate: Gookin noted in 1674 that the dormitory had cost "between three and four hundred pounds" to erect. He also provided the fullest description of the structure, stating that it was "a house of brick . . . strong and substantial, . . . large enough to receive and accommodate about twenty scholars with convenient lodgings and studies."[30]

The Commissioners wasted no time in putting the Indian College to use. In September 1656 they opened the building to regular Harvard students for a year. This directive was renewed in 1657 and remained in effect thereafter. To judge from the published correspondence between the two parties, the confederation never told the corporation that the structure was being used in this manner. As Kellaway has observed, the Commissioners obviously recognized that London "could not fall in with such a facile diversion of . . . [missionary] funds from their proper purpose." The number and names of the undergraduates who lived in the Indian College can no longer be determined, nor can the amount of housing revenue that entered the Harvard coffers. "We cannot tell who roomed there or what the study rents were," Samuel Eliot Morison has written.[31]

The College was presumably the place of residence for the small number of English and Indian students who attended Harvard in preparation for missionary service. John Stanton, the son of Thomas Stanton, Sr., was the only Englishman who went to Harvard at Company expense prior to King Philip's War. In 1654 the Commissioners convinced the elder Stanton to permit John and Thomas, Jr., to be "fitted for future service . . . in teaching such Indian children as shall be taken into the college for that end." By this time both sons had "good skill in the Indian language." Thomas, Jr., apparently never received a Cambridge education. John spent several years at Elijah Corlet's grammar school before entering Harvard in 1658. College life did not appeal to him—Chauncy accused him of "intolerable negligence"—and he dropped out a year or two later. He then returned to his Stonington home. Shortly thereafter he decided to resume his education with Abraham Pierson in Branford. In September 1661 John attended the Commissioners' meeting in Plymouth and presented a "testimonial letter from Mr. Pierson of his good carriage and proficiency in learning." The confederation agreed to resume his funding, on the condition that he reimburse the corporation if he "refuse[d] to be employed in the Indian work." Pierson received allocations of £25 for Stanton's maintenance from 1661 to 1663. John then disappears from the missionary sources, apparently without repaying the money. The Commissioners had wasted over £200 of Company funds on his education in the two Cambridge institutions and with Pierson.[32]

At least five natives studied at Harvard during the lifetime of the Indian College. Two were from Martha's Vineyard: Joel, the son of Hiacoomes, and Caleb Cheeschaumuck, both members of the Class of 1665. Prior to their matriculation, they studied with Peter Folger on the Vineyard and then with Corlet in Cambridge. There is no reason to think that the two Indians followed a simplified curriculum at either Cambridge institution. Corlet and/or Chauncy wrote testimonials about their Latin proficiency that were appended to *A further Accompt* and *A further Account;* and Winthrop, Jr., told Boyle that he had conversed with them in Latin and that he had heard them recite Greek. The two natives died young. Shortly before the 1665 commencement service, Joel and several other persons were shipwrecked on Nantucket and murdered by Indians who wanted their goods; Gookin later noted that some of the culprits were executed for the crime. Caleb succumbed to consumption several months after receiving his degree. He is the only Indian known to have graduated from Harvard in the colonial period.[33]

The third of the five Indian students at Harvard was John Wampas, who matriculated in 1665. He was probably the son of Wamporas, whose variant names include Wampas. "Wholly indisposed to follow learning," John left the institution in 1667 or 1668 and went to sea. After King Philip's War he became a speculator in Indian land. The fourth Indian was in residence in 1675. His existence is established in a Guildhall Library manuscript cited by Kellaway. This native was surely the "Eleazar" who styled himself "Indus Senior Sophista" in October 1678, when he composed a Latin elegy and a Greek epitaph for Thomas Thacher, minister in Third (Old South) Church, Boston. The fifth was an unidentified "Indian youth maintained and educated at the college in New England" in 1684. Only one other Indian, Benjamin Larnell, is known to have attended Harvard prior to the Revolution, in this case after the demolition of the Indian College. Larnell, a resident of the former Plymouth Colony, entered Harvard after graduating from the Boston Latin School; he died in 1714 before completing his degree.[34]

The Indian College did not survive the seventeenth century. In November 1693 the Harvard corporation ordered that the structure be destroyed, provided the costs did not exceed £5. No one was willing to undertake the task for such paltry compensation. In September 1695 the Commissioners for Indian Affairs requested that the building be demolished because "it is gone to decay and become altogether useless," adding that "any Indians [who] should hereafter be sent to the college . . . should enjoy their studies rent free." The edifice nevertheless remained standing until May 1698, when Samuel Sewall noted that "the old brick college, commonly called the Indian college, is pulled to the ground." The bricks were then used for the construction of the original Stoughton College at Harvard. The saints did not have to honor the promise to provide a "rent free" college education to the only Indian who subsequently attended Harvard in the colonial period—Larnell's expenses were covered by a bequest from Boyle.[35]

The foregoing examination of the confederation's actions raises an obvious question: Did the Commissioners defraud the New England Company? Kellaway concludes that "on the whole the Company was well served" by the United Colonies; but Jennings contends that the Commissioners "took advantage of their agency to divert mission funds to ends of their own" and that the corporation "transmitted much more money than was ever accounted for in mission records or activity."[36] Jennings's assessment is the more accurate. There is abundant evidence for the Commissioners' dishonesty: their decision to distribute to the orthodox colonies "one half at least" of the arms and ammunition sent from London for public auction in 1652; their claim that the colonies had reimbursed the corporation for these weapons (not even Kellaway believes this one); their suspiciously poor improvement of the Mouche benefaction and other investments in New England; their use of the New England Company's press and the Indian College for nonmissionary purposes; and their refusal to inform the corporation that the press and the dormitory were being used in this manner.

The other New England institution that supervised Eliot's mission was the Massachusetts General Court, which held civil jurisdiction over the praying Indians. The Apostle believed that the subordination of the proselytes to the General Court placed obligations on both parties. He expected the natives to seek redress through the colony's court system and to obey its laws, including those that proscribed behavior that was not criminal in traditional Algonquian society, most notably powwowing and working on Sundays (Eliot is silent on the subject of blasphemy). In order to strengthen the colony's power over the proselytes, he persuaded the General Court to create the Indian Superintendency in 1658. The Superintendent was a magistrate appointed by the court to adjudicate minor civil and criminal cases in the praying towns. At the same time Eliot demanded that the General Court protect the proselytes from land-grabbing settlers and from native marauders. His many petitions on the Indians' behalf show that he expected the colony to take these obligations seriously. For him, subordination to the General Court did not mean subjugation by it.

The Indian Superintendency and the Massachusetts General Court

By the time of King Philip's War, the court's authority extended to the Indians in the fourteen praying towns and in the semiofficial ones at and around Quabag and Nashaway. Most of these natives had submitted to the government before Eliot tried to evangelize them: the 1644 act of submission included the residents of the future old towns at Natick, Punkapoag, Nashobah, and Wamesit as well as the settlements at Quabag and Nashaway; and the 1668 act embraced the Indians in the new towns at Manchage, Chabanakongkomun, Quantisset, and Wabquisset. The inhabitants of three old towns (Okommakamesit, Hassanamesit, and Magunkog) and three new ones (Waeuntug, Maanexit, and Pakachoog) were not covered by either act of submission. The mission introduced the natives in these six settlements to the rule of the General Court.

After establishing the institution in 1658, the General Court exercised its authority over the praying towns primarily through the Superintendency. The court had created a precursor to the position in 1647, when at Eliot's request it directed "one or more of the magistrates" to hold quarterly sessions for important civil and criminal cases originating in the Christian Indian settlements. As indicated in

Chapter 3, the language barrier and other factors prevented any of the magistrates from carrying out the directive. Eliot revived his proposal for English supervision in late August 1656, asking the Commissioners to appoint "some agents . . . in Massachusetts [Bay] to promote and forward the work among the Indians, both in respect of their government and encouraging some meet instruments for their further help and instruction." The United Colonies referred the matter to the General Court, which clearly did nothing about it because Eliot was obliged to repeat his request to the Commissioners in September 1657, suggesting on this occasion that Gookin and Humphrey Atherton of Dorchester be named the "agents." Once again the confederation turned the matter over to Massachusetts Bay. The court did not act until May 1658, when it established the Superintendency and gave it authority over all "Indians subject to us, especially those of Natick and Punkapoag."[37]

Eliot never explained why he revived the plan in 1656. One likely reason was his sciatica, which appeared in mid-August 1656, two weeks before his first petition to the Commissioners. The onset of the disease probably convinced him that he needed to arrange for substitute English supervision over the praying towns during his convalescence. A second was that the growing scope of the mission placed severe demands on his time even when he was able to travel: Natick, Punkapoag, Hassanamesit, Nashobah, Okommakamesit, and Wamesit had been formed, or were in the process of formation, by the mid-1650s. A third reason was that since 1655 the Commissioners had been debating the possibility of abolishing the salary for Francis Eliot, who instructed the proselytes in carpentry and in plant and animal husbandry. These, among others, were made duties of the Superintendent. The Apostle may have feared that he would be without such assistance should his brother's services be terminated. Eliot miscalculated if this was his reasoning, for the creation of the Superintendency was surely the event that removed Francis from the New England Company payroll.

In the 1658 action, the court instructed the Superintendent to "appoint Indian commissioners [evidently the 'rulers' and 'chief rulers' in the praying towns] in their several plantations to hear and determine all such matters that do arise among themselves, as one magistrate may do among the English." This provision presumably meant that Indian commissioners, like Puritan magistrates, were empowered to hear civil suits under 20 shillings and to punish minor criminal infractions such as drunkenness, sabbath-breaking, and petty theft. The praying town rulers were already adjudicating such matters, as the 1654 incident involving Totherswamp's drunken son shows. The 1658 directive also stated that the Superintendent "with the said commissioners, shall have the power of a county court." The county courts of the day ruled on civil actions between 20 shillings and £10 and on more serious criminal cases not extending to life, limb, and banishment.

Atherton was named Superintendent in the same 1658 action that created the office; Gookin was in England at the time. Atherton had only one known previous connection with the mission: in 1657 he was the recipient of Eliot's petition that Dorchester assign land to the Punkapoag Indians. After his appointment Atherton served on several of the committees created to investigate the Natick-Dedham boundary dispute. He received a corporation salary of £10 or £15 between 1658 and his death in 1661, which occurred when he was thrown from his horse after a collision with a cow. At the time of the accident, he was also major general of the colony's forces. Eliot said little about Atherton's performance as Superintendent except that it was inferior to Gookin's. The Apostle's decision to recommend Atherton in 1657 was curious. In the words of one recent scholar, the Dorchester man was "probably" the "military leader most hostile to Native Americans." In 1648 and 1650 he led expeditions authorized by the Commissioners into the Narragansett Country, and in 1659 he founded the Narragansett Proprietors—sometimes called the Atherton Company—to defraud the Rhode Island Indians of their lands.[38]

At Eliot's request Gookin was named Superintendent in November 1661; he retained the office until his death in 1687, when he was replaced by Thomas Prentice, the last person to hold the position. Gookin claimed in his *Historical Collections* that he had been the colony's first Superintendent, serving as such from 1656 until leaving for England in 1657. If so, he worked in an unofficial capacity because the General Court did not create the post until 1658. His association with the mission may have commenced with Eliot's initial Nonantum sermon in October 1646. Explicit evidence of Gookin's involvement did not surface until 1651, when he participated in a question and answer session with a visiting Vineyard Indian. In 1653 he served on a committee that studied the Natick-Dedham dispute, and in 1656 he sponsored Eliot's first petition for expanding Wamesit's boundaries. The latter action was perhaps Gookin's basis for claiming that he was the Superintendent in 1656. His corporation salary began at £15 in 1662, rose to £20 several years later, and remained at this level until King Philip's War. He complained that these amounts were inadequate compensation for his time and expenses, which included entertaining Indian rulers who occasionally came to his Cambridge home for advice. In 1663 the New England Company suggested that his stipend be eliminated. The Commissioners and Eliot protested to London, and the corporation dropped the idea. The Apostle's intervention on Gookin's behalf was not surprising: the two were best friends, and their families were eventually united by the marriage of Eliot, Jr., and Elizabeth Gookin in 1666.[39]

Daniel Gookin was born around 1612 into an English family that moved to County Cork, Ireland, either shortly before or soon after his birth. He spent most of the period between 1631 and 1643 in Virginia. In May 1642 he and seventy-three other tidewater Puritans signed a letter asking Massachusetts Bay to provide them with ministers; several months later, the Bay Colony sent William Tompson of Braintree, John Knowles of Watertown, and Thomas James, formerly of Charlestown, to Virginia; in 1643 Gookin and the three ministers were among the many persons who left the colony after Governor William Berkeley expelled dissenters. Gookin moved to Boston (he may have lived briefly in Annapolis en route to New England) and was soon admitted into full church membership. Shortly thereafter he settled in Roxbury but retained his affiliation with the Boston congregation. In the fall of 1648 he moved permanently to Cambridge, induced by the town's promise of 500 acres of land at Shawshin (Billerica), and was immediately accepted into the Cambridge church. He was elected a deputy in 1649 and in 1651 and an assistant from 1652 until 1676, when he was voted out of office for defending the loyal praying Indians during King Philip's War. After many years as a captain in the Cambridge train-band, Gookin was chosen sergeant-major of the Middlesex regiment in 1676 and major general of the colony's forces in 1681.[40]

Gookin made brief trips to England in 1650 and 1655 and a lengthy one from 1657 through 1660. The latter journey is noteworthy in two respects. First, he planned to sail from Boston in the ship that carried Thomas Mayhew, Jr., Jonathan Ince, and Nathaniel Pelham to their deaths. Gookin took a different passage because the captain of the ill-fated vessel treated him "somewhat unkindly" about his accommodations. Second, he returned to Massachusetts Bay in July 1660 on the same boat as Marmaduke Johnson and regicides Edward Whalley and William Goffe. Gookin harbored the regicides in his Cambridge home until late February 1661, when they left for New Haven by way of Hartford. Protecting Whalley and Goffe made Gookin a diplomatic liability for Massachusetts Bay. The General Court concealed his name, as it did Eliot's, from the royal commissioners, referring to the two men simply as the "persons appointed to govern and instruct" the praying Indians "in civility and religion."[41]

Gookin had four known holdings in Indian land besides the tract at Billerica. First, in May 1657 the General Court awarded him 500 acres at an unspecified location for "public service done." During his absence in the late 1650s, the court allotted these acres in Southertown, the expansionist outpost on the west bank of the Pawcatuck River that Massachusetts Bay had established in 1658 and then placed within Suffolk County. The royal commissioners voided Gookin's title in 1665 as punishment for aiding the regicides; nevertheless, he managed to retain possession of the land until he sold it in 1672. Second, in 1665 the court awarded him for public service 500 acres at a location of his choosing; he picked land adjacent to Nashobah. Third, Gookin was one of the leading proprietors who purchased the land for Worcester from Sagamores John and Solomon in 1674. His personal stake in the town apparently amounted to only 50 acres. Fourth, the Okommakamesit Indians gave him 120 acres of praying town land in 1677 as an expression of "the love and duty" they "owe[d] unto him." All totaled, Gookin's holdings in native land were sufficiently modest that it would be difficult to argue that he viewed the Superintendency as a vehicle for personal aggrandizement at the Indians' expense. Furthermore, there is no evidence in John Frederick Martin's careful study of the land syndicates in seventeenth-century New England, *Profits in the Wilderness,* that Gookin was an active or silent partner in the Atherton Company or in any other syndicate.[42]

On two occasions Gookin wrote summaries of his duties as Superintendent: in 1664 for the benefit of the Commissioners, who were then trying to dissuade the corporation from ending his stipend, and in 1674 for inclusion in his *Historical Collections.* He explained that his chief responsibilities were approving the rulers whom the Indians had chosen and holding courts with these officials. Gookin's courts were normally held at Natick; Waban, Captain Tom, and Captain Josiah attended the sessions. Eliot reported that Gookin conducted his sessions in English to "further the Indians in learning law and government in . . . [that] tongue." This may have been a necessity, since the missionary sources contain no indication that the Superintendent spoke any Algonquian dialect. Gookin's duties also included teaching, or arranging for others to teach, Indian men to plow and perform other tasks and women to spin and sew. At every court session he made a point to "encourage the diligent and shame the idle" because "the sin of idleness is so riveted in them." Finally, Gookin issued warrants against Englishmen suspecting of stealing from the praying Indians or selling alcohol to them.[43]

Little else is known about Gookin's courts. He explained that his sessions handled civil and criminal matters internal to the praying Indians except "appeals, life, limb, banishment, and cases of divorce." His courts punished natives for breaking the sabbath and for failing to obey rulers, attend lectures and schools, and pay tithes to rulers and teachers. Drunkenness was another common infraction. It was known to have been a problem in several prewar settlements—Wamesit, Pantucket, Hassanamesit, Nashobah, and Nashaway—and was probably one in all of them. Powwowing was also punished in Gookin's courts. This was the only routine offense that he did not permit the rulers to adjudicate at the local level as well as the only one for which the penalty is known ("the procurer, five pounds, and every person present, twenty pence").[44]

Gookin was a conscientious official who wanted to improve the quality of the mission by educating the proselytes about the behavioral norms they were expected to follow and by punishing persons who violated those norms. But, like Eliot, he was unable to devote much time to the Indian work. Gookin did not conduct courts at Wamesit until 1670, and then but once a year, and he apparently held only one session in any of the new towns, at Wabquisset in September 1674. The central courts at Natick presumably met more frequently; however, even in the case of Natick, Gookin was often out of contact with the town's residents. In 1671 he remarked that he had not seen or spoken with "any Natick Indian for several months." As a result, the native rulers had to use their own discretion in dealing with sabbath-breaking, powwowing, and other infractions. The paucity of sources about praying town self-governance makes it difficult to know how actively the rulers punished miscreants. The only specific evidence comes from Natick, where Waban and Totherswamp performed acceptably in Eliot's judgment, and from Punkapoag, where Ahawton did not. Gookin provided a similarly mixed assessment at a more general level, writing in *The Historical Collections* that "some . . . rulers are very careful and zealous."[45]

Before and after the creation of the Superintendency, the General Court exercised its authority over the praying Indians in three other ways. The first was by enacting—but not necessarily by enforcing—legislation. Most of these actions, like the ones that regulated the fur, liquor, land, and firearm trades, were intended to apply to all Indians within the colony, whether Christian or not.[46] Only a few provisions were explicitly or implicitly missionary in purpose: the 1644 sabbath law, the 1646 blasphemy and idolatry statutes, the 1647 directive that created the precursor of the Superintendency, the 1652 ruling that authorized the praying Indians to receive land for towns "as the English have," and the 1658 action that established the Superintendency.

The second was through the colony's court system, where cases were heard by individual magistrates, by the commissioners for small causes in towns without magistrates, by the county courts, by the Court of Assistants, and by the full General Court. The prewar court records I have consulted contain few civil and criminal actions involving known proselytes. The civil cases were typically boundary disputes between Indian and English towns (Natick-Dedham and Okommakamesit-Marlborough were the major cases in point) or minor actions between individuals and/or small groups. There were even fewer criminal cases heard in the colony's court system. The only known instance of a praying Indian being tried for a serious crime with or against another native is the case of Sarah Ahawton's adultery in 1668. There is no clear example prior to the war of a proselyte committing a felony against a colonist, with the possible exception of a native called Samuel, son of "William of Natick," who was accused of trying to rape a Cambridge woman in 1671. He evidently fled before he could be arrested.[47]

The third way the General Court exercised its jurisdiction was by ruling on Eliot's petitions, most of which pertained to praying town land and to protection from marauders. The General Court approved his requests for creating six of the old towns (the land for Punkapoag was awarded by Dorchester) and granted most of his known petitions for enlarging or defending the boundaries of the old towns. The only exceptions in the case of boundaries were his 1658 and 1669 requests that Natick receive 800 acres already assigned to Simon Bradstreet and that the town be given two cedar swamps in the Nipmuck Country; in both of these instances, the court had legitimate reasons for turning the Apostle down. The General Court also approved each of Eliot's extant appeals for protecting natives who had submitted to the government. There are three well-documented instances of this sort: in 1648 Massachusetts Bay dispatched soldiers to defend Nashowanon and his people (but not the aggrieved Quabag Indians in question because William Pynchon had indicated that the latter were not within the colony's jurisdiction); in 1661 the court sent troops to "terrify the enemies of [the self-proclaimed] Wossamegon"; and in 1668 the colony protected the Quantisset Indians against Quaiapen.[48]

Overall, the General Court's policy toward the mission is best characterized as benign neglect. As the previous paragraph indicates, the court was prepared to defend the praying Indians. There is no evidence, however, that it ever did so on its own volition but only at Eliot's request. Moreover, the General Court did not create its primary missionary office, the Superintendency, until 1658, and then only after two years of prodding by the Apostle. Before and after that time, the court generally ignored the praying Indians except when Eliot made petitions on their behalf, and when they surfaced in other types of cases in the English legal system. The mission had no greater priority for the colony's lay leaders than it did for the ministers.

The Apostle seems to have been satisfied with the General Court's role in supervising the mission, perhaps because the assembly granted most of his prewar requests for the mission. He never complained about the court in his extant sources, in contrast to his many criticisms of the Bay Colony's ministers and the Commissioners of the United Colonies. But whether he realized it or not, Eliot made no onerous demands upon the General Court prior to King Philip's War. The creation of the Superintendency required nothing more than legislative action—the Superintendent's salary was paid by the corporation. The actions that established, preserved, and enlarged praying town boundaries often irritated colonists who coveted the native lands under dispute. Nevertheless, the General Court could placate disgruntled settlers with compensatory grants elsewhere. The court did run a certain risk when it sent soldiers into the interior to protect Indians from their native antagonists. But because these antagonists never engaged the Massachusetts troops in battle, the colony did not have to decide if it was willing to shed English blood to defend Indians under its jurisdiction.

Eliot did not put Massachusetts Bay to a stern test until some seven weeks after the start of King Philip's War. In mid-August 1675, he presented the council of magistrates with an impassioned petition, the purpose of which was to convince the colony that selling war captives into foreign slavery was a "dangerous merchandise." Plymouth had already begun this practice, and he did not want "the thing [to] be acted" in Massachusetts Bay. Eliot proposed two alternatives. The first, which he clearly preferred, was to keep war prisoners in permanent or temporary slavery in Massachusetts Bay so that they could be properly instructed in Christianity. He quoted Matthew 5:7 ("Blessed are the merciful, for they shall obtain mercy") and Deuteronomy 23:15–16 (which he accurately paraphrased as "a fugitive servant from a pagan master might not he delivered to his master, but be kept in Israel for the good of his soul"). The second was to execute the captives. "If they deserve to die," he wrote, "it is far better to be put to death under godly governors, who will take religious care that means may be used, that they may die penitently" rather than to "sell them away from all means of grace."[49]

The petition was to no avail, for Massachusetts Bay eventually sold at least 200 war captives—most of them pagans—into slavery in the West Indies or in North Africa. From the standpoint of the magistrates, the practice was a way to recover some of the costs of the war and remove potential threats to the colony's security. The Apostle, for his part, remained true to his convictions and tried to undo the damage. He arranged for the return of Joseph (the brother of Sampson) from slavery in Jamaica, and he attempted to retrieve a group of captives from the British port at Tangier.[50]

In this particular instance, Eliot may come off poorly in comparison to the magistrates. Selling captives into foreign slavery was possibly a more humane practice than executing them, a measure the Apostle countenanced even though he preferred assigning prisoners of war to domestic servitude. But regardless of how its provision about execution is construed, Eliot's petition shows how much he valued the redemption of Indians: he could not abide the prospect of sending pagans, even those who had taken English lives, "away from the light of the Gospel . . . unto a place, a state, a way of perpetual darkness, to the eternal ruin of their souls." A less ambiguous example of Eliot's commitment to Indian instruction can be seen in his attitudes about native land. He recognized that missions could not flourish in places where they were already established, or take root in locations where they did not yet exist, unless the colonial governments pursued a just land policy.

The Mission and the Dispossession of the Indians

That Eliot's program stripped the praying Indians of their land is an article of orthodoxy in the literature. The point under debate among historians is whether Eliot deliberately pursued this objective or achieved it inadvertently. Francis Jennings claims that the Apostle viewed the Indian work as an "instrument of expansion," and Neal Salisbury states that one of "Eliot's economic and political goals" was "expropriating Indian land for occupation by settlers." James Axtell and Alden Vaughan are critical of such interpretations of Eliot's purpose. The former argues that the Apostle's "goals were [not] tainted by a barely hidden political agenda," and the latter maintains that scholars who regard the mission as "a quasi-militaristic arm of Puritan aggression" have misconstrued Eliot's "motives and methods."[51]

The mission's role in English expansion is vastly exaggerated, quite apart from the question of Eliot's motivation. To the best of my knowledge, Salisbury is the only historian who attempts to document the claim that the Indian work dispossessed the proselytes, and the seven sources he cites do not support his conclusion that "praying Indians were induced to part with substantial portions of their land."[52] It may be that scholars see no reason to document the point. Any map that shows the locations of the fourteen praying towns and the semiofficial settlements around Quabag and Nashaway consists of a series of black dots in the midst of a huge white background. The conclusion that begs to be drawn from such a map is that when they moved into reservations, the praying Indians lost whatever external land they considered their own. This conclusion—if it is indeed the basis for the claim that the mission dispossessed the natives—can be challenged in two ways.

The first is at the level of Puritan legal theory. Prior to emigration, John Winthrop, John Cotton, and others worked out four interrelated justifications for the occupation of Indian land: the epidemic of 1616–1619 was an act of divine providence that opened the coast for English settlement; biblical texts such as Genesis 1:28, Genesis 9:1, and Psalms 115:16 assigned "dominion over the earth" to those willing to "subdue" it; the royal charter awarded title to the English planters; and the natural-law doctrine of *vacuum domicilium* declared that uninhabited or unimproved land was legally vacant. At best, these justifications gave natives the rights over only those lands that they "possessed" through the construction of buildings or other artificial structures, or over those that they had "improved" through cultivation. Thus in legal theory, the Indians had lost most of their land long before Eliot began his work.[53]

The mission, in fact, increased rather than diminished the property rights that praying Indians held in legal theory. In 1652 the General Court made its fullest prewar statement about English and Indian land rights. Although occasioned by the Natick-Dedham dispute, the statement went beyond it in significance. The court declared that "all the tracts of land within the jurisdiction of this court . . . shall be accompted the just right of such English as already have or hereafter shall have grant of lands from this court." The court then made two exceptions. The first was the familiar acknowledgment that all "Indians within this jurisdiction," whether Christian or pagan, had "just right" to lands that they had "subdued" through "possession or improvement." The second pertained to lands assigned for praying towns: "it is ordered that if, upon good experience, there shall be a competent number of Indians brought on to civility, so as to be capable of a township, they shall have grant of lands undisposed of for a plantation, as the English have." Christian Indians therefore did not have to construct buildings or plant crops on a tract of praying town land in order to be given legal title to it, just as colonists were not required to do these things before receiving authorization to create an English town. In this sense, the mission gave to praying Indians a legal right that pagan Indians did not hold, namely, ownership of land that had not been "subdued" through "possession or improvement."[54]

The other way to challenge the claim that the missionary work dispossessed the proselytes is by examining the specific historical situations in the places where the mission existed prior to King Philip's

War. Doing so excludes large sections of Massachusetts Bay from consideration. Eliot and his Indian evangelists were unable to establish even the semblance of a mission in the areas north and west of Quabag and Nashaway. The same point applies to Indian territories outside the colony. Except for laying the foundation for the work of William Leveritch, Richard Bourne, and other missionaries among the Nausets, Eliot and his native associates failed in their attempts to carry his program beyond the boundaries of the Bay. Most of their activity took place in coastal Massachusetts and along the Great Trail. In order to investigate the situations in these and the other locations where Christian Indian settlements stood in prewar Massachusetts Bay, the idea of dispossession must be redefined. Rather than ask what lands proselytes forfeited in legal theory, we need to see what lands they lost in actual fact after moving into reservations, and whether or not they were compensated for their loss.

When construed in this manner, the concept of dispossession hardly pertains to the Nipmucks living in the seven new towns, in the villages around Nashaway and Quabag, and in the old towns at Hassanamesit and Magunkog. First of all, there were only six English towns in the Nipmuck Country before King Philip's War. As explained in Chapter 6, the lands for these settlements were purchased from Indians. The fact that some native parties were dissatisfied with the terms of the sales was not the fault of the mission. A thorough study of local land records might reveal that there were many absentee English holdings in the Nipmuck territories: the General Court's published records indicate that the assembly made numerous awards in unspecified locations to individuals and groups as compensation for public service or for some other reason. But until such a study is undertaken and the results known, it cannot be said that the Nipmuck proselytes lost any lands before the war except for those that they sold to colonists. Furthermore, the court never assigned reservation land for the seven new towns. This point also applies to Nashaway and Weshakim as well as to the Quabag-area settlements, with the possible exception of Putikookuppog. The General Court did create reservations for the Hassanamesit and Magunkog Indians. Nevertheless, no English town stood near either of these two settlements prior to the war, and unless absentee awards gobbled up the adjacent lands, there is no reason to assume that the Hassanamesit and Magunkog proselytes lost their land prior to King Philip's War.

Eliot's program did not disinherit the residents of Natick, Punkapoag, and Nashobah. These Indians had sold or otherwise lost nearly all of their land in Massachusetts Bay before he began his work in 1646. In fact, the mission probably expanded, rather than reduced, the territory the Massachusett and Pawtucket proselytes occupied within the Bay Colony. Evidence presented in Chapter 3 suggests that in 1646 the Nonantum Indians were confined to "the compass of [a] hill," the Neponsets to the forty-acre tract that Cutshamekin had withheld from Dorchester in a 1636 transaction, and the Musketaquid Pawtuckets to "this side the Bear Swamp or the east side of Mr. Flint's farm." In the late 1640s, the mission preserved these places of residence and may even have enlarged Nonantum, if Shepard was correct when he stated in 1647 that the General Court assigned "hundreds of acres" to the Nonantum proselytes. In the 1650s, the Indians at Nonantum, Neponset, and Musketaquid moved into praying towns—Natick, Punkapoag, and Nashobah, respectively—that were thousands of acres in size.

The standard claim about the prewar dispossession of the praying Indians seems appropriate only in the cases of Wamesit and Okommakamesit. The General Court assigned the land for Wamesit in 1653. This action was followed by the awards that created nearby Billerica and Chelmsford in 1656 and by the grant that established Dunstable in 1673. The court evidently made these three awards without compensating the Wamesit Indians. The colony did not need a mission to justify the three grants; legal theory provided pretext enough. Nevertheless, the localization of the Wamesits on a reservation clearly facilitated English expansion in the area. A similar situation existed at Okommakamesit. In 1656 the General Court created Marlborough and placed the town within lands occupied by, but not yet formally assigned to, the praying Indians; and in 1658 the legislature sustained the English title when it awarded 6,000 acres in the area to Okommakamesit. The proselytes apparently received no payment except for the land for the Marlborough church, which a local Indian identified as "Anamaks" (possibly Owussumag) sold for an undisclosed amount in 1663.[55]

Thus there is considerable evidence against the argument that the Indian work was an instrument of expansion. When the question is viewed from the standpoint of Puritan legal theory, the mission did not extinguish native rights to uninhabited or uncultivated land within

Massachusetts Bay. Those rights had been extinguished before the mission began. When the problem is examined on a case-specific basis, Eliot's work played no discernible role in dispossessing proselytes except at Wamesit and Okommakamesit. The other praying Indians had either lost their land before the mission commenced or retained it (aside from sales) through the time of the war. Furthermore, from both the theoretical and the practical viewpoints, the mission improved the situation of praying Indians. The General Court's 1652 policy statement awarded title to land that proselytes had not "subdued" in the legal sense of the word, and the creation of Natick, Punkapoag, and Nashobah enlarged the holdings of the coastal proselytes.

This body of evidence creates a problem for historians who allege that Eliot viewed the mission as a vehicle for dispossession. If such was his goal, he achieved it only at Wamesit and Okommakamesit. Scholars who make this claim about the Apostle's motivation face other difficulties as well. Eliot expected proselytes to live in praying towns because stability of residence and sedentary agriculture were important components of civilized life. He wanted the General Court to award the land for these towns so that he could have a legal basis for defending or enlarging their boundaries as circumstances warranted. His acts of intervention at Wamesit and Okommakamesit were notable cases in point. Yet at the same time, the Apostle almost certainly believed that proselytes had rights to their unimproved lands outside the praying towns. In 1662 he and John, Jr., approved the sale of eight square miles of land at or near the future town of Mendon by four Christian Indians. The description of the terrain in the deed indicates that the land was unimproved ("trees and timber woods, underwoods standing, lying, and growing thereon with all the meadows, swamps, river ponds, and brooks"). Many similar examples surfaced in the postwar period, when with Eliot's approbation Waban, Black James, and other survivors sold tracts of depopulated land in the Nipmuck Country and in the area to the east of Boston.[56]

Eliot also championed the land interests of natives who lived outside the Bay Colony. He defended Pomham against the royal commissioners in 1666 after concluding that the Gortonists had used "force and fraud" to dispossess the sachem. He asked the Commissioners of the United Colonies in 1671 to provide "the praying Indians near Plymouth" with "land of their own competent to live upon." He was probably referring to Cotton's proselytes in the area around Bridgewater, Taunton, and Middleboro, where the apostate Josias Wompatuck had sold large tracts of land to English and Indian buyers. Most importantly, Eliot admonished the Commissioners in the dedicatory epistle to *Indian Dialogues* to make sure "in all your respective colonies . . . that due accommodations of lands and waters may be allowed them ['the Indians'], whereupon townships and churches may be (in after ages) able to subsist; and suffer not the English to strip them of all their lands, in places fit for the sustenance of man." He did not tell the Commissioners which "Indians" he had in mind, probably because he intended the admonition to apply to all natives in the orthodox colonies. Nevertheless, his words had special relevance to English expansion in Plymouth, for at this time he was greatly concerned about the plight of the Pokanokets. Eliot finished writing *Indian Dialogues* in mid-1671, shortly before he drafted "Instructions from the Church at Natick to William and Anthony," his plan for a mediated peace between the Pokanokets and Plymouth.[57]

The Apostle was greatly distressed when King Philip's War began four years later. He thought that the conflict could have been prevented if Plymouth had treated the Pokanokets fairly on the matter of land. "I humbly request," he told Winthrop, Jr., in a letter written about a month after the hostilities commenced, "that one effect of this trouble may be to humble the English to do the Indians justice and no wrong about their lands." Eliot's willingness to acknowledge that the Old Colony had done the Pokanokets "wrong about their lands" distinguished him from most of his contemporaries and from some modern scholars as well. He also informed Winthrop in the letter that the war might be brought to an end through a negotiated settlement that protected the natives' property interests: "I make bold to request that Captain [George] Denison [of Stonington] may have free hand, without offense to the English, to plead the Indians' cause." The Apostle then explained that a settlement might induce the Pokanokets to accept a mission. "Our doing them justice about their lands," he wrote, "may, by the blessing of God, open their hearts to the Word of God, which I do earnestly desire may be another effect of this great motion."[58]

Eliot knew that more English lives would be lost if King Philip's War continued on its course. Like other colonists, he recognized that the Indians' skill at forest warfare made them formidable enemies. "We find that all the craft is in [the] catching of them," he explained to

Winthrop, "and that in the meanwhile they give us many a sore nip." Eliot also suspected, as he indicated in his petition against foreign slavery, that the practice of selling captives away would prove "an effectual prolongation of the war" because bellicose natives would never surrender to accept such a fate. At the same time, he was horrified about the loss of Indian lives. Pagans could not be redeemed if they were killed in battle. One of the Apostle's reasons for drawing up the ill-fated peace initiative in 1671 had been to prevent Metacom and his people from "be[ing] destroyed" in armed conflict against English might. The same fear returned in 1675. "When we came," he told the Massachusetts magistrates in the petition against slavery, "we declared to the world, and it is recorded, yea we are engaged by our letters patent to the King's majesty, that the endeavor of the Indians' conversion, not their extirpation, was one great end of our enterprise, in coming to these ends of the earth." "All men (of reading)," he continued, "condemn the Spaniard for cruelty, upon this point, in destroying men and depopulating the land. The country is large enough, here is land enough for them and us too."

Conclusion:
The Apostle and the Indians

James Axtell has proposed a paradigm for assessing European missionary programs in colonial North America. He suggests that missionaries should be evaluated in "offensive terms" by determining "how well . . . they succeed[ed] in changing the native cultures to their own cultural goals and style" and that proselytes should be judged in "defensive terms" by seeing how successfully they "maintain[ed] their cultural vitality, integrity, and independence."[1] Axtell's paradigm is a good starting point for appraising Eliot's mission, provided the frame of reference is clarified in two ways.

The first is by excluding from consideration those settlements that were barely exposed to the mission prior to King Philip's War: the old towns at Magunkog and Wamesit, the seven new praying towns, and the semiofficial settlements around Quabag and Nashaway. The focus must fall on the five remaining old towns, particularly on Natick, the best documented of them all. The second is by correcting a common mischaracterization of Eliot's cultural objectives. Scholars often accuse the Apostle of seeking to destroy all aspects of traditional Indian culture in order to replace them with their English counterparts. Neal Salisbury, to give one well-known example, claims that for Eliot "native culture lacked intrinsic value" and that the Apostle demanded that proselytes "reject . . . their entire ethnic and cultural identity" and "act like English men and women" in all respects. Eliot certainly thought that there were many inadequacies in Indian culture;

nevertheless, he did not expect proselytes to repudiate their entire way of life. From the outset of the mission, he wanted the praying Indians to retain traditional medical remedies "virtuous in the way of physic" and to share them with the English. He also preserved the Massachusett language because of its present and future value to the mission. In fact, as Stephen Guice points out, Eliot did not attempt to fit Massachusett into Indo-European rules of phonology, morphology, and syntax; rather, he tried to understand it on its own terms. In this respect he differed from many other early modern Catholic and Protestant missionaries who studied Indian dialects.[2] Moreover, Eliot learned to tolerate certain traditional native practices (soon to be identified) that he initially tried to eliminate.

As explained at the start of Chapter 3, Eliot pursued three main cultural objectives in addition to the central one of changing the natives' religion. The praying Indians generally adapted to his demands about grooming. John Wilson noted in 1652 that "most" Natick residents wore English clothing, and Daniel Gookin wrote in 1674 that "many" of "the Christian and civilized Indians . . . follow[ed] the English mode in their habit" except for retaining traditional ornaments, a practice the Superintendent did not condemn. The fact that the proselytes conformed to Eliot's grooming standards, however, did not necessarily mean that they accepted his rationale for them. Dressing in English fashion was a way for Christian Indians to advertise their connections with English power. In 1665, for example, the Massachusetts council of magistrates warned the Mohawks that they should not harm the proselytes, who were "clothed in English apparel" and wore their hair "in the manner of the English."[3]

Sexual behavior was a second point of focus. In this case, the praying Indians did not need to make as many behavioral changes as the Puritans thought they did. Polygamy was never widely practiced in aboriginal society, and "incest, rape, sodomy, buggery, [and] bestiality" were probably no more common among Indians than among colonists. Only in the area of nonmarital sex did English values differ significantly from traditional native ones. Roger Williams observed in 1643 that the Rhode Island Indians did not object to sexual relations between unmarried persons, and Eliot's many complaints in the early years of the mission about the prevalence of "lust" suggest that natives in Massachusetts Bay had no scruples about the matter either. The praying Indians who delivered conversion narratives in the 1650s often claimed that they had learned to control their "lusts." It is difficult to know whether they were also speaking for less advanced proselytes, and even whether they were being truthful about themselves. Tantalizing evidence that traditional heterosexual mores continued in the praying towns surfaced in the case of Sarah Ahawton. Ann Marie Plane has suggested that Sarah committed adultery on the advice of older Punkapoag women, who were following a time-honored Indian remedy for marriages gone bad.[4]

Eliot's third major cultural objective was to persuade the proselytes to lead settled lives. Natick was a year-round residential community; however, the town's inhabitants built few English-style houses because they preferred to live in wigwams, and they did not entirely abandon traditional subsistence practices in favor of European forms of plant and animal husbandry. The natives in the other old towns likewise continued to live in wigwams (aside from a few families at Hassanamesit) and to hunt and fish in conjunction with English types of agriculture; it is uncertain if these settlements were full-time places of residence. The Christian Indians evidently followed Puritan gender roles—men were responsible for working the fields and tending the animals, and women for spinning and weaving—but with insufficient enthusiasm. Gookin lamented in his *Historical Collections* that the proselytes fell "very short of the English both in diligence and providence."[5]

The natives' progress in religion was similarly uneven. Many "praying Indians" wore the Christian faith loosely, and others not at all. Eliot stated in the 1650s that Natick had "profane" and "unsound" residents, and Gookin later acknowledged that "sundry" persons in the old towns were "not of so good conversation as the Christian religion requires." Furthermore, powwowing almost certainly continued in the old towns, at least among a segment of the population. But at the same time, some proselytes were well schooled in Puritan doctrine. The Indians who were accepted into the Roxbury church in 1659 possessed a level of Christian knowledge comparable to that exhibited by colonists in their conversion narratives. The same point presumably applied to the individuals later admitted into full membership in the Natick and Hassanamesit churches, and to younger natives attending English or Indian schools. Yet even the leading proselytes gave the Christian religion their own twist. In the mid-1680s Eliot published in Cambridge a short tract entitled *Dying Speeches*

& *Counsels Of such Indians as dyed in the Lord.* The work contains his translations of the farewell narratives of eight praying Indians: Waban, Piumbuhhou, Old Jacob, Anthony, John Owussumag, Sr., John Speene, Nehemiah (possibly Captain Tom's son), and Black James. In these "dying speeches," as well as in the conversion narratives in the 1650s, proselytes often remarked that their souls would be transported to heaven following the deaths of their bodies. This Christian doctrine resembled the Algonquian teaching that the "dream souls," as opposed to the "clear souls," of the deceased traveled to the southwest or the south and entered Cautantowwit's house. In their conversion and deathbed narratives, the natives less frequently mentioned the theological companion to the immortality of the soul, the resurrection of the body. The likely reason was that this doctrine had no traditional analogue. As Roger Williams observed, the Narragansetts readily accepted the Christian doctrine of the soul's immortality but had problems with the concept of the body's resurrection.[6]

The emphasis that the leading proselytes placed on the immortality of the soul might suggest that they accepted only those Christian doctrines that were consonant with traditional Indian beliefs. The conversion and farewell narratives, however, indicate that the speakers certainly understood that the resurrection of the body was part of their Christian faith, as were other doctrines inconsistent with their past beliefs, like monotheism, original sin, and justification by faith. Nevertheless, the Christian beliefs and practices that were most meaningful to Waban, Piumbuhhou, and other long-term participants in the mission were those that could be interpreted in a traditional manner. The immortality of the soul is perhaps the best example. Others were prayer, the figure of Jesus the shaman, and the sense that supernatural power suffused the universe.[7]

The credit for perceiving and stressing these theological points of overlap surely belonged to the leading proselytes and not to Eliot. As many scholars correctly point out, the Apostle was not a perceptive student of traditional Indian culture. His writings contain only two neutral observations about native culture beyond his many descriptive comments about the Massachusett language: he noted in 1666 that the Indians' music was in harmony but not in rhyme and meter and in 1670 that their medicine "altogether use[d] the root and not the herb." Eliot was also capable of misconstruing traditional culture. He was not quite correct about medicine, for natives in the region occasionally used herbal remedies, and he wrongly characterized sachemic government as "tyranny." In a 1981 essay, William Simmons offered a plausible explanation for the Apostle's shortcomings as an ethnographer. In contrast to Roger Williams and the younger Thomas Mayhew, who were astute observers of Indian culture, Eliot approached the natives from a position of political, economic, and social superiority. "Puritans who were most knowledgeable about Indians," Simmons noted, lived "in a context where relationships between the cultures were most equal and where English domination had yet to be established."[8]

In general, one is struck by the extent to which the mission was shaped by the Indians rather than by Eliot. The proselytes continued to reside in wigwams and to hunt and fish. Eliot came to tolerate these traditional practices; he had to adjust to the Indians, and not vice versa. Moreover, many persons in the old towns were barely Christianized, and even the elite proselytes, while conversant with the full range of Puritan beliefs and practices, had an affinity for ones that were consistent with the past. Other features of the natives' old way of life also survived in the praying towns. The Natick Indians elected Cutshamekin, a traditional leader, their ruler of one hundred; and the proselytes in other towns also chose sachems as their rulers and chief rulers, although not to the extent that scholars commonly allege. Furthermore, excavations or disturbances of the Indian cemeteries at Natick, Punkapoag, and Hassanamesit—the three most Anglicized communities—reveal that material objects were sometimes interred with the bodies. This traditional practice violated the Puritan prohibition of grave goods. The conditions of the sites do not establish if the leading praying Indians were buried in this manner. Nevertheless, they were surely aware that the practice continued in the settlements and, at the very least, condoned it.[9]

Eliot's contributions to the mission were nonetheless important, and not only in the ways that he would have recognized—providing biweekly instruction in civility and religion, administering the sacraments at Natick, preparing translations, defending the boundaries of the praying towns, publicizing the mission in London, and contributing portions of his corporation salary to it. Whether he fully realized it or not, the Apostle improved the material condition of the old-town Indians, particularly those who were residing along the coast when he began his work. In the secondary literature, Eliot's mission is condemned for facilitating the Bay Colony's territorial, political, and economic growth. His program was not irrelevant to the colony's growth. His work played a part in dispossessing the Okommakamesit and Wamesit Indians; it brought the Okommakamesits, the Hassanamesits, and the Magunkogs—whose sachems had not signed either the 1644 or the 1668 act of submission—under the authority of the General Court; and it provided a labor force, especially in the 1660s, when the Mohawk threat drove proselytes to work for the colonists by "hoeing, reaping, picking hops, cutting wood, making hay, and making stone fences, and like necessary employments."[10] These considerations notwithstanding, the mission is more accurately understood as a way of counteracting English domination rather than abetting it.

A proper assessment of the mission's role in this respect must distinguish the precontact period from the early settlement period. No historian would argue that the natives were materially better off after the birth of the mission than they were before English colonization began. Prior to contact, the Indians controlled the use of land, participated as they pleased in the exchange of wampum and gifts with other native groups, and lived under the rule of sachems who governed consensually in conjunction with counselors. After the start of Eliot's work in 1646, the proselytes resided on reservations, competed in the English economy, and accepted the authority of the General Court. The contrast between the precontact and the missionary situations might suggest that Eliot's program was responsible for bringing about these changes. In point of fact, however, the damage occurred during the twenty or so years of English colonization that preceded the start of the Indian work. The proselytes, on balance, were better off materially after the birth of the mission than they were during the early settlement period.

By 1646 Puritan legal theory had extinguished Indian rights to unimproved or uninhabited lands within the colony, and even apart from the question of theory, the settlers by then had acquired most of the coastal land. As explained in Chapter 8, the mission enhanced the legal rights of praying Indians and enlarged the territory occupied by the Massachusett and Pawtucket proselytes. Many future old-town Indians, moreover, were already subject to the General Court when Eliot's work commenced. The Apostle used the court's authority to defend these praying Indians, as well as those later brought under the colony's control, from their English and native antagonists. Had it not been for Eliot's intervention, the General Court might not have protected the proselytes, since this body never acted on their behalf except at his request. Finally, by the time the mission began, the natives in eastern Massachusetts were dependent upon the English economy through their earlier participation in the fur trade and through the sale of land to colonists. The mission bettered the economic condition of the proselytes. Through wage labor, apprenticeships, and cottage industries, as well as through consumer goods supplied free of charge by the New England Company, the natives were able to overcome the collapse of the coastal fur trade and the loss of their land base.[11]

In sum, the old praying towns must be assessed at two levels. One is from the standpoint of cultural change. By Axtell's measure, the proselytes were more successful at "maintaining their own vitality, integrity, and independence" than Eliot was at restructuring the native way of life to his "cultural goals and style." The praying Indians retained many aspects of their traditional culture, thus giving reservation life a familiar feel. The other is in political and economic terms. Relative to the early settlement period, the mission improved the fortunes of the Indians. These conclusions challenge two claims often found in the secondary literature: that Eliot's program eradicated much of traditional native culture, and that it aggrandized Puritan power at the Indians' expense.

In the mid-1680s Eliot began to prepare for the survival of the mission after his death. In 1683, after years of trying, he persuaded the Natick Indians to ordain their own pastor, Daniel Tokkohwompait; and at about the same time, he convinced Daniel Gookin, Jr., minister at Sherborn, to deliver monthly sermons at Natick through an interpreter. Eliot's growing infirmity saddened the praying Indians. "You are now grown aged," Daniel Tokkohwompait wrote in English in March 1684, in a letter signed by Waban, William Ahawton, James the Printer, and twelve other Natick residents, "soe that we are deprived of seeing your face and hearing your voice (especially in the Winter Season) soe frequently as formerly." The purpose of this letter was to ask Eliot to secure an increase in the younger Gookin's corporation salary. The letter is more significant, however, because it begins with a poignant expression of gratitude to the Apostle: "God hath made you to us and our nation a spiritual father, we are inexpresably ingaged to you for your faithful constant Indefatigable labours, care and love, to and for us, and you have alwaies manifested the same to us as wel in our adversity as prosperity, for about forty years makeing know [sic] to us the Glad tidings of Salvation of Jesus Christ."[12]

Scholarship about the mission hardly prepares us to expect that natives would develop such affection for Eliot. Yet over the course of his long missionary career, the Apostle gave the praying Indians many reasons to admire him. He protected the proselytes against other natives and against his own people; he learned the Massachusett language, in contrast to virtually all other colonists in prewar Massachusetts Bay; he came to know the praying Indians as individuals (his writings, like the elder Gookin's, abound in biographical details about the proselytes); and unless one wishes to dismiss as insincere the natives' statement in the March 1684 letter, he brought the praying Indians "the Glad tidings of Salvation of Jesus Christ."

The Apostle showed his concern for the Indians in other ways as well. His standard descriptive adjective for the natives was "poor." For example, on three occasions he recalled his reasons for beginning the Indian work in 1646. The glory of God is mentioned in one of the lists, and the missionary obligation under the charter is noted in two of them. The only reason found in all three lists is his "pity" or "compassion" for the "poor Indians." However condescending it may sound to modern ears, Eliot's choice of words indicates that he viewed the natives with sympathy and not contempt. His most commonly used pejorative adjective was "wild," a term that he and other Puritans probably inherited from the figure of the "wild man" in late medieval and Renaissance literature. Nevertheless, Eliot did not liken the natives to wild animals who needed taming, in contrast to both Michael Wigglesworth, who wrote that the mission "brought to civility . . . those that lived like beasts (or worse)," and Cotton Mather, who praised the Apostle for "humaniz[ing] these miserable animals, and . . . circurat[ing] them." For Eliot, the Indians' "wildness" obscured their virtues but not their humanity. As he told Jonathan Hanmer in 1654, "there is in them [the natives] a great measure of natural ingenuity and ingeniosity, only it is drowned out in their wild and rude manner of living; but by culture, order, government, and religion they begin to be furbished up."[13]

Eliot's use of the expression "furbish up" in the letter to Hanmer is also noteworthy. James Axtell has observed that English colonists characteristically spoke of missionary programs as exercises in the "reduction" as opposed to the "elevation" of Indians. In 1646, for example, the General Court asked Eliot and other elders to "reduce them [the Nonantum Indians] to civility of life." Axtell further remarks that "to my knowledge, only two [English] missionaries during the whole colonial period ever expressed their goal as one of elevation—both only once—and even their aberrance was wholly out of character." The exceptions were eighteenth-century figures, John Sergeant ("raise them [the Indians], as far as possible, to the condition of a civil, industrious, and polished people") and Eleazar Wheelock ("endeavors were used to raise them up"). While it may be true in general, Axtell's observation does not apply to the Apostle. On at least eight occasions, Eliot used the expressions "furbish up" and "train up" to describe his missionary objectives.[14]

The Apostle can be distinguished from his contemporaries in other ways as well. His writings never placed the natives among the natural curiosities of the New World in the dehumanizing manner of Francis Higginson's *New-Englands Plantation* (1630), William Wood's *New Englands Prospect* (1634), Thomas Morton's *New English Canaan* (1637), and John Josselyn's *New-Englands Rarities Discovered* (1672) and *Two Voyages to New-England* (1674). He also did not use the praying Indians as object lessons for sluggish Puritans, as did Thomas Shepard, John Cotton, and the English divines who contributed prefaces to the Eliot tracts; nor, like Increase Mather and many others, did Eliot use pagan natives as symbols of what "Indianizing" colonists might or had become—lazy and lustful degenerates who lived beyond the pale of civilized institutions. In fact, Eliot betrayed no fear that he might be corrupted by the native "heart of darkness." He considered moving to Wamesit in the late 1640s and to Natick at several occasions after the town's creation in 1650, and he recognized the value of Indian medicine even though it was administered by powwows.[15]

The most subtle indication of Eliot's attitudes toward the Indians was his argument for an American millennium in "The learned Conjectures." In the 1970s and 1980s, Sacvan Bercovitch and other scholars claimed that seventeenth-century New England Puritan eschatology was one of the principal sources of American exceptionalism. This claim has been challenged by Dwight Bozeman, who concludes that the idea that the millennium could begin or had begun in Massachusetts Bay was absent in the 1630s and 1640s, and by Reiner Smolinski, who finds no evidence of it in seventeenth-century sources written after the Restoration. The idea probably surfaced only in the 1650s, and then in only two texts. One was Edward Johnson's "Wonder-Working Providence." The Indians were irrelevant to Johnson, who gave all the credit to the saints. From their perch at the "western end of the world," they had constructed "the porch of the glorious building" soon to be erected in England. The other was Eliot's "Learned Conjectures." Eliot's conviction that Massachusetts Bay was the "eastern gate" to the kingdom required more than a particular theory of the natives' ancestry; it also required an ability to affiirm that the Indians, not the saints, were the ones who made New England a special place in biblical prophecy.[16]

Clearly, Eliot had a greater respect for the Indians' intelligence and character than did his contemporaries, and he had a stronger sense of justice than they did. It had not always been so. If an argument advanced in Chapter 2 is correct, he was no different in outlook than others in the colony when he began his mission in 1646. The Apostle was transformed by his exposure to the natives: he learned to appreciate their humanity and to sympathize with their problems. The Bay Colony's ministers and magistrates never underwent a similar transformation. The mission in Massachusetts Bay was not a "main end" of settlement before 1646, and it did not become one thereafter except for members of the Eliot and Gookin families. The colony's clerical and lay leaders were not hostile to the Indian work: various ministers helped the Apostle from time to time, particularly in the early years of the mission; and the magistrates (often in conjunction with the deputies) granted most of his petitions prior to King Philip's War. But because they never interacted with the Indians to the extent that he did, the ministers and magistrates never came to share Eliot's sympathy for the native people.

APPENDIX ONE

• • •

John Cotton's Lectures on Revelation and Canticles

John Cotton lectured on all twenty-two chapters of the Book of Revelation. The dates for these lectures cannot be fixed with precision. He was preaching on Revelation 4 by late 1638 or early 1639 and on Revelation 13 in early 1640. If he held to the same schedule, he would have reached the book's final chapter in early to mid-1641.[1] Only portions of the lectures on Revelation survive in any form:

Cotton's lectures on Revelation 16 were "taken from his own mouth" and published by John Humphrey under the title *The Powring Out of the Seven Vials* (London, 1642, 1645). John Winthrop, Sr., said that the publication of this work "much grieved" Cotton because he had not "perused and corrected the copy."

Cotton reworked his lecture on Revelation 20:5–6 and published it as *The Churches Resurrection* (London, 1642).

Cotton's lectures on Revelation 13 were printed as *An Exposition upon the Thirteenth Chapter of the Revelation* (London, 1655, 1656). According to its title page, the work was "taken from his mouth in short-writing, and some part of it corrected by himself soon after the preaching thereof." James Maclear plausibly suggests that William Aspinwall, a repatriated Massachusetts man, was responsible for seeing the work through the press. Maclear also observes that Aspinwall could not have been the person who transcribed the lectures on Revelation 13 because he was living in Rhode Island at the time, having been exiled from Massachusetts Bay for supporting Anne Hutchinson.

Thomas Shepard's manuscript notes on Cotton's lectures on Revelation 4:1–2, 4:9–11, 5:12–13, 6:1–4, and 6:7–11 are available at the New England Historic Genealogical Society, Boston. George Selement has edited and published the lecture on Revelation 4:1–2.

Samuel Sewall used a source he called Cotton's "manuscript on the Revelation" and cited its discussions of Revelation 6:12, 12:7–9, 15:8, 18:21, and 20:7–9.[2]

Cotton preached on the Book of Canticles in the early 1620s in his Lincolnshire church. These lectures were published as *A Brief Exposition of the whole Book of Canticles* (London, 1642, 1648). He delivered the American lectures on Canticles around 1645 and later edited them for what proved to be posthumous publication under the title *A Brief Exposition with Practical Observations upon the Whole Book of Canticles, Never Before Published* (London, 1655).[3]

APPENDIX TWO

. . .

Variant Indian Personal and Place Names in the Missionary History of Massachusetts Bay

Personal Names

Ahawton: Ahauton, Ahhaton, Mahanton, Nabanton, Nahanton, Nahauton, Old Ahawton
Anaweakin: Annuweekit, Anuweekin
Attawans: Ahatawance, Nattahatawans, Tahattaware, Tattawans, Tohatooner
Black James: Walamachin, Willy Machin
Captain Josiah: Pennahannit, Pennakennit
Captain Tom: Poliquanum, Poquanum, Wattasacompanum, Wutaskompanum
Chickataubut: Chickkatawbut, Obtakiest
Cutshamekin: Cuchamakin, Cutchamaquin, Cutshamacke, Kitshamake, Kutshamekin, Quoshamakin
Daniel Tokkohwompait: Takawompait, Tookuwompbait
James Rumney Marsh: James Muminquash, James C ıssumag, James Quanapaug, James Quanapohit
James the Printer: Wawaus, Wowaus
Job Nesutan: Nassott, Noistenus
John Lyne: John a Line, John Alline
John Sassamon: Sassaman, Sausiman, Sosoman, Wussausman
John Thomas: Naanischow
Joseph Tuckawillipin: Tuckup William, Tuhapawillin, Tuppukkoowillin
Josias Wompatuck: Josiah, Womputik
Mascononomo: Mashanomet, Massaconomet, the "sagamore of Agawam"
Mattaumpe: Maliompe, Netamp, Netop
Monoco: "One-eyed John"
Monotunkquanit: Monatunkanet
Nashowanon: Nashacowam, Shoanan, Sholan, Shoniow, Showanon

Nausquonit: Nosannowitt
Numphow: Mempho, Nobhow, Numphon
Old Jethro: Tantamous
Owussumag: Awussamag, Onomog, Oquannamaug, Owanamaug
Passaconaway: Papassaconnaway, Papisseconeway
Petavit: Peneovot, Petahheg, Petakhey, Robin
Peter Jethro: Animatohu, Hantomush
Piumbuhhou: Piambow, Piam Boohan
Pomham (Nipmuck): Pomhaman, Pumham
Sagamore George: George Rumney Marsh, Winnepurkitt
Sagamore James: Monowampate
Sagamore John (Nipmuck): Horowaninit
Sagamore John (Pawtucket): Wonohaquaham
Sagamore John (Pennacook): Point Ahau, Puntahhun
Sagamore Sam: Shoshanim, Upchatuck, Uskatuhgun
Simon Beckom: Betokom, Pottoquam
Solomon (of Pakachoog): Wooamaskochu
Squamaug: Daniel, Misquamaug, Scumuck, Squamuck
Totherswamp: Todorsway, Toteswamp, Tutaswampe
Waban: Waaubon, Waawbon, Wakan
Wamporas: Wampas, Wampoowas
Wannalancett: Nanaleucet
Webbacowet: Wabbacowites, Wabbakoxets
William Awinian: Manawianut
William of Sudbury: Naaos, Naoas, Nataous, Nattous
Wossamegon (Nipmuck): Matchippa, Ousamequin, Wesamequen, Wesawegun

Place Names

Italics indicate English town in existence before King Philip's War.

Ashquoach: Quabag Old Fort, Brimfield
Chabanakongkomun: Chachaubunkkakowok, Chobonakonkon, Dudley, Webster
Hassanamesit: Hassanamisco, Grafton
Maanexit: Thompson (Conn.)
Magunkog: Magunkaquog, Magunkuhquok, Magwongkommuk, Ashland, Hopkinton
Manchage: Monuhchogok, Sutton
Musketaquid: *Concord*
Nashaway: Nashaurreg, Nashauwog, *Lancaster*
Nashobah: Nashop, Nayhop, Littleton
Neponset: Channit, Cohannet, *Dorchester,* Dorchester Mill
Nonantum: Nonanetum, Noonanetum, *Newton (Cambridge Village),* Watertown Mill

Okommakamesit: Ogkoohquonkam, Ogquonikongquamesit, Whipsufferage, Whipsuppenicke, *Marlborough*
Pakachoog: Packachooge, Auburn
Pantucket: Panatukit, Pautucket, Pawtucket, Lowell
Punkapoag: Blue Hill, Pakemit, Pakeunit, Pankapoag, Ponipog, Canton, Stoughton
Putikookuppog: Fiskdale
Quabag: *Brookfield*
Quantisset: Quanetusset, Quantiske, Pomfret (Conn.)
Quassuck: Sturbridge
Quinebaug: Qunnubbagge
Quobagud: Quobacutt, East Brookfield
Wabquisset: Wabuhquoshish, North Woodstock (Conn.)
Waeuntug: *Mendon*, Uxbridge
Wamesit: Waymesick, Lowell
Wekabaug: West Brookfield
Weshakim: Washacum, Sterling

APPENDIX THREE

Population Figures and Permanent and Temporary Personnel in the Prewar Settlements

This information is taken primarily from Eliot in Ford, ed., *Some Correspondence,* pp. 27–30; Eliot, *Brief Narrative,* pp. 5–8; Temple, *History of North Brookfield,* pp. 26–31; and Gookin, *Historical Collections,* pp. 184–194. Gookin lists populations by families and not by heads; he assumes five persons per family (p. 186). Figures in parentheses indicate population size in 1674 according to Gookin. Italicized names indicate nonresident teachers.

The Old Praying Towns

Hassanamesit (60)
    RULERS: Anaweakin, Petavit
    TEACHERS: Joseph Tuckawillipin (pastor of the church), Monotunkquanit
    OTHER PROMINENT RESIDENTS: Piumbuhhou (ruling elder in the church), James the Printer and Sasomet (teachers at Waeuntug), William of Sudbury (deacon in the church), Captain Tom (ruler of the new towns), *James Speene (teacher at Pakachoog),* Joseph and Sampson (brothers)

Magunkog (55)
    RULER: Pomham
    TEACHERS: Simon, Wohwohquoshadt, *Job Kattananit Nashobah (50)*

Nashobah (50)
    RULERS: Attawans, John Attawans, Sr., Captain Josiah (also marshall-general of the old and new praying towns)
    TEACHER: John Thomas

Natick (not listed)
    RULERS: Cutshamekin, Waban, Totherswamp, Peter, Piumbuhhou, Thomas Speene, Sr., Captain Tom, Moshosinan
    TEACHERS: Totherswamp, Nishohkou, Ponampam, Samuel (son of Monotunkquanit), John Speene, Anthony
    OTHER PROMINENT RESIDENTS: Wamporas, Robin Speene, Monequasson, Nookau, John Sassamon, William of Sudbury, Job Nesutan, Owussumag, Monotunkquanit

Okommakamesit (50)
    RULER: Owussumag
    TEACHERS: Nausquonit, Solomon

Punkapoag (60)
    RULERS: Josias Wompatuck, Squamaug (regent to Jeremy, son of Josias), Ahawton
    TEACHERS: William Awinian, William Ahawton

Wamesit (75)
    RULERS: Numphow, John Lyne
    TEACHERS: Mystic George, Samuel Numphow, Simon Beckom
    OTHER PROMINENT RESIDENT: Sagamore John (possibly John Lyne)

The New Praying Towns

Chabanakongkomun (45)
    TEACHER: Joseph (brother of Sampson)
    OTHER PROMINENT RESIDENT: Black James (constable of the new towns)

Maanexit (100)
    TEACHER: John Moqua

Manchage (60)
    TEACHER: Waabesktamin

Pakachoog (100)
    SACHEMS: Sagamore John, Solomon
    TEACHER: *James Speene*
    OTHER PROMINENT RESIDENT: Matoonas (constable)

Quantisset (100)
: TEACHERS: *Monotunkquanit, Joseph Tuckawillipin,* Daniel (probably Daniel Tokkohwompait)

Wabquisset (150)
: TEACHER: Sampson

Waeuntug (not listed)
: TEACHERS: *James the Printer, Sasomet*

The Semiofficial Settlements

Nashaway and Weshakim (75–80)
: SACHEMS: Nashowanon, Sagamore Matthew, Sagamore Sam
: TEACHER: Peter Jethro
: OTHER PROMINENT RESIDENT: Monoco

Pantucket (not listed)
: SACHEMS: Passaconaway, Wannalancett
: TEACHER: Peter Jethro

Quabag-area villages and sachems (not listed)
: ASHQUOACH: Quancunquasit
: PUTIKOOKUPPOG: Wattalloowekin, Nakin, Konkewasco
: QUASSUCK: Nanaswhat
: QUOBAGUD: the "aged sachem," David
: WEKABAUG: Shattoockquis, Mattaumpe
: SPECIFIC LOCATIONS UNCERTAIN: Wompontupont, Wossamegon

APPENDIX FOUR

· · ·

Principal Nonantum and Neponset Indians

The following list is taken primarily from Shepard, ed., *The Clear Sun-shine of the Gospel;* and from the Indian narratives printed in Eliot and Mayhew, Jr., *Tears of Repentance,* and in Eliot, *A further Account of the progress of the Gospel.*

Nonantum Indians
    Anthony, Totherswamp, and Wamporas (brothers)
    John, Robin, and Thomas Speene (brothers)
    Piumbuhhou
    Waban

Neponset Indians
    Ahawton and William Ahawton (father and son)
    Cutshamekin and Josias Wompatuck (uncle and nephew)
    Job Nesutan
    John Sassamon
    Monequasson
    Nishohkou
    Nookau
    Ponampam

APPENDIX FIVE

• • •

Eliot's Massachusett Publications

Asterisks denote editions no longer extant.

"Primer and Catechism." Cambridge, 1654,* 1662,* 1669, 1686 or 1687. The third edition, the only one extant in its entirety, was published as *The Indian Primer*. The title page and several other portions of the fourth edition are not extant.
The First Book of Moses called Genesis. Cambridge, 1655.
The Gospel of Matthew. Cambridge, 1655.*
The Psalter (in metrical translation). Cambridge, 1658 or 1659,* 1663 or 1664,* 1682.*
A Christian Covenanting Confession. Cambridge, 1660 or 1661. Republished at a later date, probably around 1670.
The New Testament of Our Lord and Saviour Jesus Christ. Cambridge, 1661. Rev. ed. Cambridge, 1680.
The Holy Bible Containing the Old Testament and the New. Cambridge, 1663. Rev. ed. Cambridge, 1685.
A Call to the Unconverted. By Richard Baxter. Cambridge, 1664,* 1688.
The Practice of Piety. By Lewis Bayly. Cambridge, 1665, 1685.
"Our Indians' A B C." Cambridge, 1671.*
The Logick Primer. Cambridge, 1672.
The Sincere Convert. By Thomas Shepard. With Grindal Rawson. Cambridge, 1689.

Abbreviations

. . .

AAS   American Antiquarian Society, Worcester, Mass.
MHS   Massachusetts Historical Society, Boston.
MHSC   Massachusetts Historical Society, *Collections*. (Cited by series and volume numbers.)
MHSP   Massachusetts Historical Society, *Proceedings*. (Cited by cumulative volume number only.)
MSA   Massachusetts State Archives, Boston. (Cited by microfilm reel and position number.)
NEHGR   *New England Historical and Genealogical Register.*
NEQ   *New England Quarterly.*
PCSM   *Publications of the Colonial Society of Massachusetts.* Transactions or Collections. (Cited by cumulative volume number only.)
RCP   Nathaniel B. Shurtleff and David C. Pulsifer, eds., *Records of the Colony of New Plymouth* (1855–1861; reprint ed. New York: AMS Press, 1968).
RMB   Nathaniel B. Shurtleff, ed., *Records of the Governor and Company of the Massachusetts Bay in New England* (1853–1854; reprint ed. New York: AMS Press, 1968).
WJ   James K. Hosmer, ed., *Winthrop's Journal: "History of New England," 1630–1649* (New York: Charles Scribner's Sons, 1908).
WMQ   *William and Mary Quarterly,* third series.
WP   Allyn B. Forbes et al., eds., *The Winthrop Papers, 1498–1649* (Boston: Massachusetts Historical Society, 1929–1947).

Principal Printed Sources

∴

The Eliot Tracts

The following are listed in chronological order. Citations in notes do not include the names of the authors or the editors of the Eliot tracts.

[Shepard, Thomas.] *The Day-Breaking, If Not the Sun-Rising of the Gospell with the Indians in New-England.* London, 1647. In MHSC 3:4 (1834): 1–23.

———, ed. *The Clear Sun-shine of the Gospel Breaking Forth upon the Indians in New-England.* London, 1648. In MHSC 3:4 (1834): 25–67.

Winslow, Edward, ed. *The Glorious Progress of the Gospel amongst the Indians in New England.* London, 1649. In MHSC 3:4 (1834): 69–98.

Whitfield, Henry, ed. *The Light appearing more and more towards the perfect Day.* London, 1651. In MHSC 3:4 (1834): 101–147.

———, ed. *Strength out of Weaknesse.* London, 1652. In MHSC 3:4 (1834): 149–196.

Eliot, John, and Thomas Mayhew, Jr. *Tears of Repentance: Or, A further Narrative of the Progress of the Gospel amongst the Indians in New-England.* London, 1653. In MHSC 3:4 (1834): 197–260.

Eliot, John. *A Late and Further Manifestation of the Progress of the Gospel amongst the Indians in New-England.* London, 1655. In MHSC 3:4 (1834): 261–287.

———. *A further Accompt of the Progresse of the Gospel amongst the Indians in New-England.* London, 1659.

———. *A further Account of the progress of the Gospel Amongst the Indians in New England.* London, 1660.

———. *A Brief Narrative of the Progress of the Gospel amongst the Indians in New England, in the Year 1670.* London, 1671. In *Old South Leaflets* 1:21 (Boston: Old South Meeting House, n.d.), pp. 1–11.

Other Principal Sources

Bowden, Henry W., and James P. Ronda, eds. *John Eliot's Indian Dialogues: A Study in Cultural Interaction.* Westport, Conn.: Greenwood Press, 1980. Original publication: Cambridge, 1671.

Eames, Wilberforce, ed. *John Eliot and the Indians, 1652–1657: Being Letters Addressed to Reverend Jonathan Hanmer of Barnstaple, England.* New York: Adams and Grace Press, 1915.

Eliot, John. "An Account of Indian Churches in New-England" (1673). First published in MHSC 1:10 (1809): 124–129.

———. *Dying Speeches & Counsels Of such Indians as dyed in the Lord.* Cambridge [ca. 1685].

——— *The Indian Grammar Begun: Or, An Essay to bring the Indian Language into Rules.* Cambridge, 1666. In MHSC 2:9 (1822): 243–312.

———. "The learned Conjectures of Reverend John Eliot touching the Americans." In Thomas Thorowgood, *Jews in America, or Probabilities that Those Indians Are Judaical* (London, 1660), pp. 1–27 (separate pagination).

"Eliot's Letters to Boyle." In MHSC 1:3 (1794): 177–188.

Ford, John, ed. *Some Correspondence between the Governors and Treasurers of the New England Company in London and the Commissioners of the United Colonies in America, the Missionaries of the Company, and Others between the Years 1657 and 1712, to Which Are Added the Journals of the Rev. Experience Mayhew in 1713 and 1714.* London: Spottiswoode and Company, 1896.

Gookin, Daniel. *An Historical Account of the Doings and Sufferings of the Christian Indians in New England, in the Years 1675, 1676, 1677* (1677). First published in AAS, *Transactions and Collections* 2 (1836): 429–525.

———. *The Historical Collections of the Indians in New England* (1674). First published in MHSC 1:1 (1792): 141–227.

Hill, Don Gleason, and Julius H. Tuttle, eds. *The Early Records of the Town of Dedham, Massachusetts.* Dedham: The Dedham Transcript, 1886–1936.

"Letter from Rev. John Eliot, 1664." In NEHGR 9 (1855): 131–133.

"Letters of John Eliot." In MHSP 17 (1879–80): 245–253.

"Letters of the Rev. John Eliot." In NEHGR 36 (1882): 291–299.

New Englands First Fruits. London, 1643.

Powicke, F. J. "Some Unpublished Correspondence of the Rev. Richard Baxter and the Rev. John Eliot, 'The Apostle to the American Indians,' 1656–1682." *Bulletin of the John Rylands University Library* 15 (1931): 138–176, 442–466.

Pulsifer, David C., ed. *Acts of the Commissioners of the United Colonies of New England.* Vols. 9–10 in RCP.

Shurtleff, Nathaniel B., ed. *Records of the Governor and Company of the Massachusetts Bay in New England.* Cited as RMB.

Thorowgood, Thomas. *Jews in America, or Probabilities that Those Indians Are Judaical*. London, 1660. Introductory material and body of text separately paginated.

Winship, George Parker, ed. *The New England Company of 1649 and John Eliot*. Boston: Publications of the Prince Society, 1920.

Notes

1. The Context of the Mission

1. WJ 1:49–50. For the oath, see RMB 1:351–352 (see also p. 39); for Skelton and Higginson, see RMB 1:36^f–37^f; for Cradock, see RMB 1:384; for the charter, see RMB 1:17, and Samuel Eliot Morison et al., "The Royal Charter, or Patent, of the Colony of the Massachusetts Bay," MHSP 62 (1930): 235–236; and for the seal, see Matt B. Jones, "The Early Massachusetts-Bay Colony Seals," AAS, *Proceedings* 44 (1935): 13.
2. John Winthrop in WP 2:111, 114, 117, 138; and John Cotton, *Gods Promise to His Plantations* (London, 1630), in *Old South Leaflets* 3:53 (Boston: Old South Meeting House, n.d.), pp. 14–15.
3. Andrew Delbanco, *The Puritan Ordeal* (Cambridge: Harvard University Press, 1989), p. 105; Theodore Dwight Bozeman, *To Live Ancient Lives: The Primitivist Dimension in Puritanism* (Chapel Hill: University of North Carolina Press, 1988), p. 97; Winthrop, "A Modell of Christian Charity" (1630), in WP 2:282–293; Cotton in Everett Emerson, ed., *Letters from New England: The Massachusetts Bay Company* (Amherst: University of Massachusetts Press, 1976), pp. 127–131; and Richard Mather, "Arguments tending to prove . . ." (1635), in Increase Mather, *The Life and Death of That Reverend Man of God, Mr. Richard Mather* (Cambridge, 1670), pp. 12–19.
4. Eliot in "Learned Conjectures," p. 26 (mispaginated 18), and in *Tears of Repentance*, p. 216; and "Petition of Rev. John Eliot" (1675), in RCP 10:452. For statements by others, see *Memoirs of Captain Roger Clap* (Boston, 1731), in Alexander Young, ed., *Chronicles of the First Planters of the Colony of Massachusetts Bay* (1846; reprint ed. Williamstown, Mass.: Corner House, 1978), p. 364; John Endecott in *Strength out of Weaknesse*, p. 189; the General Court in RMB 4(2): 265; Gookin, *Historical Collections*, p. 223; and Increase Mather, *A Brief History of the Warr with the Indians in New-Eng-*

land (Boston, 1676), in Richard Slotkin and James K. Folsom, eds., *So Dreadfull a Judgment: Puritan Responses to King Philip's War* (Middletown, Conn.: Wesleyan University Press, 1978), p. 82.

5. Francis Jennings, *The Invasion of America: Indians, Colonialism, and the Cant of Conquest* (1975; reprint ed. New York: Norton, 1976), pp. 53, 238, and "Goals and Functions of Puritan Missions to the Indians," *Ethnohistory* 18 (1971): 207.
6. Winthrop in WP 2:111, 112, 126, 146; Saltonstall, Jr., in Emerson, ed., *Letters from New England*, p. 92; Cotton, *Gods Promise*, p. 14; and *New Englands First Fruits*, pp. 23–24. For the authorship of *New Englands First Fruits*, see Raymond P. Stearns, *The Strenuous Puritan: Hugh Peter, 1598–1660* (Urbana: University of Illinois Press, 1954), p. 167.
7. David C. Stineback, "The Status of Puritan-Indian Scholarship," NEQ 51 (1978): 83–84; Neal Salisbury, *Manitou and Providence: Indians, Europeans, and the Making of New England, 1500–1643* (New York: Oxford University Press, 1982), p. 178; James Axtell, *The Invasion Within: The Contest of Cultures in Colonial North America* (New York: Oxford University Press, 1985), p. 219; and John Canup, *Out of the Wilderness: The Emergence of an American Identity in Colonial New England* (Middletown, Conn.: Wesleyan University Press, 1990), pp. 151–152. I take the term "affective model" from the use of the word "affect" in the quotations by Matthew Cradock in note 8 below and by Edward Winslow in Chapter 2, note 28.
8. Cradock in RMB 1:384, 387, 390; and John White, *The Planters Plea* (London, 1630; reprint ed. New York: Da Capo Press, 1968), pp. 27, 35–36 (see also pp. 5, 7, 65–66).
9. Axtell, *Invasion Within*, pp. 136–178; Shepard in *Day-Breaking*, p. 15; and *New Englands First Fruits*, p. 1.
10. White, *Planters Plea*, p. 53 (see also p. 27); Hopkins in WP 3:106; Eliot in *Glorious Progress*, p. 88, and in *Clear Sun-shine*, p. 50; and Shepard in *Day-Breaking*, p. 4.
11. For the first reason, see Eliot in *Glorious Progress*, p. 90, and Shepard in *Day-Breaking*, p. 15; for the second, see Eliot in *Clear Sun-shine*, p. 50; for the third, see White, *Planters Plea*, pp. 38–39; and for the fourth, see Eliot in Eames, ed., *John Eliot and the Indians*, p. 7.
12. Alden T. Vaughan, "Early English Paradigms for New World Natives," in *Roots of American Racism: Essays on the Colonial Experience* (New York: Oxford University Press, 1995), pp. 34–54; Williams, *The Hireling Ministry None of Christs* (London, 1652), in *The Complete Writings of Roger Williams* (New York: Russell and Russell, 1963), 7:168; *New Englands First Fruits*, pp. 8–9; and Cradock in RMB 1:397 (see also p. 386).
13. Howes and Copeland in WP 3:77, 4:157–158; and White, *Planters Plea*, pp. 11, 52–53.
14. For the assumptions, see Francis Higginson in Emerson, ed., *Letters from New England*, p. 38; Shepard in *Day-Breaking*, p. 15; and *New Englands*

First Fruits, pp. 1–2, 23–24. For Williams, see Glenn W. LaFantasie et al., eds., *The Correspondence of Roger Williams* (Hanover, N.H.: University Press of New England, 1988), p. 750; and Alden T. Vaughan, ed., *William Wood: New Englands Prospect* (Amherst: University of Massachusetts Press, 1977), p. 110. For Dunster, see Thomas Lechford, *Plaine Dealing: Or, Newes from New-England* (London, 1642), in MHSC 3:3 (1833): 105–106. For the children, see *New Englands First Fruits,* p. 3; WJ 1:111, 115; and J. Franklin Jameson, ed., *Johnson's Wonder-Working Providence, 1628–1651* (1910; reprint ed. New York: Barnes and Noble, 1967), p. 80.

15. Shepard in *Day-Breaking,* p. 15.
16. James F. Maclear, "New England and the Fifth Monarchy: The Quest for the Millennium in Early American Puritanism," WMQ 32 (1975): 229–234; Bozeman, *To Live Ancient Lives,* pp. 216–217, 229; and Francis J. Bremer, *Congregational Communion: Clerical Friendship in the Anglo-American Puritan Community, 1610–1692* (Boston: Northeastern University Press, 1994), pp. 123–129. For textual and dating problems in Cotton's two series of lectures, see Appendix 1. No thorough text-critical study of Cotton's eschatological writings exists.
17. Bozeman, *To Live Ancient Lives,* pp. 198–217 (quotations on pp. 206, 229n, 250). Cotton's English lectures were published as *A Brief Exposition of the whole Book of Canticles* (London, 1642, 1648). It is important to understand how Bozeman and I use the words "millennium" and "millennialism." The former is the kingdom of biblical prophecy and not a synonym for "working model" of a successful civil and ecclesiastical order; and the latter is the conviction that the millennium is both imminent and terrestrial, rather than an alternative term for "eschatology," the branch of theology that interprets, in various ways, the millennium and the other "last things" of biblical prophecy.
18. Bozeman, *To Live Ancient Lives,* pp. 9–10, 237–262 (quotations on pp. 11, 207, 261).
19. Ibid., pp. 217–236 (quotations on pp. 229–233). The millennial version of the "errand into the wilderness" thesis is perhaps best associated with two works by Sacvan Bercovitch: *The Puritan Origins of the American Self* (New Haven, Conn.: Yale University Press, 1975), pp. 35–108, and *The American Jeremiad* (Madison: University of Wisconsin Press, 1979), pp. 3–92.
20. For the hastening arrival of Armageddon, see Cotton's *An Exposition upon the Thirteenth Chapter of the Revelation* (London, 1655), p. 93; *The Churches Resurrection* (London, 1642), p. 30; *The Bloudy Tenent Washed, and made white in the bloud of the Lambe* (London, 1647), p. 148; and *The Powring Out of the Seven Vials* (London, 1642), first part of the sermon on the sixth vial, p. 10 (mispaginated 23), and second part of the sermon on the sixth vial, p. 15 (mispaginated 42). For the location of Armageddon, see ibid., fourth part of the sermon on the sixth vial, p. 2; and for the identity and activities of the ten kings, see ibid., second part of the sermon on the sixth

vial, p. 4 (mispaginated 30), fourth part of the sermon on the sixth vial, pp. 1–3, and *An Exposition*, p. 81.

21. For the national conversion of the Jews and its role as a precondition to the millennium, see Cotton, *A Brief Exposition with Practical Observations upon the Whole Book of Canticles, Never before Printed* (London, 1655), pp. 184–189 (quotation on p. 185); *Churches Resurrection*, pp. 8, 13; and *Powring Out*, first part of the sermon on the sixth vial, pp. 8–9, 13 (mispaginated 21–22, 26), and fourth part of the sermon on the sixth vial, p. 6. For the destruction of the Ottoman Empire and the repatriation to Palestine, see ibid., first part of the sermon on the sixth vial, pp. 8–13 (mispaginated 21–26); and *Brief Exposition with Practical Observations*, pp. 183–187.

22. Cotton, *Churches Resurrection*, p. 20; *Powring Out*, sermon on the seventh vial, p. 11; and Bozeman, *To Live Ancient Lives*, p. 256. For Cotton's distinction between "reformation" and "resurrection" (the latter was his term for millennial restoration), and for his insistence that Massachusetts could not achieve the latter until the Middle Advent, see *Churches Resurrection*, pp. 17–22.

23. Cotton, *Brief Exposition with Practical Observations*, pp. 24–50, 202–207; *Churches Resurrection*, pp. 4–6; *Powring Out*, sermon on the third vial, pp. 16–22 (quotation on pp. 20–21); and *An Exposition*, pp. 17–18. See also the undated and anonymous discussion of Cotton's views, entitled "How Far Moses Judicialls Bind Mass[achusetts]," in MHSP 36 (1902): 282–284.

24. For Jerusalem, see Cotton, *Brief Exposition with Practical Observations*, pp. 91–93, 179–235, and *Powring Out*, first part of the sermon on the sixth vial, pp. 8, 13 (mispaginated 21, 26); for Europe and New England, see *Churches Resurrection*, pp. 12–30; and for the pagan nations, see *Powring Out*, sermon on the seventh vial, pp. 6–14, and the sources cited in note 27 below. Cotton thought that England and Scotland were making important contributions to the coming transformation of Europe. He stated in *The Powring Out* that the work in progress in the British "corner of the world" would be extended to "the very gates of Rome itself." The work in question, however, was the destruction of the episcopal polity and not the establishment of the millennium, an honor he assigned to the Christianized Jews. Sermon on the fifth vial, p. 7; first part of the sermon on the sixth vial, p. 8 (mispaginated 23); and sermon on the seventh vial, p. 16.

25. For the second coming, see *Powring Out*, first part of the sermon on the sixth vial, p. 13 (mispaginated 26), and third part of the sermon on the sixth vial, pp. 2–3. Cotton apparently took the word "millennium" in its literal sense of "one thousand years." Ibid., second part of the sermon on the sixth vial, p. 15 (mispaginated 42), and third part of the sermon on the sixth vial, p. 3; and *Churches Resurrection*, pp. 3–15.

26. Cotton, *Powring Out*, sermon on the seventh vial, pp. 10–11, and *The Way of Congregational Churches Cleared* (London, 1648), in Larzer Ziff, ed., *John Cotton on the Churches of New England* (Cambridge: Harvard Univer-

sity Press, 1968), p. 274; WJ 2:30; and Shepard in *Day-Breaking*, p. 14, and in *Clear Sun-shine*, p. 62. Puritans used the word "Gentile" in the biblical sense of "non-Jew" or "non-Israelite" and not in the Spanish sense of "non-Christian." Mercator's famous sixteenth-century map placed the straits of Anian in the approximate location of the Bering Straits. For the Tartar-origins view, see Lee E. Huddleston, *Origins of the American Indians: European Concepts, 1492–1729* (Austin: University of Texas Press, 1967), especially pp. 114–117; and David S. Katz, *Philo-Semitism and the Readmission of Jews into England* (London: Oxford University Press, 1982), pp. 135–136. Brerewood and Purchas modified a continental version of the theory, which held that the Tartars were the remnants of the lost tribes of Israel, by teaching instead that Tartary (sometimes called Scythia) was exclusively a Gentile region.

27. Cotton, *Powring Out*, first part of the sermon on the sixth vial, p. 9 (mispaginated 22), and fourth part of the sermon on the sixth vial, p. 8; Cotton ms. fragment on Revelation 15:8 quoted in Samuel Sewall, *Phaenomena quaedam Apocalyptica* (Boston, 1697), pp. 52–53; and Shepard in *Clear Sunshine*, p. 60. For the occasional exceptions, see Cotton, *Powring Out*, fourth part of the sermon on the sixth vial, p. 12; *The Way*, p. 274; *Bloudy Tenent Washed*, p. 148; *Brief Exposition with Practical Observations*, pp. 185–186; and WJ 2:30. Shepard said that he took the 1690 date from Brightman, who also taught the Jews-then-Gentiles sequence. See *The Workes of That Famous, Reverend, and Learned Divine, Mr. Tho: Brightman* (London, 1644), pp. 517–519.

28. Williams, *Christenings make not Christians, or a Brief Discourse concerning that name Heathen, commonly given to the Indians* (London, 1645), in *Complete Writings*, 7:40. For the development of Williams's eschatology, see W. Clark Gilpin, *The Millenarian Piety of Roger Williams* (Chicago: University of Chicago Press, 1979), pp. 60–62. For the Indians' Gentile ancestry, see Williams, *A Key into the Language of America* (London, 1643), in *Complete Writings*, 1:87–88 (see also p. 84); *Christenings*, p. 31; and LaFantasie et al., eds., *Correspondence of Roger Williams*, p. 429. For Williams's earlier interest in the lost tribes theory, see ibid., p. 30; and Thomas Thorowgood, *Iewes in America, or Probabilities That the Americans are of that Race* (London, 1650), pp. 5–6. For the commissioning of apostles, see Williams, *The Bloudy Tenent of Persecution* (London, 1644), in *Complete Writings*, 3:307; *Hireling Ministry*, pp. 175–177; and *The Bloody Tenent yet More Bloody* (London, 1652), in *Complete Writings*, 4:370–371. For the imminent Middle Advent, see *Christenings*, p. 32; and *Mr. Cottons Letter Lately Printed, Examined and Answered* (London, 1644), in *Complete Writings*, 1:317–318. For the two preconditions to the Middle Advent, see *Hireling Ministry*, pp. 168–169. For the nonmilitary destruction of Catholicism, see *Bloudy Tenent*, pp. 360–364; *Queries of Highest Consideration* (London, 1644), in *Complete Writings*, 2:269; and *Hireling Ministry*, pp. 158–162. For the occasional conversions,

see *Bloody Tenent yet More Bloody*, pp. 370–371; and *Hireling Ministry*, p. 168.
29. Williams, *Christenings*, p. 37 (see also pp. 40–41); *Bloody Tenent yet More Bloody*, pp. 371–374; *Hireling Ministry*, pp. 158–161; and *The Examiner defended in A Fair and Sober Answer* (London, 1652), in *Complete Writings*, 7:270–274.
30. Williams, *A Key*, p. 85, and *Christenings*, p. 35.
31. Shepard in *Day-Breaking*, p. 15. Eliot's unrevealing statement reads: "The Lord must reign in these latter days, and more eminently and observably overtop all instruments and means: and I trust he will mightily appear in this [missionary] business, as in other parts of the world." *Glorious Progress*, p. 89. For Eliot's acknowledgments of his debt to Cotton, see *Light appearing*, pp. 127, 137–138, 140–141; *Strength out of Weaknesse*, p. 173; and "Learned Conjectures," pp. 24–25 (irregular pagination).
32. Gary B. Nash, "Notes on the History of Seventeenth-Century Missionization in Colonial America," *American Indian Culture and Research Journal* 2 (1978): 5; and Cotton in Emerson, ed., *Letters from New England*, p. 164. In 1637 the court gave English towns "the power . . . to restrain Indians . . . from profaning the Lord's day." The probable purpose of this directive was to regulate native conduct in English towns on Sundays rather than to authorize local officials to inspect Indian villages for violations of sabbath decorum. RMB 1:209. For the war captives, see WJ 1:227–228; and Winthrop, Sr., and Copeland in WP 3:457, 4:157, 159.
33. For Sagamore John, see Cotton, *The Way*, pp. 277–278; WJ 1:115; *New Englands First Fruits*, pp. 2–3; and Howes in WP 3:74. Several scholars wrongly report that John's brother, Sagamore James, also underwent a deathbed conversion to Christianity. For Squanto, see Neal Salisbury, "Squanto: Last of the Patuxets," in David G. Sweet and Gary B. Nash, eds., *Struggle and Survival in Colonial America* (Berkeley: University of California Press, 1981), pp. 228–245. For Wequash, see *New Englands First Fruits*, pp. 5–7 (irregular pagination); WJ 2:69; and Williams, *A Key*, pp. 86–87. Wequash should not be confused with Wequash Cook, a Pequot–Eastern Niantic.
34. *New Englands First Fruits*, pp. 2, 4, 7 (mispaginated 15), 8.
35. Ibid., pp. 2–8 (quotations on pp. 5, 7); Eliot in *Clear Sun-shine*, p. 55, and in Powicke, "Some Unpublished Correspondence," pp. 157–158; Shepard in *Day-Breaking*, p. 15; Cotton, *The Way*, pp. 272–273; Cotton ms. fragment on Revelation 15:8 quoted in Sewall, *Phaenomena*, p. 52; and Winslow in *Glorious Progress*, p. 75. For the Indian testimony, see *Tears of Repentance*, pp. 229, 232, 253–254, 256; and *Further Account*, pp. 10, 27, 47, 63, 72.
36. Eliot in *Clear Sun-shine*, p. 50, and in Powicke, "Some Unpublished Correspondence," pp. 157–158; and Cotton in Emerson, ed., *Letters from New England*, p. 164. For Eliot's unsuccessful sermon in September 1646, see Shepard in *Day-Breaking*, p. 4. For Wilson, see Jameson, ed., *Johnson's Wonder-Working Providence*, p. 264; and Ponampam in *Further Account*, p. 54.

Brown clearly preached to the Indians after the birth of the mission. For his possible efforts before that time, see Captain Tom in ibid., p. 27. There is no conclusive evidence that Williams preached to Indians during his residence in Plymouth and Massachusetts Bay, even though he had studied the language for this purpose. See LaFantasie et al., editorial note in *Correspondence of Roger Williams*, p. 11.

37. Winslow in *Glorious Progress*, p. 75; Cotton, *The Way*, pp. 274–275; and *New Englands First Fruits*, pp. 1–2. See also Eliot, *Indian Grammar Begun*, p. 312; and Shepard in *Day-Breaking*, p. 16.
38. Lechford, *Plaine Dealing*, p. 80; Cotton, *The Way*, p. 274; and Cotton ms. fragment on Revelation 15:8 quoted in Sewall, *Phaenomena*, p. 52. Cotton did not discuss the missionary implications of the sequence in any of the publications derived from his lectures on Revelation and Canticles. Lechford's remark and the ms. fragment on Revelation 15:8 are the only pre-1646 evaluations of the matter known to me. In 1641 Winthrop noted the sequence but did not comment on its implications for the nonexistent mission. WJ 2:30. Increase Mather stated that even after the birth of the mission, some colonists used the sequence to justify their nonparticipation in the Indian work. *Brief History of the Warr*, p. 82.
39. Shepard in *Clear Sun-shine*, p. 45.
40. Alden T. Vaughan, *New England Frontier: Puritans and Indians, 1620–1675* (1965; 1979; 3rd ed. Norman: University of Oklahoma Press, 1995), pp. 236–240; Stineback, "The Status," pp. 83–85; Henry Warner Bowden, *American Indians and Christian Missions: Studies in Cultural Conflict* (Chicago: University of Chicago Press, 1981), pp. 112–116; and Dane Morrison, *A Praying People: Massachusett Acculturation and the Failure of the Puritan Mission, 1600–1690* (New York: Peter Lang, 1995), pp. 37–41.

2. *The Submission of the Sachems and the Birth of the Mission*

1. WJ 2:81; RMB 2:26–27; and Howard M. Chapin, ed., *Documentary History of Rhode Island: Being the History of the Towns of Providence and Warwick to 1649 and of the Colony to 1647* (Providence: Preston and Rounds, 1916), pp. 146–147.
2. Robert E. Wall, Jr., *Massachusetts Bay: The Crucial Decade, 1640–1650* (New Haven, Conn.: Yale University Press, 1972), pp. 122–128 (quotation on p. 122); and LaFantasie et al., editorial note in *Correspondence of Roger Williams*, pp. 208–215.
3. Williams, *A Key*, pp. 80, 85–88; and *New Englands First Fruits*, pp. 5–7.
4. The fradulent charter is printed in NEHGR 11 (1857): 41–43.
5. WJ 2:198. For the 1644 charter, see John R. Bartlett, ed., *Records of the Colony of Rhode Island and Providence Plantations in New England* (Providence: A. Crawford Greene, 1856–1865), 1:143–146.
6. Williams, *Christenings*, pp. 39–40. A person identified only as "I. H." (prob-

ably John Humphrey, a Massachusetts man who had repatriated in 1641) saw the work through the press.

7. Wall, *Massachusetts Bay,* pp. 128–129; and WJ 2:123–124. At the time wampum was valued at 5 shillings per fathom. Williams, *A Key,* pp. 234–235.
8. RMB 2:40; and Winthrop, Sr., in WP 4:410. See also WJ 2:125.
9. RCP 9:11, 14–15; and WJ 2:134–136.
10. Wall, *Massachusetts Bay,* pp. 130–152.
11. RMB 2:55–56, 73; "Covenant signed by Passaconaway," in MSA 30:3; and WJ 2:156–157, 160. The five sachems reportedly responded to the various injunctions in nearly the same manner as Pomham and Sacononoco.
12. Jennings, *Invasion of America,* p. 235, and "Goals and Functions," p. 202. The following studies do not explain how the submissions of 1644 came about: Vaughan, *New England Frontier;* Salisbury, *Manitou and Providence;* Axtell, *Invasion Within;* Elise M. Brenner, "To Pray or To Be Prey, That is the Question: Strategies for Cultural Autonomy of Massachusetts Praying Town Indians," *Ethnohistory* 27 (1980): 135–152, and "Strategies for Autonomy: An Analysis of Ethnic Mobilization in Seventeenth Century Southern New England" (Ph.D. diss., University of Massachusetts, 1984); and Morrison, *Praying People.* In an earlier essay, Salisbury noted that the sachems "perhaps, as Jennings has suggested, . . . took their cue from the fate of Miantonomi." "Red Puritans: The 'Praying Indians' of Massachusetts Bay and John Eliot," WMQ 31 (1974): 30. James Drake observes that the sachems submitted in order to receive protection; however, he does not explore the circumstances that led to the action. "Symbol of a Failed Strategy: The Sassamon Trial, Political Culture, and the Outbreak of King Philip's War," *American Indian Culture and Research Journal* 19 (1995): 120.
13. For the death of Chickataubut, see WJ 1:111. The approximate death dates for the Squaw and for Cutshamekin can be inferred from the times when their names disappear from the sources as active participants in colonial affairs, as opposed to deceased ones in disputed land transactions. The Squaw vanishes after the act of submission, and Cutshamekin in late 1651. For Sagamores John, James, and George, see D. Hamilton Hurd, ed., *History of Middlesex County, Massachusetts* (Philadelphia: J. W. Lewis and Co., 1890), 1:9; Sidney Perley, ed., *The Indian Land Titles of Essex County, Massachusetts* (Salem, Mass.: Essex Book and Print Club, 1912), pp. 11–12; and George F. Dow, ed., *Records and Files of the Quarterly Courts of Essex County, Massachusetts* (Salem, Mass.: Essex Institute, 1911–1921), 1:25, 29, 42. For Masconomono, see ibid., 3:400; WJ 1:50; and Samuel G. Drake, *The Aboriginal Races of North America* (15th ed. New York: John B. Alden, 1880), p. 111.
14. Dudley in Emerson, ed., *Letters from New England,* pp. 68–69; WJ 1:111, 114–115; and Salisbury, *Manitou and Providence,* pp. 103–105. Salisbury surmises that the first epidemic was bubonic or the more lethal pneumonic plague (pp. 101–102). William Cronon suspects chicken pox; see his *Changes in the Land: Indians, Colonists, and the Ecology of New England* (New York:

Hill and Wang, 1983), p. 87. Hepatitis A and Type Two (or malignant confluent) smallpox have also been proposed: see respectively Arthur J. and Bruce D. Spiess, "The New England Pandemic of 1616–1622: Cause and Archaeological Implication," *Man in the Northeast,* no. 34 (1987): 71–83; and Timothy L. Bratton, "The Identity of the New England Indian Epidemic of 1616–19," *Bulletin of the History of Medicine* 62 (1988): 351–383.

15. Salisbury, *Manitou and Providence,* pp. 180–181, 184, 192–193, 199–202 (quotations on pp. 192–193, 202); and RMB 1:112. For the raids, see WJ 1:66–68. For Cambridge and the other towns, see RMB 1:196, 201, 252, 292; Hurd, ed., *History of Middlesex County,* 1:8; and WP 4:42, 104–105.
16. RMB 1:181, 252, 2:36, 44; WJ 1:59, 62; and Howes in WP 3:74. The colony otherwise prohibited Indians, except for servants, from using guns or ammunition. RMB 1:76, 127, 196, 206, 2:16. Cutshamekin and Masconomo continued to receive exemptions after their submission. RMB 2:148, 163, 3:65, 78, 235, and 4(1): 54.
17. Salisbury, *Manitou and Providence,* pp. 187–188, 199–200.
18. WJ 1:76, 186, 189, 192–194; and LaFantasie et al., eds., *Correspondence of Roger Williams,* p. 176. See also Salisbury, *Manitou and Providence,* pp. 214–218; and Vaughan, *New England Frontier,* pp. 150–152.
19. WJ 2:74–75, 122–123; and Salisbury, *Manitou and Providence,* p. 230.
20. WJ 2:156.
21. Dudley in Emerson, ed., *Letters from New England,* p. 69; and Salisbury, *Manitou and Providence,* pp. 190–191.
22. Gookin, *Historical Account,* p. 463; Vaughan, ed., *William Wood: New Englands Prospect,* pp. 100–101; Thomas Morton, *New English Canaan* (Amsterdam, 1637; reprint ed. New York: Da Capo Press, 1969), p. 34; WJ 2:75; and RMB 2:23–24, 27. For the three other references to Passaconaway and his sons, see WJ 1:91, and William Hilton and Giles Firmin in WP 3:449, 4:191. For Passaconaway's death, see Chapter 6, note 19.
23. RMB 3:365–366, 4(1):210 (Nashowanon's death); Eliot in MHSP 3 (1855–1858): 312 (Matchippa); and WJ 2:160. The Nipmucks were also called Nipnets, Neipnets, Nipmugs, and Nipusts in Puritan sources. Some scholars wrongly equate Wossamegon and Massasoit. William Wood distinguished the two sachems in the "small nomenclator" at the end of *New Englands Prospect;* moreover, Wossamegon and Massasoit made different marks. Compare RCP 10:450 with Bartlett, ed., *Records of Rhode Island,* 1:47.
24. Eliot in MHSP 3 (1855–1858): 312–313; Pynchon in James Savage, ed., *The History of New England from 1630 to 1649 by John Winthrop, Esquire* (Boston: Little, Brown, and Co., 1853), 2:384–387; and Gookin, *Historical Collections,* p. 148.
25. WJ 2:156; and Gookin, *Historical Collections,* p. 149. For Titicut, see RCP 10:157, and Drake, *Aboriginal Races,* p. 108.
26. RMB 2:84, 134, 3:6–7, 56–57.
27. Jennings, *Invasion of America,* p. 235; Nash, "Notes," p. 6; Stineback, "The

Status," p. 84; Axtell, *Invasion Within*, pp. 138–139; and Brenner, "To Pray or To Be Prey," p. 140, and "Strategies for Autonomy," pp. 98–99.
28. Winslow in *Glorious Progress*, p. 75; and WJ 2:156.
29. Eliot in *Clear Sun-shine*, p. 50; WJ 2:276; and RCP 9:45–49 (quotations on pp. 46, 49). Jennings improbably concludes from Eliot's terse statement about the response to the sermon that Cutshamekin and his men "badly heckled" him. *Invasion of America*, pp. 238–239.
30. Shepard in *Day-Breaking*, pp. 3–8 (quotations on pp. 4, 7).
31. RMB 2:166, 178–179, 3:85, 100.
32. RMB 2:176–177, 3:98; and Jennings, *Invasion of America*, pp. 241–242. For the existing law, see John D. Cushing, ed., *The Laws and Liberties of Massachusetts, 1641–1691* (Wilmington, Del.: Scholarly Resources, 1976), p. 1.
33. For the punishment of powwowing, see Gookin, *Historical Collections*, pp. 154, 178, 192; for Sawcer, see RMB 3:363, 4(1): 213, and John Noble and Joseph F. Cronin, eds., *Records of the Court of Assistants of the Colony of the Massachusetts Bay, 1630–1692* (Boston: The County of Suffolk, 1901–1908), 3:34–38; and for King and Gatchell, see ibid., 1:201, 253–254. None of the three convicted blasphemers was executed: Sawcer escaped from prison before his trial, King received twenty lashes and an unspecified jail sentence, and Gatchell lost his tongue. There were also several cases of colonists indicted for blasphemy but acquitted of the crime. Ibid., 3:211; RMB 4(1): 244–245; and Samuel Eliot Morison et al., eds., *The Records of the Suffolk County Court, 1671–1680*, PCSM 29–30 (1933): 114–115.
34. Cotton in Emerson, ed., *Letters from New England*, p. 164, and in *Bloudy Tenent Washed*, pp. 147–148.
35. Jennings, *Invasion of America*, p. 241; Salisbury, "Red Puritans," pp. 30–31, and "Religious Encounters in a Colonial Context: New England and New France in the Seventeenth Century," *American Indian Quarterly* 16 (1992): 502–503; and William S. Simmons, "Conversion from Indian to Puritan," NEQ 52 (1979): 216–217. Jennings and Simmons cite only the blasphemy and idolatry laws, and Salisbury includes the June 1644 directive that "enjoined" Indians to receive instruction on Sundays. The sabbath directive did not constitute a law—there was no provision for punishing noncompliance. Its purpose was to encourage rather than to compel natives to accept Christian instruction, and it was directed as much to the elders as to the Indians.
36. Jennings, *Invasion of America*, p. 244; RMB 3:93–98 (quotation on pp. 96–97); and WJ 2:309–315. See also RMB 2:171, 175, 185; and WJ 2:289, 292. For a fuller discussion of the diplomacy in London, see Wall, *Massachusetts Bay*, pp. 157–224.
37. Jennings, *Invasion of America*, pp. 236–238; WJ 2:283–284; and Shepard in *Day-Breaking*, pp. 3–4.
38. Jennings, *Invasion of America*, pp. 235–238; and Eliot in W. H. Whitmore and W. S. Appleton, eds., *A Report of the Record Commissioners Containing*

the *Roxbury Land and Church Records* (2nd ed. Boston: Rockwell and Churchill, 1884), pp. 187, 189, 190.
39. Eliot ms. quoted in Cotton Mather, *Magnalia Christi Americana* (1852; reprint ed. Carlisle, Penn.: Banner of Truth Trust, 1979), 1:335–336; and Eliot, "Learned Conjectures," p. 22. For Eliot's life in England, see Samuel Eliot Morison, *Builders of the Bay Colony* (1930; rev. ed. Boston: Houghton Mifflin, 1958), pp. 291–294; Ola E. Winslow, *John Eliot: "Apostle to the Indians"* (Boston: Houghton Mifflin, 1968), pp. 5–22; and Rae Demler Burchfiel, "The Character of John Eliot: A Study in the Nurture of Values" (Ph.D. diss., Boston College, 1987), pp. 79–154.
40. Franklin B. Dexter, ed., *Extracts from the Itineraries and Other Miscellanies of Ezra Stiles* (New Haven, Conn.: Yale University Press, 1916), p. 215; WJ 1:70, 94–95; Eliot in Whitmore and Appleton, eds., *Report of the Record Commissioners*, p. 76; and Morison, *Builders of the Bay Colony*, p. 291.
41. Cotton Mather, *The Triumphs of the Reformed Religion in America: The Life of the Renowned John Eliot* (Boston, 1691), pp. 60–61, 142; and Nehemiah Adams, *The Life of John Eliot* (Boston: Massachusetts Sabbath School Society, 1847), pp. 321–322.
42. For the justification of Williams's banishment, see John Cotton, "A Reply to Mr. Williams His Examination," in *Complete Writings of Roger Williams*, 2:43; for the proceedings against Hutchinson, see David D. Hall, ed., *The Antinomian Controversy, 1636–1638: A Documentary History* (1968; rev. ed. Durham, N.C.: Duke University Press, 1990), pp. 311–388; for the two committees, see RMB 1:223, and "Propositions concerning Evidence of God's Love," in WP 4:286–287; for the "Bay Psalm Book," see Bozeman, *To Live Ancient Lives*, pp. 139–150; for the election sermon, see Winslow, *John Eliot*, p. 38; for the 1669 synod and Roxbury's opposition to the Half-Way Covenant, see Robert G. Pope, *The Half-Way Covenant: Church Membership in Puritan New England* (Princeton, N.J.: Princeton University Press, 1969), pp. 32–33, 159, 206–214; and for the Reform Synod, see Williston Walker, ed., *The Creeds and Plaforms of Congregationalism* (New York: Charles Scribner's Sons, 1893), p. 417n.
43. Eliot in *Light appearing*, p. 124. Eliot's wife, Anne, is sometimes called Hannah, and his daughter, Hannah, is occasionally called Anne, in both seventeenth- and twentieth-century sources. For Eliot, Jr., see Eliot in Eames, ed., *John Eliot and the Indians*, pp. 25–26, and Gookin, *Historical Collections*, p. 171; for Joseph, see RCP 10:207, 245; and for Samuel, see Winslow, *John Eliot*, p. 158. For Benjamin, see [no author], *History of the Town of Dorchester, Massachusetts* (Boston: E. Clapp, 1859), p. 219; G. F. Clark, "Who Was the First Minister of Mendon?" NEHGR 35 (1881): 157–159; and M. Halsey Thomas, ed., *The Diary of Samuel Sewall* (New York: Farrar, Straus, and Giroux, 1973), p. 147.

44. Eliot in Emerson, ed., *Letters from New England*, p. 106, and in Whitmore and Appleton, eds., *Report of the Record Commissioners*, p. 189. For the 1645 Narragansett-Mohegan war, see Vaughan, *New England Frontier*, pp. 168–171; for the treaty with the Pequots, see WJ 1:142, and Jennings, *Invasion of America*, p. 233 (see also pp. 190–196); and for the chaplaincy, see WJ 1:218, and RMB 1:195.
45. Gookin, *Historical Collections*, p. 168; and WJ 2:319. The 1643 date apparently originated in 1912 in an undocumented assertion by James deNormandie, in "John Eliot, the Apostle to the Indians," *Harvard Theological Review* 5 (1912): 359.
46. Eliot in *Clear Sun-shine*, p. 50.
47. Eliot in *Glorious Progress*, p. 90, in *Indian Grammar Begun*, p. 312, and in *Light appearing*, p. 121; and Jennings, *Invasion of America*, p. 234. The teacher is not named in the Massachusetts sources. William Tooker is almost certainly correct in surmising that he was an Indian named Cockenoe, who lived on Long Island from 1649 until his death in 1690. *John Eliot's First Indian Teacher and Interpreter* (New York: F. P. Harper, 1896).
48. Mather, *Triumphs of the Reformed Religion*, p. 86; and Eliot, *Indian Grammar Begun*, p. 312. For the details about the Massachusett language, see Stephen A. Guice, "The Linguistic Work of John Eliot" (Ph.D. diss., Michigan State University, 1990), pp. 128, 132–133, 145, 149; and Ives Goddard and Kathleen J. Bragdon, *Native Writings in Massachusett* (Philadelphia: American Philosophical Society, 1988), pp. 492–493.

3. The Early Development of the Mission

1. *The Day-Breaking* is anonymous. The MHS edition of the work incorrectly identifies Eliot as the author. The evidence in Shepard's favor is extremely strong. See Thomas Werge, *Thomas Shepard* (Boston: Twayne Publishers, 1987), pp. 13, 121. Shepard's authorship is assumed throughout this narrative.
2. RMB 2:166, 3:85; and Shepard in *Clear Sun-shine*, p. 61. The Nonantum code is in *Day-Breaking*, pp. 20–21.
3. Eliot in *Clear Sun-shine*, pp. 50, 53.
4. Eliot in ibid., p. 56, and in *Light appearing*, p. 142; Ponampam and Peter in *Tears of Repentance*, pp. 242, 246; Shepard in *Day-Breaking*, p. 18; Abraham Pierson, *Some Helps for the Indians* (Cambridge, 1658), in Connecticut Historical Society, *Collections* 3 (1895): 51; and RMB 2:56.
5. Monequasson in *Tears of Repentance*, p. 239. For several of Eliot's denunciations of long hair, see "Learned Conjectures," pp. 27–28; and Eliot ms. quoted in Mather, *Triumphs of the Reformed Religion*, pp. 35–36.
6. Shepard in *Day-Breaking*, pp. 3, 19; Jennings, *Invasion of America*, pp. 239–241; WJ 2:319; and Waban in *Tears of Repentance*, p. 231.
7. WJ 2:319; Eliot in *Clear Sun-shine*, pp. 51–55 (quotation on p. 55); and

Salisbury, "Red Puritans," p. 36. The missionary sources do not contain a transcript of the Neponset code. Portions of it appear in *Clear Sun-shine*, pp. 51–55.

8. Eliot in *Clear Sun-shine*, pp. 53–54.
9. Eliot in *Light appearing*, pp. 140–141.
10. Eliot in *Clear Sun-shine*, pp. 52–54, in *Light appearing*, pp. 132, 139, in *Strength out of Weaknesse*, p. 173, and in Bowden and Ronda, eds., *John Eliot's Indian Dialogues*, p. 125.
11. Eliot in *Strength out of Weaknesse*, p. 173, in *Tears of Repentance*, p. 232, and in *Dying Speeches*, p. 2.
12. Shepard in *Day-Breaking*, p. 8; John Speene in *Further Account*, p. 58; Monequasson in *Tears of Repentance*, p. 234; Cutshamekin in MSA 30:15; and Eliot in Bowden and Ronda, eds., *John Eliot's Indian Dialogues*, p. 125.
13. James Axtell, "The Power of Print in the Eastern Woodlands," in *After Columbus: Essays in the Ethnohistory of Colonial North America* (New York: Oxford University Press, 1988), pp. 92–99; and Peter Wogan, "Perceptions of European Literacy in Early Contact Situations," *Ethnohistory* 41 (1994): 407–429 (especially pp. 412–419). For the Massachusetts Bay details, see Shepard in *Day-Breaking*, pp. 3, 18, 21; Eliot in *Clear Sun-shine*, p. 59, in *Light appearing*, p. 144, and in *Strength out of Weaknesse*, p. 167; and Dunster in MHSC 4:1 (1852): 253. Waban's son Thomas, a prominent praying Indian after King Philip's War, was presumably not the son of Waban educated at Dedham in the 1640s. Thomas was approximately twenty-five years of age in 1686. See Perley, ed., *Indian Land Titles of Essex County*, p. 10.
14. Elise M. Brenner, "Sociopolitical Implications of Mortuary Ritual Remains in 17th-Century Native Southern New England," and Constance A. Crosby, "From Myth to History, or Why King Philip's Ghost Walks Abroad," both in Mark P. Leone and Parker B. Potter, Jr., eds., *The Recovery of Meaning: Historical Archaeology in the Eastern United States* (Washington, D.C.: Smithsonian Institution Press, 1988), pp. 147–181, 183–209 (especially pp. 192–198); Shepard in *Day-Breaking*, p. 17; and Anthony in *Further Account*, pp. 11, 47–48.
15. For the code and for Shepard's comments, see *Clear Sun-shine*, pp. 38–41.
16. Shepard in ibid., pp. 38–39. For Waban's marriage, see Drake, *Aboriginal Races*, p. 113. For sample land transactions, see RMB 1:196, 201; MSA 30:1; and W. B. Trask et al., eds., *Suffolk Deeds* (Boston: Rockwell and Churchill, 1880–1904), 1:34.
17. Eliot in *Glorious Progress*, p. 88; and RCP 10:141.
18. Eliot in *Clear Sun-shine*, pp. 58–59, and in *Strength out of Weaknesse*, p. 171 (see also p. 166); and RMB 2:188–189, 3:105–106.
19. Eliot's petitions are in MSA 30:12, 15a. See also RMB 1:106, 2:85, 258, and 3:139–140; Shepard in *Day-Breaking*, p. 11, and in *Clear Sun-shine*, p. 47;

Eliot in ibid., pp. 54–55; and RCP 9:104. The "malignant drunken" George was probably not Sagamore George. The former seems to have been a Massachusett Indian rather than a Pawtucket.

20. WJ 2:319; Cotton, *The Way*, pp. 200, 273; and Eliot in *Clear Sun-shine*, p. 53, and in *Glorious Progress*, p. 84. The sermon texts can be identified from the questions the Indians asked in the late 1640s: see *Glorious Progress*, pp. 84–86, 91–92; and *Light appearing*, pp. 128–130, 132–133. For the analogies, see Shepard in *Day-Breaking*, pp. 6–8, 12–13; John Speene in *Further Accompt*, p. 16; and Nishohkou in *Further Account*, pp. 7, 43. For the Nipmucks, see Monotunkquanit and Captain Tom in ibid., pp. 24, 27, 63, 65; Eliot in *Glorious Progress*, p. 88; William of Sudbury in *Tears of Repentance*, pp. 232–234; and Owussumag in MSA 30:129a. Owussumag should not be confused with John Owussumag, Sr., who was apparently his son or brother. The former died in 1674 and the latter in the winter of 1684–85. See Eliot in Ford, ed., *Some Correspondence*, p. 28; Gookin, *Historical Collections*, p. 186; Eliot, *Dying Speeches*, p. 9; and RMB 5:531–532. William of Sudbury (Nataous) fathered James the Printer and three other prominent Christian Indians. See Richard W. Cogley, "A Seventeenth-Century Native American Family: William of Sudbury and His Four Sons" (forthcoming, NEHGR). Captain Tom was also known as Wutasakompanum and Poquanum (Poliquanum). Gookin, *Historical Account*, p. 476; Eliot in *Further Accompt*, p. 19, and in *Tears of Repentance*, pp. 253–254. Ponampam, Nishohkou, and the Speene brothers, whom I classify as Massachusett Indians, may have been Nipmucks who had moved inland to Nonantum or Neponset.

21. Eliot in *Strength out of Weaknesse*, p. 170; and Shepard in *Day-Breaking*, p. 15. For Waban and Totherswamp, see Shepard in *Clear Sun-shine*, pp. 62–63; Monotunkquanit and Captain Tom in *Further Account*, pp. 25, 27, 63; and William of Sudbury in *Tears of Repentance*, p. 233.

22. Eliot in *Glorious Progress*, pp. 81–83, and in *Light appearing*, pp. 123–124; and Shepard in *Clear Sun-shine*, p. 62.

23. Eliot in *Light appearing*, pp. 125, 130.

24. Pynchon in Savage, ed., *History of New England*, 2:384–388; WJ 2:343–344; and J. H. Temple, *History of North Brookfield, Massachusetts* (North Brookfield: privately printed, 1887), pp. 30, 35.

25. Eliot in *Glorious Progress*, p. 83 (see also *Light appearing*, p. 139); Shepard in *Clear Sun-shine*, p. 39; and Gookin, *Historical Collections*, p. 154. For background on the powwows, see Kathleen J. Bragdon, *Native People of Southern New England, 1500–1650* (Norman: University of Oklahoma Press, 1996), pp. 200–230.

26. Eliot in *Light appearing*, p. 139; and Salisbury, "Red Puritans," p. 38. For Eliot's efforts to evangelize Uncas, Ninigret, and Massasoit, see Chapter 7. For the Pokanonet alliances, see Vaughan, *New England Frontier*, Appendix I; and RCP 2:133. Historians have long assumed that Massasoit was the father of Wamsutta (Alexander) and Metacom (King Philip). There is good

evidence that Wamsutta and Metacom were the children of Massasoit's son Moanam, who predeceased his father. See Betty Groff Schroeder, "The True Lineage of King Philip (Sachem Metacom)," NEHGR 144 (1990): 211–214. For the Mohegans, see Chapter 2, note 18 (Hartford treaty), and RCP 9:29–30, 45–46 (1644 and 1645 alliances). For the Eastern Niantics, see Timothy J. Sehr, "Ninigret's Tactics of Accommodation: Indian Diplomacy in New England, 1637–1675," *Rhode Island History* 36 (1977): 44–53.

27. Shepard in *Clear Sun-shine*, pp. 42–43, 61 (Nausets and "Narragansett sachem"); Eliot in ibid., p. 58, and in *Glorious Progress*, p. 81 (Titicut Indians); and Eliot in *Light appearing*, p. 123 (Pennacooks).

28. Eliot in *Glorious Progress*, pp. 81, 88, 90, and in *Light appearing*, pp. 122, 123–124.

29. Eliot in *Light appearing*, p. 134, and in *Late and Further Manifestation*, pp. 270–271. Elise Brenner claims that the Apostle deliberately localized the praying Indians in a series of small settlements in order to prevent the proselytes from "unit[ing] and challeng[ing] their mutual domination by the colonists." Eliot's original plan, however, was to create a single central settlement; he abandoned the idea because he could not find a suitable location and because the natives preferred to live in places of their own choosing. "Strategies for Autonomy," p. 118.

30. Whitfield in *Light appearing*, p. 107. That Pelham was the recipient of Eliot's letter is clear from *Glorious Progress*, p. 89, and *Light appearing*, p. 125. The published version of this letter (*Glorious Progress*, pp. 87–88) incorrectly dates it as 1649 instead of 1648. For a discussion of these and other problems in Eliot's extant correspondence, see Richard W. Cogley, "The Letters of John Eliot, Puritan Minister and Indian Evangelist" (forthcoming, *The Bulletin of the Congregational Library*).

31. Lechford, *Plaine Dealing*, p. 80 (see also pp. 88–92, 111, 115, 120, 124); Robert Baillie, *A Dissuasive from the Errours of the Time* (London, 1645), p. 60 (see also p. 69); and Williams, *Christenings*, p. 36. Salisbury lists William Castell's 1641 petition to Parliament as another example of a work that condemned Massachusetts Bay for the absence of a mission. This does not seem accurate. The purpose of Castell's petition was to mobilize the English colonies, and particularly Virginia, to save the Indians from Catholicism. The petition mentions Massachusetts Bay once and in this case only to excuse the saints because epidemic disease had left them with "few Indians" to evangelize. "Red Puritans," p. 30.

32. Shepard in *Day-Breaking*, pp. 14–15, and in *Clear Sun-shine*, pp. 37, 45; Eliot in *Light appearing*, p. 126; and Cotton, *The Way*, pp. 268–279 (quotations on pp. 268, 276). According to Jennings, "the primary function of the mission was to make an impression in England." He argues that the colony used the Indian work to "recover lost influence" in London following the diplomatic successes of Williams and Gorton in 1643–44 and the publication of the works of Lechford and Baillie. *Invasion of America*, pp. 238, 244

(see also pp. 234–235). That Massachusetts Bay used the mission for diplomatic advantage is undeniable. The major problem with claiming that such was its "primary function" is that the colony sustained the Indian work long after the political events that purportedly inspired it had passed.
33. Shepard in *Day-Breaking*, p. 22; Marshall et al. in *Clear Sun-shine*, p. 35; Eliot and Dury in *Glorious Progress*, pp. 87, 97; William Kellaway, *The New England Company, 1649–1776: Missionary Society to the American Indians* (New York: Barnes and Noble, 1962), p. 32; and WJ 2:309.
34. Raymond P. Stearns, "The Weld-Peter Mission," PCSM 32 (1937): 193, 214–216.
35. Weld's statements are in PCSM 14 (1913): 125–126, and in NEHGR 36 (1882): 68–69. Figures are given in English money. Matthew Cradock died shortly before Weld and Peter arrived in London in September 1641. If he was the "Mr. Cradock" in question, then he left a portion of his estate to the mission.
36. RCP 9:193, 195. For the Armine annuity and the £10 payment to Eliot in 1647, see RMB 2:189, 3:106; and RCP 9:204.
37. Leo Francis Stock, ed., *Proceedings and Debates of the British Parliaments respecting North America* (Washington, D.C.: Carnegie Institution, 1924), 1:203, 209; Kellaway, *New England Company*, pp. 12–16; and C. H. Firth and R. S. Rait, eds., *Acts and Ordinances of the Interregnum: 1642–1660* (London: Gaunt and Sons, 1911), 2:197–200.
38. Bernard Bailyn, ed., *The Apologia of Robert Keayne: The Self-Portrait of a Puritan Merchant* (New York: Harper and Row, 1964), p. 25. For the Commissioners' meetings, see Gookin, *Historical Collections*, p. 213; for the surveying costs, see RMB 3:301, 4(1): 136–137; and for Eliot's contributions, see the sources cited in Chapter 8, note 15.
39. For the quotation, see Eliot in *Clear Sun-shine*, p. 58; for interior partitions, see Shepard in ibid., p. 62; for fencing, see Eliot and Shepard in ibid., pp. 59, 61–62, and Eliot in *Glorious Progress*, p. 87; for grooming, see Eliot in ibid., p. 87, and Shepard in *Clear Sun-shine*, pp. 40, 45, 46; and for English skills, see Eliot in ibid., p. 59. For Heath, Parke, Jackson, and Willard, see Shepard in ibid., pp. 38–41, 46, 65; Eliot in *Light appearing*, p. 141, and in *Strength out of Weaknesse*, p. 167; and "Letters of the Rev. John Eliot," p. 297. For cottage industries and market activities, see Eliot in *Clear Sun-shine*, p. 59, and in *Glorious Progress*, p. 80; and Cotton, *Bloudy Tenent Washed*, p. 148. For servants, see Shepard in *Day-Breaking*, p. 18, and Eliot in *Clear Sun-shine*, pp. 58–59; for harvesting, see Eliot in ibid., 59; and for Waban, see Abiel Holmes, "The History of Cambridge," in MHSC 1:7 (1800): 26.
40. Eliot in *Clear Sun-shine*, p. 51 (Sunday worship and catechism); Shepard in *Day-Breaking*, p. 22, and Eliot in *Clear Sun-shine*, p. 59 (Nonantum and Neponset schools); Shepard in *Day-Breaking*, p. 3, Eliot in *Glorious Progress*, p. 88, and Thomas Peters in WP 5:150 (dame and town schools); and

Eliot and Shepard in *Clear Sun-shine*, pp. 51–54, 58, 60 (disciplinary problems).
41. Shepard in *Day-Breaking*, p. 17, and in *Clear Sun-shine*, p. 48 (see also pp. 64, 66); Dury in *Glorious Progress*, p. 97; and Whitfield in *Light appearing*, p. 146 (see also p. 145). For similar statements, see Stephen Marshall et al. in *Clear Sun-shine*, pp. 32–34; Cotton in [John Elmeston], *A Censure of That Reverend and Learned man of God Mr. John Cotton* (London, 1656), p. 55 (mispaginated 54); and Richard Mather in *Tears of Repentance*, pp. 224–225.
42. Eliot in *Glorious Progress*, p. 86 (see also p. 84); and Shepard in *Day-Breaking*, pp. 15, 21, and in *Clear Sun-shine*, pp. 60, 66.
43. Shepard in *Day-Breaking*, p. 13 (see also pp. 9, 14, 16, 18); and Shepard and Eliot in *Clear Sun-shine*, pp. 53–54, 60, 65–66.
44. Shepard in *Day-Breaking*, p. 22, and in *Clear Sun-shine*, p. 63; and Eliot in ibid., p. 51, and in Bowden and Ronda, eds., *John Eliot's Indian Dialogues*, p. 104.
45. Williams, *A Key*, p. 229; Axtell, *Invasion Within*, p. 169; WJ 2:319–320; Ponampam in *Further Account*, p. 56; George E. Tinker, *Missionary Conquest: The Gospel and Native American Cultural Genocide* (Minneapolis: Fortress Press, 1993), p. 26; and Shepard in *Clear Sun-shine*, p. 63. For Wequash, see *New Englands First Fruits*, p. 6.
46. For divisions within couples, see Eliot in *Clear Sun-shine*, pp. 55–56, in *Glorious Progress*, p. 86, and in *Light appearing*, p. 132; for divisions among siblings, see Eliot in ibid., p. 125, Anthony in *Further Account*, p. 10, and John Speene in *Tears of Repentance*, pp. 246–247; for pagan parents with Christian children, see Shepard in *Day-Breaking*, p. 7; for Christian parents with pagan children, see Shepard in ibid., p. 10, and Robin Speene in *Tears of Repentance*, p. 248; and for the adulterous woman, see Shepard in *Clear Sun-shine*, p. 63. Sources from the 1650s refer to a third Speene brother besides John and Robin. See John Speene in *Tears of Repentance*, p. 247, and in *Further Account*, p. 59. This brother was surely called Thomas, since a source from the 1660s mentions a Thomas Speene, Jr. See Hill and Tuttle, eds., *Early Records*, 4:251.
47. Eliot in Powicke, "Some Unpublished Correspondence," p. 158; Ponampam in *Further Account*, pp. 20–21, 55–56; John Speene in ibid., p. 58, and in *Tears of Repentance*, pp. 246–247; Monequasson in ibid., p. 237; and Anthony in ibid., p. 256, and in *Further Account*, pp. 10, 47.
48. Charles L. Cohen, "Conversion among Puritans and Amerindians: A Theological and Cultural Perspective," in Francis J. Bremer, ed., *Puritanism: Transatlantic Perspectives on a Seventeenth-Century Anglo-American Faith* (Boston: MHS, 1993), pp. 239–244 (quotations on pp. 242, 243). For the natives' questions, see *Glorious Progress*, pp. 84–85; and *Light appearing*, p. 130 (see also *Clear Sun-shine*, p. 55). For the problem of language, see

Shepard in *Day-Breaking,* pp. 5, 13; Waban in *Tears of Repentance,* p. 231; Monotunkquanit and Waban in *Further Account,* pp. 25, 31, 65, 72; and Williams, *A Key,* pp. 207–208. For Ponampam, Magus, Captain Tom, and Anthony, see *Tears of Repentance,* pp. 241, 252, 253; and *Further Account,* pp. 10, 48.

4. The Mission and the Millennium

1. The letters to Winslow are in *Light appearing,* pp. 119–133; and *The Christian Commonwealth* is in MHSC 3:9 (1846): 127–164. For dating of the treatise, see ibid., p. 135; and Eliot in Eames, ed., *John Eliot and the Indians,* p. 7. Eliot sent the manuscript to Ferdinando Nicolls, a minister in Exeter. Ibid., p. 7. James Holstun suggests that Nicolls or Hugh Peter was the "server of the season." *A Rational Millennium: Puritan Utopias of Seventeenth-Century England and America* (New York: Oxford University Press, 1987), p. 327n. James Maclear proposes the repatriate William Aspinwall. "New England and the Fifth Monarchy," p. 253.
2. Bozeman, *To Live Ancient Lives,* pp. 263–280.
3. Eliot, *Christian Commonwealth,* pp. 130–134. Eliot made similar statements in *Light appearing,* pp. 120, 127, 131, and in *Tears of Repentance,* pp. 212–216. For Nimrod, see Eliot, "Learned Conjectures," pp. 6–10. Eliot called the millennium the "kingdom," a word Puritans often used in a nonmillennial sense. His concomitant references to the Middle Advent in passages cited later in this chapter indicate that for him the "kingdom" in question was the millennium.
4. Eliot in "Account of Indian Churches," p. 128, and in *Light appearing,* p. 127.
5. Eliot in *Light appearing,* p. 131, and in *Christian Commonwealth,* p. 142. For Eliot's brief contemporary discussions of the millennial church order, see "Learned Conjectures," pp. 17, 27 (mispaginated 23). For his other discussions of scriptural law, see *Christian Commonwealth,* pp. 157–164; "Memoir of Hugh Peters," in NEHGR 5 (1851): 292; Eames, ed., *John Eliot and the Indians,* p. 7; and [Eliot], "From Natick in New-England, 4 July 1651," in Marchamont Needham, ed., *Mercurius Politicus, Sept. 18–25* (London, 1651), p. 1091.
6. Eliot, *Christian Commonwealth,* pp. 147, 148, 159. The formal organization of Eliot's millennial order is most fully described in Holstun, *Rational Millennium,* pp. 145–158.
7. Eliot in *Light appearing,* pp. 120–121, and in *Christian Commonwealth,* pp. 129, 134. Bozeman first observed that statements about "the coming of Christ" in Eliot's early Interregnum sources were references to the Middle Advent and not to the second coming. *To Live Ancient Lives,* pp. 266, 275–277.
8. Eliot, *Christian Commonwealth,* pp. 133, 138. For England's geographical

location and/or the migrations of Japheth, see Eliot in ibid., pp. 133n, 139n, in *Light appearing*, p. 119, in Thorowgood, *Jews in America*, p. 33, and in "Learned Conjectures," pp. 9–10; and for the references to Jerusalem, see ibid., p. 20, and Eliot in Thorowgood, *Jews in America*, p. 53.

9. Eliot in *Light appearing*, pp. 127, 131, and in *Christian Commonwealth*, pp. 136, 138.

10. Cotton, "Sermon upon A Day of Publique thanksgiving" (1651), in Francis J. Bremer, "In Defense of Regicide: John Cotton on the Execution of Charles I," WMQ 37 (1980): 110–115, 122–124 (quotations on p. 114). For Cotton's earlier use of the "sea of glass" image, see *Powring Out*, sermon on the second vial, pp. 2–3 (mispaginated 18–19), and sermon on the third vial, p. 2. In 1651 Cotton drafted a short proposal that clarified some of the terms for the proposed national church. *Certain Queries Tending to Accommodation and Communion of Presbyterian & Congregationall Churches* (London, 1654).

11. Cotton, "Sermon upon A Day," pp. 117–120. The Cotton and Cromwell letters are in W. H. Whitmore and W. S. Appleton, eds., *The Hutchinson Papers* (1865; reprint ed. New York: Burt Franklin, 1967), 1:262–267. According to Roger Williams and Samuel Sewall, Cotton told Cromwell in 1651 or 1652 that the conquest of the Spanish possessions in the West Indies would hasten the fulfillment of the sixth vial of divine wrath against Antichrist (Revelation 16:12). Although updated in light of a contemporary event, this reported statement indicates that Cotton continued to think that the Middle Advent lay in the future: the sixth vial was preparatory to the millennium but was not the millennium itself. LaFantasie et al., eds., *Correspondence of Roger Williams*, p. 428; and Thomas, ed., *Diary of Samuel Sewall*, p. 359.

12. For discussions of the movement, see Maclear, "New England and the Fifth Monarchy," especially pp. 239–240, 249–253, 255–257; and B. S. Capp, *The Fifth Monarchy Men: A Study in Seventeenth-Century English Millenarianism* (Totowa, N.J.: Rowman and Littlefield, 1972). The movement's name was derived from the vision in Daniel 7–11 of the rise and fall of four monarchies and the appearance of a fifth, the "everlasting dominion of the Son of Man." The use of the five monarchies typology was no necessary index of participation in the movement. Cotton used the typology throughout his lectures on Revelation, as did Anne Bradstreet in her unfinished poem, "The Four Monarchies," which she wrote in the 1640s.

13. For the epithet, see Thorowgood, *Jews in America*, p. 24 (introductory material). The terminus a quo for the composition of Eliot's "Learned Conjectures" is the death of Cotton on December 23, 1652, and the terminus ad quem is the expiration of the Old Style year 1652 in late March 1653. See "Learned Conjectures," pp. 21, 27 (mispaginated 23); and "Letters of the Rev. John Eliot," p. 297. The existing studies of Eliot's eschatology do not fully appreciate the significance of "The learned Conjectures."

14. Winslow and Dury in *Glorious Progress*, pp. 72–74, 93–95; and Dury, "An

Epistolicall Discourse," in Thorowgood, *Iewes in America*, pp. e–e2. The Latin translation of Menasseh's book made changes in the Spanish original to make his messianism less offensive to Christian readers, and the English translation made even more changes for the same purpose. See Henry Mechoulan and Gerard Nahon, eds., *Menasseh ben Israel, The Hope of Israel: The English Translation by Moses Wall, 1652*, trans. Richenda George (New York: Oxford University Press, 1987), especially pp. 62–64, 115n. Aside from a different title page and a slight rearrangement of the component parts, the 1652 edition of Thorowgood's book is identical to the 1650 one. The revised version of 1660 (*Jews in America* as opposed to *Iewes in America*) made many changes.

The distinction between "Israelites" and "Jews" may require clarification. Prior to the division of the monarchy in the tenth century B.C.E., the twelve tribes of Jacob were called collectively the "Israelites." After the division of the monarchy, the word "Israelites" was generally restricted to the ten tribes who settled the northern kingdom of Israel (or Ephraim). The term "Jews" eventually came to refer to the descendants of the two tribes that inhabited the southern kingdom of Judah (Judea). The Assyrian conquest of the northern kingdom in the eighth century B.C.E. led to the disappearance of the Israelites (hence the expression "the ten lost tribes of Israel"). Puritans were aware of the distinction between "Israelites" and "Jews" even though they sometimes used the words in a biblically imprecise fashion.

15. Menasseh, *The Hope of Israel* (London, 1650), "To the courteous Reader" (n.p.) and pp. 20, 22, 37–40; Dury, "Epistolicall Discourse," pp. e–e2, [e4]; and Thorowgood, *Iewes in America*, p. 3.

16. Menasseh, *Hope of Israel*, "To the courteous Reader" (n.p.) and pp. 25–26, 56, 83. Menasseh wrote at one point in *The Hope of Israel* that the lost tribes had preceded the Tartars into America, and at another that they had followed them. According to Dury's summary of letters written by the rabbi in the late 1640s, Menasseh thought that the lost tribes had been the first to arrive. Ibid., pp. 21, 86; and Dury, "Epistolicall Discourse," p. e2. For Thorowgood's list of vestiges, see *Iewes in America*, pp. 1–35; for Dury's, see *Glorious Progress*, pp. 93–95; and for Winslow's, see ibid., p. 73. Thorowgood did not explicitly state that there had been no pre-Columbian Gentile migration to America; however, this assumption clearly underlies his argument against the Tartarian-origins view as well as his discussion entitled "How such a remnant [of Israelites] should enpeople so great a part of the world." *Iewes in America*, pp. 37–40, 45–48. In his appendix to *The Glorious Progress*, Dury was open to the possibility of Gentile settlement in the New World, as evidenced by qualifying phrases like "at least a remnant of the generation of Jacob in America" and "a sprinkling at least of Abraham's seed in these parts" (pp. 93, 94). These qualifiers are absent in his longer and later "Epistolicall Discourse." Winslow's brief discussion seems to presuppose that the lost tribes were exclusively responsible for peopling ancient America.

17. Dury in *Glorious Progress*, p. 93. For Menasseh's views on a restoration in Palestine, see *Hope of Israel*, "To the Parliament," p. A4^v, "To the courteous Reader" (n.p.), and pp. 62–70, 83–84; and for Dury's, see "Epistolicall Discourse," pp. d3–[d4]^v, e2^v–[e4]. The title page to Thorowgood's *Digitus Dei* stated that the book "foret[old] the calling of the Jews, and the restitution of them into their own land, and the bringing back of the ten tribes from all the ends and corners of the earth, and that great battle to be fought." This statement is absent on the 1650 title page of *Iewes in America* and is not discussed in the body of either the 1650 or the 1652 edition of the work.
18. Eliot in *Light appearing*, pp. 119–120. For Broughton, who used the Joktanite theory for a different purpose, see Katharine R. Firth, *The Apocalyptic Tradition in Reformation Britain* (New York: Oxford University Press, 1979), pp. 153–163 (especially p. 161). Eber, the putative progenitor of the Hebrews, was Shem's great-grandson. According to the biblical genealogies, Eber's older son Peleg initiated the line of descent that led to Abraham, Isaac, and Jacob, and through Jacob to the twelve tribes of Israel who accompanied Moses into the Promised Land and who later divided into the Israelites and the Jews. Eber's younger son Joktan produced the line, or so Eliot and Broughton thought, that eventually settled in the New World. Thus the Joktanites were Semites and Hebrews but not Israelites or Jews—a point overlooked or confused by contemporary scholars of Eliot's eschatology. The Mosaic Law originated in Peleg's line, not Joktan's. For this reason, circumcision and other vestiges of the Law could be cited as evidence of Israelite but not Joktanite settlement in America. The Hebrew language, however, was presumed to have been common to both lines of descent.
19. Eliot in *Light appearing*, pp. 126–128. For the Nonantum sermon(s), see Shepard in *Day-Breaking*, p. 22, and in *Clear Sun-shine*, p. 62; and for Cromwell, see WJ 2:272–273, and Francis Murphy, ed., *William Bradford: Of Plymouth Plantation, 1620–1647* (New York: Random House, 1981), pp. 383–384. Although Ezekiel 37 explicitly includes the lost tribes among the "dry bones," Puritans were capable of reading the text in a nonliteral fashion. In "A Modell of Christian Charity," for instance, John Winthrop interpreted Ezekiel's vision as an allusion to the regeneration of human nature through the power of divine grace. WP 2:290. It was presumably in this sense that Eliot had used the text in 1646.
20. Eliot in Thorowgood, *Jews in America*, p. 27 (introductory material) and pp. 33–34, and in "Learned Conjectures," p. 20. Eliot's other letters to Thorowgood are excerpted in *Jews in America*.
21. Eliot, "Learned Conjectures," pp. 5–19 (quotations on pp. 10, 16, 17, 18).
22. Ibid., pp. 1, 19–20.
23. Ibid., pp. 18, 20. For Eliot's intricate interpretation of the ancient promises to Shem, see ibid., pp. 3–17. A foreshadowing of his argument that America belonged to the eastern world appeared in a 1650 letter excerpted in Thorowgood's *Jews in America*, pp. 32–33. At the time he wrote this letter, however,

Eliot had not yet concluded that America was part of the eastern world. He located New England in the western world as late as 1652. See *Tears of Repentance,* p. 212.

24. Eliot in "Learned Conjectures," pp. 1–2, 18–19, and in *Light appearing,* pp. 119–120. At the time he wrote the letter to Winslow, Eliot had not yet assigned America to the eastern world. Hence, the "eastern nations" in question were the Asian ones. Eliot's doctrine of the simultaneous redemption of the Israelites and Joktanites left only the progeny of Noah's son Ham, the supposed ancestor of the sub-Saharan peoples, at the end of the Jews-then-Gentiles sequence. For Eliot's brief remarks about the posterity of Ham, see "Learned Conjectures," pp. 4, 10, 12, 17.
25. Eliot in *Light appearing,* pp. 121, 127, 131.
26. Eliot in ibid., p. 139, and in "Learned Conjectures," p. 27 (mispaginated 23).
27. Eliot in *Light appearing,* p. 131, and in *Christian Commonwealth,* p. 133.
28. Eliot's discussions of Natick mention only the civil and ecclesiastical components of the millennium, never the legal one. He probably thought that the Indian rulers were not sufficiently familiar with the Bible to administer "Scripture law" at Natick. In *The Christian Commonwealth,* he stated that the application of Israelite law "must be by the wisdom and discretion of the judges, guided by the light of the Scriptures" (p. 163).
29. The two prefaces are in *Tears of Repentance,* pp. 212–216. For the dating of *Tears of Repentance,* see "Letters of the Rev. John Eliot," p. 297. Cromwell began to actively support the mission at about the time the tract was published; however, it is unclear if Eliot's preface had anything to do with that fact. Kellaway, *New England Company,* p. 28.
30. Timothy J. Sehr, "John Eliot, Millennialist and Missionary," *The Historian* 46 (1983–1984): 195; Holstun, *Rational Millennium,* pp. 115–158; Maclear, "New England and the Fifth Monarchy," pp. 243–248 (quotations on pp. 245, 247); Philip F. Gura, *A Glimpse of Sion's Glory: Puritan Radicalism in New England, 1620–1660* (Middletown, Conn.: Wesleyan University Press, 1984), p. 135; Bozeman, *To Live Ancient Lives,* pp. 272–275; and Eliot, *Christian Commonwealth,* p. 135.
31. Eliot in *Strength out of Weaknesse,* p. 171; and Jameson, ed., *Johnson's Wonder-Working Providence,* pp. 34, 59, 63, 269–270.
32. "Copy of the Elders' Advice about the Addresses" (1660), in Whitmore and Appleton, eds., *Hutchinson Papers,* 2:50–51. It is no longer possible to determine when Eliot learned that the publication of *The Christian Commonwealth* had been delayed. He thought that the work was in print at the time he wrote "The learned Conjectures" in early 1653; see infra, p. 27 (mispaginated 23). The General Court's censure of *The Christian Commonwealth* in May 1661 is discussed in Chapter 5. It bears mention at this point, however, that there is no reason to question the sincerity of Eliot's court-ordered acknowledgment that monarchy was a "lawful" and an "eminent form of government." His participation in "The Elders' Advice" predated the court's action,

and his eschatology after the Restoration indicates that he was not dissembling to the court.
33. Eliot in Thorowgood, *Jews in America*, p. 34. For testimony to the popularity of the Tartarian-origins view and/or the unpopularity of the lost tribes theory in seventeenth-century Massachusetts, see Mather, *Magnalia*, 1:249; William Hubbard, *A General History of New England*, in MHSC 2:5–6 (1815): 26–28; Increase Mather, *A Dissertation concerning the Future Conversion of the Jewish Nation* (London, 1709), pp. 32–33; Paul J. Lindholdt, ed., *John Josselyn, Colonial Traveler: A Critical Edition of Two Voyages to New-England* (Hanover, N.H.: University Press of New England, 1988), pp. 88–89; and Gookin, *Historical Collections*, pp. 144–146. To the best of my knowledge, the only other seventeenth-century Bay Puritans who endorsed the lost tribes theory were John Oxenbridge of First Church, Boston, and Samuel Sewall. For Oxenbridge, see Sewall, *Phaenomena*, p. 54; and for Sewall, see Conclusion, note 16. In his discussion of the Indians' origins at the start of *The Historical Collections*, Gookin stated that it was "not impossible, and perhaps not . . . improbable" that some Israelites had settled among a larger Gentile population in the New World (pp. 145–146). The fact that Gookin calls the natives "Gentiles" elsewhere in his narrative (pp. 143, 154, 223) suggests that he did not take the possibility of an Israelite migration too seriously.
34. Eliot's letter is in Richard Baxter, *Reliquiae Baxterianae* (London, 1696), 2:293–295. For references to the Middle Advent in Eliot's Restoration-era sources, see Powicke, "Some Unpublished Correspondence," pp. 171, 450.
35. Eliot, *The Communion of Churches: Or, The Divine Management of Gospel-Churches by the Ordinance of Councils* (Cambridge, 1665), preface (n.p.) and p. 37; and Raymond P. Stearns, "Correspondence of John Woodbridge, Jr., and Richard Baxter," NEQ 10 (1937): 572, 578. For the revised edition, which is not extant, see Eliot in Powicke, "Some Unpublished Correspondence," p. 166; and for Baxter's objections, see ibid., pp. 160–163, 167–170, 442–446, 446–449, 456–461.
36. Eliot, *Communion of Churches*, pp. 6, 34. For Eliot's scriptural justification for a hierarchy of councils, see ibid., pp. 12–13, 20–21; and for the addition of magistrates, see Eliot in Powicke, "Some Unpublished Correspondence," p. 166.
37. Eliot, *Communion of Churches*, pp. 3, 23–24; and Baxter in Powicke, "Some Unpublished Correspondence," pp. 156, 159. For the importance of a Nonconformist alliance against the Anglican enemy, see Eliot in ibid., pp. 167, 171. Eliot's *Communion of Churches* resembled Cotton's *Certain Queries* in that each proposed a strategy for uniting the Presbyterians and the Congregationalists. Eliot thought that his platform would endure "until the world's end," whereas Cotton offered his as a temporary expedient rather than as a permanent feature of the millennium. Eliot, *Communion of Churches*, p. 2.
38. "Letters of John Eliot," p. 247; and Eliot in Powicke, "Some Unpublished

Correspondence," pp. 174–175 (see also pp. 163–164), and in *Communion of Churches*, pp. 33–34. For the destruction of Anglicanism and Catholicism in Europe, see Eliot in ibid., pp. 13, 22, 26, 37, 38, in Powicke, "Some Unpublished Correspondence," pp. 175, 450, 453, and in *Reliquiae Baxterianae*, 2:295.

39. The ambiguity of 1 Samuel 8–10, which recounts the birth of the ancient Israelite monarchy, probably helped Eliot accommodate the Restoration into his eschatology. The text contains contradictory statements: that the monarchy originated with the elders, who (in a verse quoted in *The Christian Commonwealth*) asked Samuel to " "make us a king to judge us like all the nations (8:5), and that it originated with God (10:1–2).

40. Eliot in *Communion of Churches*, pp. 16–17, in *Reliquiae Baxterianae*, 2:294, and in "Learned Conjectures," pp. 7–8; and Walter Charleton, *The Immortality of the Human Soul* (London, 1657), p. 45. For seventeenth-century assumptions about the Hebrew language and for proposals for a universal language, see Katz, *Philo-Semitism*, pp. 43–88 (especially p. 60); and Thomas C. Singer, "Hieroglyphs, Real Characters, and the Idea of Natural Language in English Seventeenth-Century Thought," *Journal of the History of Ideas* 50 (1989): 49–70.

41. Eliot in *Reliquiae Baxterianae*, 2:294. For the advancement of learning tradition in England, see Charles Webster, *The Great Instauration: Science, Medicine, and Reform, 1626–1660* (New York: Holmes and Meier, 1976); and Firth, *Apocalyptic Tradition*, pp. 204–215, 225–228, 242–245.

42. Eliot in *Reliquiae Baxterianae*, 2:295, in *Communion of Churches*, p. 17, and in "Account of Indian Churches," p. 128.

43. Eliot in *Communion of Churches*, p. 16, and in Powicke, "Some Unpublished Correspondence," p. 171. For additional evidence that Eliot thought that the European branch of the millennium was to begin in England, see ibid., pp. 174–175; *Reliquiae Baxterianae*, 2:293; and "Letters of John Eliot," p. 247. For New England's location at the "ends of the earth," see Eliot in Bowden and Ronda, eds., *John Eliot's Indian Dialogues*, p. 119, in *Indian Grammar Begun*, p. 245, and in Powicke, "Some Unpublished Correspondence," p. 454; and "Petition of Rev. John Eliot" (1675), in RCP 10:452.

44. Eliot in Thorowgood, *Jews in America*, p. 34; Mather, *Triumphs of the Reformed Religion*, p. 85; and Thomas, ed., *Diary of Samuel Sewall*, p. 279.

5. The Natick Mission

1. Eliot in *Light appearing*, pp. 134, 138; "The declaration of the towne of Dedham" (1662), in Hill and Tuttle, eds., *Early Records*, 4:253; and RMB 3:246, 4(1): 75–76.

2. For the statement in 1650, see Eliot ms. quoted in Hurd, ed., *History of Middlesex County*, 1:516; for Wamporas, see Eliot in *Strength out of Weaknesse*, pp. 166–167, and in *Late and Further Manifestation*, p. 270; for the

Neponsets, see Eliot in ibid., p. 270, and "Letters of the Rev. John Eliot," pp. 295–296; and for the sermons, see Eliot in *Strength out of Weaknesse,* p. 175, and Monequasson in *Tears of Repentance,* pp. 235, 238.

3. For the "fair house," the bridge, the fort, the meetinghouse, and the schoolhouse, see Eliot in *Light appearing,* pp. 138, 143; Eliot, John Wilson, and John Endecott in *Strength out of Weaknesse,* pp. 168, 171, 174, 177–178, 190–191; Richard Mather and Eliot in *Tears of Repentance,* pp. 224, 227, 256; [Eliot], "From Natick in New-England," p. 1091; Eliot, "Natik case drawen up in defence of the pore Indians" (1662), in Hill and Tuttle, eds., *Early Records,* 4:259; and William Biglow, *History of the Town of Natick, Mass.* (Boston: Marsh, Capen, and Lyon, 1830), p. 25. For the sawmill, see Eliot and Endecott in *Strength out of Weaknesse,* pp. 174, 191; Joshua Fisher in Hill and Tuttle, eds., *Early Records,* 4:262 (see also p. 13); and Gookin, *Historical Account,* p. 512. The ms. copy of Gookin's *Historical Collections* is missing a portion of his discussion of Natick. The persons who prepared the MHS edition of the work in 1792 stated that "we have filled up the chasm with some particulars collected from other authors, and from tradition." In this case, the editors suppose that the "fair house" served as both a meetinghouse and a schoolhouse throughout the prewar period (p. 181). This supposition does not square with the sources cited in this note, which establish that these were three separate structures.

4. For the fences, see "Letters of the Rev. John Eliot," p. 296; Eliot, "Natik case drawen up," p. 256; and Eliot in Hill and Tuttle, eds., *Early Records,* 4:268. For the streets, see Wilson in *Strength out of Weaknesse,* p. 177. For crops, see Eliot in ibid., p. 168, in *Light appearing,* p. 143, and in Thorowgood, *Jews in America,* p. 53; Gookin, *Historical Collections,* p. 150; and "Letters of the Rev. John Eliot," p. 296. For animals, see ibid., p. 296; the Commissioners in NEHGR 36 (1882): 375; William Kellaway, "Arms and Ammunition for New England, 1652," *Journal of the Arms and Armour Society* 3:7 (1960): 201; and Virginia Anderson, "King Philip's Herds: Indians, Colonists, and the Problem of Livestock in Early New England," WMQ 51 (1994): 606–608, 613–614.

5. John Speene in *Tears of Repentance,* p. 246; "Letters of the Rev. John Eliot," p. 298; Eliot in *Light appearing,* p. 126; and RCP 9:203. For men, see Mather in *Tears of Repentance,* p. 224; Eliot in *Light appearing,* p. 139; Wilson and Endecott in *Strength out of Weaknesse,* pp. 177, 179, 191; and "Letters of the Rev. John Eliot," p. 296. For women, see Eliot in Thorowgood, *Jews in America,* pp. 53–54; and for English goods, see Eliot in *Light appearing,* pp. 137–138, 143, and "Letters of the Rev. John Eliot," pp. 294, 297–298.

6. Eliot in *Tears of Repentance,* p. 227, and in *Late and Further Manifestation,* p. 270; Gookin, *Historical Collections,* pp. 181, 188; and Trask et al., eds., *Suffolk Deeds,* 6:288–289. Elise Brenner argues that there was little "full-time sedentism" in prewar Natick, and that the settlement was an "unbounded area in which and through which the praying Indian community

moved about seasonably, stopping periodically in the town center for Eliot's visits, for formal church occasions, and for burying the dead." "Strategies for Autonomy," pp. 131, 169. For a critical assessment of Brenner's argument, see Richard W. Cogley, "Was Natick a Residential Praying Town in the Period before King Philip's War?", *Bulletin of the Massachusetts Archaeological Society* 59 (1998): 31–35.

7. RMB 3:306, 385, 4(1): 148, 234; and Morrison, *Praying People*, pp. 135–136. For Eliot's authorization, see Hill and Tuttle, eds., *Early Records*, 4:266; and for Dedham's views, see ibid., 4:253–254, 261–269.

8. For the first attempt, see RMB 4(1): 408–410, 428, and Eliot, "Natik case drawen up," p. 260; for the grant to Russell, see RMB 4(1): 304, 370–371; and for the second attempt, see "An Expedient for the Ishuing of the Case" (1660), in Hill and Tuttle, eds., *Early Records*, 4:247–249. In 1669 Eliot asked the General Court to trade the 80 acres of meadow for two cedar swamps so that the Indians could make shingles and clapboards. This petition was denied, doubtless because the Apostle had rejected the other provisions of the committee's recommendation in 1660. "The humble Petition of John Eliot in the behalf of the poor Indians of Natick & Magwonkkommuk" (1669), in Biglow, *History of Natick*, pp. 34–35.

9. Eliot, "Natik case drawen up," pp. 255–261; and Allin in Hill and Tuttle, eds., *Early Records*, 4:264. For the suits made by Dedham and the actions by the Suffolk County Court, see ibid., 4:250–252; and for the General Court order, which Eliot misdated as 1654 instead of 1652, see RMB 3:281–282, 4(1): 100–101.

10. RMB 4(2): 49, 282–283; and "The petition of us whose names are heere unto subscribed" (1662), in Hill and Tuttle, eds., *Early Records*, 4:275–276. For the continued animosity, see the statements by Allin, Eliot, and others in ibid., 4:279–285; RMB 4(2): 431–432, 5:485–486; and George Parker Winship, "Samuel Sewall and the New England Company," MHSP 67 (1945): 101. For the figure of Natick's 4,000 total acres, see Edward Tyng et al., in Hill and Tuttle, eds., *Early Records*, 4:273; and RMB 5:485–486.

11. For Keayne, see Bailyn, ed., *Apologia of Robert Keayne*, pp. 24–26, and RMB 2:283, 3:181–182, 188–189, and 4(1): 6–7; for Bradstreet, see RMB 3:193, 413, 4(1): 270, 362–363, and Eliot, "Natik case drawen up," p. 260; and for Sherborn, see RMB 5:37, 227–230, and Gookin et al. in MSA 30:305.

12. Eliot in *Strength out of Weaknesse*, p. 171, and in *Late and Further Manifestation*, p. 275; Wilson and Endecott in *Strength out of Weaknesse*, pp. 178, 190; Tyng et al. in Hill and Tuttle, eds., *Early Records*, 4:273; and Daniel Mandell, "'To Live More Like My Christian English Neighbors': Natick Indians in the Eighteenth Century," WMQ 48 (1991): 556n, 564. The MHS edition of Gookin's *Historical Collections* suggests that 29 families lived at Natick in 1674 (pp. 180, 195.)

13. Eliot in *Strength out of Weaknesse*, pp. 171–172, and in *Light appearing*, p. 139; Holstun, *Rational Millennium*, p. 154; Chapter 3, note 11; and

Nishohkou in *Further Account*, pp. 39–40. For Attawans, see Eliot in *Brief Narrative*, p. 7; for Totherswamp, see Eliot in *Late and Further Manifestation*, p. 273; for Peter, see Eliot in *Tears of Repentance*, p. 245; for Piumbuhhou, see Eliot, *Dying Speeches*, p. 4; and for Thomas Speene, Sr., see John Speene in *Tears of Repentance*, p. 247. Peter was probably from Neponset because he said in 1652 that "I believe that God calls us to Natick." Deciding to move to Natick was more of a problem for Neponset than for Nonantum Indians. Peter in *Tears of Repentance*, p. 246. Piumbuhhou was also known as Piambow and as Piam Boohan. Eliot in Ford, ed., *Some Correspondence*, p. 28, and in *Dying Speeches*, p. 4. Gookin mistakenly thought that Piumbuhhou and Piambow were different Indians. *Historical Collections*, pp. 184–185.

14. Eliot in *Strength out of Weaknesse*, pp. 172–174. For similar phrasing, see *Light appearing*, p. 127, and *Christian Commonwealth*, p. 139; and for Cutshamekin's embassy, see Eliot in *Strength out of Weaknesse*, p. 173. For Indian references to the three final last things, see *Light appearing*, pp. 129–130, 132–133; *Tears of Repentance*, pp. 230–231, 233, 237, 240, 247, 253, 257; *Late and Further Manifestation*, pp. 279–280; and *Further Account*, pp. 16, 28, 52.

15. The accounts of Wilson and Endecott are in *Strength out of Weaknesse*, pp. 176–179, 189–191. See also Eliot in ibid., pp. 174–175; and "Letters of the Rev. John Eliot," p. 292. *Strength out of Weaknesse* was reprinted, under the title *The Banners of Grace and Love Displayed in the farther Conversion of the Indians in New-England*, in London in 1657.

16. Holstun, *Rational Millennium*, pp. 153–154; Bozeman, *To Live Ancient Lives*, p. 274; and Eliot, "Learned Conjectures," p. 18. I have not found a single reference to the system of tens through thousands, let alone an endorsement of it, in any non-Eliot source written in Massachusetts Bay in the 1650s. For the repatriates, see Maclear, "New England and the Fifth Monarchy," pp. 249–250; and Gura, *Glimpse of Sion's Glory*, pp. 137–144. For Johnson's views about the civil order in Massachusetts Bay, see Jameson, ed., *Johnson's Wonder-Working Providence*, pp. 30–32, 140–141.

17. RMB 4(2): 5–6.

18. RMB 4(1): 449–454, 4(2): 33, 199. The 1661 and 1663 dedicatory prefaces, which were included only in the copies of the Indian Bible sent to England, are printed in AAS, *Transactions and Collections* 5 (1874): 393–401, and also in MHSC 1:7 (1801): 222–228. The 1663 preface was written by Simon Bradstreet and Thomas Danforth, the Bay Colony's delegates to the United Colonies at the time. RCP 10:311. Authorship of the 1661 preface is unknown.

19. Eliot in *Christian Commonwealth*, p. 135 (see also pp. 140–141), and in "Account of Indian Churches," p. 128; and Chapter 4, note 32.

20. Eliot in Ford, ed., *Some Correspondence*, p. 28; Gookin, *Historical Collections*, pp. 183–184 and Chapter 6, note 58.

21. Eliot in *Tears of Repentance*, p. 232, and in *Brief Narrative*, p. 5; Gookin,

"The Examination of Sarah Ahhaton" (1668), in MSA 30:152–153; and RMB 4(2): 407–408.
22. Eliot in *Late and Further Manifestation,* pp. 273–275.
23. For the missing document, see Eliot in Eames, ed., *John Eliot and the Indians,* p. 22; and for the general duties of rulers, see Eliot in *Late and Further Manifestation,* p. 273, and in *Brief Narrative,* p. 3. For the rulers of tens, see "Letters of the Rev. John Eliot," p. 298; Eliot in *Strength out of Weaknesse,* p. 171, and in "Account of Indian Churches," p. 125; and Gookin, *Historical Collections,* pp. 178–179.
24. Eliot in *Tears of Repentance,* p. 227.
25. For Massachusett-language instruction, see Chapter 3, note 40; and Eliot in *Light appearing,* p. 144, in *Strength out of Weaknesse,* pp. 168, 170, and in *Indian Grammar Begun,* pp. 250–251. For standard English practice, see E. Jennifer Monaghan, "Literacy Instruction and Gender in Colonial New England," *American Quarterly* 40 (1988): 24–25, 28; and for the literacy figures, see RCP 10:242, and Kathleen J. Bragdon, "'Another Tongue Brought In': An Ethnohistorical Study of Native Writings in Massachusett" (Ph.D. diss., Brown University, 1981), p. 55. For the transition to English, see Gookin, *Historical Collections,* pp. 219–222; RCP 10:368–339; Winship, ed., *New England Company of 1649,* p. 185; and the Commissioners in Ford, ed., *Some Correspondence,* p. 59.
26. For Monequasson, see Eliot and Endecott in *Strength out of Weaknesse,* pp. 169–170, 190; RCP 10:167; and Eliot in *Tears of Repentance,* p. 234, and in *Late and Further Manifestation,* p. 273. For Sassamon, see William Hubbard, *The Present State of New-England* (London, 1677), in Samuel G. Drake, ed., *The History of the Indian Wars in New England* (1865; reprint ed. New York: Kraus Reprint Co., 1969), 1:60; and Eliot in Whitmore and Appleton, eds., *Report of the Record Commissioners,* p. 192. For Nesutan, see Gookin, *Historical Account,* p. 444. Eliot noted that one of the culprits in the incident with Totherswamp's son was "my interpreter, whom I have used in translating a good part of the Holy Scriptures." Jill Lepore suggests that Sassamon was the individual in question. Gookin, however, said that Nesutan was Eliot's primary assistant in translating the Bible. Eliot in *Late and Further Manifestation,* p. 274; Lepore, "Dead Men Tell No Tales: John Sassamon and the Fatal Consequences of Literacy," *American Quarterly* 46 (1994): 494; and Gookin, *Historical Account,* p. 444.
27. Salisbury, "Red Puritans," p. 42n; Eliot in *Reliquiae Baxterianae,* 2:293; and Kenneth Miner, "John Eliot of Massachusetts and the Beginnings of American Linguistics," *Historiographia Linguistica* 1 (1974): 177. For Nesutan, see Gookin, *Historical Account,* p. 444; for Sassamon, see Mather, *Brief History of the Warr,* p. 87; and for James the Printer, see Hubbard, *Present State of New-England,* 1:249, and RCP 10:244.
28. Gookin, *Historical Collections,* p. 169. For the dates of publication for the first, second, and fourth editions, see RCP 10:120, 278; and "Eliot's Letters to Boyle," p. 187.

29. Eliot in *Light appearing*, p. 121, in Thorowgood, *Jews in America*, pp. 52–53, and in *Further Accompt*, p. 2. See also Wilson in *Strength out of Weaknesse*, p. 178. For the approximate date of publication for the translation of the Psalms, see Eliot in *Further Accompt*, p. 20; and RCP 10:219.
30. RCP 10:106, 123, 140, 243; Usher quoted in Winship, ed., *New England Company of 1649*, p. 34; and Eliot in *Further Accompt*, pp. 2–3.
31. Eliot in *Strength out of Weaknesse*, p. 169, and in *Further Accompt*, p. 20; and Endecott in ibid., p. 4. For Eliot's sciatica, see Samuel Danforth in Whitmore and Appleton, eds., *Report of the Record Commissioners*, p. 198; Eliot in Powicke, "Some Unpublished Correspondence," pp. 154–155, in Eames, ed., *John Eliot and the Indians*, p. 25, and in Thorowgood, *Jews in America*, p. 54; and "Letters of John Eliot," p. 245.
32. For the printing schedule of the first edition of the Bible, see George Parker Winship, *The Cambridge Press, 1638–1692* (Philadelphia: University of Pennsylvania Press, 1945), pp. 208–240. An English translation of the two intertestamental expositions was made by James Hammond Trumbull and privately printed in an untitled edition of 35 copies in 1865; a copy is available at the Boston Athenaeum. The metrical Psalter printed between the two testaments was probably identical to the three separately published editions of the Psalms in meter. No copy of any of the separate editions has survived.
33. Williams, *Bloody Tenent yet More Bloody*, pp. 371–373, and *George Fox Digg'd out of His Burrowes* (Boston, 1676), in *Complete Writings*, 5:465; and James Hammond Trumbull, "The Indian Tongue and Its Literature as Fashioned by Eliot and Others," in Justin Winsor, ed., *The Memorial History of Boston* (Boston: J. R. Osgood and Co., 1880–1881), 1:473. For Exodus 3:14, see Guice, "Linguistic Work," p. 133; for the loan words, see Miner, "John Eliot," p. 176; and for an example of the "eelpot" legend, see Biglow, *History of Natick*, pp. 84–85.
34. For Baxter's *Call*, see Eliot in Powicke, "Some Unpublished Correspondence," pp. 154–155, and in *Reliquiae Baxterianae*, 2:293; and N. H. Keeble, *Richard Baxter: Puritan Man of Letters* (New York: Oxford University Press, 1982), pp. 73–74. For Bayly's *Practice*, see Baxter in *Reliquiae Baxterianae*, 2:290–291; Eliot in Thomas Birch, ed., *The Works of the Honourable Robert Boyle* (London, 1772), 6:510; and Winship, ed., *New England Company of 1649*, pp. 108–109. For Shepard's two works, see "Letter from Rev. John Eliot, 1664," pp. 132–133.
35. Eliot in Birch, ed., *Works*, 6:510, and in *Indian Grammar Begun*, p. 245; and Miner, "John Eliot," p. 170. I wish to thank Martha Ann Selby for enhancing my understanding of contemporary scholarship about the Massachusett language.
36. Eliot, *The Logick Primer* (Cambridge, 1672), p. A3; Miner, "John Eliot," pp. 176, 180; Guice, "Linguistic Work," pp. 179–183; and Perry Miller, *The New England Mind: The Seventeenth Century* (1939; Boston: Beacon Press,

1961), pp. 114, 120. For "Our Indians' A B C," see "Letters of John Eliot," p. 249; and Kellaway, *New England Company,* p. 140. For the lectures on theology and logic as well as the Boyle and Armine gifts, see Eliot in *Brief Narrative,* p. 4; "Eliot's Letters to Boyle," p. 177; "Letters of John Eliot," p. 249; Gookin, *Historical Collections,* p. 183; and Guice, "Linguistic Work," p. 146.

37. Eliot in *Strength out of Weaknesse,* pp. 170, 175; Wilson in ibid., p. 178; and Gookin, *Historical Collections,* p. 183. For the visitation schedule, see Eliot in *Strength out of Weaknesse,* p. 174; and for the Sunday and weekday lectures, see Gookin, *Historical Collections,* p. 183. For the identities of the teachers before 1660, see Totherswamp in *Tears of Repentance,* p. 231; and Nishohkou, Monotunkquanit, and Ponampam in *Further Account,* pp. 7, 25, 42, 55. For John Speene and Anthony, see Eliot in Ford, ed., *Some Correspondence,* pp. 27–28, in *Brief Narrative,* p. 5, and in *Dying Speeches,* pp. 7, 11; and Gookin, *Historical Collections,* p. 184. For prophesying, see "Letters of John Eliot," p. 248. For sermon texts that Eliot took from books other than Genesis, Psalms, and Matthew, see the following citations in the native narratives of the 1650s: *Tears of Repentance,* p. 241 (Exodus 4:12); *Further Account,* pp. 21, 56 (1 Chronicles 28:9); ibid., p. 40 (Isaiah 58:13); *Tears of Repentance,* p. 254 (Ezekiel 37:4); ibid., pp. 234, 240–242, 249, and *Further Account,* pp. 20, 55 (Malachi 1:11); ibid., pp. 41, 43 (Luke 16:19–31, 18:1–8); ibid., pp. 7–8, 22, 42–44, 53, 56–57 (John 3:6, 5:40, 6:53–55, 14:6, 15:16); *Tears of Repentance,* p. 242 (Hebrews 12:8); and ibid., pp. 235, 237, 257 (James 1:5–6, 22). The Indian speakers rarely identified these passages, or the ones from Genesis, Psalms, and Matthew, by chapter or by chapter and verse.

38. Bowden and Ronda, eds., *John Eliot's Indian Dialogues,* p. 144. For preparations for the sabbath, see Eliot, "What should a Christian do, to keep perfectly holy the Sabbath day?"; for the worship format and the seating arrangements, see Gookin, *Historical Collections,* p. 183; for Psalm-singing, see Wilson and Endecott in *Strength out of Weaknesse,* pp. 178, 190, and Eliot, *Indian Grammar Begun,* p. 250; and for fast and thanksgiving days, see Eliot in *Late and Further Manifestation,* p. 273, and in "Account of Indian Churches," pp. 126, 128.

39. Eliot in "How can I walk with God all the day long?", in *Clear Sun-shine,* p. 51, in *Strength out of Weaknesse,* p. 170, and in Bowden and Ronda, eds., *John Eliot's Indian Dialogues,* p. 80; Shepard in *Day-Breaking,* p. 13; and Robert James Naeher, "Dialogue in the Wilderness: John Eliot and the Indian Exploration of Puritanism as a Source of Meaning, Comfort, and Ethnic Survival," NEQ 62 (1989): 358–359.

40. Eliot in *Light appearing,* p. 142, and in *Strength out of Weaknesse,* p. 165.

41. "Letters of the Rev. John Eliot," pp. 296–297; and Eliot in *Tears of Repentance,* pp. 227–228, 250.

42. Eliot in *Tears of Repentance,* pp. 228, 243–244; and Cotton in [Elmeston], *Censure of That Reverend and Learned man of God,* p. 55 (mispaginated

54). The procedures for forming a new church are described in Robert G. Pope, introduction to *The Notebook of the Reverend John Fiske, 1644–1675,* PCSM 47 (1974): pp. xi–xiv.
43. Eliot in *Tears of Repentance,* pp. 228, 244.
44. Eliot in ibid., pp. 243, 245.
45. Waban and William of Sudbury in ibid., pp. 232, 234; Eliot in *Strength out of Weaknesse,* p. 170; Shepard in *Clear Sun-shine,* p. 63; and George Selement, "The Meeting of Elite and Popular Minds at Cambridge, New England, 1638–1645," WMQ 41 (1984): 35, 46–47. For native references to the catechism, see *Tears of Repentance,* pp. 242, 247, 253, 255, 257; for scriptural references by Indians, see note 37 above; and for Old Jacob, see Eliot, *Dying Speeches,* p. 5.
46. Ponampam and Nishohkou in *Tears of Repentance,* pp. 243, 252 (see also p. 241); and Holstun, *Rational Millennium,* p. 111. For native statements about lust in *Tears of Repentance,* see pp. 229, 237–238, 247–248, 250, 253–254, 258; for gambling, see pp. 229, 248; for long hair, see pp. 234, 239; for sabbath-breaking, see pp. 246, 252; for neglect of labor, see pp. 246, 252; for the inward/outward distinction, see pp. 232, 247, 250, 254, 256–257, 259; for fear of damnation, see pp. 229, 235, 240, 242, 249, 251, 253; and for human inability, see pp. 229, 233, 237, 246, 248, 253–254, 257.
47. Mather's statement is in *Tears of Repentance,* pp. 219–225. For Dorchester and Wenham, see Pope, introduction to *Notebook of the Reverend John Fiske,* p. xii.
48. Eliot in *Tears of Repentance,* pp. 215–216.
49. Eliot in *Late and Further Manifestation,* pp. 271–276, and in Eames, ed., *John Eliot and the Indians,* p. 22.
50. Eliot and Walton in *Late and Further Manifestation,* pp. 276, 284.
51. Eliot in ibid., pp. 285–286.
52. Eliot in *Further Accompt,* pp. 6–8 (irregular pagination), 20; and John Speene in ibid., pp. 14–15.
53. For the 1647 epidemic, see Eliot in Whitmore and Appleton, eds., *Report of the Record Commissioners,* p. 190; for consumption, see Gookin, *Historical Collections,* p. 173, and the Commissioners in Ford, ed., *Some Correspondence,* p. 14; and for other diseases, see Eliot in *Light appearing,* pp. 133–134, in *Strength out of Weaknesse,* p. 165, and in *Tears of Repentance,* p. 259, and "Letters of the Rev. John Eliot," p. 296. For the individuals in question, see *Tears of Repentance,* pp. 239, 247–248, 259–260; *Strength out of Weaknesse,* pp. 166–167; "Letters of the Rev. John Eliot," p. 296; and *Further Account,* pp. 18, 22, 28, 40, 57, 59, 63, 69.
54. Harold van Lonkhuyzen, "A Reappraisal of the Praying Indians: Acculturation, Conversion, and Identity at Natick, Massachusetts, 1646–1720," NEQ 63 (1990): 417; and Cohen, "Conversion among Puritans and Amerindians," pp. 253–254. For native statements about Jesus the shaman, see Waban and Captain Tom in *Further Accompt,* pp. 9, 19.
55. Eliot in *Further Account,* pp. 1–2.

56. Eliot in ibid., pp. 2, 29, 30, 35.
57. Eliot in ibid., p. 35. For the admission of new members into an existing church, see Charles L. Cohen, *God's Caress: The Psychology of Puritan Religious Experience* (New York: Oxford University Press, 1986), pp. 140–147.
58. Eliot in *Further Account*, pp. 35–37, 45–46, 54, 67–68.
59. Nishohkou in ibid., p. 5. For native statements about lust in *Further Account*, see pp. 4, 9, 11–12, 22, 26, 38, 48, 71; for the internal-external distinction, see pp. 17, 32, 58; for fear of damnation, see pp. 5, 7, 13, 22–23, 26, 28, 52, 61; for human inability, see pp. 18, 28–29, 34, 44, 57, 60, 62, 70, 74; for polytheism, see pp. 9–10, 17, 38, 47, 55, 66, 68 (compare *Tears of Repentance*, pp. 232–233, 250); for powwowing, see pp. 4, 9, 27, 31, 38, 58 (compare *Tears of Repentance*, pp. 248, 254); for "running wild," see pp. 3, 5, 12, 22, 24, 32, 38, 55, 64; for desire for sacraments, see pp. 7–8, 20, 23, 43–44, 53, 61–62, 67; and for original sin, see pp. 3, 9, 13, 17, 23, 26–27, 37, 46–47, 56–57, 63, 68, 71 (compare *Tears of Repentance*, pp. 229–230, 236, 239, 254). In 1652 several Indians had spoken of "running away" from the mission; however, none of them characterized his pre-Christian life as "running wild." In 1659 the only native speakers who stated that they had read a given biblical passage were the teacher Nishohkou and the future teacher John Speene. For their narratives, see *Further Account*, pp. 3–9, 37–44 (especially pp. 7, 42), and pp. 16–20, 57–62 (especially pp. 59, 61).
60. Cohen, "Conversion among Puritans and Amerindians," pp. 242, 252, 254–256; and Selement, "The Meeting of Elite and Popular Minds," pp. 36, 44. For published Puritan conversion narratives, see Selement and Bruce C. Woolley, eds., *Thomas Shepard's Confessions*, PCSM 58 (1981); Mary Rhinelander McCarl, "Thomas Shepard's Record of Relations of Religious Experience, 1648–1649," WMQ 48 (1991): 432–466; Edmund Morgan, ed., *The Diary of Michael Wigglesworth, 1653–1657* (New York: Harper and Row, 1965), pp. 107–125; and Pope, ed., *Notebook of the Reverend John Fiske*. All or virtually all of these narratives were accepted by the various churches. For a fuller discussion of the Puritan "affective cycle," see Cohen, *God's Caress*, especially pp. 111–33, 201–241.
61. Eliot in *Further Account*, pp. 74–76.
62. Eliot in ibid., pp. 1–2, and in Powicke, "Some Unpublished Correspondence," p. 159. For the 1660 date, see Gookin, *Historical Collections*, p. 181.
63. Eliot in "Account of Indian Churches," pp. 125–126, in Ford, ed., *Some Correspondence*, pp. 27–29, and in *Brief Narrative*, p. 5.
64. Eliot in "Account of Indian Churches," p. 125, and in *Light appearing*, pp. 122, 134; and Baxter in Powicke, "Some Unpublished Correspondence," p. 456. For Eliot and the sacraments, see RCP 10:275; and Eliot in Powicke, "Some Unpublished Correspondence," pp. 164–165, and in "Account of Indian Churches," p. 125. For the date of Daniel's ordination, see "New England Chronology," in NEHGR 8 (1854): 19.
65. Cohen, "Conversion among Puritans and Amerindians," pp. 254–255. Two

other scholars, however, are prepared to dismiss the Christian knowledge of the leading proselytes. Salisbury claims that the conversion narratives in the 1650s "lack . . . intellectual content. There is no indication that the converts understood either the Word, except as it applied to themselves, or the most basic tenets of Puritan theology." George Tinker contends that the native speakers had no "genuine understanding of Christian doctrine" and that their knowledge of theology was "sophomoric" and "reflect[ed] the level of discourse one might rightly expect of young adolescent catechists with a minimal grasp of any deeper complexities." Such judgments are not persuasive. Neither scholar provides any evidence that he has looked at the contemporaneous Puritan conversion narratives, which were on the whole no more theologically sophisticated than their native counterparts. Salisbury, "Red Puritans," pp. 49–50; and Tinker, *Missionary Conquest,* pp. 38, 39, 41.
66. Mather in *Tears of Repentance,* p. 221.

6. *The Remaining Praying Towns*

1. RMB 3:281–282, 4(1): 100–101; and Gookin, *Historical Collections,* p. 179.
2. Eliot in Thorowgood, *Jews in America,* p. 53; Gookin, *Historical Collections,* p. 184; and Punkapoag deed in MHSC 1:2 (1793): 9.
3. Gookin, *Historical Collections,* pp. 166, 184; and Eliot in Powicke, "Some Unpublished Correspondence," p. 158, in *Brief Narrative,* p. 5, and in Bowden and Ronda, eds., *John Eliot's Indian Dialogues,* p. 122. For the territorial claims of the Massachusett sachems, see Drake, *Aboriginal Races,* p. 108, and RCP 10:157; for Cotton, Jr., see his ms. "Diary of preaching to the Indians" at the MHS, and his letter in Ford, ed., *Some Correspondence,* p. 47; for Squamaug's status as ruler in 1668, see Gookin, "Examination of Sarah Ahhaton," in MSA 30:152–153; and for the genealogy of the Massachusett sachems, see Trask et al., eds., *Suffolk Deeds,* 5:450–452, and James Blake, ed., *Annals of the Town of Dorchester* (Boston: David Clapp, 1846), 2:25.
4. For Hingham, see Trask et al., eds., *Suffolk Deeds,* 5:451–452; for Braintree, see Drake, *Aboriginal Races,* p. 108; and for sample sales in Plymouth, see ibid., p. 109, Trask et al., eds., *Suffolk Deeds,* 5:462–464, and RCP 12:238.
5. Eliot in Ford, ed., *Some Correspondence,* p. 28, and in *Brief Narrative,* p. 5; and Gookin, *Historical Collections,* pp. 171, 184.
6. "The humble petition of John Eliot of Roxbury on behalfe of some Indians" (1654), ms. at the AAS, in "Grafton, Mass. Local Records," Folder 2; and RMB 3:348, 4(1): 192.
7. Eliot in Ford, ed., *Some Correspondence,* pp. 28–29, and in *Brief Narrative,* pp. 5–6; Gookin, *Historical Collections,* pp. 185, 191, 193; and Winthrop in MHSP 72 (1957–1960): 63.
8. "Letters of John Eliot," p. 248; Eliot in Ford, ed., *Some Correspondence,*

p. 29, and in *Dying Speeches*, p. 4; "The Diary of John Hull," in AAS, *Transactions and Collections* 3 (1857): 231; and Gookin, *Historical Collections*, p. 185.

9. Eliot in Ford, ed., *Some Correspondence*, p. 28, and in *Brief Narrative*, p. 6; and Gookin, *Historical Collections*, pp. 185–186. For Solomon in 1657, see Trask et al., eds., *Suffolk Deeds*, 3:144a.

10. Sumner Chilton Powell, *Puritan Village: The Formation of a New England Town* (1963; Garden City, N.Y.: Anchor Books, 1965), pp. 150–177 (especially p. 172); and RMB 4(1): 296, 317, 363.

11. Eliot in *Brief Narrative*, p. 6; Gookin in *Historical Collections*, p. 185, and in *Historical Account*, pp. 455–461 (quotations on pp. 455, 456); and Drake, *Aboriginal Races*, p. 265. Moseley was also responsible for atrocities against praying Indians from the old towns of Wamesit and Nashobah. For a recent discussion of his actions, see Jenny Hale Pulsipher, "Massacre at Hurtleberry Hill: Christian Indians and English Authority in Metacom's War," WMQ 53 (1996): 468, 471–473, 479–480.

12. "The Humble Petition of John Eliot in the behalfe of the praying Indians . . . of Marlborough" (1663), ms. at the New England Historic Genealogical Society, Boston, in "Davenport Family Papers," A/D38, folder one; RMB 4(2): 82–83; and Gookin, *Historical Collections*, pp. 219–221.

13. Eliot in Ford, ed., *Some Correspondence*, p. 29, and in *Brief Narrative*, p. 7; and Gookin in *Historical Collections*, pp. 184, 188, and in *Historical Account*, p. 482.

14. "The humble Petition of John Eliot in the behalf of the poor Indians of Natick & Magwonkkommuk," p. 35; RMB 4(2): 465; Eliot in Ford, ed., *Some Correspondence*, p. 29, and in *Brief Narrative*, p. 8; and Gookin in *Historical Collections*, pp. 188–189, and in *Historical Account*, p. 480.

15. The Eliot and Gookin sources, as well as the General Court records, sometimes use the words "Wamesit" and "Pantucket" interchangeably. The identity of the settlement can normally be determined either by descriptions of the location (Wamesit was south of the Merrimack River along the Concord River, and Pantucket was further up the Merrimack) or by references to known residents. Also helpful in distinguishing between the settlements is Catherine C. Carlson, *Archival and Archaeological Research Report on the Configuration of the Seven Original 17th Century Praying Indian Towns of the Massachusetts Bay Colony* (Amherst: University of Massachusetts Archaeological Services, 1986), pp. 70–85. The present-day town of Wamesit is near but not on the location of the praying town of the same name.

16. Eliot in *Strength out of Weaknesse*, p. 168; "Letters of the Rev. John Eliot," p. 295; and Eliot ms. quoted in Lawrence Shaw Mayo, ed., *The History of the Colony and Province of Massachusetts-Bay by Thomas Hutchinson* (1764; Cambridge: Harvard University Press, 1936), 1:397–398. For the Willard expedition, see RMB 3:288, 4(1): 98–99, 109.

17. RMB 3:301, 406, 4(1): 136–137, 268, and 4(2): 16, 108–109; and Gookin, *Historical Collections*, p. 186. For the location of the 1653 award, see

Carlson, *Archival and Archaeological Research Report*, pp. 73, 80. Eliot's May 1656 petition was conveyed to the court by Gookin. See MHS Photostats, 1651–1657. In 1660 Wamesit and Chelmsford, with Eliot's approval, amicably agreed to exchange some land on the west side of the Concord River. RMB 4(1): 430–432.

18. Eliot in Ford, ed., *Some Correspondence*, pp. 29–30, and in *Brief Narrative*, p. 8; Drake, *Aboriginal Races*, pp. 267–268; and Gookin in *Historical Collections*, p. 186, and in *Historical Account*, pp. 485, 492. For Numphow's marriage, see Carlson, *Archival and Archaeological Research Report*, p. 74; and for his place of residence in 1660, see RMB 4(1): 431.

19. For the Pantucket residence of Passaconaway and Wannalancett, see Gookin in *Historical Collections*, p. 187, and in *Historical Account*, p. 463; for Naticot, see RMB 4(2): 51, and Passaconaway's 1662 petition in Nathaniel Bouton, *The History of Concord* (Concord, N.H.: Benning W. Sanborn, 1856), pp. 25–26; for Passaconaway's warning to the Pennacooks, see Hubbard, *Present State of New-England*, 1:48–49; and for Wannalancett during and after King Philip's War, see Bouton, *History of Concord*, pp. 28–30. The Naticot petition in 1662 marks Passaconaway's final appearance as a living figure in the sources consulted for this study.

20. Eliot in Ford, ed., *Some Correspondence*, pp. 29–30, and in *Brief Narrative*, pp. 7–8; and Gookin, *Historical Collections*, p. 188. See also Charles Cowley, *Illustrated History of Lowell* (Boston: Lee and Shepard, 1868), p. 19.

21. Gabriel Druillettes, "Narrative of the Journey made in behalf of the Mission of the Abnaquois" (1651), in R. G. Thwaites, ed., *The Jesuit Relations and Allied Documents* (1896–1901; reprint ed. New York: Pageant Book Co., 1959), 36:82–111 (quotation on p. 91); Eliot in Powicke, "Some Unpublished Correspondence," p. 455; and RCP 9:199–200. For the ensuing discussion of diplomatic and military history, I am indebted to Gordon M. Day, "The Ouragie War: A Case History in Iroquois-New England Indian Relations," in Michael K. Foster, Jack Campisi, and Marianne Mithun, eds., *Extending the Rafters: Interdisciplinary Approaches to Iroquoian Studies* (Albany: State University of New York Press, 1984), pp. 40–48; Neal Salisbury, "Toward the Covenant Chain: Iroquois and Southern New England Algonquians, 1637–1684," in Daniel K. Richter and James H. Merrell, eds., *Beyond the Covenant Chain: The Iroquois and Their Neighbors in Indian North America, 1600–1800* (Syracuse, N.Y.: Syracuse University Press, 1987), pp. 63–69; and Colin G. Calloway, *The Western Abenakis of Vermont, 1600–1800* (Norman: University of Oklahoma Press, 1990), pp. 67–74.

22. RCP 9:200–203; and Salisbury, "Toward the Covenant Chain," p. 65.

23. Day, "Ouragie War," p. 47; Gookin, *Historical Collections*, pp. 164–166; "Diary of John Hull," p. 219; and the Massachusetts council in MSA 30:127. For the deaths of Numphow's brother and John Thomas's father, see Eliot in Ford, ed., *Some Correspondence*, p. 29, and in *Brief Narrative*, p. 7; and Gookin, *Historical Collections*, p. 188.

24. The Commissioners in Ford, ed., *Some Correspondence,* pp. 13, 20; RMB 4(2): 329–330; and Boyle in Ford, ed., *Some Correspondence,* p. 26 (see also p. 27n). For the 1669 allocation, see Kellaway, *New England Company,* p. 118; and for the musket and fowling piece, see RCP 10:162–163.
25. Chapter 2, note 16, and RCP 9:105, 148–149 (exemptions to sachems and attempts to control the gun trade); RCP 9:137–138, 149, and RMB 2:264, 268, 3:131, 164 (1648 and 1649 allocations to Eliot); Nishohkou in *Further Account,* pp. 5, 40 (disarming at Neponset); and RCP 10:122, 140 (Eliot's 1654 and 1655 requests).
26. Gookin, *Historical Collections,* p. 166; Jean Pierron, "Of the War of the Agnies with the Nation of the Loups," in Thwaites, ed., *Jesuit Relations,* 53:137; and Eliot in Ford, ed., *Some Correspondence,* p. 30, and in *Brief Narrative,* pp. 7–8.
27. John Pynchon in Carl Bridenbaugh, ed., *The Pynchon Papers,* PCSM 60 (1982): 80; Salisbury, "Toward the Covenant Chain," p. 67; Gookin, *Historical Collections,* p. 166; and Eliot in *Brief Narrative,* p. 5.
28. Gookin, *Historical Collections,* pp. 162–164, 166. For the postwar attacks on Natick and Hassanamesit, see RMB 5:165–166; RCP 10:390–391; and Gookin in NEHGR 18 (1864): 178, and in *Historical Account,* pp. 518–520. For Monoco and James Rumney Marsh, see ibid., p. 489; and [Gookin], "James Quanapohit's Relation" (1676), in Temple, *History of North Brookfield,* p. 114. James Rumney Marsh's praying town of residence is not known to me.
29. Gookin, *Historical Collections,* pp. 166–167; Eliot in Ford, ed., *Some Correspondence,* pp. 28–30, and in *Brief Narrative,* pp. 5–8; and Pierron, "Of the War of the Agnies," pp. 137–153.
30. Eliot in Ford, ed., *Some Correspondence,* pp. 29–30, and in *Brief Narrative,* pp. 7–8; and Gookin, *Historical Collections,* pp. 162–163, 186–187.
31. "Letters of the Rev. John Eliot," p. 295; John Endecott in *Strength out of Weaknesse,* p. 191; and Eliot in Thorowgood, *Jews in America,* pp. 53–54. For the "aged sachem," see Eliot in *Light appearing,* pp. 125, 130; and for the Narragansetts and Mohegans, see RCP 9:158–159.
32. See the sources cited in note 28 above and in notes 33 and 40 below.
33. MSA 30:138–140; and RMB 4(2): 357–359.
34. LaFantasie et al., eds., *Correspondence of Roger Williams,* pp. 576–577; and RMB 4(2): 378, 385–386. The act of submission is in MSA 30:146.
35. Eliot in Powicke, "Some Unpublished Correspondence," p. 454; and Gookin, *Historical Collections,* pp. 189–194. For the native missionaries to the Nipmucks, see Eliot in *Brief Narrative,* p. 4; and "Letters of John Eliot," pp. 248–250.
36. Eliot in Ford, ed., *Some Correspondence,* p. 29, and in *Brief Narrative,* pp. 8–9; and Gookin, *Historical Collections,* pp. 189–190, 192–193. For the son of Matoonas, see Hubbard, *Present State of New-England,* 1:44, 98; and Samuel G. Drake, introduction to *The Old Indian Chronicle; Being a Collec-*

tion of Exceedingly Rare Tracts, Written and Published in the Time of King Philip's War (1867; reprint ed. New York: AMS Press, 1976), pp. 64–65.
37. Gookin, *Historical Collections,* pp. 189–194.
38. Ibid., pp. 189, 194.
39. RMB 4(2): 109–110. One of the 1715 sources says that the sachems gave Eliot the land, and the other that he purchased it from them. Convers Francis, *Life of John Eliot, the Apostle to the Indians* (1836; reprint ed. New York: Harper and Brothers, 1849), pp. 354–355.
40. Eliot's letter to Endecott is in MHSP 3 (1855–1858): 312–313. Another contemporary source provides slightly different details about the 1661 raid. "Mercurius de Quabaconk, or a declaration of the dealings of Uncas and the Mohegin Indians, to certain Indians the inhabitants of Quabaconk" (1661), in MSA 30:85. The Mohegans made less well-documented attacks on Nipmuck Indians in 1659 and 1660. See Eliot, "The case of the Nipmuk Indians" (1659), in Drake, *Aboriginal Races,* pp. 144–145; and the postscript to Eliot's letter to Endecott.
41. RMB 4(2): 22–23; and RCP 10:268–269. For the enmity between the Mohegans and Pocumtucks, see RMB 4(1): 299–300.
42. RMB 3:365–366, 4(1): 210.
43. "Letter from Rev. John Eliot, 1664," p. 131; Bowden and Ronda, eds., *John Eliot's Indian Dialogues,* pp. 63–94 (especially p. 94); and Gookin, *Historical Collections,* pp. 193–194. For Sagamore Sam's accession, see RMB 5:39.
44. For the raid on Mendon, see Hubbard, *Present State of New-England,* 1:97–98.
45. Gookin, *Historical Account,* pp. 436 (quotation), 449, 454–455, 462, 475–477, and "James Quanapohit's Relation," pp. 112–118 (especially p. 114). See also Drake, *Aboriginal Races,* p. 265.
46. For Sagamore Sam, Monoco, and Mattaumpe, see Thomas, ed., *Diary of Samuel Sewall,* p. 23. For Captain Tom, see ibid., p. 18; Eliot in Whitmore and Appleton, eds., *Report of the Record Commissioners,* pp. 194–195; and Gookin, *Historical Account,* pp. 527–528. For Sagamore John and Matoonas, see Hubbard, *Present State of New-England,* 1:286–287; and Thomas, ed., *Diary of Samuel Sewall,* p. 19. For Peter Jethro and Old Jethro, see ibid., p. 23; Gookin, *Historical Account,* p. 473; and Increase Mather, *Historical Discourse Concerning the Prevalency of Prayer* (Boston, 1677), p. 6. For Sampson and Joseph, see Gookin, *Historical Account,* p. 449. For James the Printer, see Thomas, ed., *Diary of Samuel Sewall,* p. 18; "Eliot's Letters to Boyle," p. 181; and Grindal Rawson and Samuel Danforth, Jr., "Account of an Indian Visitation, A.D. 1698," in MHSC 1:10 (1809): 134. For Joseph Tuckawillipin and William of Sudbury, see Gookin, *Historical Account,* p. 477. For Nehemiah, see [?], *A True Account of the Most Considerable Occurrences that have happened in the Warre between the English and the Indians in New-England* (London, 1676), in Drake, ed., *Old Indian Chronicle,* p. 269.

47. Philip Ranlet, "Another Look at the Causes of King Philip's War," NEQ 61 (1988): 79–100; Neal Salisbury, "Indians and Colonists in Southern New England after the Pequot War: An Uneasy Balance," in Laurence M. Hauptman and James D. Wherry, eds., *The Pequots in Southern New England: The Fall and Rise of an American Indian Nation* (Norman: University of Oklahoma Press, 1990), p. 93; and Jennings, *Invasion of America*, p. 309.
48. For nonresident English shareholders, see John Frederick Martin, *Profits in the Wilderness: Entrepreneurship and the Founding of New England Towns in the Seventeenth Century* (Chapel Hill: University of North Carolina Press, 1991), pp. 25, 88, 209–210, 327.
49. Jennings's claim about the armed missionaries to the Nipmucks rests on a misleading use of the sources. See Richard W. Cogley, "Idealism vs. Materialism in the Study of Puritan Missions to the Indians," *Method and Theory in the Study of Religion* 3 (1991): 176–177.
50. No copy of the 1643 or 1644 deed for Lancaster survives. See Dennis A. Connole, "Land Occupied by the Nipmuck Indians of Central New England, 1600–1700," *Bulletin of the Massachusetts Archaeological Society* 38 (1976): 17. Later evidence of the transaction appears in RMB 3:302–303, 4(1): 139–140. For the 1667 purchase of additional land for Lancaster, see RMB 4(2): 340; for Sudbury, see Powell, *Puritan Village*, p. 105; for Mendon, see Trask et al., eds., *Suffolk Deeds*, 6:288–289; for Brookfield, see Harry A. Wright, ed., *Indian Deeds of Hampden County* (Springfield, Mass.: privately printed, 1905), pp. 57–60, and RMB 4(2): 342, 5:568; and for Worcester, see William Lincoln, *History of Worcester, Massachusetts* (Worcester: Charles Hersey, 1862), pp. 303–304.
51. For the embassy, see the documents in George M. Bodge, *Soldiers in King Philip's War* (1906; reprint ed. Baltimore: Genealogical Publishing Co., 1976), pp. 88, 90, 104; and for Uncas, see Douglas E. Leach, *Flintlock and Tomahawk: New England in King Philip's War* (1958; reprint ed. New York: Norton, 1966), pp. 45, 56–57, 76.
52. Eliot in Bowden and Ronda, eds., *John Eliot's Indian Dialogues*, p. 80, and in Powicke, "Some Unpublished Correspondence," p. 454.
53. Eliot in *Brief Narrative*, pp. 5, 7; and Gookin, *Historical Collections*, p. 186. For population figures, see Appendix 3.
54. WJ 2:343. For the systems of trails, see Levi Badger Chase, *The Bay Path and along the Way* (N.P.: privately printed, 1919); Harral Ayres, *The Great Trail of New England* (Boston: Meador Publishing Co., 1940); and Temple, *History of North Brookfield*, pp. 24–26.
55. Gookin, *Historical Collections*, pp. 184–192.
56. Ibid., pp. 184–189 (quotations on pp. 185, 188); and Chapter 5, note 4.
57. "The humble Petition of John Eliot in the behalf of the poor Indians of Natick & Magwonkkommuk," p. 34; Lindholdt, ed., *John Josselyn, Colonial Traveler*, p. 105; and Gookin, *Historical Collections*, pp. 162, 184, 219. For the

seed money, see RCP 10:280, 382; and for apprenticing the Indians, see RCP 10:251, 397–398, and RMB 4(2): 23.
58. Eliot, "Account of Indian Churches," pp. 128–129. Aside from the references in this document, the Apostle mentioned the numerical terms on only three or four occasions after the mid-1650s: *Communion of Churches*, pp. 9–10; *Brief Narrative*, p. 7; and *Dying Speeches*, pp. 2, 4. In a widely cited study, Susan L. MacCulloch claimed that "in almost every [known] case" the rulers of praying towns were sachems or sagamores. The sources indicate that such was true about half the time. Cutshamekin, Josias Wompatuck, Attawans, and John Attawans, Sr., were "sachems of the blood"; Numphow was a "prince of the blood"; Owussumag was the "sachem of Marlborough"; Captain Tom was "an ancient sachem" and "of the chief sachem's blood of the Nipmuck Country"; John and Solomon were "sagamores"; and John Lyne was possibly the Pennacook Indian known as "Sagamore John." Nevertheless, there were twelve rulers in the fourteen settlements who are not identified as sachems or sagamores in the documentary record. MacCulloch, "A Tripartite Political System among the Christian Indians of Early Massachusetts," *Kroeber Anthropology Society Papers* 34 (1966): 67. For Josias, Numphow, and Attawans, see Eliot in *Brief Narrative*, pp. 5, 7; for Owussumag, see MSA 30:129a; for Captain Tom, see Eliot, "Account of Indian Churches," p. 128, and Gookin, *Historical Collections*, p. 193; and for John and Solomon, see ibid., pp. 192–193.
59. Eliot in "Account of Indian Churches," pp. 126–127, and in *Brief Narrative*, p. 8; and Gookin in *Historical Account*, p. 436, and in *Historical Collections*, p. 189. For nonresident church members, see ibid., p. 189; Eliot in Ford, ed., *Some Correspondence*, pp. 28–29, and in *Brief Narrative*, p. 7; and note 8 above. MacCullough states that the teachers were "usually" the sons of rulers in instances "for which there is information." "Tripartite Political System," p. 67. The Numphows at Wamesit and the Ahawtons at Punkapoag clearly exemplified this pattern. There were similar cases elsewhere: Petavit's sons Joseph and Sampson were teachers in towns other than the one in which their father resided, and the Nashobah teacher John Thomas was the son-in-law of Attawans. More than twenty persons who served as teachers, however, are not specified as sons of rulers in the sources.
60. Eliot in "Account of Indian Churches," p. 128, and in *Brief Narrative*, p. 3.
61. Eliot in *Brief Narrative*, pp. 3–4; "Letters of John Eliot," p. 246; and the Commissioners in Ford, ed., *Some Correspondence*, p. 36.
62. For the 1650s, see "Letters of the Rev. John Eliot," p. 292; and Eliot in *Tears of Repentance*, p. 216, and in "Learned Conjectures," p. 25 (mispaginated 19). For the early 1670s, see Eliot in *Brief Narrative*, p. 4, and in Bowden and Ronda, eds., *John Eliot's Indian Dialogues*, p. 59; "Letters of John Eliot," p. 250; and Thomas Mayhew, Sr., in Ford, ed., *Some Correspondence*, p. 41.
63. Shepard in *Day-Breaking*, p. 15.

7. Missionary Work outside Massachusetts Bay

1. Mayhew, Jr., in *Light appearing*, p. 109. For the colonization of the islands, see Jennings, *Invasion of America*, p. 230.
2. Simmons, "Conversion from Indian to Puritan," p. 215; and Mayhew, Jr., and Eliot in *Light appearing*, pp. 113, 139.
3. Mayhew, Jr., in *Light appearing*, pp. 111–113, and in *Glorious Progress*, pp. 77–78.
4. Mayhew, Jr., in *Strength out of Weaknesse*, p. 187, and in *Light appearing*, p. 116.
5. Mayhew, Jr., in *Light appearing*, pp. 114, 116, and in *Strength out of Weaknesse*, pp. 185–187; and Simmons, "Conversion from Indian to Puritan," pp. 209–210.
6. Mayhew, Jr., in *Strength out of Weaknesse*, pp. 186–188, in *Light appearing*, pp. 115–116, and in *Tears of Repentance*, pp. 203, 206–208.
7. Eliot in *Glorious Progress*, pp. 82, 84, in *Clear Sun-shine*, pp. 56–57, and in Bowden and Ronda, eds., *John Eliot's Indian Dialogues*, pp. 88–89. For Webbacowets, see Eliot in *Clear Sun-shine*, p. 55; for the husband and wife, see Shepard in *Day-Breaking*, p. 19; for Robin Speene, see Eliot in *Tears of Repentance*, p. 248; and for Black James, see Eliot, *Dying Speeches*, pp. 11–12. In late 1646 Eliot publicly confronted a powwow, probably at Neponset, "with a stern countenance and unaccustomed terror." Later the Apostle spoke to him "more courteously and lovingly" in private. Shepard in *Day-Breaking*, p. 19. It is easy to imagine Mayhew, Jr., doing the former but not the latter.
8. Eliot in *Clear Sun-shine*, pp. 50–51, and in "Account of Indian Churches," p. 126. For the new towns as well as Pantucket and Nashaway, see Gookin, *Historical Collections*, p. 192; and Eliot in *Light appearing*, p. 135, in Ford, ed., *Some Correspondence*, p. 30, and in Bowden and Ronda, eds., *John Eliot's Indian Dialogues*, pp. 88–89.
9. For population figures, see James P. Ronda, "Generations of Faith: The Christian Indians of Martha's Vineyard," WMQ 38 (1981): 370.
10. Eliot in *Further Accompt*, p. 7; Gookin, Mayhew, Sr., and Cotton, Jr., in *Historical Collections*, pp. 202–203, 205–207; and Bragdon, *Native People of Southern New England*, p. 11.
11. RCP 10:275; Eliot in *Brief Narrative*, p. 2, and in "Account of Indian Churches," p. 126; Cotton, Jr., and Mayhew, Sr., in Gookin, *Historical Collections*, pp. 204–205; and Luca Codignola, "The Holy See and the Conversion of the Indians in French and British North America, 1486–1760," in Karen O. Kupperman, ed., *America in European Consciousness, 1493–1750* (Chapel Hill: University of North Carolina Press, 1995), p. 219.
12. Eliot in *Glorious Progress*, p. 81, and in *Light appearing*, pp. 122–123; and Jennings, *Invasion of America*, pp. 245–247. See also Cogley, "Idealism vs. Materialism," p. 169n. For the Apostle's efforts on the younger Mayhew's

behalf, see Eliot in *Light appearing,* pp. 128, 132, 143–144; "Letters of the Rev. John Eliot," pp. 293–294; and RCP 9:196, 198. For Mayhew's visits to the mainland, see Eliot in *Light appearing,* p. 125, and in *Late and Further Manifestation,* p. 276; John Wilson in *Strength out of Weaknesse,* p. 176; Gookin, *Historical Collections,* pp. 155–156; and Waban in *Tears of Repentance,* p. 231.

13. RCP 10:121–122, and "Letters of the Rev. John Eliot," p. 293 (Armine annuity); RCP 10:121–122, 163, 356 (Eliot's corporation salary); RCP 9:205, and the Commissioners in NEHGR 36 (1882): 375 (first contact with Mayhew, Jr.); RCP 10:120, 141, 167, 189 (salary for Mayhew, Jr.); RCP 10:189, 205, 218, 356 (salary for Mayhew, Sr.); and RCP 10:210, and Mayhew, Sr., in MHSC 4:7 (1865): 34, and in Ford, ed., *Some Correspondence,* p. 41 (complaints).
14. "Letters of the Rev. John Eliot," pp. 298–299, RCP 10:140, 167, 189, and "Letters of John Eliot," p. 246 (Francis Eliot); RCP 10:189, 330 (Eliot, Jr.); RCP 10:245, 262 (Joseph Eliot); RCP 10:205, 291, 293, 313, 331, and Winthrop in MHSP 16 (1878): 218 (Mayhew's widow); and RCP 10:206, 219, 277, 289, 296 (Matthew Mayhew).
15. "Letters of the Rev. John Eliot," p. 298, and RCP 10:189, 356 (representative allocations to Indian teachers and rulers in Massachusetts Bay); RCP 10:123–124, 167, 331, 356 (sample awards to native personnel on the islands); RCP 10:331, 356 (Waban); and RCP 10:167, 262 (Folger).
16. Eliot in *Tears of Repentance,* pp. 255–256, and RCP 10:378 (Anthony); "Letters of the Rev. John Eliot," p. 295 (Quinebaug); RCP 10:189 (corn); RCP 10:218 (church examination); Gookin, *Historical Collections,* pp. 157–158 (aborted journey; thanks to John Carter of George Mason University for providing me with information about the Massawomacks); RCP 10:123–124, 141 (supplies); and RCP 10:189 (£80).
17. Margaret Connell Szasz, *Indian Education in the American Colonies, 1607–1783* (Albuquerque: University of New Mexico Press, 1988), p. 106.
18. James Hammond Trumbull and Charles J. Hoadly, eds., *The Public Records of the Colony of Connecticut* (1850–1890; reprint ed. New York: AMS Press, 1968), 2:8.
19. Ibid., 1:265, 531; and RCP 10:128, 141.
20. For Blinman, see RCP 9:196, 10:182, 190; and Samuel Eliot Morison, *The Founding of Harvard College* (Cambridge: Harvard University Press, 1935), p. 367. For Tompson, see RCP 10:218, 246, 263, 277, 294; and John Winthrop, Jr., "Rough draft of proposals to the corporation for Ninecraft's Indian business" [1661 or 1662], in MHSC 5:9 (1885): 45.
21. Trumbull and Hoadly, eds., *Public Records of Connecticut,* 2:574–576.
22. Winship, ed., *New England Company of 1649,* p. 34; RCP 10:186–187; Trumbull and Hoadly, eds., *Public Records of Connecticut,* 2:111; and Blackleech in MHSC 4:7 (1865): 150–151.
23. "Extracts of Letters to Rev. Thomas Prince," in Connecticut Historical Soci-

ety, *Collections* 3 (1895): 275–276; and Eliot, "Natik case drawen up," p. 260. See also Eliot in *Further Accompt*, p. 2.

24. Eliot in *Light appearing*, p. 140, and in *Clear Sun-shine*, p. 57; and "Letters of the Rev. John Eliot," p. 294. For the Mohegan raids, see RCP 9:97–102.
25. Trumbull and Hoadly, eds., *Public Records of Connecticut*, 2:157–158; Gookin and Fitch in *Historical Collections*, pp. 208–209; "Letters of John Eliot," p. 248; and RCP 10:353, 356.
26. RCP 9:196, 10:120, 176, 288. For sample salary payments to Pierson, see RCP 10:109, 331.
27. Fitch in Gookin, *Historical Collections*, p. 208; Pierson, *Some Helps for the Indians*, pp. 11–12; and Pierson in Connecticut Historical Society, *Collections* 21 (1924): 159.
28. RCP 10:247, 278; E. B. O'Callaghan et al., eds., *Documents Relating to the Colonial History of the State of New York* (Albany: Weed, Parsons, and Co., 1883), 14:610–611; Kellaway, *New England Company*, pp. 104–105; and James in MHSC 4:7 (1865): 485–486.
29. For the appeal of revivalism, see William S. Simmons, "The Great Awakening and Indian Conversion in Southern New England," in William Cowan, ed., *Papers of the Tenth Algonquian Conference* (Ottawa: Carleton University Press, 1979), pp. 25–36.
30. Bartlett, ed., *Records of Rhode Island*, 2:3–4, 10; and Gookin, *Historical Collections*, p. 210.
31. Shepard in *Clear Sun-shine*, p. 61; LaFantasie et al., eds., *Correspondence of Roger Williams*, pp. 281, 282n; and Eliot and Carr in Bartlett, ed., *Records of Rhode Island*, 2:134–135, 138. Carr stated that Pomham "ordinarily takes counsel" with Eliot. Ibid., p. 138. The missionary sources contain no evidence of prior communication between Pomham and Eliot, except perhaps in a 1651 incident discussed in note 33 below.
32. Eliot in *Strength out of Weaknesse*, p. 170; and LaFantasie et al., eds., *Correspondence of Roger Williams*, p. 281.
33. Eliot in *Light appearing*, pp. 135–137, and in *Strength out of Weaknesse*, p. 173; and LaFantasie et al., eds., *Correspondence of Roger Williams*, p. 333.
34. LaFantasie et al., eds., *Correspondence of Roger Williams*, pp. 409, 410, 413; and Eliot in *Light appearing*, pp. 139–140. Williams took the Indians' request to Cromwell, who certainly qualified as one of the "high sachems of England." Cromwell directed the orthodox colonies to notify Rhode Island of any plans to invade the Narragansett Country. LaFantasie et al., editorial note in *Correspondence of Roger Williams*, p. 414.
35. RCP 10:125–127, 130–133; and LaFantasie et al., editorial note in *Correspondence of Roger Williams*, pp. 403–407 (quotation on p. 407).
36. Eliot in *Christian Commonwealth*, p. 132, and in *Light appearing*, p. 139; "Letters of the Rev. John Eliot," pp. 294–295; and Waban in *Further Account*, p. 31. Eliot's December 1652 letter to Steele certainly "branded" Nini-

gret "for refusing to pray and be converted." This letter was not published in the seventeenth century, however, so Williams could not have seen it in printed form in England.
37. Ranlet, "Another Look at the Causes," p. 85n; and Gorton in RMB 4(2): 253.
38. "Letters of the Rev. John Eliot," pp. 294–295.
39. Winthrop, "Rough draft of proposals," pp. 45–47; Boyle in RCP 10:273; Winship, ed., *New England Company of 1649*, p. 32; and Robert C. Black III, *The Younger John Winthrop* (New York: Columbia University Press, 1966), p. 247. For the interest in projects for the Indians and the English poor, see J. R. Jacob, "The New England Company, the Royal Society, and the Indians," *Social Studies of Science* 5 (1975): 450–455.
40. Gookin, *Historical Collections*, p. 210.
41. Richard Bourne and John Cotton, Jr., in ibid., pp. 196–199; and Shepard in *Clear Sun-shine*, pp. 42–43.
42. Eliot in *Brief Narrative*, p. 2; Leveritch in *Strength out of Weaknesse*, p. 181; "Letters of the Rev. John Eliot," p. 298; and RCP 10:141, 183, 205.
43. Bourne in Gookin, *Historical Collections*, pp. 196, 199. For sample payments to Bourne and his Indians, see RCP 10:205, 296, 317, 356 (see also "Letter from Rev. John Eliot, 1664," p. 132); for the ordination of Bourne, see Eliot in *Brief Narrative*, pp. 1–2; and for biographical background, see M. F. Ayer, "Richard Bourne, Missionary to the Mashpee Indians," NEHGR 62 (1908): 139–143. Jennings wrongly reports that Eliot "fradulently [took] credit" for Bourne's work. *Invasion of America*, p. 246n; and Cogley, "Idealism vs. Materialism," pp. 179–180.
44. Frederick L. Weis, "The New England Company of 1649 and Its Missionary Enterprises," PCSM 38 (1959): 149; and Kellaway, *New England Company*, pp. 147, 233–234, 247. In 1657 Samuel Newman, minister at Rehoboth, received seed money from the Commissioners to hire a language teacher in preparation for Indian work. Newman subsequently disappears from the missionary sources. RCP 10:183.
45. Cotton, Jr., in Gookin, *Historical Collections*, p. 200; and RCP 10:331, 356.
46. Eliot in Whitmore and Appleton, eds., *Report of the Record Commissioners*, p. 196, and in MHSP 50 (1916–1917): 78; "Eliot's Letters to Boyle," pp. 180–181; "Letters of John Eliot," p. 253; and Experience Mayhew in NEHGR 39 (1885): 12.
47. Eliot in *Glorious Progress*, p. 81; and Hubbard, *Present State of New-England*, 1:47.
48. "Letter from Rev. John Eliot, 1664," pp. 131–132; "Letters of the Rev. John Eliot," p. 298; Harvard records in PCSM 31 (1935): 150; and James N. Arnold, ed., *The Records of the Proprietors of the Narragansett, Otherwise Called the Fones Reports* (Providence: Narragansett Historical Publishing Co., 1894), pp. 6–7.
49. "Letter from Rev. John Eliot, 1664," p. 132. For the 1662 treaty with Rhode Island, see Lepore, "Dead Men Tell No Tales," p. 494; for the renewal of the

1621 mutual assistance pact, see RCP 4:25; for the 1664 and 1665 transactions, see Drake, *Aboriginal Races,* pp. 194, 198; and for the actions in 1666, see W. Noel Sainsbury et al., eds., *Calendar of State Papers, Colonial Series: America and the West Indies* (1860–1939; reprint ed. Vaduz, Liechtenstein: Kraus Reprint Co., 1964), 5 (1661–1668): 380, and RCP 12:237. The letter to Prince, printed in MHSC 1:2 (1793): 40, is undated and the author is not identified. George D. Langdon, Jr., dates the letter as 1672 and names Sassamon as the author. Jennings plausibly argues against Langdon for a 1662 date but does not speculate about authorship. Langdon, *Pilgrim Colony: A History of New Plymouth, 1620–1691* (New Haven, Conn.: Yale University Press, 1966), pp. 161–162; and Jennings, *Invasion of America,* 290n.

50. Gookin, *Historical Account,* p. 440; John Easton, "A Relacion of the Indyan Warre" (1676), in Charles H. Lincoln, ed., *Narratives of the Indian Wars, 1675–1699* (New York: Barnes and Noble, 1913), p. 7; Hubbard, *Present State of New-England,* 1:60–61; Increase Mather, *A Relation Of the Troubles which have hapned in New-England, By reason of the Indians there. From the Year 1614 to the Year 1675* (Boston, 1677), p. 74; Jennings, *Invasion of America,* pp. 294–295, 295n; RCP 12:230; and Eliot in Whitmore and Appleton, eds., *Report of the Record Commissioners,* pp. 192–193.

51. "Letter from Rev. John Eliot, 1664," p. 131; and Eliot in Bowden and Ronda, eds., *John Eliot's Indian Dialogues,* p. 121, and in MHSC 5:1 (1871): 425. Cotton Mather claimed that during a meeting between the two men, "the monster [Metacom] entertained . . . [Eliot] with contempt and anger, and . . . took a button upon the coat of the reverend man, adding that he cared for his gospel, just as much as he cared for that button." *Triumphs of the Reformed Religion,* pp. 106–107. The Apostle's less sensationalistic accounts of his contact(s) with the sachem make Mather's story highly improbable.

52. Bowden and Ronda, eds., *John Eliot's Indian Dialogues,* pp. 120–149. The meeting occurred after the defection of Squamaug in 1669 or 1670 and before the composition of *Indian Dialogues* in mid-1671. See ibid., p. 122; and Eliot in Powicke, "Some Unpublished Correspondence," p. 462. See also Eliot, "Instructions from the Church at Natick to William and Anthony" (1671), in MHSC 1:6 (1800): 201.

53. Bowden and Ronda, eds., *John Eliot's Indian Dialogues,* pp. 121–122 (first objection), pp. 123–126 (second objection), and pp. 127–129 (third objection). For Weymouth, see Eliot in *Light appearing,* p. 133.

54. Eliot in Bowden and Ronda, eds., *John Eliot's Indian Dialogues,* p. 149, in "Instructions from the Church at Natick," p. 201, and in MHSC 5:1 (1871): 425; and Easton, "Relacion of the Indyan Warre," p. 10.

55. To the best of my knowledge, Ranlet is the only historian who discusses Eliot's plan for peace. "Another Look at the Causes," pp. 92–93. Ranlet's interpretation of the plan differs from mine in almost every respect.

56. Hugh Cole in MHSC 1:6 (1799): 211. The Taunton agreement is printed in

full and discussed in Hubbard, *Present State of New-England*, 1:54–55, and in Mather, *Brief History of the Warr*, p. 151. The document is summarized in RCP 5:63.
57. Eliot's letter to Prince is in Francis, *Life of John Eliot*, pp. 267–268. For the disputes over disarmings and the preparations for war, see RCP 5:63–64, 73–75; and MHSC 1:5 (1798): 193–197. Eliot also told Prince in the letter that the Bay Colony's recent execution of an Indian murderer was an "act of eminent justice . . . [which] will strike more terror into them [the Pokanokets] than ten disarmings." This was surely a reference to the execution of Matoonas's son. Metacom was suspected of complicity in the murder, even though he almost certainly had nothing to do with it. See John Pynchon in Bridenbaugh, ed., *Pynchon Papers*, p. 87.
58. Eliot, "Instructions from the Church at Natick," pp. 201–203.
59. James Walker in MHSC 1:6 (1799): 197–198; and RCP 5:76–77.
60. RCP 5:77–79.
61. RCP 10:124; and Jennings, *Invasion of America*, p. 249. For Cotton's possible work among the Pokanokets, see Langdon, *Pilgrim Colony*, p. 158; for the Pokanoket claim over the islands, see Gookin, *Historical Collections*, p. 148; and for John Gibbs, see Drake, *Aboriginal Races*, p. 202.
62. RCP 10:123; the royal commissioners in *Collections of the New York Historical Society for the Year 1869*, p. 86; and Axtell, *Invasion Within*, p. 146. For Uncas and the Quinebaugs, see RCP 10:429–430.
63. Lepore, "Dead Men Tell No Tales," p. 498.
64. Ibid., pp. 497–498; Leach, *Flintlock and Tomahawk*, p. 21; Jennings, *Invasion of America*, p. 249; Salisbury, "Indians and Colonists," p. 93; and Drake, "Symbol of a Failed Strategy," p. 129.

8. The Supervision of the Mission

1. Kellaway, *New England Company*, pp. 21–29. The corporation apparently did not pay for the tenth and final Eliot tract, *A Brief Narrative*.
2. Kellaway, *New England Company*, p. 30; Whitfield in *Light appearing*, p. 107; Allen in *Strength out of Weaknesse*, p. 194; Mather in *Tears of Repentance*, p. 222; Eliot, "Learned Conjectures," p. 25 (mispaginated 19); RCP 10:118; and Peter in MHSC 4:6 (1863): 116.
3. Kellaway, *New England Company*, pp. 27–40, especially p. 36, and "The Collection for the Indians of New England, 1649–1660," *Bulletin of the John Rylands University Library* 39 (1956–1957): 444–462, especially pp. 461–462. Figures in English money.
4. Kellaway, *New England Company*, pp. 41–46, 51n; Jennings, *Invasion of America*, p. 244; and Lynn Ceci, "Native Wampum as a Peripheral Resource in the Seventeenth-Century World-System," in Hauptman and Wherry, eds., *Pequots in Southern New England*, pp. 61–62. The 1662 charter is in Sainsbury et al., eds., *Calendar of State Papers*, 5 (1661–1668): 71–73. For

the 1640s, see Firth and Rait, eds., *Acts and Ordinances of the Interregnum*, 2:198; and WJ 2:30.
5. Kellaway, *New England Company*, pp. 17–21, 47–51.
6. Ibid., pp. 43–45, 52–59 (especially pp. 52, 56). Figures in English money.
7. RCP 9:161–167, 10:319, 336.
8. RCP 9:165–166, 193; and Kellaway, *New England Company*, pp. 67–69. For the shipwreck, see "Letters of the Rev. John Eliot," p. 292, and the Commissioners in NEHGR 36 (1882): 374–375; for Cotton and Wilson, see Winship, ed., *New England Company of 1649*, p. lxix; and for Rawson, see RCP 9:205–206, 10:167, 206. Inventories of the four shipments may be found in Kellaway, *New England Company*, pp. 64–66, and in NEHGR 36 (1882): 374–375.
9. RCP 10:133, 138–139, 165–166 (requests); and RCP 10:136–137, 163 (responses).
10. RCP 10:137–139, 162–163, 165–166, 184–186. Figures in English money. For the 1652 shipment of arms and ammunition, which included a small quantity of tools and cloth evidently designated for the Indians, see Kellaway, "Arms and Ammunition for New England," pp. 198–203, and *New England Company*, pp. 69–70; and for the distribution of the weapons and the alleged reimbursement of the Company, see RCP 10:33–34, 104–105, 120–121, 424–425.
11. RCP 10:185, 195–196; and Kellaway, *New England Company*, pp. 71–76.
12. For 1659, see RCP 10:215–216, 217, and Winship, ed., *New England Company of 1649*, p. 62; and for 1661 and 1662, see RCP 10:254–255, 260, 273. Figures in English money.
13. Boyle in Ford, ed., *Some Correspondence*, p. 23; Winship, ed., *New England Company of 1649*, p. 152; and Kellaway, *New England Company*, pp. 71–72, 76–80.
14. RCP 10:118, 160; Winship, ed., *New England Company of 1649*, p. 17; and "Letters of John Eliot," pp. 248–249. For the scolding letters to Eliot, see RCP 10:121–122, 140.
15. "Letters of the Rev. John Eliot," p. 293; "Letters of John Eliot," pp. 246, 249; "Eliot's Letters to Boyle," p. 181; Eliot quoted in Winship, ed., *New England Company of 1649*, p. 115; Kellaway, *New England Company*, pp. 94–95; and "Anecdote of Rev. John Eliot, of Roxbury," MHSC 1:10 (1809): 186–187.
16. For Thorowgood, see *Jews in America*, pp. 3–4 (introductory material); for Nicolls, see RCP 9:204, and Eliot in Eames, ed., *John Eliot and the Indians*, pp. 6–7, 11; for Hanmer, see Eliot in ibid., pp. 9, 11 (see also pp. 17–18); for Eliot's promise, see RCP 10:121; and for Jessey, see "Letters of John Eliot," pp. 245–246.
17. "A Letter from New England, from Mr. Eliot," in *Severall proceedings in Parliament: from Thursday the 25 of Septemb. to Thursday the 2 day of October, 1651* [London, 1651], postscript; "Letters of the Rev. John Eliot,"

p. 294; and RCP 10:104, 138. For the 1670 and 1671 reimbursements, see "Letters of John Eliot," p. 246, and Winship, ed., *New England Company of 1649*, pp. 139, 146–147; and for Boyle's £30 gift, see ibid., p. 165, and "Eliot's Letters to Boyle," p. 187. Figures in English money. The 1651 "Letter from New England, from Mr. Eliot" was published, without the postscript, in *Strength out of Weaknesse*, pp. 165–168.
18. "Letters of the Rev. John Eliot," pp. 292, 297–298; and RCP 10:104, 122.
19. "Letter from Rev. John Eliot, 1664," pp. 131–133. For the 1663 cessation of payments to schoolteachers, see ibid., p. 132; for Eliot's initial request that Johnson be reappointed, see RCP 10:292; for the Company's advice about Gookin's salary, see RCP 10:314; and for the Commissioners' responses to Eliot's 1664 requests, see RCP 10:317–318, and Trumbull's annotation to Eliot's 1664 letter.
20. "Letters of John Eliot," pp. 247–251; and Winship, ed., *New England Company of 1649*, pp. 146–147. The charge for "powder and shot" was approximately £6. Kellaway, *New England Company*, p. 118.
21. "Letters of the Rev. John Eliot," p. 292; Winship, ed., *New England Company of 1649*, p. 18; Kellaway, *New England Company*, p. 63; RCP 10:138; and RMB 4(1): 324.
22. Morison, *Founding of Harvard College*, pp. 342–349; and Winship, *Cambridge Press*, especially pp. 225–228, 269–270, 327–329, 338. The cost of the press sent by the corporation in 1659 or 1660 is not known.
23. Green in MHSC 5:1 (1871): 423; Winship, *Cambridge Press*, p. 351; Marmaduke Johnson, "Accounts relating to the printing of Eliot's Indian Bible," ms. in the Historical Society of Pennsylvania, Misc. Collections, Box 11C; and Kellaway, *New England Company*, p. 145.
24. Chauncy in Ford, ed., *Some Correspondence*, pp. 64–65; and Winship, ed., *New England Company of 1649*, p. 128. Green controlled both Indian College presses between 1664 and 1675. Over fifty nonmissionary works were printed during these years by "Samuel Green." A determination of which ones he printed on the Glover press, and which on the Company press, would require a skilled analysis of typeface. Eliot did not misuse the Company's press. The three nonmissionary works he published in New England, *The Communion of Churches, The Harmony of the Gospels*, and *A Brief Answer to a Small Book Written by John Norcot against Infant Baptism*, were produced on the press that Johnson brought back from England in 1665.
25. The Commissioners and the corporation in Ford, ed., *Some Correspondence*, pp. 13, 17, 33.
26. Eliot, *Indian Grammar Begun*, p. 247.
27. Axtell, *Invasion Within*, p. 183; Gookin, *Historical Collections*, p. 173; and Kellaway, *New England Company*, p. 114. For the Vineyard Indians, see the discussion of Joel and Caleb in note 33 below, and RCP 10:280–281; for the Pequot, see Daniel Weld in MHSC 5:1 (1871): 409; and for the girl, see RCP

10:167, 207. Weld boarded his own students, and Corlet's lived with Thomas Danforth.
28. Dunster in MSA 30:9; and Cotton, *Bloudy Tenent Washed*, p. 148.
29. RCP 9:194, 198, 216; and Chapter 3, note 37.
30. RCP 10:104–105, 107, 128–129, 168; and Gookin, *Historical Collections*, p. 176. The glass was part of a shipment of goods that had arrived with Winslow's letter. Many scholars have been misled by Gookin's claim (ibid.) that the corporation had instructed the confederation to build the Indian College. The Company had simply proposed that six Indians be educated at Harvard. Gookin's figure of £300–£400 is the only known estimate of the actual cost of constructing the building. Coincidentally or not, the Commissioners did not begin itemizing their missionary expenditures until 1656, by which time the structure was complete. For other descriptions of the Indian College, see the royal commissioners in *Collections of the New York Historical Society for the Year 1869*, p. 87; the General Court in RMB 4(2): 198; and Robert N. Toppan and A. T. S. Goodrick, eds., *Edward Randolph* (1898–1909; reprint ed. New York: Burt Franklin, 1967), 2:256.
31. RCP 10:168, 190; Kellaway, *New England Company*, p. 110; and Samuel Eliot Morison, *Harvard College in the Seventeenth Century* (Cambridge: Harvard University Press, 1936), p. 359. Four of Eliot's sons attended Harvard while the Indian College was standing. Given their connections, they probably lived in the building. If such was the case, Eliot was not misusing Company property. He intended his sons for missionary service, and he paid their educational expenses. See the financial records in John L. Sibley, *Biographical Sketches of Graduates of Harvard University* (Cambridge: Charles William Sever, 1873, 1881), 1:477, 530, 2:60–61.
32. RCP 10:128, 167, 189, 206, 219, 228, 252, 263, 265, 277, 296.
33. Chauncy in Ford, ed., *Some Correspondence*, pp. 13–14; Gookin, *Historical Collections*, p. 173; and Winthrop in MHSP 16 (1878): 218–219. The Commissioners spent roughly £45 on Joel and Caleb during their first year at Harvard. RCP 10:277. The confederation's records do not itemize the two Indians' subsequent educational expenses.
34. For John Wampas, see the Commissioners in Ford, ed., *Some Correspondence*, pp. 13–14, 21; Morison, *Harvard College in the Seventeenth Century*, pp. 356–357; and Jean M. O'Brien, *Dispossession by Degrees: Indian Land and Identity in Natick, Massachusetts, 1650–1790* (New York: Cambridge University Press, 1997), pp. 75–78. Wamporas had a son who was living with Isaac Heath in Roxbury in 1651. Eliot in *Strength out of Weaknesse*, p. 167. John Wampas was probably the "John" who was studying with Corlet in 1663. RCP 10:310–311. For Eleazar, see Kellaway, *New England Company*, p. 113, and Mather, *Magnalia*, 1:496–497; for the fifth Indian, see Winship, ed., *New England Company of 1649*, p. 207; and for Larnell, see Morison, *Harvard College in the Seventeenth Century*, pp. 357n, 486. The Commissioners' published records contain no expenditures of any kind for the Har-

vard educations of Wampas, Eleazar, and the unidentified Indian. Nathaniel Saltonstall, the author of a notoriously inaccurate account of King Philip's War, said that Metacom's "privy councilor" (whom he distinguished from Sassamon) had been "formerly educated at Cambridge." Saltonstall failed to indicate which Cambridge institution the Indian allegedly attended. *The Present State of New-England With Respect to the Indian War* (London, 1675), in Lincoln, ed., *Narratives of the Indian Wars*, p. 31. The Commissioners' records contain numerous references to native students "at Cambridge." I take these to be references to Indians attending Corlet's grammar school.

35. Thomas, ed., *Diary of Samuel Sewall*, p. 394. For the 1693 and 1695 actions, see PCSM 15–16 (1925): 346, 352.
36. Kellaway, *New England Company*, p. 75 (see also p. 70); and Jennings, *Invasion of America*, pp. 243n, 247.
37. RCP 10:168, 182; and RMB 4(1): 334.
38. RMB 4(1): 362, 408–409, 428 (Dedham-Natick dispute); RCP 10:205, 219, 246, 263 (stipend); and Eliot, "Account of Indian Churches," p. 129 (Atherton's performance). For the quotation and for the Atherton Company, see Martin, *Profits in the Wilderness*, pp. 20n, 62–73; and for the expeditions, see Samuel H. Brockunier, *The Irrepressible Democrat: Roger Williams* (New York: Ronald Press, 1940), pp. 188, 192.
39. RMB 4(2): 34 (appointment of Gookin); Yasuhide Kawashima, *Puritan Justice and the Indian: White Man's Law in Massachusetts, 1630–1763* (Middletown, Conn.: Wesleyan University Press, 1986), p. 29 (Prentice); Gookin, *Historical Collections*, p. 177 ("first" Superintendent); William French in *Strength out of Weaknesse*, p. 193 (Vineyard Indian); RMB 3:306, 4(1): 148 (Natick-Dedham); Chapter 6, note 17 (Wamesit); RCP 10:277, 296, 318, 330, 356, and Gookin, *Historical Collections*, pp. 179–180 (stipend); and RCP 10:291, 294, 314, and "Letter from Rev. John Eliot, 1664," p. 132 (possible termination of stipend).
40. Jon Butler, "Two 1642 Letters from Virginia Puritans," MHSP 84 (1972): 105–106; Guy Loran Lewis, "Daniel Gookin, Superintendent and Historian of the New England Indians" (Ph.D. diss., University of Illinois, 1973), pp. 235–236; McCarl, "Thomas Shepard's Record," pp. 452–455; and Frederick W. Gookin, *Daniel Gookin: Assistant and Major General of the Massachusetts Bay Company* (Chicago: Lakeside Press, 1912), pp. 78–79.
41. Gookin, *Historical Collections*, p. 203; and RMB 4(2): 199. Gookin was elected an assistant in 1658 and 1659 even though he was in England.
42. For Southertown, see Gookin, *Daniel Gookin,* pp. 111–114; Sainsbury et al., eds., *Calendar of State Papers,* 5 (1661–1668): 345; and RMB 4(1): 353. For Nashobah, see RMB 4(2): 282, 315–316, 388; for Worcester, see Lincoln, *History of Worcester,* pp. 13–14, 303–304; and for Okommakamesit, see RMB 5:216–217.
43. Gookin in RCP 10:381–382, and in *Historical Collections*, pp. 177–179; and "Eliot's Letters to Boyle," p. 185. Two of Gookin's warrants (mss. 329 and

614 in the Ayer Collection, Newberry Library) are printed in Norman Lewis, "English Missionary Interest in the Indians of North America, 1578–1700" (Ph.D. diss., University of Washington, 1968), pp. 276, 427–428.

44. Gookin in *Historical Collections*, pp. 154, 177, 192, and in RCP 10:382. For alcohol abuse, see "Letters of the Rev. John Eliot," p. 295; Eliot in *Brief Narrative*, p. 6; and Gookin, *Historical Collections*, pp. 188, 191, 194. Tithing was the only form of taxation imposed on praying Indians; they were not rated by the colony.

45. Gookin in *Historical Collections*, pp. 184, 186, 188, 192, and in MHSC 1:6 (1799): 199. Given the frequent absence of Gookin and Eliot, it is hard to agree with Jennings that "the mission Indians were kept under tight controls from the very beginning." *Invasion of America*, p. 240n. For a fuller argument against Jennings on this point, see Brenner, "To Pray or To Be Prey," pp. 140–148.

46. For a survey of the laws regarding trade and other matters, see Kawashima, *Puritan Justice and the Indian*, pp. 76–82.

47. For examples of minor civil actions, see RMB 3:386, 4(1): 228, and MSA 30:129, 129a; and for Samuel, see Noble and Cronin, eds., *Records of the Court of Assistants*, 3:210. My judgment about the paucity of prewar civil and criminal cases involving known Christian Indians is based on the following sources: *Records of the Court of Assistants*; RMB; MSA 30; Dow, ed., *Records and Files of the Quarterly Courts of Essex County*; Joseph H. Smith, ed., *Colonial Justice in Western Massachusetts (1639–1702): The Pynchon Court Record* (Cambridge: Harvard University Press, 1961); Morison et al., eds., *Records of the Suffolk County Court*; the folio index cards to the Middlesex County Court records in the MSA; *Old Norfolk County Records, 1648–1681*, in *Essex Antiquarian* 1–13 (1897–1909), and in *Essex Institute Historical Collections* 56–68 (1920–1932) and 70 (1934); and *The Notarial Records of William Aspinwall, 1644–1651*, in *Boston Records* 32 (1903). The surviving manuscript and printed sources rarely indicate whether or not a given Indian was Christian. For this reason, it would be difficult if not impossible to determine how the colony's court system treated praying Indians relative to pagan ones in civil and criminal actions, and how it treated proselytes relative to colonists.

48. Chapter 5, notes 1, 8, 10–11, and Chapter 6, notes 2, 6, 10, 14, 17 (praying town land); and Chapter 3, note 24, and Chapter 6, notes 33–34, 40–41 (protection).

49. "Petition of Rev. John Eliot" (1675), in RCP 10:451–453. For Plymouth's policy, see Easton, "Relacion of the Indyan Warre," p. 13; [Saltonstall], *Present State of New-England With Respect to the Indian War*, pp. 30, 34; and RCP 5:173.

50. For Massachusetts Bay, see Almon Wheeler Lauber, *Indian Slavery in Colonial Times within the Present Limits of the United States* (1913; reprint ed.

New York: AMS Press, 1969), pp. 109, 126; for Joseph, see Gookin, *Historical Account,* p. 449; and for Tangier, see "Eliot's Letters to Boyle," p. 183.
51. Jennings, *Invasion of America,* p. 249; Salisbury, "Religious Encounters," p. 507; Axtell, *Invasion Within,* pp. 138–147, and "Were Indian Conversions Bona Fide?" in *After Columbus,* pp. 101–102 (quotation on p. 101); and Vaughan, *New England Frontier,* "Introduction to Second Edition," xviii, xxxiii–xxxv (quotation on p. xxxv), and "Introduction to the Third Edition," lv–lix.
52. Salisbury, "Indians and Colonists," p. 84. Two of Salisbury's citations are for actions that took place before the birth of the mission: MSA 30:15, and RMB 2:159/3:73. A third, which he lists as "MHS photostats 6, May 21, 1646," is evidently a misprint for the Eliot-Gookin petition, dated May 21, 1656, that asked the General Court to enlarge Wamesit's boundaries. See Chapter 6, note 17. Two other citations (*Suffolk Deeds* 1:93, 205) are for sales in 1648 and 1652 by Indians not known to be part of the mission at the time, Cato and Sagamore George. A sixth, Hurd, ed., *History of Middlesex County,* [3]:609, is for a 1656 sale by Captain Josiah and several other Christian Indians of land south of Sudbury. The transaction involved only ten acres. The seventh is Drake, *Aboriginal Races,* pp. 108–109, which covers various deeds signed by Josias Wompatuck, most of them after his apostasy. Furthermore, Salisbury does not explain that these actions (with the exception of the misdated one) pertained to sales of land by natives. The actions were not seizures of praying Indian land, if such is the impression that he wishes to convey to readers.
53. For discussions of Puritan justifications for occupying Indian land, see Salisbury, *Manitou and Providence,* pp. 190–202; and Patricia Seed, *Ceremonies of Possession in Europe's Conquest of the New World, 1492–1640* (New York: Cambridge University Press, 1995), pp. 16–40. For the meaning of "possession" and "improvement" in Puritan legal theory, see James Warren Springer, "American Indians and the Law of Real Property in Colonial New England," *American Journal of Legal History* 30 (1986), pp. 45–46. The four pre-emigration justifications were repeated after settlement began. For a later instance of the argument from epidemic disease, which was updated to take into account the smallpox contagion of the 1630s, see Winthrop, Sr., in WP 3:172; for a post-emigration example of the justification from the scriptural passages in question, see RMB 3:282, 4(1): 101; for citations of the argument from the charter, see Gookin, *Historical Collections,* p. 179, and Winthrop, Sr., in WP 4:101; and for later appeals to *vacuum domicilium,* see Cotton, "Reply to Mr. Williams," p. 46, and Winthrop, Sr., in WP 4:101. As far as I can determine, the pre-emigration argument most relevant to the mission, the "spirituals for temporals" one (see Chapter 1, note 6), was never advanced by any Bay Puritan after colonization began.
54. RMB 3:281–282, 4(1): 100–101. Jennings writes, "In legal theory at the time

[that is, prior to the arrival of the royal commissioners in the mid-1660s], no Indian in the colony's jurisdiction had clear title to as much as an acre until the General Court made its minuscule restitution of reservation land." *Invasion of America,* p. 243 (see also p. 286). This statement does not accurately represent Puritan legal theory, which acknowledged that Indians had right to lands they "possessed" or had "improved." Moreover, there were many instances prior to the arrival of the royal commissioners when pagan and Christian Indians sold fresh land to colonists or received retroactive payments for land donated to or occupied by the English during the early settlement period.

55. The deed is printed in Charles Hudson, *History of the Town of Marlborough* (Boston: T. R. Marvin and Son, 1862), pp. 40–41.
56. Trask et al., eds., *Suffolk Deeds,* 6:288–289. For a discussion of the postwar sales, see O'Brien, *Dispossession by Degrees,* pp. 65–90.
57. "Letters of John Eliot," p. 248; and Bowden and Ronda, eds., *John Eliot's Indian Dialogues,* p. 60. For the composition of *Indian Dialogues,* see "Letters of John Eliot," p. 249. I have found no indication that the Commissioners acted on either of Eliot's requests.
58. Eliot in MHSC 5:1 (1871): 425. I know of no evidence that Denison or anyone else subsequently chose to "plead the Indians' cause." For seventeenth-century defenses of Plymouth's land policy, see Hubbard, *Present State of New-England,* 1:44, 56, 2:66; Mather, *Brief History of the Warr,* pp. 89, 145–146, 152; Josiah Winslow quoted in ibid., pp. 146–147; and [Saltonstall], *Present State of New-England With Respect to the Indian War,* p. 26. For twentieth-century ones, see Vaughan, *New England Frontier,* pp. 310–312, 351–352; David Bushnell, "The Treatment of the Indians in Plymouth Colony," NEQ 26 (1953): 210; and Ranlet, "Another Look at the Causes," p. 95.

Conclusion

1. Axtell, "Some Thoughts on the Ethnohistory of Missions," in *After Columbus,* p. 56.
2. Salisbury, "Red Puritans," pp. 28, 29, 50; and Guice, "Linguistic Work," pp. 8–15, 58–63, 99, 113, 124–126, 132, 138, 145, 188.
3. Wilson in *Strength out of Weaknesse,* p. 178; Gookin, *Historical Collections,* p. 152; and the Massachusetts council in MSA 30:127.
4. Williams, *A Key,* p. 228; and Ann Marie Plane, "'The Examination of Sarah Ahhaton': The Politics of Adultery in an Indian Town of Seventeenth-Century Massachusetts," in Peter Benes, ed., *Algonkians of New England: Past and Present* (Boston: Boston University Press, 1993), pp. 18–21.
5. See Chapter 5, note 6; and Chapter 6, note 56.
6. Eliot in *Strength out of Weaknesse,* p. 166, and in *Late and Further Manifestation,* p. 273; Gookin, *Historical Account,* p. 515; and Williams, *A Key,*

pp. 84, 144. For the two souls, see Crosby, "From Myth to History," p. 205n; and Bragdon, *Native People of Southern New England*, pp. 190–191. Eliot wrote and published *Dying Speeches* between the death of Owussumag, Sr., in the winter of 1684–85 and the visit of John Dunton in the summer of 1686. See RMB 5:531–532; and W. H. Whitmore, ed., *John Dunton's Letters from New England, 1686* (Boston: Publications of the Prince Society, 1867), p. 193.

7. For prayer, see Chapter 5, note 39; for Jesus the shaman, see Chapter 5, note 54; and for supernatural power, see Bowden, *American Indians and Christian Missions*, pp. 118–119.

8. Eliot, *Indian Grammar Begun*, p. 250; "Eliot's Letters to Boyle," p. 177; and William S. Simmons, "Cultural Bias in the New England Puritans' Perception of the Indians," WMQ 38 (1981): 68–69. I have not been able to determine if Eliot was correct about native music.

9. There is no evidence that Eliot knew that proselytes interred objects with corpses. For the exaggerated claim about the numbers of sachems who served as praying town rulers, see Chapter 6, note 58; for the Natick gravesites, see Brenner, "Strategies for Autonomy," pp. 229–233, 290–292; for the Punkapoag cemetery, see the summary of Brona Simon's research in Brenda J. Baker, "Pilgrim's Progress and Praying Indians: The Biocultural Consequences of Contact in Southern New England," in Clark Spencer Larsen and George R. Milner, eds., *In the Wake of Contact: Biological Responses to Conquest* (New York: Wiley-Liss, 1994), pp. 39, 42–43; and for Hassanamesit, see Frederick C. Pierce, *History of Grafton, Worcester County, Massachusetts* (Worcester: Charles Hamilton, 1879), p. 318. Experts are not in agreement about the meaning of grave goods in pre- and postcontact society. For a review of recent literature, see Bragdon, *Native People of Southern New England*, pp. 236–247.

10. Gookin, *Historical Collections*, p. 162.

11. Scholars recognize that by 1646 the Indians in eastern Massachusetts had lost much of their land, their economic independence, and their political autonomy. As Salisbury has written in a representative passage, "by the time Eliot began preaching to a group of Indians, the group had typically . . . sold or otherwise lost much of its land under the incessant pressure of English immigration; it had become economically dependent on the English; and it had submitted to the political authority of the colonial government." Salisbury and other historians rightly include these anterior conditions among the reasons why Eliot was able to establish a foothold among the natives along the coast. But scholars have tended to overlook these conditions when assessing the impact of the mission, as though the praying Indians had managed to retain their land and their economic and political autonomy until the Apostle began his work. For example, despite what he says in the quotation given above, Salisbury brands the Indian work a tool of expansion, chides the mission for supplying colonists with native laborers, and claims that Eliot's

program "suddenly destroyed" the Indians' traditional "legal mechanisms." See his "Red Puritans," pp. 33, 35, and "Indians and Colonists," p. 84.
12. The Indians' letter is in Ford, ed., *Some Correspondence,* pp. 74–76. For Gookin, Jr., see Kellaway, *New England Company,* pp. 120, 236–237. My judgment about authorship of the letter is based on a comparison of the hand that composed it with the signatures in the manuscript photocopy of the letter in the New York Public Library, catalogued under Eliot, "Personal Mss. (misc.)."
13. Michael Wigglesworth, "God's Controversy with New-England" (1662), in MHSP 12 (1871–1873): 84; Cotton Mather, *India Christiana* (Boston, 1721), p. 29; and Eliot in Eames, ed., *John Eliot and the Indians,* p. 21. For Eliot's three lists of reasons for beginning the mission, see "Learned Conjectures," p. 26 (mispaginated 18); *Indian Grammar Begun,* p. 312; and Gookin, *Historical Collections,* p. 170. For the figure of the wild man, see Vaughan, "Early English Paradigms," pp. 35–38.
14. Axtell, *Invasion Within,* p. 135; and RMB 2:178. For Eliot's use of "train up," see *Strength out of Weaknesse,* p. 170; Eames, ed., *John Eliot and the Indians,* p. 8; "Letters of John Eliot," p. 248; "From Natick in New-England," p. 1091; "Account of Indian Churches," p. 128; *Late and Further Manifestation,* p. 285; and *Brief Narrative,* p. 3. The Apostle apparently used the phrase "furbish up" only once, in the letter to Hanmer cited in the previous note. Vaughan has noted another problem with Axtell's well-known observation: in the seventeenth century, the word "reduce" did not mean "bring down" but "bring" or "bring back." Vaughan, review of *Invasion Within,* WMQ 43 (1986): 663; and *The Oxford English Dictionary* (2nd ed. Oxford: Clarendon Press, 1989), 13:431–433.
15. The classic examples of "Indianizers" were Thomas Morton at Merry Mount (Mount Wollaston, Quincy) and Joshua Tift (Tefft), who married a Pokanoket, fought on the Indian side in King Philip's War, and was hanged and then drawn and quartered by Rhode Island in 1676. For a recent discussion of the Puritan fear of "Indianism," see Canup, *Out of the Wilderness,* pp. 88–172.
16. Reiner Smolinski, "*Israel Redivivus:* The Eschatological Limits of Puritan Typology in New England," NEQ 63 (1990): 357–396. For Bercovitch and Bozeman, see Chapter 1, note 19; and for Johnson, see Chapter 4, note 31. Smolinski determines that Samuel Sewall was the only prominent second- or third-generation colonist who believed that the millennium could begin in the New World (pp. 378–480). An advocate of the lost tribes theory, Sewall thought that Mexico City—not Boston—would be the inaugural location because the settlement of Sephardic Jews in the region provided an opportunity for the reunion of Israel and Judah in the capital of the Antichrist's American empire. Although Smolinski does not note the point, Sewall credited Eliot with first recognizing the importance of the Indians in an argument for a distinctively American millennium. For Mexico City, see "The Letter-

Book of Samuel Sewall," in MHSC 6:1 (1886): 178, and 6:2 (1888): 272–273; and Sewall, *Phaenomena*, p. 8. For the lost tribes and Sewall's acknowledged debt to Eliot, see ibid., pp. A2, 2, 4, 34–35; and "Letter-Book," 1:176–177.

Appendix 1

1. For lecturing on all twenty-two chapters, see Samuel Whiting, "Concerning the Life of the Famous Mr. Cotton," in Young, ed., *Chronicles of the First Planters*, p. 429; for Revelation 4, see George Selement, "John Cotton's Hidden Antinomianism: His Sermon on Revelation 4:1–2," NEHGR 129 (1975): 282; and for Revelation 13, see Thomas Allen, "To the Reader," in Cotton, *An Exposition*. John Winthrop's journal contains a reference, under a spring 1641 date, to Cotton's lecture on Revelation 15:8. WJ 2:30. This entry reads like a later insertion of Winthrop's; moreover, it is unlikely that Cotton needed over a year to advance from Revelation 13 to Revelation 15.
2. [John Humphrey], "To the Christian Reader," in Cotton, *Powring Out*, p. A2; WJ 2:69–70; Maclear, "New England and the Fifth Monarchy," pp. 250, 253; Selement, "John Cotton's Hidden Antinomianism," pp. 278–294; and Sewall, *Phaenomena*, pp. 29–30, 52–53.
3. For the dating of the English lectures on Canticles, see Ann Kibbey, *The Interpretation of Material Shapes in Puritanism: A Study of Rhetoric, Prejudice, and Violence* (New York: Cambridge University Press, 1986), pp. 150–151; and for the dating of the American lectures, see Bozeman, *To Live Ancient Lives*, p. 251.

Index

Abenakis, Eastern, 148–153
Advancement of learning, 98, 101
Affective model, 5–6, 18, 19–20, 22, 40, 51, 181, 186–187
"Aged sachem" at Quobagud, 62, 64, 154, 158
Ahawton, 56, 106, 141, 230
Ahawton, Sarah, 116, 117, 230, 242
Ahawton, William, 106, 116, 142, 198, 200, 201–203, 246
Alcohol, 60, 116–117, 125, 156, 157, 160, 226, 229, 230
Allin, John, 40, 41, 47, 72, 110, 113, 127, 134
American exceptionalism, 248–249
Anaweakin, 142
Anderson, Virginia, 107
Anian, Straits of, 84, 271n26
Anongaich, 60–61
Anthony, 58, 74, 75, 180, 243; as teacher, 124–125; as prospective church member, 126, 132, 133; family, 132; and Metacom, 198, 200, 201–203
Apprenticeships, 58, 119, 167–168, 246
Armageddon, 12, 80, 85, 191, 287n17
Armine, Lady Mary, 69, 70, 124, 178, 179
Arnold, William and Benedict, 23, 24, 27
Ashurst, Henry, 209, 213, 215
Aspinwall, William, 82, 114, 251, 284n1
Atherton, Humphrey, 140, 196, 225, 226
Attawans, 58, 59, 64, 112, 145

Attawans, John, Sr., 145
Auquontis, 65, 187, 188
Awinian, William, 142
Axtell, James, 6, 57, 73, 219, 240, 246, 247–248; on Eliot, 205, 233

Baillie, Robert, 67–68
Baxter, Richard, 98, 99, 137–138, 208; translated, by Eliot, 122
Bayly, Lewis: *Practice of Piety*, translated, 122, 217
Beckom, Simon, 147, 153
Ben Israel, Menasseh, 84–85, 86, 89
Bercovitch, Sacvan, 248, 269n19
Bible: knowledge of, by Indians, 61, 119, 124, 125, 128, 135; translations of, by Eliot, 115, 120–121, 124, 161, 195–196, 212, 213, 217
Black James, 156, 157, 162, 163, 175, 237, 243
Blackleech, John, 183
Blasphemy, 28, 29, 42–43, 58, 224
Blinman, Richard, 182
Bourne, Richard, 194, 218
Boyle, Robert: as corporation governor, 122, 123, 150, 192, 208, 209, 212, 217; as benefactor to mission, 124, 214, 223
Bozeman, Dwight, 2, 45, 248; on Cotton, 10–12, 13; on Eliot, 76–77, 79, 94–95, 114, 284n7

324 · Index

Bradstreet, Simon, 46, 111, 209, 216, 231, 293n18
Bragdon, Kathleen, 118, 119, 121, 177
Brenner, Elise, 58, 281n29, 291n6, 316n45
Brightman, Thomas, 10–11, 271n27
Broughton, Hugh, 85
Brown, Edmund, 20, 170
Brown, James, 202–203
Burial practices, 58, 73, 174, 244

Canonicus, 23, 27, 34, 155
Captain Josiah, 145, 229
Captain Tom, 61, 75, 105, 142, 143, 155, 280n20; as ruler, 116, 156, 162, 163, 168, 229; as prospective church member, 126, 132, 133; family, 132, 161; and King Philip's War, 161
Carpentry, 58, 71, 107, 167, 179, 225
Carr, Robert, 187–188
Catechism: oral, of Indians, 61, 71, 125, 130, 136; manuscript, by Eliot, 118, 119, 128; written, by Pierson and by Thomas James, 185–186
Ceci, Lynn, 209
Chabanakongkomun, 155, 157, 164, 169
Charles I, execution of, 76, 95, 114; Eliot on, 77, 79–80, 82–83, 91, 173, 190, 191; Cotton on, 81–82
Charles II, restoration of, 96, 115; Eliot on, 96, 99–100, 102, 115, 191–192, 288n32
Charleton, Walter, 100–101
Chauncy, Charles, 217, 222
Cheeschaumuck, Caleb, 134, 222
Chickataubut, 31, 32, 110
Christian Commonwealth, 76–81, 95, 96, 113, 114–115, 190, 191
Christian Covenanting Confession, 123
Church: admission into, in Massachusetts Bay, 9, 126–127, 131; apostolic, 11, 13, 16–17, 81; procedures for formation of, in Massachusetts Bay, 133–134
Civility, 17, 41, 71, 118, 140, 234, 237, 247; defined, 6–7
Cloth and clothing, English, 58, 68, 107, 178, 210, 211, 215, 241
Cohen, Charles, 74–75, 132, 135, 138
Commissioners, royal, 115, 141, 187–188, 205, 228, 318n54
Commissioners for Indian Affairs, 210, 223
Commissioners of the United Colonies, 71, 209; and Mohegans, 29, 35, 60–61, 65, 159; and Rhode Island Indians, 29, 41, 120, 189–190, 192, 226; and Massachusett and Pawtucket Indians, 35, 41, 59; and New England Company, 70, 209–212, 215–216; and Eliot, 107, 115, 120, 150, 178–180, 204, 212–215, 225, 237–238; and New France, 148–149; misuse of corporation funds and property by, 211, 212, 217, 221, 223
Communion of Churches, 98–99, 101–102
Congregationalism: as millennial form of organization, 13, 78, 92, 95, 98; as missionary obstacle, 21–22, 67–68, 99. *See also* Independency
Constables, 116, 117, 156, 160, 168
Conversion: defined, 6, 9; Indians' progress toward, 72–73, 92, 97, 126, 129, 131
Corlet, Elijah, 179, 219, 221, 222
Cotton, John, 30, 47, 48, 210, 234; missionary theology, 2, 3, 4, 16–17, 18, 20, 42–43, 68, 248; Revelation and Canticles lectures, 9–10, 251–252; and Eliot's eschatology, 9, 12, 18, 76–77, 78, 81, 99–100, 289n37; political views, 14, 77, 81–82, 99; and Natick, 112–113, 127. *See also* Jews-then-Gentiles sequence
Cotton, John, Jr., 141, 177, 194, 195, 204, 214, 237
Cradock, Matthew, 1, 5, 7, 69
Cromwell, Oliver, 82, 83, 96, 288n29, 308n34; Eliot's preface to, 92–93, 94, 95, 96, 97
Crosby, Constance, 58
Cutshamekin: relations with Massachusetts Bay, 30–39; family, 31, 54–55, 56, 72; land sales by, 32, 57, 199; and other Indian groups, 34–35, 37, 38–39, 41, 63–64, 188–189; and Eliot's mission, 40–41, 43, 51, 54–56, 64, 73, 91, 106, 112–113, 178, 198–199

Danforth, Samuel, 46, 130
Danforth, Samuel, Jr., 195
Danforth, Thomas, 210, 215, 293n18
Day, Gordon, 149
Delbanco, Andrew, 2
DeMontezinos, Antonio, 84
Denison, Daniel, 47, 210
Denison, George, 47, 238

Discipline, 54–55, 55–56, 61, 72, 74, 117, 131, 136, 199
Disease: smallpox (1633–34), 19, 32, 36, 132, 317n53; "plague" (1616–1619), 31–32, 36, 132, 234, 274n14; sciatica, 120, 124, 131, 225; smallpox (1649, 1652), 132; dysentery, 132; tuberculosis, 132, 219; Christian Indian interpretation of, 132, 243; kidney stones, 142; on Martha's Vineyard, 173–174
Druillettes, Gabriel, 148–149
Dry bones, 84, 86, 89, 103
Dudley, Thomas, 32, 36, 46, 47
Duke William (Black William), 19
Dunster, Henry, 4, 8, 57, 69, 216, 219, 220
Dury, John, 67, 68, 72, 83–85, 86
Dying Speeches, 242–243

Easton, John, 197, 200, 204–206
Economic activity, among proselytes, 71, 167–168, 245, 246
Eleazar, 222
Eliot, Francis, 45, 179, 225
Eliot, John: nonmissionary biography, 2, 45–47, 48–49, 213, 313n24; conventional missionary objectives, 4–5, 6–7, 53–54, 65, 71–73, 97, 104, 107–108, 117, 129, 131, 237, 240–243, 246; protects natives from marauders, 37–38, 63–64, 155–156, 159, 231; family, 46, 47–48, 314n31; language study and language ability, 49, 50–51, 119, 123, 127, 241, 247; general attitudes about Indians, 49, 91–92, 171, 247–249; petitions for magisterial supervision of the mission, 59–60, 224–225; visitation schedule, 61, 124, 145; plans for central praying town, 65–66, 75, 103, 105; full-time Indian ministry, 65–66, 137–138, 169, 248; Massachusett-language works, 68, 119–122, 154, 180, 183, 185, 196, 213, 214, 217–219, 260; as apologist and fund-raiser, 68–69, 170, 213; petitions for creating, defending, or enlarging praying towns, 105, 109–111, 140–141, 142, 143–144, 145, 146, 159, 231, 298n8; toleration of traditional native culture, 108, 243–244; complaints about clerical participation in the mission, 169–170, 231; aids or encourages other English missionaries, 178, 183, 184, 186, 194; defends Indian land outside Massachusetts Bay, 187–188, 237–238; petition against slavery, 232–233, 239
Eliot, John, Jr., 47–48, 132, 133, 134, 142, 169, 179, 198, 237
Eliot, Joseph, 48, 169, 179
Eliot tracts, 52, 67–69, 189, 248; publication of, 66–67, 92, 113, 131, 132, 133, 169, 207–208
Endecott, John, 1, 34, 113, 216

Fast days, fasting, 112, 125, 131–132
Fifth Monarchy eschatology, 82–83, 96, 114–115
Fitch, James, 182, 184, 212
Floyd, Richard, 209
Folger, Peter, 134, 179, 222
Fur trade, 32, 36, 148, 149, 230, 246

Gambling, 58, 72, 128
Gender roles, gender identity, 53–54, 107, 117–118, 119, 125, 242
Gentiles: conversion of, 14–16; Indians as, 15–16, 84, 97; Indians as, for Eliot, 18, 85, 87, 88–89, 90, 102. *See also* Jews-then-Gentiles sequence
George (Massachusett Indian), 60
Glover, Habbakuk, 47, 142, 170
Goddard, Ives, 119, 121
Gookin, Daniel, 107–108, 116, 241, 247, 289n33; early involvement in mission, 41, 226–227; duties as Superintendent, 117, 168, 228–229; visits to praying Indians, 147–148, 153–154, 156, 157, 158; absence from praying towns, 162, 229; holdings in Indian land, 164, 227, 228; salary, 214, 227; biography, 226–228
Gookin, Daniel, Jr., 214, 246
Gorton, Samuel, 24, 187; and Massachusetts Bay, 27, 29, 43–44, 191; and Warwick Commission, 29–30, 44; and Eliot, 45, 187–188, 188–189
Green, Samuel, 119, 216, 217
Grooming, 6, 53–54, 58, 128, 176, 241
Guice, Stephen, 119, 121, 123–124, 241
Guns: legislative restrictions upon Indian possession of, 33, 150, 230, 275n16; disarmings of Indians, 34, 37, 150, 162,

Guns (*cont.*)
200–201; distributions of, to Eliot and/or Gookin, 149–150, 215; shipments of, for auction, 211
Gura, Philip, 94

Hanmer, Jonathan, 213
Harvard College, 60, 110, 216; and the mission, 4, 8, 68, 69, 70, 119, 196, 217, 219. *See also* Indian College
Hassanamesit, 142, 152, 161, 164, 167, 235, 244; church at, 102, 142–143
Heath, Isaac, 41, 71, 130
Hiacoomes, 172–177
Hiacoomes, Joel, 134, 222
Higginson, Francis, 1, 248
Holden, Randall, 29, 44, 45, 51
Holstun, James, 94, 111, 114, 129, 284n1
Hooker, Thomas, 45, 48, 183
"How can I walk with God all the day long?", 121
Husbandry, English, 33, 58, 71, 106–107, 167, 192, 225, 229, 242

Idolatry, 42–43, 58, 134, 146, 156, 160, 224, 229, 242
Immortality of the soul, 243
Ince, Jonathan, 169, 177, 227
Independency, Independents, in England, 66, 67, 207, 209; Cotton on, 81–82, 289n37; Eliot on, 99, 102
Indian College, 216, 219–223
Indian Dialogues, 56, 57, 73, 125, 170, 175–176, 198–200, 215, 219, 238
Indian Grammar Begun, 123
Indian Primer, 119–120, 218, 219
"Instructions from the Church at Natick to William and Anthony," 201–204, 238, 239

Jackson, Edward, 71, 73
James, Thomas, 186
James the Printer, 119, 142, 158, 219, 246; and King Philip's War, 144, 161
Japheth, 80, 81, 83
Jennings, Francis, 50, 54, 197–198, 209, 223, 276n29, 316n45, 317n54; on Eliot's motives, 3, 49, 178, 233, 309n43; on submissions of 1644, 31, 35; on blasphemy and idolatry laws, 42–43; on birth of mission, 44–45, 281n32; on King Philip's War, 162–163, 204

Jerusalem. *See* Palestine
Jessey, Henry, 207, 213
Jethro, Peter, 153, 160, 161
Jews: conversion of, 13, 80, 81; readmission of, into England, 81. *See also* Jews-then-Gentiles sequence
Jews-then-Gentiles sequence, 15–16, 18, 21, 22, 49, 51, 72–73, 89–90, 273n38, 288n24
Johnson, Edward, 95, 114, 249
Johnson, Marmaduke, 214, 216, 217, 228
Joktan. *See* Gentiles, Indians as
Joseph (brother of Sampson), 142, 157, 161
Josselyn, John, 167, 248

Kattananit, Job, 143, 145, 155, 161
Keayne, Robert, 71, 110
Kellaway, William, 68, 70, 213, 215, 221, 222, 223
King Philip. *See* Metacom
King Philip's War: praying Indians during and after, 147, 160–162, 196, 237, 246–247; enslavement of Indian captives, 161, 232–233, 239; causes of Nipmuck belligerence, 162–165; causes of Pokanoket belligerence, 162, 200, 204–206; Eliot's attempts to prevent and end, 200–204, 238–239

LaFantasie, Glenn, 190
Land: loss of, by coastal Indians, 32–33, 56–57, 59, 141–142, 236; Bay Colony's policy toward, 32, 33, 109, 110, 230; native views of, 34, 35; mission and Indian loss of, 233–239; Puritan theory about native rights to, 234, 236–237
Language: choice of, for Indian instruction, 8, 117–118, 144, 195–196, 219; as obstacle to missionary work, 21, 27, 75, 169, 183; Massachusett, compared to Indo-European languages, 50–51, 121, 123; and legal proceedings, 60, 229; Hebrew, 87, 100–101, 287n18; universal, 98, 100–101
Larnell, Benjamin, 222–223
Law: biblical, 7, 14, 78, 80, 83, 92; English, 24, 44, 78, 79, 83; Mosaic, vestiges of, in Indian cultures, 85, 86, 87, 287n18; codes of, at Neponset, Nonantum, and Musketaquid, 41, 52–54, 58, 279n7

"Learned Conjectures," 83, 86–90, 93, 94, 95–96, 97, 208, 248–249
Lechford, Thomas, 21, 67–68
Lepore, Jill, 205, 294n26
L'Estrange, Hamon, 96–97
Leveritch, William, 127, 194
Literacy: appeal of, to Indians, 57, 138, 197, 219; rate of, among Eliot's Indians, 118
Logick Primer, 123–124, 219
Lost tribes of Israel, 83–85; Eliot on, 81, 85–88, 89–90, 96–97, 103, 131
Lyne, John, 147, 153

Maanexit, 158, 164
MacCulloch, Susan, 305nn58,59
Maclear, James, 82, 94, 251, 284n1
Magunkog, 145, 161, 235
Magus, 75, 126
Mahican Indians, 148–153
Manchage, 155, 158, 164
Mandell, Daniel, 111
Martin, John Frederick, 228
Mascononomo, 30, 31, 32, 33, 35, 38, 59
Massachusetts Bay Colony, 1–2; charter, 2, 3, 5, 25, 43, 114, 170, 181, 234, 239, 247; missionary legislation, 18–19, 39, 41–44, 51, 59–60, 140, 230, 234, 272n32, 276n35; covets Narragansett Country, 23, 25–26, 28, 30, 228; accepts Indian submissions, 27–28, 30, 37, 154, 155–156, 224; diplomatic use of Eliot's mission, 30, 43–45, 51, 115, 228; non-missionary legislation for Indians, 32, 33, 60, 150, 230, 234; ecclesiastical controversies, 47, 81, 99; and missionary financing, 68–69, 70, 71, 208–209, 210, 219; censures Eliot's radicalism, 114–115; exercise of judicial jurisdiction over Christian Indians, 59–60, 116, 224–231; and Mohawks, 148, 149, 241; and Metacom, 203–204
Massasoit, 37, 64–65, 196, 205; family, 281n26
Massawomack Indians, 180
Mather, Cotton, 47, 103, 210, 247
Mather, Increase, 210, 248
Mather, Richard, 3, 22, 47, 48, 129; and Eliot's mission, 40, 72, 92, 127, 129, 138, 208
Matoonas, 157, 161, 164, 311n57
Mattaumpe, 161, 164

Mayhew, Experience, 177, 194, 196
Mayhew, Thomas, 172, 177, 179, 180, 195
Mayhew, Thomas, Jr., 67, 92, 181, 204, 205, 227; personal relations with Eliot, 120, 127, 130, 178; methods, compared to Eliot's, 172–173, 175–176, 244; compensation, 178–180; family, 177, 179
Medicine: Indian, 64, 173–174, 175–176, 241; English, 68, 101, 173–174, 180, 210
Metacom, 155, 196–206
Miantonomi, 23, 24, 27, 28–29, 31, 34–35
Middle Advent, 11, 13, 16, 17, 76, 79, 81, 95, 97, 113
Millennium: Eliot on, in general, 4, 75, 103–104, 117, 129–130, 248–249, 284n3; English Puritan views about, 10; Cotton on, 10–15, 75, 80–82; exaggerated significance of, in American Puritan scholarship, 11–12, 13, 94–95, 248–249; civil order of, for Eliot, 77–79, 96, 98, 101–102, 113–114, 115, 168; ecclesiastical order of, for Eliot, 78, 92, 98–99; legal order of, for Eliot, 78, 79, 288n28; imminence of, in England, for Eliot, 79–81, 83, 90, 91–92; imminence of, among Indians, for Eliot, 88–94; disintegration of Eliot's Interregnum views about, 96–97; Eliot's vision of, after Restoration, 97–103; defined, 269n17
Miner, Kenneth, 119, 121, 123, 124
Minor, John, 181–182
Missionaries, Eliot's native, 61–62, 148, 154–155, 156, 158, 160, 169, 170, 188–189, 190–191, 198–199
Missionaries, English (exclusive of Eliot): on Martha's Vineyard, Nantucket, and Chappaquiddick, 172–175, 177; in Connecticut, 181–184; in New Haven and on Long Island, 184–186; in Plymouth, 194–195, 204
Missionary work: place of, in royal and proprietary charters, 2, 24, 181, 186–187; Bay colonists' general attitudes toward, 2–4, 51, 170–171, 215, 231, 246, 249, 273n38; delay of, in Massachusetts Bay, 18–22
Mohawk Indians, 184; harass Indians in Massachusetts Bay, 145, 149, 152, 153, 167; Algonquian-French alliance against, 148–153

Mohegan Indians, 28–29, 34, 63; and Christianity, 64–65, 183–184, 186, 189, 190, 193; and praying Indians, 157–158, 159, 164, 205
Monequasson, 54, 57, 74, 106, 119, 131, 132; as teacher, 118, 124; as prospective church member, 126, 127, 128
Monoco, 152, 160, 161
Monotunkquanit, 61, 105, 133, 142, 156
Morison, Samuel Eliot, 48, 221
Morrison, Dane, 109
Morton, Thomas, 36, 248, 320n15
Moseley, Samuel, 144, 300n11
Mouche benefaction, 184, 212
Music, 125, 243
Musketaquid, Musketaquid Indians, 58–59, 66, 71, 145, 236
Mystic George, 147

Naeher, Robert James, 125–126
Narragansett Indians, 37, 41, 151; and Christianity, 65, 186, 187–193; and Quantisset Indians, 155–156, 193. *See also* Canonicus, Miantonomi
Nash, Gary, 18
Nashaway, Eliot's mission at, 152, 158, 159–160, 163, 176, 235. *See also* Nashowanon
Nashobah, 59, 112, 142, 144–145, 152, 228, 236
Nashowanon, 30, 36, 37–38, 164, 231; and Eliot, 62, 63, 64
Natick, 164, 225, 246–247; founding of, 66, 75, 105–106; eschatological meaning of, 90–95, 97, 113–114; boundaries and boundary disputes, 105, 108–111, 226, 230, 231; English buildings in, 106, 107, 113; size and population of, 110, 111; civil government of, 111–113, 116–117, 229–230; church at, 123, 136–137, 246; religious instruction, devotions, and worship in, 124–126; evaluation of conversion narratives (1652), 126–129; doctrinal examination (1654), 130–131; fast-day exhortations (1658), 131–132, 180; evaluation of conversion narratives (1659), 132–136, 180; nonresident church members, 137, 142, 168
Nauset Indians, 65, 193–195
Nehemiah, 161, 162, 243
Neponset Indians, 66, 140, 150, 259; Eliot's first sermon to, 20, 40–41, 44–45, 49–50, 51; growth of mission among, 54–58, 61, 71–75; and Natick, 105–106
Nesutan, Job, 118, 119, 124, 127, 214
New England Company: charters and official names, 70, 208, 220; and United Colonies, 70, 209–212; shipments of goods by, 107, 210–211, 214; payments for Eliot's Algonquian and English-language missionary works, 119, 212, 213, 215, 216–219; fund-raising and investments, 207, 208, 209, 212; bills and rates of exchange, 211–212
New Englands First Fruits, 4, 6, 7, 19–20, 21, 25
New Netherland, 130, 177, 189, 211
Niantics, Eastern, 151, 193; and First Great Awakening, 186. *See also* Ninigret
Nicolls, Ferdinando, 213, 284n1
Ninigret, 65, 130, 155, 197; and Eliot, 188, 189–192; and Winthrop, Jr., 192–193
Nipmuck Country: English towns in, 162, 164, 235; postwar land sales in, 237
Nipmuck Indians: submissions to Massachusetts Bay, 36, 155–156; early interest of, in the mission, 61, 62–64, 66, 154; raids against, 63–64, 152, 154, 155, 159; in old and new praying towns, 138–139, 142, 145, 156–158, 165; and King Philip's War, 160–165
Nishohkou, 112, 124, 132, 280n20; as prospective church member, 126, 129, 132, 133, 134
Nonantum Indians, 66, 176, 259; Eliot's first sermon to, 41, 49–50, 51; growth of mission among, 52–58, 61, 71–75; and Natick, 66, 105
Nookau, 126
Nowell, Increase, 2, 43, 160
Numphow, 147, 149, 151
Numphow, Samuel, 147, 153

Okommakamesit, Okommakamesit Indians, 142, 143, 228; boundary dispute with Marlborough, 143–144, 164, 183, 230, 236
Old Jacob, 128, 243
Old Jethro, 161, 164
"Our Indians' A B C," 123, 215, 219
Owussumag, 61, 105, 126, 143, 236
Owussumag, John, Sr., 243, 280n20

Pakachoog, 157, 164
Palestine, 13, 14, 80, 85, 88, 99, 102
Pantucket, 65–66, 148–153, 176. *See also* Passaconaway; Wannalancett
Parke, William, 71, 214
Parliaments, 25, 70, 82, 83, 100, 115, 188, 220, 281n31
Passaconaway, 30, 36–37, 38–39; and Eliot, 62, 64, 146, 147
Pawtucket Indians, 59, 165; and Massachusetts Bay, 30–36
Pawtuxet. *See* Sacononoco
Pelham, Herbert, 67, 209
Pelham, Nathaniel, 177, 227
Pennacook Indians, 65, 151, 148–153, 165. *See also* Passaconaway; Wannalancett
Pequot Indians, 34, 48–49, 149, 184, 219; and Christianity, 9, 19, 50, 182–183, 192
Petavit, 142, 143
Peter, 112, 126
Peter, Hugh, 2, 208, 215; as agent of Massachusetts Bay, 4, 25, 43, 69–70, 207
Pierron, Jean, 151, 153
Pierson, Abraham, 53, 120, 134, 184–186, 221–222
Piumbuhhou, 112, 116, 132, 143, 160, 293n13; as prospective church member, 132, 133, 134
Plane, Ann Marie, 242
Plymouth Colony, 23, 24, 39; and Pokanokets, 65, 197, 200–201, 202–203, 205–206; and Indian slavery, 232
Pocumtuck, Pocumtuck Indians, 62, 110, 148–153, 159
Podunk Indians, 183
Pokanoket Indians, 116, 152; and First Great Awakening, 186; and Eliot, 196–200, 201–206, 238–239. *See also* Massasoit; Metacom; Plymouth Colony
Polygamy, 58, 73–74, 241
Polytheism, 75, 134, 243
Pomham (Narragansett), 24, 27–28, 34, 35, 36; and Eliot, 187–188, 188–189
Pomham (Nipmuck), 145, 161, 162
Ponampam, 74, 75, 124, 132, 280n20; as prospective church member, 126, 127, 129, 133
Powwowing. *See* Idolatry
Powwows, 64; Eliot on, 64, 173, 175–176; Mayhew, Jr., on, 172–175
Praying towns (general): "old" and "new" defined, 140, 145, 158; populations of, 165, 168; locations of, 165–167, 235; rulers in, 168, 179, 225–226, 229–230, 244; churches in, 168, 242; teachers in, 168–169, 179, 214; and submissions to Massachusetts Bay, 224; dispossession of residents in, 235–236. *See also* Economic activity
Prentice, Thomas, 161, 226
Presbyterianism, Presbyterians, 66, 207, 209; Cotton on, 81–82, 289n37; Eliot on, 98, 99, 102
Presses, printing, 216–217
Primitivism, 11, 16–17, 45, 76, 77–78, 115
Prince, Thomas, 197, 201, 202, 203
Pummakummin, 154, 205
Punkapoag, Punkapoag Indians, 140–141, 142, 180, 225, 230, 236, 242, 244; and Natick, 105–106, 116; sales of land by, 108, 141–142, 164, 238
Putikookuppog, 158–159, 235
Pynchon, William, 2, 38, 46, 63–64, 149, 231

Quabag, Quabag Indians, 152, 164, 231, 235; and Eliot's mission, 37–38, 62–64, 158–159, 163
Quaiapen, 155, 163, 231
Quantisset, Quantisset Indians, 155–156, 156–157, 164, 193, 231

Ranlet, Philip, 162, 191, 310n55
Rawson, Edward, 46, 113, 210, 211
Rawson, Grindal, 122
Remonstrants, 44
Resurrection of the dead, 15, 76, 113, 243
Rhode Island Colony: charters of, 23, 26, 29, 186–187; residents' lack of missionary interest, 187, 193
Roman Catholicism, 7, 146, 177; destruction of, 12–13, 16, 80; alleged corruption of apostolic Christianity by, 13
Roxbury, church of, 46–47; and Natick church, 130, 133, 134, 136
Rumney Marsh, James, 153

Sabbath: observance of, enjoined upon Indians, 28, 58, 117, 121, 125, 156, 160, 183, 224, 226, 272n32, 276n35; violations of, by Indians, 56, 128, 198, 229; observance of, in praying towns, 72, 126

Sachem, office of, 33–34, 54, 56, 65, 245; Eliot's interpretation of, 55, 64–65, 91, 112, 157–158, 173, 190, 198–199, 205, 244
Sacononoco, 23, 27–28, 34–35, 36
Sagamore George, 31, 59
Sagamore James, 31, 32, 272n33
Sagamore John (Nipmuck), 157, 161, 164, 228
Sagamore John (Pawtucket), 19, 31, 32
Sagamore John (Pennacook), 147
Sagamore Matthew, 160, 164
Sagamore Sam, 160, 161, 164
Sakonnet Indians, 195, 200, 202
Salisbury, Neal, 32, 33; on diplomacy, 34–35, 149, 151, 274n12; on Eliot's mission, 54, 65, 119, 233, 240, 276n35, 281n31, 299n65, 319n11; on King Philip's War, 162
Sampson, 142, 143, 157, 161, 232
Samuel (son of Monotunkquanit), 124
Samuel (son of "William of Natick"), 230
Sassamon, John, 118, 119, 124, 196, 219, 294n26; and Metacom, 198, 201, 202, 205, 214–215
Schools: Massachusett-language, 57, 71, 117–118, 219; English dame and grammar, 57–58, 68, 71, 219
Second coming, 11, 15, 76, 113, 125
Sehr, Timothy, 94
Selement, George, 128, 135, 251
Servitude, Indian, 59, 60, 71, 119
Sewall, Samuel, 103, 210, 252, 289n33, 320n16
Sexuality, sexual mores, 121, 128, 134, 241–242; Puritan attempts to regulate, among Indians, 28, 53, 58, 74, 116
Shattoockquis, 164
Shawomet, Shawomet Indians, 200. *See also* Gorton, Samuel; Pomham (Narragansett)
Shem, 81, 83, 85, 88
Shepard, Thomas, 128, 135, 251; missionary theology of, 6, 7, 9, 15–16, 19, 72–73, 248; as missionary companion of Eliot, 41, 52, 62, 187, 193; as publicist for mission, 52, 66, 68, 72, 278n1; works of, translated, 122, 217
Simmons, William, 172, 174, 244
Sin, original, 75, 129, 135, 243
Smolinski, Reiner, 248–249
Sokoki Indians, 148–153

Solomon (of Okommakamesit), 143
Solomon (of Pakachoog), 157, 164, 228
Speaking in tongues, 8, 21
Speene, James, 157, 161
Speene, John, 57, 105, 107, 109, 243; family, 74, 110, 132, 280n20; as teacher, 124–125; as prospective church member, 126, 131, 133
Speene, Robin, 74, 126, 132, 175
Speene, Thomas, Sr., 74, 112, 132, 283n46
Spinning and weaving, 58, 107, 150, 167, 229, 242
Squamaug, 141
Squanto, 19
Squaw Sachem. *See* Pawtucket Indians
Stanton, Thomas, Sr., 120, 181, 185; sons of, 134, 221–222
Stearns, Raymond, 69, 70
Steele, William, 209
Subsistence practices, Indian, 6, 53, 108, 167, 242, 244
Superintendency, Indian: precursor to, 59–60, 224–225; creation of, 224–226, 230, 231. *See also* Gookin, Daniel
Szasz, Margaret Connell, 181

Tartars. *See* Gentiles: Indians as
Ten Commandments, 28, 43, 50, 124
Ten kings, of biblical prophecy, 12–13, 80, 82, 99–100
Tens through thousands, system of, 83, 293n16; in praying towns 56, 92, 111–112, 116, 168; as primitive institution, 77–78, 115
Theology, Christian: Indian difficulties with, 74–75, 135, 243; Indians' acceptance of, 129, 132, 134, 138, 242, 243
Theology, natural, 41, 61
Thomas, John, 145
Thorowgood, Thomas, 83–87, 96–97, 103, 207, 213
Tinker, George, 74, 299n65
Titicut Indians, 38–39, 65
Tokkohwompait, Daniel, 137, 157, 246
Tompson, William (of New London), 182, 185, 193
Tools and utensils, metal: appeal of, to Indians, 58; and Eliot's mission, 68, 107, 214; and other missions, 178, 180, 194, 210
Totherswamp, 58, 60–61, 73, 74, 132; as ruler and teacher, 112, 117, 124, 230;

and inebriated son, 116–117, 118, 130, 226; as prospective church member, 126, 127
Treat, Samuel, 195
Tribute, 155, 157–158, 198, 204, 205; and Cutshamekin, 55, 56, 91, 199
Trumbull, James Hammond, 121, 215
Tuckawillipin, Joseph, 142, 143, 156, 161, 177
Tupper, Thomas, 194–195
Tuspequin, 198, 204

Uncas. *See* Mohegan Indians
Usher, Hezekiah, 120, 211–212

Van Lonkhuyzen, Harold, 132
Vaughan, Alden, 7, 233, 320n14
Venner, Thomas, 82, 96, 114, 115

Waban, 41, 52, 58, 64, 71, 72, 109, 191, 237, 246; as ruler, 54, 56, 59, 112, 116, 117, 141, 168, 179, 229, 230; sons of, 57, 279n13; as missionary, 61, 73; as prospective church member, 126, 127, 128, 132, 133, 134
Wabquisset, Wabquisset Indians, 155, 157–158, 164, 205, 229
Waeuntug, 158, 164
Walker, James, 202–203, 205
Wall, Robert, Jr., 24
Walton, William, 130
Wamesit, Wamesit Indians, 71, 146–147, 153–154, 167, 169, 227, 229, 236; and Mohawks, 148, 149–150, 151, 152, 153, 215
Wampanoag Indians, 172, 175, 177, 204
Wampas, John, 222
Wamporas, 53, 57, 58, 73, 74, 105, 132, 222
Wamsutta, 197
Wannalancett, 36, 147, 153–154
Warwick Commission, 25–26, 29, 43–44
Webbacowet, 33, 59, 175
Wequash, 19, 25, 73–74
Weld, Daniel, 219
Weld, Thomas, 46, 47, 48, 215; as agent of Massachusetts Bay, 4, 25–26, 43, 69–70, 207
Weshakim, 160, 163, 235

Weymouth Indians, 132
"What should a Christian do, to keep . . . the Sabbath day?", 121
White, John, 5, 6, 7, 8
Whitfield, Henry, 67, 72, 207
Wigglesworth, Michael, 247
Wigwams, 71, 107–108, 242, 244
Willard, Simon, 58, 62, 71, 146, 159, 190, 192
William of Sudbury, 61, 105, 126, 127, 128, 143; family, 142, 143, 280n20; and King Philip's War, 161, 162
Williams, Roger, 46, 67–68, 202–203; and missionary work, 8, 16–17, 20, 187, 193; diplomatic embassies to London, 16, 23–27, 29, 189; eschatology, 16–17, 26–27, 68, 83; and Eliot, 47, 121, 187, 190–191, 244; observations about Narragansetts, 73, 75, 241, 243; letters to Massachusetts Bay, 156, 189–192
Wilson, John, 19, 20, 46, 49; and Eliot's mission, 54–55, 113, 127, 134, 135, 193, 210
Winslow, Edward, 20, 21, 40; as agent of Massachusetts Bay, 30, 43–44, 66–67; and lost tribes theory, 67, 83–86; and New England Company, 70, 207, 209, 214, 220
Winthrop, John, 1–2, 9, 69, 166, 234; and missionary work, 2, 3, 4, 40, 189; and Narragansett Indians, 23, 28, 35–36, 40, 43–44; and Massachusetts Bay sachems, 33, 35–36, 38
Winthrop, John, Jr., 32, 46, 69, 142, 179; and Narragansett Country, 188, 192–193, 196
Winthrop, Margaret, 46, 146
Wogan, Peter, 57
Wompatuck, Josias, 31, 35, 38, 110, 141–142, 199, 238; and Christianity, 106, 141, 195; and Mohawks, 152, 153
Wompontupont, 37
Wood, William, 36, 248
Work habits, English: Eliot on, 6, 53, 107, 194; in praying towns, 71, 107, 117, 128, 135, 167, 229, 242
Wossamegon, 30, 36, 37, 38, 158, 159, 168, 231